INFORMATION SYSTEMS
ACTION RESEARCH

INTEGRATED SERIES IN INFORMATION SYSTEMS

Series Editors

Professor Ramesh Sharda
Oklahoma State University

Prof. Dr. Stefan Voß
Universität Hamburg

Other published titles in the series:

E-BUSINESS MANAGEMENT: *Integration of Web Technologies with Business Models/* edited by Michael J. Shaw

VIRTUAL CORPORATE UNIVERSITIES: *A Matrix of Knowledge and Learning for the New Digital Dawn/* Walter R.J. Baets & Gert Van der Linden

SCALABLE ENTERPRISE SYSTEMS: *An Introduction to Recent Advances/* edited by Vittal Prabhu, Soundar Kumara, Manjunath Kamath

LEGAL PROGRAMMING: *Legal Compliance for RFID and Software Agent Ecosystems in Retail Processes and Beyond/* Brian Subirana and Malcolm Bain

LOGICAL DATA MODELING: *What It Is and How To Do It/* Alan Chmura and J. Mark Heumann

DESIGNING AND EVALUATING E-MANAGEMENT DECISION TOOLS: *The Integration of Decision and Negotiation Models into Internet-Multimedia Technologies/* Giampiero E.G. Beroggi

INFORMATION AND MANAGEMENT SYSTEMS FOR PRODUCT CUSTOMIZATION/ Thorsten Blecker et al

MEDICAL INFORMATICS: *Knowledge Management and Data Mining in Biomedicine/* edited by Hsinchun Chen et al

KNOWLEDGE MANAGEMENT AND MANAGEMENT LEARNING: *Extending the Horizons of Knowledge-Based Management/* edited by Walter Baets

INTELLIGENCE AND SECURITY INFORMATICS FOR INTERNATIONAL SECURITY: *Information Sharing and Data Mining/* Hsinchun Chen

ENTERPRISE COLLABORATION: *On-Demand Information Exchange for Extended Enterprises/* David Levermore & Cheng Hsu

SEMANTIC WEB AND EDUCATION/ Vladan Devedžić

INFORMATION SYSTEMS ACTION RESEARCH

An Applied View of Emerging Concepts and Methods

edited by

Ned Kock

 Springer

Ned Kock
Texas A & M International University
Laredo, Texas, USA

Library of Congress Control Number: 2006931352

ISBN-10: 0-387-36059-X (HB)   ISBN-10: 0-387-36060-3 (e-book)
ISBN-13: 978-0387-36059-1 (HB) ISBN-13: 978-0387-36060-7 (e-book)

Printed on acid-free paper.

Printed in the United States of America.

9 8 7 6 5 4 3 2 1

springer.com

CONTRIBUTING AUTHORS

David Avison

David Avison is Distinguished Professor of Information Systems at ESSEC Business School, near Paris, France after being Professor at the School of Management at Southampton University for nine years. He is also visiting professor at Brunel University in England. He is joint editor (with Guy Fitzgerald) of Blackwell Science's Information Systems Journal now in its 16th volume. He has authored over twenty books, including the best selling book "Information Systems Development: Methodologies, Techniques and Tools" (also with Guy Fitzgerald) published by McGraw-Hill (4th edition 2006) and "Research in Information Systems: A Handbook for Research Supervisors and their Students" (edited with Jan Pries-Heje) Butterworth Heinemann (2005) as well as a large number of papers in learned journals, edited texts and conferences. He is Vice Chair of the International Federation of Information Processing (IFIP) Technical Committee 8, previously Chair of its working group 8.2 on the impact of IS/IT on organizations and was past President of the UK Academy for Information Systems. He is joint program chair of International Conference in Information Systems (ICIS) 2005 in Las Vegas and has chaired several other international conferences.

C. Richard Baker

C. Richard Baker is Professor of Accounting in the School of Business at Adelphi University, Garden City, New York. Prior to joining Adelphi University, he was Professor and Chair of the Accounting Department at the

University of Massachusetts Dartmouth. He also has held professorial positions at Columbia University and Fordham University in New York City. His research interests concentrate on the regulatory, legal and ethical aspects of professional accounting and auditing. He is the author of over 90 academic papers and other publications. He holds a Ph.D. from the Graduate School of Management at UCLA and he is a Certified Public Accountant in New York State.

Richard L. Baskerville

Richard L. Baskerville is professor of information systems and chairman in the Department of Computer Information Systems, Robinson College of Business, Georgia State University. His research specializes in security of information systems, methods of information systems design and development, and the interaction of information systems and organizations. His interest in methods extends to qualitative research methods. Baskerville is the author of "Designing Information Systems Security" (J. Wiley) and more than 100 articles in scholarly journals, professional magazines, and edited books. He is an editor for The European Journal of Information Systems and serves on the editorial boards of The Information Systems Journal, Journal of Information Systems Security, and the International Journal of e-Collaboration. Baskerville's practical and consulting experience includes advanced information system designs for the U.S. Defense and Energy Departments. He is president of the Information Systems Academic Heads International, former chair of the IFIP Working Group 8.2, a Chartered Engineer under the British Engineering Council, a member of The British Computer Society and Certified Computer Professional. Baskerville holds degrees from the University of Maryland (B.S. summa cum laude, Management), and the London School of Economics, University of London (M.Sc., Analysis, Design and Management of Information Systems, Ph.D., Systems Analysis).

Simon Bell

Simon Bell is a Senior Lecturer in Information Systems in the Systems Department at the UK Open University. He has wide ranging experience in working with diverse communities on developing information systems and products valued by these communities. As co-author of three books on the Multiview approach and three books on the Imagine approach, he has worked with diverse ethnic and cultural groups on information systems development in many countries including Nigeria, Nepal, Bangladesh, Lebanon, Bulgaria, China and the UK. As a consultant and a co-researcher he has worked on projects funded by the World Bank, the European Union and the UK Department for International Development for over twenty years. Recently he has been invited to talk about the methods he has developed in Finland France and the USA.

Peter Checkland

Peter Checkland gained a first in chemistry at Oxford in the 1950s. He joined 1CI when it was developing a new industry: making synthetic fibres from nylon and polyester polymers. Working first as a technologist then as a manager, Peter remained with ICI for fifteen years. When he left to start a second career in university teaching and research, he was manager of a 100-strong research and development group.

Joining the postgraduate Department of Systems Engineering at Lancaster University, Peter Checkland led what became a thirty-year programme of action research in organizations outside the university. Initially the research theme was to determine the possibility of using the well-developed methods of systems engineering in management problem situations rather than in the technically defined problem situations in which the methods had been refined. This attempt at transfer failed, and the action research moved in a different direction. The work finally established Soft Systems Methodology (SSM) as an approach to tackling the multi-faceted problems which managers face; in doing this, it also established the now well-recognised distinction between 'hard' and 'soft' systems thinking. SSM is now taught and used around the-world. Its development through action research is described in many papers and in four books: Systems Thinking, Systems Practice (1981); Soft Systems Methodology in Action (with J. Scholes, 1990); Systems, Information and Information Systems (with Sue Holwell 1998) and SSM: A 30-Year Retrospective (1999).

Peter Checkland's work has been recognized in a number of awards: he holds 6 honorary doctorates from City University, the Open University, Erasmus University (The Netherlands), and Prague University of Economics, A Most Distinguished and Outstanding Award from the British Computer Society, and the Gold Medal of the UK Systems Society.

Paulo Rupino da Cunha

Paulo Rupino da Cunha is Assistant Professor at the University of Coimbra, Portugal. He holds a Ph.D. and an M.Sc. in Informatics Engineering. His main research interests are Information Systems Design, Quality Management and Information Systems, Design of Business Models and Strategy, Enterprise Application Integration and IT Investment Valuation. He is the

Vice-President of Instituto Pedro Nunes, an Innovation and Technology Transfer organization providing specialized consulting, training and business incubation. For a period of three years, he was the elected Coordinator of the Informatics Engineering Chapter for the centre region of Portugal of the Portuguese Engineering Association, and for a two year term he held the Vice-Presidency of the Department of Informatics Engineering of the University of Coimbra.

Robert Davison

Robert Davison received the BA and MA degrees from the University of Nottingham, UK, and the Ph.D. degree in Information Systems from the City University of Hong Kong. He is an Associate Professor of Information Systems at the City University of Hong Kong. His work has appeared in the Information Systems Journal, IEEE Transactions on Engineering Management, IEEE Transactions on Professional Communication, Information Technology & People, Information & Management, MIS Quarterly, Group Decision & Negotiation and the Communications of the ACM. Dr. Davison's research interests span the academic and business communities, examining the impact of GSS on group decision making and communication, particularly in cross-cultural settings, as well as the ethical values of IT professionals. He also actively applies an action research perspective to research in organisational contexts. He has recently completed editing special issues of the Communications of the ACM (Global Applications of Collaborative Technologies) and IEEE Transactions on Engineering Management (Cultural Issues and IT Management). Dr. Davison is the Editor in Chief of the Electronic Journal of Information Systems in Developing Countries.

Antonio Dias de Figueiredo

Antonio Dias de Figueiredo is Full Professor of MIS at the University of Coimbra, Portugal, since 1984. He obtained his Ph.D. in Computer Science from the University of Manchester, U.K., in 1976. He created and was the first chair of the Department of Informatics Engineering of the University of Coimbra, and was vice-president for Western Europe of the Intergovernmental Informatics Program of UNESCO, Paris. He has participated in various European projects and acted on various occasions as a consultant to the European Commission in matters regarding strategies for information technologies in education. He was awarded an Honoris Causa by the Portuguese Open University and the Sigillum Magnum by the University of Bologna, Italy. He is the author of over 200 papers, has contributed to several books, and is a member of the editorial board of various national and international journals. His current research interests centre on the philosophy of engineering and technology, IS research methods, action research, e-collaboration, context design in socio-technical systems, and virtual learning contexts.

Bob Dick

In the distant past Bob Dick has been shop assistant, electrician, draftsperson, recruitment officer, and industrial psychologist. For the past 30 years he has been academic, publisher, consultant, and facilitator. He enjoys his consultancy and facilitation, which primarily help people learn action research, qualitative evaluation, change management, and the communication and facilitation skills which are a foundation for these. In this work he uses highly participative methods to help others to improve their practice while also trying always to improve his own. In his spare time he reads, thinks and writes. He lives in the leafy western suburbs of Brisbane with his partner of 31 years, Camilla, in a house frequently overrun by grandchildren.

R. Brent Gallupe

R. Brent Gallupe is Professor of Information Systems, Director of the Queen's Executive Decision Center, and Associate Dean – Faculty at the School of Business, Queen's University at Kingston, Canada. He also holds an on-going Visiting Professor appointment at the University of Auckland, New Zealand. His current research interests are in computer support for groups and teams, the management of international information systems, and knowledge management systems. His work has been published in such journals as Management Science, MIS Quarterly, Information Systems Research, Academy of Management Journal, Sloan Management Review, and Journal of Applied Psychology.

Christopher Gronski

Christopher Gronski is currently pursuing his Ph.D. in information systems at the Richard Ivey School of Business at the University of Western Ontario. He is a BA and MBA graduate of the University of Toronto/Rodman School of Management and holds a post graduate diploma in information technology. Prior to returning to academia, Christopher spent over a decade in various technologically oriented roles, flavoring his academic work to date decidedly towards the practitioner. His current research focus is the firm level use of information systems for competitive advantage. He has presented his work as part of the conference proceedings of the Administrative Sciences Association of Canada.

Varun Grover

Varun Grover is the William S. Lee (Duke Energy) Distinguished Professor of Information Systems in the Department of Management at Clemson University. He holds a degree in electrical engineering from I.I.T., New Delhi, an MBA, and a Ph.D. in MIS from the University of Pittsburgh. Dr. Grover has published extensively on the effective use and impact of information systems with over 150 publications in refereed journals such as MIS Quarterly, Journal of MIS, and Information Systems Research, among others. He has consistently been ranked as one of the top 3 most productive IS researchers based in publications in major journals. He currently serves as the Senior Editor of MIS Quarterly, Journal of AIS and Database.

Ola Henfridsson

Ola Henfridsson is a research manager of the Telematics Group at the Viktoria Institute, Göteborg, Sweden. He is also an associate professor in Informatics at the School of Information Science, Computer and Electrical Engineering, Halmstad University. Dr. Henfridsson holds a Ph.D. in Informatics from Umeå University, Sweden, since 1999. He has published his research in DATA BASE, Information Systems Journal, Information Technology & People, Information and Organization, MIS Quarterly and other journals. Dr. Henfridsson serves at the editorial boards of MIS Quarterly and Scandinavian Journal of Information Systems.

Ellen D. Hoadley

Ellen D. Hoadley is an Associate Professor of Management Information Systems at Loyola College in Maryland. Her research areas include business process reengineering, requirements determination in systems analysis, and the use of color in the human/computer interface. Dr. Hoadley has published in Communications of the ACM, Journal of Business and Economic Perspectives, and Journal of Knowledge and Process Management among others. Dr. Hoadley is currently the Director of the Lattanze Center @ Loyola College that seeks to provide opportunities for academics, students, and practitioners to share problems and knowledge for the benefit of the field.

Sue Holwell

Sue Holwell has been a member of the Open Systems Research Group at the Open University since 2002. She teaches postgraduate and undergraduate courses in information systems and systems thinking. Prior to joining the Open University, Sue lectured at Cranfield University and Lancaster University. She has been an active action researcher for many years, collaborating with Peter Checkland, including on this program of research. She is co-author, with Checkland, of "Information, Systems and Information Systems" and has published about action research, soft systems methodology, and information systems. Before joining academia she worked for 20 years in IS/IT in the Australian Public Service.

Ned Kock

Ned Kock is Associate Professor and Chair of the Department of MIS and Decision Science at Texas A&M International University. He holds degrees in electronics engineering (B.E.E.), computer science (M.S.), and management information systems (Ph.D.). Ned has authored several books, and published in a number of journals including Communications of the ACM, Decision Support Systems, European Journal of Information Systems, IEEE Transactions, Information & Management, Information Systems Journal, Information Technology & People, Journal of Organizational Computing and Electronic Commerce, MIS Quarterly, and Organization Science. Ned has been working as a systems analyst and organizational development consultant for over 20 years, having provided consulting, training and systems development services to a number of organizations including Hong Kong & Shanghai Bank, PricewaterhouseCoopers, Johnson & Johnson, Rio de Janeiro State Construction Company, Westaflex, New Zealand Ministry of Agriculture and Fisheries, True North, Day & Zimmermann, Lockheed Martin, Bristol-Myers Squibb, Texas International Education Consortium, and the European Commission. He is the Editor-in-Chief of the International Journal of e-Collaboration, Associate Editor of the Journal of Systems and Information Technology, and Associate Editor for Information Systems of the journal IEEE Transactions on Professional Communication. His research interests include action research, ethical and legal issues in technology research and management, e-collaboration, and business process improvement.

Rajiv Kohli

Rajiv Kohli is an associate professor of Management Information Systems at the College of William & Mary. He received his Ph.D. from the University of Maryland, Baltimore County. For over 15 years, he has worked or consulted with IBM Global Services, SAS Corporation, United Parcel Service, AM General, MCI Telecommunications, Westinghouse Electronics, Wipro Corporation and Godrej Industries (India), in addition to several healthcare organizations. Prior to joining full-time academia in 2001, he was a Project Leader in Decision Support Services at Trinity Health. Dr. Kohli's research is published in MIS Quarterly, Management Science, Information Systems Research, Journal of Management Information Systems, and Communications of the ACM among other journals. He is a co-author of "IT Payoff: Measuring Business Value of Information Technology Investment" published by Financial Times Prentice-Hall. Dr. Kohli has been a recipient of several grants in information systems research.

Allen S. Lee

Allen S. Lee is Professor of Information Systems and Associate Dean for Research and Graduate Studies in the School of Business at Virginia Commonwealth University. At MIS Quarterly, he has served as Associate Editor, Senior Editor, and Editor-in-Chief. As a scholar in the discipline of information systems who is a proponent of qualitative, interpretive, and case-based research approaches and their integration with quantitative, positivist, and sampling-based research approaches, Dr. Lee has presented papers at numerous research conferences and in university research seminars around the world. He has earned degrees from Cornell University, the University of California at Berkeley, and the Massachusetts Institute of Technology.

Rikard Lindgren

Rikard Lindgren is a member of the management group at the Viktoria Institute, Göteborg, Sweden. He is also an Associate Professor at the IT University of Göteborg. Professor Lindgren has published his research in MIS Quarterly, Information and Organization, European Journal of Information Systems, Information Systems Management, Scandinavian Journal of Information Systems, and other journals in the information systems discipline. He won an award for the best paper published in the European Journal of Information Systems in 2003.

Peter Marshall

Professor Peter Marshall is Head of School and Woolworth's Chair in IT and Systems at the University of Tasmania in Australia. He is a committed qualitative researcher who believes in holistic and organisationally informed IS research in which the personal, social and political factors are fully investigated and taken as an integral and essential part of the Information System's phenomena. Peter is currently guiding a team of researchers involved in several action research based initiatives with respect to the formulation of

IT Strategy in SMEs in Tasmania. He collaborates regularly with Associate Professor Judy McKay at Swinburne University in Melbourne concerning matters regarding Information Systems research and the philosophy of Information Systems. Judy and Peter have recently published "Strategic Management of e-Business", an MBA level text in Information Systems.

Maris G. Martinsons

Maris G. Martinsons is a professor of management at the City University of Hong Kong. He received his Bachelor of Applied Science (Engineering Science) and M.B.A. degrees from the University of Toronto, and a Ph.D. (Industrial and Business Studies) from the University of Warwick. Maris is among the most active and influential management scholars in the Asia-Pacific region. His research and insights have appeared in leading English language journals and have been translated into Chinese, French, Japanese, Latvian, and Russian. His professional interests focus on the strategic and cultural issues associated with managing information (technology), knowledge, and organizational change.

Judy McKay

Associate Professor Judy McKay is currently Academic Leader of the Information Systems Group in the Faculty of Information & Communication Technologies at Swinburne University of Technology in Melbourne, Australia. She joined the staff at Swinburne in 2004 after academic appointments in Information Systems at Monash University, Edith Cowan University and Curtin University of Technology. She has a Bachelor of Arts (majoring in Linguistics), and postgraduate qualifications in Education, Business and Information Systems. She was awarded a Ph.D. from the University of Queensland, after an action research study into the issue of differences in perspective when adequately determining the information requirements of managers. She has published approximately 80 articles in international and national journals and conferences in the fields of organisational problem solving, information requirements analysis, IS Management, IS Strategy and IS Governance. In 2004, she co-authored her first book, "Strategic Management of eBusiness," with Peter Marshall.

Darren Meister

Darren Meister is an assistant professor in information systems and Robert V. Brouillard faculty fellow at the Richard Ivey School of Business. He obtained his Ph.D. from the University of Waterloo and also previously attended the University of Cambridge as a Rotary Foundation Scholar. Darren's research focus is on the integration of technology and organizational processes, particularly for technology adoption and adaptation, interorganizational systems, and knowledge management. His work has been published in: MIS Quarterly, Management Science, IEEE Transactions of Engineering Management, Information Technology & People, and International Journal of Technology Management.

Michael D. Myers

Michael D. Myers is Professor of Information Systems and Associate Dean (Postgraduate and Research) at the University of Auckland Business School, New Zealand. His main research interests are concerned with the social and organizational aspects of information systems, and the use of qualitative research methods in IS. He currently serves as Editor in Chief of the University of Auckland Business Review and Editor of the ISWorld Section on Qualitative Research. He previously served as Senior Editor of MIS Quarterly from 2001–2005, as Associate Editor of Information Systems Research from 2000–2005, and as Associate Editor of Information Systems Journal from 1995–2000. His research articles have been published in many journals and books. He won the Best Paper award (with Heinz Klein) for the most outstanding paper published in MIS Quarterly in 1999. He also won the Best Paper Award (with Lynda Harvey) for the best paper published in Information Technology & People in 1997. He currently serves as the President-Elect of the Association for Information Systems (AIS) and as Chair of the International Federation of Information Processing (IFIP) Working Group 8.2 which concerns the interaction between information systems and organizations.

Ravi Narayanaswamy

Ravi Narayanaswamy is a doctoral student of Information Systems in the department of Management at Clemson University. He holds a MS in Information systems, and an MBA in Marketing. Prior to pursuing his doctoral work, he worked in diverse areas with some of the leading multinational firms. While his primary interests are methodological, his research focuses on topics such as project management, outsourcing, and culture.

Peter Axel Nielsen

Peter Axel Nielsen is associate professor in Information Systems at the Department of Computer Science at Aalborg University. Over the past years he has been engaged in action research on information systems development practice and the use of methodologies. His research interests include analysis and design techniques, object-orientation, and software process improvement. He is co-author of a book on object-oriented analysis and design and a book on software process improvement.

John T. Nosek

Dr. Nosek is Professor of Computer & Information Sciences at Temple University. He has published widely on a broad range of information technology topics. For over a decade, his main interest has been exploring ways to accelerate organizational success by transforming collaborative work. He continues to focus on development of collaborative theories and theory-based technology that will dramatically improve anytime, anyplace collaborative work by better managing the social, cognitive, and procedural complexities inherent in joint effort. Dr. Nosek is Associate Editor of the International Journal of e-Collaboration and is guest co-editor of IEEE Transactions on Professional Communications for the recent Special Issue on "Expanding the Boundaries of E-Collaboration." Dr. Nosek's work has been funded by the National Science Foundation, private companies, semi-governmental organizations and foundations, including The Ben Franklin Partnership and The Lattanze Foundation, The U.S. Navy, and The U.S. Air Force. He has also worked with a number of small and large companies, including Lockheed Martin. Dr. Nosek is a retired Navy Captain and holds degrees from The United States Naval Academy, Villanova University, and Temple University.

David J. Pauleen

David J. Pauleen (PhD) is a senior lecturer at the School of Information Management at Victoria University of Wellington, New Zealand. His work has appeared in such journals as the Journal of Management Information Systems, Sloan Management Review, Journal of Global Information Management, Leadership and Organizational Development Journal, Journal of Knowledge Management, the Journal of Information Technology, and Internet Research. He is also editor of the book, "Virtual Teams: Projects, Protocols and Processes" (2004) and currently editing the book, "Cross-Cultural Perspectives on Knowledge Management."

Trevor Wood-Harper

Trevor Wood-Harper is Professor of Information Systems and Director of Graduate Research at the School of Informatics at the University of Manchester and his research view takes a multiple perspective systems thinking stance from Enid Mumford, West Churchman and Peter Checkland's work as applied to Information Systems. He was Research Director at the University of Salford which was awarded a 6* rating in the UK 2001 Research Assessment Exercise (RAE). He is Visiting Professor of Information Systems at the Australian National University, Canberra and held visiting chairs at University of Oslo, Copenhagen Business School and Georgia State University. Wood-Harper has co-authored or co-edited 20 books & monographs and over 200 research articles in a wide range of topics including: Social Informatics; Electronic Government; Ethical Considerations in System Development; Information Systems in Developing Countries; Doctoral Research; Action Research and the Multiview Methodology. These papers and texts have been published in top international journals & publishers and he has supervised more than 25 doctoral theses successfully in the above research areas.

Pak Yoong

Pak Yoong (PhD) is an Associate Professor of Information Systems/E-commerce at Victoria University of Wellington. Pak teaches in the areas of virtual organisation, research methods and IS leadership. Pak's research, teaching, and consulting experience is in the facilitation of virtual meetings, online communities of practice, online knowledge sharing, mobile collaborations, and human resource development in information technology environments. He is currently editing the book IT Human Resource Management Challenges in the Internet Age. His work has been published in such journals as Journal of Information Technology, and People, The DATABASE for Advances for Information System, Journal of Information and Knowledge Management, Journal of Information Technology, and Internet Research.

FOREWORD

Bob Dick
Southern Cross University, Australia

Since its beginning in the mid 1940s — and prior to that if you consider the practices and not just the labels — action research has experienced times of decline and times of growth. Despite some countervailing forces it seems that we are now in a time of growth. My library alerts seem to arrive with much greater frequency than they did just a few years ago. Each year my bibliographic database shows an upward trend for action research publications. Some of the growth over the past decade and a half has been due to action research spreading into new fields, one of which is information systems.

I expect the growth to continue at least into the near future, spurred on by certain global conditions. There are pressures towards more practical outcomes from academic research. Cooperation between the academy and the world of practice is now more encouraged than I recall it being when I first embarked on an academic career. At that time it was assumed that the brightest people pursued pure research. I've since discovered that the challenges are at least as great, and probably greater, in the very applied research of which action research is a part.

In addition, globalisation has increased the pace of change for many of us. More rapid change favours research methodologies that are flexible and responsive. In corporate settings, disillusion with conventional training has in some quarters led to a growing popularity of action learning, a near cousin of action research. I don't perceive any signs that these pressures will reduce, at least in the short term.

There are three other apparent trends that I regard as more important than sheer quantity. They are: greater experimentation with different forms of action research; more emphasis on rigour in non-positivist science; and increasing theory-practice integration.

In recent decades action research has been enriched by the addition of related methodologies such as soft systems methodology and appreciative inquiry, among others. They share with other forms of action research a commitment towards both research and action. They offer action researchers more choices in the specific form of research. Information systems researchers have embraced this variety.

A commitment to participation and action has been part of action research from the beginning. There were times when this seemed to be achieved by reducing the commitment to theory building and to rigour. More recently action research authors have striven to increase the rigour without abandoning the other features: other features which to my mind are the special competency of action research. Here, the information systems field has had a strong and valuable contribution to make, both to issues of rigour and to moves to develop more explicit theory building.

In theory-practice integration, too, the information systems literature has been prominent. Design of information systems is often seen as co-design with the users. A variety of applications of action research are explored. Academics and practitioners cooperate often, and many action researchers fill both roles.

In short, information systems researchers and practitioners have been among the important recent contributors to the resurgence of action research and to its ongoing development. It is therefore appropriate that this book should address the area of information systems and should help to bridge the gap between the academy and industry. It is also appropriate that many of the authors represented here are information systems people who have been part of that development.

PREFACE

Ned Kock
Texas A&M International University, USA

The field of research known as information systems (IS) is largely dedicated to the understanding of how computer systems and related technologies (e.g., communication technologies) affect human behavior. This is done mostly in the context created by organizations and social groups; although there are examples of IS investigations involving single individuals. While the field of IS started taking shape as a distinct area of research and education in the 1960s, it builds on inventions, methods and ideas that date back at least to the 1940s. One notable invention without which the field of IS would probably not exist is the computer. Most accounts of the history of computing suggest that the first computer was the ENIAC, developed at the University of Pennsylvania in 1946.

IS research and education has come a long way since the 1960s. It is not uncommon to see IS programs in universities, particularly in colleges of business, as among the most successful in terms of student enrolment. Many doctoral programs with IS concentrations exist. There is also a vibrant and relatively large global IS research community, which congregates on a regular basis in large conferences such as the International Conference on Information Systems (ICIS). Much of what the field of IS has become up until today is due to the work of several pioneers. Among the IS pioneers are Peter Checkland (who is also an action research pioneer), Gordon Davis, Peter Keen, Scott Morton, and Charles Stabell. Today the field of IS gravitates around a few international associations, notably the Association for Information Systems (AIS).

According to most accounts, action research has emerged as a distinctive research approach soon after World War II. From its inception, it has been viewed as a research approach where the investigators try to find solutions to problems faced by their research clients – which can be individuals, groups, or organizations – while at the same time producing knowledge that can be used to develop or refine theoretical models. That is, in action research the investigators produce and refine theoretical knowledge approximately at the same time as they try to improve a problematic situation facing their research clients.

The history of action research suggests that it has been independently developed by one individual, the late Kurt Lewin, and one key institution, the Tavistock Institute of Human Relations.

Kurt Lewin received his doctorate from the University of Berlin in 1914, served in the German army during World War I, and later joined the Berlin Psychoanalytic Institute as a faculty member. He moved to the United States in 1933 and worked for approximately 10 years at the University of Iowa, later moving to the Massachusetts Institute of Technology. There he remained until his premature death in 1947. Lewin is believed to have coined the term "action research".

The Tavistock Institute was founded in London in 1946, through a grant from the Rockefeller Foundation, as an action-oriented research organization. One of the main goals of the Tavistock Institute was to develop and use innovative approaches to treating mental disorders resulting from individual exposure to events related to World War II. Of particular concern were the traumatic experiences underwent by military personnel, as well as their effects on those individuals' behavior and societal integration after their return from the battlefield.

Often action research is seen as a research approach that has been originated outside the United States, that has little to do with the American research tradition, and that is largely unrelated to the development and funding of research in the United States. In fact, in a number of disciplines (including information systems), action research finds a lot more acceptance in academic circles outside the United States than within. Some notable examples are England, Scandinavia, and Australasia.

One interesting aspect of the historical accounts outlined above is that they highlight the fact that the past relationship between action research and individuals and organizations based in the United States is a lot closer than many are led to believe – at least based on action research's scarce promotion and use in American academic circles. For example, Kurt Lewin pioneered action research while in the United States, even though his experience in Germany must have played a role in forming several of his ideas. Also, the Tavistock Institute has been founded with support from a high-profile American foundation, namely the Rockefeller Foundation. Among other things, the Rockefeller Foundation is widely known for its unwavering support of innovative social research, chiefly but obviously not exclusively in the United States.

Perhaps one of the reasons for the lack of acceptance of action research in American circles is that it is often seen as opposed to the predominant mode of research employed in business schools in the United States. (The same is largely true for American schools of science and engineering as well.) That predominant mode of research is characterized by a focus on quantification of behavioral phenomena, and the use of sophisticated quantitative analysis techniques. From an epistemological perspective, that mode of research is most closely associated with the positivist epistemology.

American business schools seem to house most academic departments dedicated to IS research and teaching, which appears to have led to an interesting situation. While action research is in many ways a very good match for IS inquiry, because of the utilitarian and problem-solving nature of most IS applications in organizations, its use in the field is dwarfed by that of research approaches that are better aligned with positivist notions. Estimates suggest that action research accounts for less than one percent of all IS research. The lion share goes to experimental, survey, and case research.

Several researchers have been concerned about the situation above, a concern that has often been enhanced by a deep interest in action research's potential to be used for IS research. One of those researchers is Richard Baskerville, perhaps the most prominent figure in the IS action research community today. Richard organized a workshop on IS action research at Georgia State University in October 1998, which I had the fortune to attend. That workshop planted the seed for the first special issue on IS action research published in 2001 by the journal *Information Technology & People*, which I guest-edited together with Francis Lau, and led me to ultimately decide to edit this book.

As it will become obvious to the readers of this book, modern IS action research is characterized by a range of views and methods. While this unavoidably goes hand-in-hand with some methodological fragmentation, it also opens up a number of opportunities for the acceptance of action research in areas that have traditionally been closed to it. It also allows for the expectation that action research can be made compatible with many epistemologies, including positivism. This latter point can be illustrated through a simple analogy. Cubism, for instance, can serve as the basis for painting employing various approaches, such as oil and acrylic painting. Similarly, I believe that positivism can serve as the basis for research employing various approaches, and action research is one of those approaches.

Yet, as it will also become clear to the readers of this book, there is no consensus among IS action researchers about action research being compatible with many epistemologies, positivism included. In fact, some openly disagree with this notion. One thing is very likely though. If cubism was practiced only by artists specializing in acrylic painting, probably those artists would be tempted to claim ownership of cubism. I wonder if something similar is not currently happening with action research in general, and IS action research in particular.

This book is organized in three main parts. Part I, made up of chapters 1 to 6, is dedicated to the discussion of methodological issues related to IS action research. Hopefully the chapters in Part I will be useful to those researchers who are preparing to conduct IS action research investigations, so that they can better plan their research projects. Part II, which comprises chapters 7 to 12, focuses on providing exemplars of empirical IS action research studies. Part II will hopefully be of value to researchers in the future as a basis for the development of their own reports on IS action research investigations. Finally, Part III, comprising chapters 13 to 18, is dedicated to the discussion of issues that are currently being debated by IS action researchers and their critics, or that are likely to form the basis for future debate.

The range of topics covered by the authors of the chapters that make up this book arguably represents the state-of-the-art of IS action research today. Moreover, several of the chapters discuss IS action research issues that have been present in longstanding debates in the field of IS, as well as many other fields. Finally, several of the chapters in this book raise issues that are likely to feature prominently in the future debate and application of action research, not only in the field of IS, but in several other fields. Among the key reasons for these positive aspects of this book is that its contributing authors are certainly among the most influential thinkers and practitioners of IS action research in the world today, not only in IS but also in a few other disciplines. Those authors are also pioneers, and their chapters will hopefully pave the way for the future.

I am indebted to the authors for their hard work, and for contributing well researched, and truly thought provoking chapters to this book. I would also like to thank the team at Springer for their support of this book project. In particular, I would like to thank Gary Folven, for taking the editorial lead on this book project at Springer, as well as Carolyn Ford for her editorial assistance. Thanks are also due to series editors Ramesh Sharda and Stefan Voss for their comments and suggestions early on this project.

I would also like to thank my colleagues at Texas A&M International University for supporting my research and scholarship. Special thanks go to my colleagues at the Department of MIS and Decision Science, for supporting my work as Department Chair; and several university administrators, for their strong commitment to the promotion of high quality research and scholarship. President Ray Keck, Provost Dan Jones, and Dean Jacky So deserve special mention in that respect. Many thanks go to Ruth Chatelain-Jardon and Jesus Carmona for helping with the development of the book's index.

Last, but certainly not least, I would like to thank my wife and children for their love and support. This book is dedicated to them.

CONTENTS

Contributing Authors   v

Foreword   xvii

Preface   xix

Part I. Methodological Issues

1. Action Research: Its Nature and Validity   3
    Peter Checkland and Sue Holwell

2. The Structure of Power in Action Research Projects   19
    David Avison, Richard Baskerville and Michael D. Myers

3. Action Is an Artifact: What Action Research and Design
    Science Offer to Each Other   43
    Allen S. Lee

4. Action Research and Design in Information Systems:
    Two Faces of a Single Coin   61
    António Dias de Figueiredo and Paulo Rupino da Cunha

5. The Three Threats of Organizational Action Research:
    Their Nature and Related Antidotes   97
    Ned Kock

6. Driven by Two Masters, Serving Both: The Interplay of
   Problem Solving and Research in Information Systems
   Action Research Projects   131
   Judy McKay and Peter Marshall

Part II. IS Action Research in Practice

7. Story Telling in Action Research Projects: Malta, Bangladesh,
   Lebanon and Slovenia   161
   Simon Bell and Trevor Wood-Harper

8. Action Research in New Product Development   193
   Ola Henfridsson and Rikard Lindgren

9. Action Research in a Virtual Setting:
   Cautions from a Failed Project   217
   Darren B. Meister and Christopher M. Gronski

10. Healthcare: Fertile Ground for Action Research   241
    Rajiv Kohli and Ellen D. Hoadley

11. Generating Data for Research on Emerging Technologies:
    An Action Learning Approach   255
    Pak Yoong, David Pauleen and Brent Gallupe

12. A Test of the Communication Flow Optimization Model
    Through an Action Research Study at a Defense Contractor   277
    Ned Kock

Part III. Current Debate on IS Action Research

13. Educing Theory from Practice   313
    Richard Baskerville

14. A Critical Assessment of Information Systems Action Research   327
    Ravi Narayanaswamy and Varun Grover

15. IS Action Research and Its Criteria   355
    Peter Axel Nielsen

16. Action Research and Consulting: Hellish Partnership or
    Heavenly Marriage?   377
    Robert M. Davison and Maris G. Martinsons

17. A Plea for Action Research in Accounting Information Systems   395
    C. Richard Baker

18. Insider as Action Researcher   405
    John Teofil Nosek

Index   421

Part I. Methodological Issues

Chapter 1

ACTION RESEARCH:
Its Nature and Validity

Peter Checkland[1] and Sue Holwell[2]
[1]*Lancaster University, UK;* [2]*The Open University, UK*

Abstract: The process of knowledge acquisition which has the strongest truth claim is the research process of natural science, based on testing hypotheses to destruction. But the application of this process to phenomena beyond those for which it was developed, namely, the natural regularities of the physical universe, is problematical. For research into social phenomena there is increasing interest in "action research" in various forms. In this process the researcher enters a real-world situation and aims both to improve it and to acquire knowledge. This paper reviews the nature and validity of action research, arguing that its claim to validity requires a recoverable research process based upon a prior declaration of the epistemology in terms of which findings which count as knowledge will be expressed.

Key words: research; action research; research methodology.

1.   INTRODUCTION

As *Systems Practice* extends its scope to include action research (AR), it is appropriate to reflect briefly on both the nature of AR and, because this is often challenged, its validity as a mode of inquiry leading to defensible and potentially transferable results. These characteristics could not of course include *replicability,* and that is the source of the challenge. Whenever sulfuric acid is added to a barium chloride solution, a white precipitate settles out. It does not matter who does it, in what part of the world, or in what circumstances; the precipitate is always formed. Chemists accept that they are investigating phenomena which are not capricious. They no longer agonize about the provenance of their discipline or the replicability of their results: they can be publicly tested. Chemists can concentrate on making substantive contributions within a taken-as-given framework.

Things are more volatile in the investigation of human and social phenomena. There it is still necessary to argue about the underlying assumptions, the modes of inquiry, and their validity. In that context AR is a mode of inquiry particularly in need of defense. This paper, which draws on and extends Checkland & Holwell (1997, Chap. 1) examines the provenance of AR and its problems. It offers a model derived from a 25-year program of AR carried out at Lancaster University and presents an argument for an appropriate form of validation which, though it does not match the magic of the replicability criterion in natural science, can sustain AR as a legitimate form of inquiry which can be defended if it meets certain criteria which are developed here.

In what follows we are concerned with the fundamentals of "action research" and use the generic shorthand AR as covering a number of versions of the approach which have acquired such names as action learning (Revans, 1972), action science (Argyris *et al.,* 1985), action inquiry (Torbet, 1991), participatory action research (Whyte, 1991), and RAAKS (rapid appraisal of agricultural knowledge systems) (Engels & Salomon, 1997). Clark (1972) provides a useful bibliography of AR up to the early 1970s, and Dash (1997) usefully surveys this field from a more recent perspective.

An initial chronological sampling of this field is provided by Lewin (1947), Blum (1955), Foster (1972), Clark (1972), Susman & Evered (1978), Hult & Lennung (1980), Argyris *et al.* (1985), Susman (1983), and Dash (1997).

2.   THE PROVENANCE OF ACTION RESEARCH

For most people who consider the matter at all, the paradigm model of organized inquiry is that provided by natural science. This is not surprising since the investigation of natural phenomena via the method of science is undoubtedly the most powerful form of knowledge generation ever devised. The development of that method is the crucial distinguishing characteristic of the civilization in which it has emerged, starting with the pre-Socratic philosophers in Ancient Greece in the 6th century BC. They postulated *rational* myths about the world, rather than myths involving supernatural beings, myths about which there cannot be much discussion. Rational myths *can* be discussed, however, and their emergence led to the development of rational methods of investigating the world, culminating eventually in the Newtonian scientific revolution of the 17th century. Our own century, with the subsuming of the Newtonian model as a limited special case of Einstein's physics, has taught us that all scientific knowledge is in fact provisional, being simply the best-tested knowledge we have at any given time. But the experimental method which generates that (provisional) knowledge is now taken as a given. This is thanks to its success, through science-based technology, in creating our worldview and our world.

The scientific method can be expressed as being based on three fundamental principles which characterize it and give it its power: reductionism, repeatability, and refutation (Checkland, 1981, Chap. 2). Scientists select a portion of the world to investigate and carry out disciplined observations in experiments. If the results of the experiments are repeatable, they count as part of the body of knowledge; and progress can be made in sequences of experiments through the testing to destruction of hypotheses. Scientific knowledge is then the accumulation of hypotheses which have not (yet) been refuted. This method of inquiry has been so successful that, in Western culture, to declare some putative knowledge as "unscientific" is often to justify dismissing it as irrelevant.

The power of scientific method lies in the *replicability* of its results; this turns its findings into "public knowledge" (Ziman, 1968) (though argument can of course still rage concerning the *interpretation* of the demonstrable experimental happenings). This replicability of experimental results stems from the fact that the phenomena investigated must be, in Keynes' phrase "homogenous through time": the inverse square law of magnetism is always, demonstrably, an inverse square law. Keynes (1938), quoted by Moggridge (1976, p. 26), was pointing out that economics should repel attempts to turn it into a pseudo-natural science precisely because unlike the typical natural science the material to which economics is applied is, in too many respects, not homogenous through time.

The point which Keynes makes highlights brilliantly the difficulties for social-scientists who would like to make use of the outstanding successful method of inquiry developed in the natural sciences. Can the method of science be applied to material which is not homogeneous through time, making complete replicability impossible? If not, what else can be done?

This is the context in which AR emerged. Kurt Lewin (1890-1947), a psychologist who became interested in human groups and their dynamics, particularly from the point of view of bringing about change in society, came to perceive "the limitations of studying complex real social events in a laboratory, the artificiality of splitting out single behavioural elements from an integrated system" (Foster, 1972). The concept emerged of a researcher immersing himself or herself in a human situation and following it along whatever path it takes as it unfolds through time. This means that the only certain object of research becomes the change process itself. This is a difficult concept for those anxious to import hypothesis-testing into social research, though it is an approach with which anthropologists and sociologists are familiar. Whyte (1991, p. 9) from the 1940s, was doing work in which "informants" in situations he researched became "active participants in the research," thus blurring the distinction between the researcher and those researched. This is something which worries natural scientists and those who would emulate their method of inquiry. As Vickers used to point out (Checkland, & Holwell, 1997, p. 19), since social phenomena are mental abstractions at a meta-level to their manifestations, even *thinking and arguing* about them can change them! On the other hand, whether the structure of our part of the cosmos corresponds to Ptolemy's earth-centered model or Copernicus' heliocentric model is entirely unaffected by our having theories about it. But Marx's theory of history changes history! Social phenomena are not, in Keynes' phrase, "homogeneous through time": hence the idea of taking part in change in organizations as a basis for research in the social world.

Probably most "interpretive" action researchers, acting on the assumption that social reality is continuously being created and recreated in a social process, would accept the notion of Argyris *et al.* (1985) that the crucial elements in a research approach which works within a specific social situation are

- a collaborative process between researchers and people in the situation,
- a process of critical inquiry,
- a focus on social practice, and
- a deliberate process of reflective learning.

This implies a very different kind of research from the testing of hypotheses. The latter process is represented in Fig. 1-1. This shows an "ideal-type" model of positivist research in which a researcher propounds a hypothesis about some part of perceived reality and then tries to test that hypothesis to destruction. It is useful to develop an alternative which covers the kind of approach Argyris and his colleagues describe, in order both to organize this kind of research and to explore the difficulties which AR faces, not least the question of its validity. This is done in the next section.

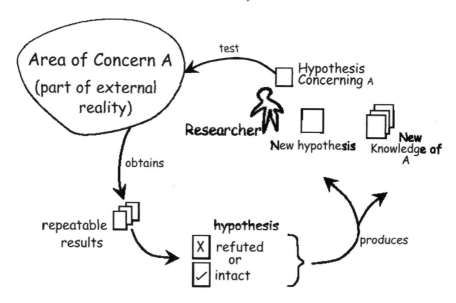

Figure 1-1. The hypothesis-testing research process of natural science

3.   THE AR PROCESS AND ITS PROBLEMS

Any research in any mode may be thought of as entailing the elements shown in Fig. 1-2 (Checkland & Holwell, 1997; after Checkland, 1985, 1991). Particular linked ideas F are used in a methodology M to investigate an area of interest A. Using the methodology may then teach us not only about A but also about the adequacy of F and M. For example, molecular orbital theory and known atomic and molecular dimensions, as a framework F, can be used via a methodology of the computer modeling of the shapes of molecules not yet synthesized in the laboratory to research potentially useful new drugs, an important A. The phlogiston theory of heat (heat as a liquid) is a failed F from the 18th Century. Figure 1-1 shows the classic form of M for research in natural science.

The change to or modification of F, M, and even A has to be expected in action research. In the 25-year program at Lancaster University which led to the emergence of soft systems methodology (SSM), the initial A was "tackling real-world problems of management" via the application of systems engineering (M). That methodology entailed, as F, *systematic* systems thinking. The methodology was found to be inadequate in that application area, and the learning led to the forming of SSM as a new M, based on a *systemic* F, which was then used for a new attack upon the original A.

This susceptibility to change F, M, and A in research in which the researcher becomes involved in the flux of real-world social situations leads to a (or probably *the*) most important principle in AR. It is a principle almost totally neglected in the literature of this area.

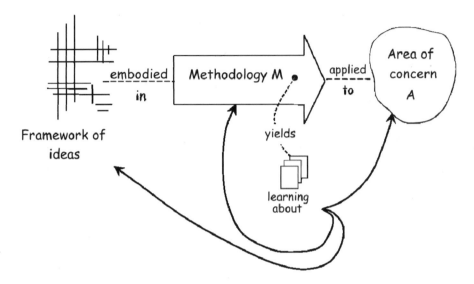

Figure 1-2. Elements relevant to any piece of research

In keeping your intellectual bearings in a changing situation in which the adequacy of F and M and the appropriateness of A are likely to be tested, it is essential to declare in advance the elements F M A in Fig. 1-2. This is the intellectual structure which will lead to findings and research lessons being recognized as such. Without that declaration, it is difficult to see how the outcome of AR can be more than anecdotal. Many literature accounts of AR leave the reader wondering about the status of that account: How is it to be distinguished from novel writing? To avoid this trap it is essential to define the epistemology in terms of which what will count as knowledge from the research will be expressed. It is the neglect of this principle which leaves AR vulnerable to positivist critics resolutely hanging on to hypothesis testing as a way of researching social phenomena. (They, for their part, have the problem of defining in testable form hypotheses and criteria necessarily expressed in ambiguous abstract terms. The hypothesis that "the designs produced in the Company would be better if design meetings were electronically supported" sounds reasonable if said quickly in everyday language; but every word in it except the articles, the preposition, and the conjunction are richly ambiguous. What would constitute a fair test? Could agreement on the criteria for refutation or survival of the hypothesis be achieved? In social situations one observer's "success" is often another's "failure.")

In constructing another "ideal-type" model of research, this time modified from Fig. 1-1 to cover AR, we have to accept that the researcher will deal not in hypothesis but in research themes within which lessons can be sought. (In the example above one such theme might be "exploration of design processes" in the Company in question or "support for design meetings.") The researcher interested in particular themes, declaring F and M (from Fig. 1-2), then enters the "social practice" of a real-world situation in which the themes are relevant and becomes involved as both participant and researcher. It will be necessary to think about that dual role and to negotiate carefully entry into the situation and his or her role in relation to that of participants. Work to effect change and "improvement" (as judged by people in the situation) can then ensue, with the researcher, however his or her role is defined, also committed to continuous reflection on the collaborative involvement and its outcomes. This will entail trying to make sense of the unfolding experience using the declared F and M. This of course may require some rethinking of earlier phases—and again, it is the declared intellectual framework of F and M which allows this to be done coherently. Finally, since real-world situations continuously evolve, the researcher must negotiate an exit from the situation and tease out the serious lessons learnt. This process, as an ideal type, is shown in Fig. 1-3.

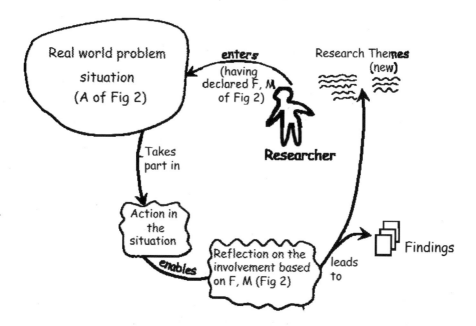

Figure 1-3. The cycle of action research in human situations

More explicitly, although still as an "ideal type" rather than a prescriptive description, Fig. 1-3 implies the process model for AR shown in Fig. 1-4. This covers entering a problem situation, declaring the epistemology in terms of which what counts as learning will be recognized, taking part in the change process, reflecting upon the experience, and recording the learning.

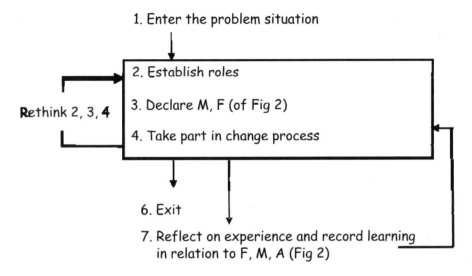

Figure 1-4. The process of action research

Obviously a process such as that in Fig. 1-4 could not produce law-like generalizations from involvement in a single situation. In any case AR does not assume that "social laws" await discovery in the same way that physical laws can be regarded as regularities of the universe which do recur whether or not they have yet been noticed and codified. But a serious organized process of AR *can* be made to yield defensible generalizations. For example, a multidisciplinary research team from Lancaster researched the contracting process in the National Health Service in the AR mode and did feel able to generalize. Using the guiding epistemology (F and M in Fig. 1-2) of soft systems methodology (SSM), a dozen pieces of action research, together with 80 semi structured interviews (structured using SSM-style activity models), were carried out. This did enable defensible generalizations about the gap between the rhetoric of "contracting" and the reality in NHS hospitals and Health Authorities to be made. This work is described by Checkland (1997).

In spite of this kind of evidence that AR can lead to results which can be generalized and transferred to other situations, however, it is obvious that AR cannot aspire to the same claim of validity as that associated with natural science (Campbell, 1988; Phillips, 1992). Achieving credibility, consensus, and coherence does not make a "truth claim" as strong as that derived from replicability of results independent of time, place, and researcher. Action researchers must pay careful attention to the claim of validity relevant to their research into phenomena not "homogenous through time."

It is useful to record the answers implicit in Fig. 1-4 to hostile questions commonly asked of AR.

3.1   What Exactly Is Being Researched?

The AR process accepts that "themes" have to replace hypotheses. Research in an organization on how to introduce a particular information system, for example, may well evolve into research on what organizational changes are first needed to make it sensible even to contemplate the introduction of a particular system. But themes need to be declared, and a link between them and a putative F and M has to be explicitly argued.

3.2   Who Is Researcher, Who Participant?

The potential merging of the roles "researcher" and "participant" in the situation has to be acknowledged; it should, ideally, be discussed, and the roles may evolve in the course of AR. We have in our practice met among participants a wide range of degrees of readinesses to take part in the critical reflection on the research as it is enacted, something which is ultimately the researcher's responsibility.

3.3   How Do You Know When to Stop?

The laboratory researcher in natural science can stop when replicable results show that a hypothesis has been refuted or has survived the tests to which it has been subjected. AR as a research mode accepts that social phenomena are "not homogenous through time"; this means that ending a piece of research in an organization is ultimately an arbitrary act. The flux of events and ideas which constitute the research situation will continue to evolve through time. It has to be the researcher's judgment that the chosen methodology (M) and its framework of ideas (F) have yielded significant learning in interaction with the area of application (A). Attempting to "write up" the results will often reveal whether or not a strong case can be made that this position has been reached.

3.4   How Can Results Be Conveyed to Others or Transferred to Other Situations?

Since any organizational situation at a particular time, with its particular participants having their own individual or shared histories, may be unique, it cannot be guaranteed that results can be made richly meaningful to people in other situations. The problem here is not only a problem for AR; it exists also, for example, for those describing case histories. Once again, the importance of the declared epistemology (via F and M) is crucial, though it is neglected as much in case histories in the literature as it is in accounts of AR. For example, Zuboff (1988), in her important and oft-cited work on the profound social effects of computerization in a bank and at a newspaper plant, used participant observation, open-ended interviews, and small group discussions. She wished to understand the interchange between "human responsiveness (feeling, perceiving, behaving) and the experienced 'life-world'" (Zuboff, 1988, p. 243): that was her main theme. She used "an extensive interview protocol designed to translate . . . themes into appropriate questions" (p. 427). Unfortunately her appendix on methodology does not include details of that protocol. With "1500 pages of field notes and transcripts," she "began to build a conceptual map of the territory" (p. 428). Had she included such maps in reporting the work, the reader would have been able to recover more of the research content and appraise the judgments being made by the researcher in the course of the work. This criterion of recoverability is sufficiently important to be considered in more detail. If it is met, it will help to justify the generalization and transferability of results from AR (or case study) research.

4.   THE IMPORTANCE OF THE "RECOVERABILITY" CRITERION

If we imagine an "ideal-type" spectrum of processes of knowledge acquisition, from experimental natural science at one end to telling stories at the other, then along that spectrum we shall have very different criteria for judging the "truth value" of their outputs or claims. For laboratory experiments in natural science the in-principle "public" repeatability of the experimental happenings, no matter who conducts the experiments, is the basis of the strong criterion which has made natural science the common model of knowledge acquisition. (Ultimately this criterion rests upon the consensus among observers acting in good faith that the happenings are what everyone agrees they are: "This voltmeter is reading 3 volts.") At the other end of the spectrum we shall have the much weaker criterion that this (research) story is "plausible." But that immediately provokes the question, Plausible to whom? What *Weltanschauung* would make this research seem "plausible"? Would another observer find its outcomes "implausible"? The problem for action researchers, knowing that the strong criterion of "repeatability" is beyond their reach, is to do better than simply settle for "plausibility."

Our argument here is that the aim in AR should be to enact a process based on a declared-in-advance methodology (encompassing a particular framework of ideas) in such a way that the process is *recoverable* by anyone interested in subjecting the research to critical scrutiny. The research described by Checkland (1997), carried out by a multidisciplinary team researching purchaser-provider interactions in the National Health Service, attempted to provide such a recoverable process. The work used SSM in the sense-making "Mode 2" form (Checkland and Scholes, 1991), with its particular framework of systemicity. The aim was to make clear to interested observers the thought processes and models which enabled the team to make their interpretations and draw their conclusions. Those observers might not accept the team's interpretations; then a debate about the work could take place which was sufficiently well structured as to be coherent. The weaker "plausibility" criterion does not offer that prospect.

It is the desirability of using the "recoverability" criterion that makes it so important, in the "ideal-type" AR in Figs. 1-3 and 1-4, to declare in advance the epistemology in terms of which a piece of AR will acquire what counts as knowledge.

The absence of an insistence on this is the greatest lacuna in the literature of AR, though the point does get made in the more philosophical literature of social science. For example, Phillips (1992, p. 108) argues that if findings are to be taken seriously, they must be supported by appropriate arguments and or evidence; there must be, in the language of Toulmin's account of reasoning (Toulmin *et al.,* 1979), an adequate "warrant" in conjunction with a particular framework which supplies "backing" for the warrant and, ultimately, the "claims."

> The *claims* involved . . . are . . . *well founded* only if sufficient *grounds* of an appropriate and relevant kind can be offered in their support. These grounds must be connected to the claims by reliable, applicable warrants, which are capable in turn of being justified by appeal to sufficient *backing* of the relevant kind. (Toulmin *et al.*, 1979, p. 27)

The AR literature has rather neglected this kind of consideration. Even as rich an account of AR as that given by Eden & Huxham (1996) does not strongly embrace this point. They usefully set out 15 characteristics of AR, which we drastically summarize below:

(i) researcher intends to change the organization;

(ii) there must be implications beyond the specific situation;

(iii) research seeks theory as an explicit concern;

(iv) any tools, techniques, or models developed need to be linked to the research design;

(v) emergent theory will emerge from both data and initial theory;

(vi) theory building will be incremental and cyclic;

(vii) presentation should acknowledge prescription and description;

(viii) there will be an orderliness in approach;

(ix) exploration of data and theory building should be explainable to others;

(x) later reporting is part of theory exploration and development;

(xi) i-x are necessary but not sufficient for valid AR;

(xii) it is used where other methods are not appropriate;

(xiii) triangulation is used if possible;

(xiv) history and context are given due weight; and

(xv) dissemination of findings goes beyond those involved in a study.

With the exception of point xi (which is a meta-level point, about the set rather than of it), these characteristics map well our experiences in the 25-year action research program at Lancaster. Points v and viii come closest to addressing our concern for the prior declaration of both theory and methodological process, but they need greater emphasis if AR is to deliver more than plausible stories.

5.   CONCLUSION

This paper has made an argument which may be summarized as follows.

1. The repeatability of results in experiments carried out by natural scientists makes the research process of natural science the most easily defended system we have of knowledge acquisition—even though the repeatability extends only to a consensus on observable happenings, not to any interpretation of them. This success apparently stems from the fact that the natural phenomena studied by natural science are themselves truly regular; they are "homogenous through time" in Keynes' (1938) phrase.

2. With the increased acceptance that "social reality" is not a given, but is the changing product of a continual intersubjective discourse, there has been in the last decade an increased interest in qualitative research. AR and its many variants are increasingly being treated as serious and appropriate alternatives to the hypothesis testing which is at the core of research methodology in natural science. But proponents of AR need to

recognize the limits to the claims they can make for the validity of their approach.

3. Unable to match the complete replicability of experimental happenings which characterize natural science, researchers investigating social phenomena via AR must at least achieve a situation in which their research process is *recoverable* by interested outsiders. In order to do this it is essential to state the epistemology (the set of ideas and the process in which they are used methodologically) by means of which they will make sense of their research, and so define what counts for them as acquired knowledge.

4. This gives well-organized AR a "truth claim" less strong than that of laboratory experimentation, but one much stronger than that of mere "plausibility," which is all that much putative AR in the literature can claim.

5. The literature of AR has so far shown an inadequate appreciation of the need for a declared epistemology and hence a recoverable research process.

Finally, we may remark on this occasion that since systems ideas are a strong component of much methodology which is relevant to qualitative research methods such as action research, it seems appropriate that *Systems Practice* should extend its cover to include interventions aimed at both acquiring knowledge and helping to bring about organizational change.

6.   AFTERWORD

Since this chapter was first published in 1998 the stream of papers and books on aspects of action research has flowed forth unabated, in many different fields – information systems, health care, education, management. See, for example, Bate (2000), Hadfield (2005), Kidd & Kral (2005), Lomax (2002), McNiff (2001) and Reed (2005).

This indicates a growing interest in this form of social research, but many publications are unspecific about both its fundamental nature and the issues concerning the validity of findings from action research. In particular there is so far little recognition of the need for prior declaration of the epistemology in terms of which knowledge will be created by the research. It is this which makes it possible for people outside the research both to recover and understand it and to judge its credibility.

ACKNOWLEDGMENT

The figures in this paper are reproduced from Checkland & Holwell (1997) by permission of J. Wiley & Sons.

This chapter is a revised version of an article by the authors, published in 1998 in volume 11, issue 1 of Systemic Practice and Action Research.

REFERENCES

Argyris, C., Putnam, R., & Smith, D. M. (1985). *Action Science - Concepts, Methods and Skills for Research and Intervention.* San Francisco: Jossey-Bass.

Bate, P. (2000). Synthesizing Research and Practice: Using the Action Research Approach in Health Care Settings. *Social Policy and Administration, 34*(4), 478-493.

Blum, F. H. (1955). Action Research - a scientific approach? *Philosophy of Science, 22*(1), 1-7.

Campbell, D. T. (1988). *Methodology and Epistemology for Social Science: Selected Papers edited by E.S. Overman.* Chicago: University of Chicago Press.

Checkland, P. (1981). *Systems Thinking, Systems Practice,* Chichester: John Wiley.

Checkland, P. (1985). From Optimizing to Learning: A Development of Systems Thinking for the 1990s. *Journal of the Operational Research Society, 36*(9), 757-767.

Checkland, P. (1991). From Framework Through Experience to Learning: the Essential Nature of Action Research. In H. Nissen, H. K. Klein & R. A. Hirschheim (Eds.), *Information Systems Research: Contemporary Approaches and Emergent Traditions* (pp. 397-403). Amsterdam: North-Holland.

Checkland, P. (1997). Rhetoric and Reality in Contracting: research in and on the NHS. In R. Flynn & G. Williams (Eds.), *Contracting for Health - Quasi-markets and the National Health Service* (pp. incomplete). London: Oxford University Press.

Checkland, P., & Holwell, S. E. (1998). *Information, Systems and Information Systems: Making Sense of the Field.* Chichester: John Wiley and Sons.

Checkland, P., & Scholes, J. (1990). *Soft Systems Methodology in Action.* Chichester: John Wiley & Sons.

Clark, A. (1972). *Action Research and Organizational Change.* London: Harper & Row.

Dash, D. P. (1997). *Problems of Action Research,* (Working Paper No. 14). University of Lincolnshire and Humberside.

Eden, C., & Huxham, C. (1996). Action Research for the Study of Organizations. In S. Clegg, C. Hardy & W. Nord (Eds.), *The Handbook of Organizational Studies* (pp. 526-542). Beverly Hills CA: Sage.

Engels, P. G. H., & Salomon, M. L. (1997). *Facilitating Innovation for Development,* Royal Tropical Institute, The Netherlands.

Foster, M. (1972). An Introduction to the Theory and Practice of Action Research in Work Organisations. *Human Relations, 25*(6), 529-556.

Hadfield, M. (2005). Knowledge Production, Its Management and Action Research. *Educational Action Research, 13*(2), 301-311.

Hult, M., & Lennung, S. (1980). Towards a Definition of Action Research: A Note and a Bibliography. *Journal of Management Studies, 17*(2), 242-250.

Keynes, J. M. (1938). Discussion of R. F. Harrod's presidential address to the Royal Economic Society. In Moggridge, D. E. (ed.) (1976), *Keynes,* Fontana/Collins, London.

Kidd, S. A., & Kral, M. J. (2005). Practising Participatory Action Research. *Journal of Counseling Psychology, 52*(2), 187-195.

Lewin, K. (1947). Frontiers in Group Dynamics: Concept, Method and Reality in Social Science; Social Equilibrium and Social Change. *Human Relations, 1*(1), 5-41.

Lomax, P. (2002). Action Research. In M. Coleman & A. R. J. Briggs (Eds.), *Research Methods in Educational Leadership.* London: Paul Chapman.

McNiff, J., with Whitehead, J. (2001). *Action Research: Principles and Practice* (2nd ed.). London: Routlege Falmer.

Moggridge, D. E. (1976). *Keynes.* London: Fontana/Collins.

Phillips, D. C. (1992). *The Social Scientist's Bestiary: A Guide to Fabled Threats to, and Defences of, Naturalistic Social Science.* Oxford: Pergamon.

Reed, J. (2005). Using Action Research in Nursing Practice with Older People: Democratizing Knowledge. *Journal of Clinical Nursing, 14*(5), 594-600.

Revans, R. (1972). *Hospitals: Communication, Choice and Change.* London: Tavistock.

Susman, G. (1983). Action Research: A Sociotechnical Systems Perspective. In G. Morgan (Ed.), *Beyond Method: Strategies for Social Research* (pp. 95-113). Newbury Park: Sage.

Susman, G., & Evered, R. D. (1978). An Assessment of the Scientific Merits of Action Research. *Administrative Science Quarterly, 23*, 582-603.

Torbet, W. R. (1991). *The Power of Balance: Transforming Self, Society and Scientific Inquiry.* Newbury Park, CA: Sage.

Toulmin, S., Rieke, R., & Janik, A. (1979). *An Introduction to Reasoning.* New York: Macmillan.

Whyte, W. F. (1991). *Participatory Action Research.* Newbury Park: Sage Publications.

Ziman, J. J. (1968). Public Knowledge, an Essay Concerning the Social Dimension of Science. London: Cambridge University Press.

Chapter 2

THE STRUCTURE OF POWER IN ACTION RESEARCH PROJECTS

David Avison[1], Richard Baskerville[2] and Michael D. Myers[3]

[1]*ESSEC Business School, France;* [2]*Georgia State University, USA;* [3]*University of Auckland, New Zealand*

Abstract: Action research is a qualitative research method that emphasizes collaboration between researchers and practitioners. The process of action research requires that choices be made determining how power is balanced in various ways between researchers and their collaborators within the host organization. We discuss three aspects of power: the procedures for initiating an action research project, those for determining authority within the project, and the degree of formalization. We analyze seven action research projects in information systems and from this analysis distil recommendations for determining power structures. These recommendations will be important to those researchers using action research in information systems.

Key words: action research, qualitative research, power, information systems

1. INTRODUCTION

Action research (AR) emphasizes collaboration between researchers and practitioners. It is an important qualitative research method for the information systems field (Baskerville and Wood-Harper, 1996; Lau, 1997; Myers, 1997; Avison et al., 1999). Action research differs from case study research in that the action researcher is directly involved in planned organizational change. Unlike the case study researcher, who seeks to study organizational phenomena but not to change them (Benbasat et al. 1987), the action researcher intervenes by creating organizational change and simultaneously studies the impact of this change (Baburoglu and Ravn, 1992). The intervention aspect of action research means that it is an especially interesting and relevant method for the area of information systems development (Avison et al., 1998).

Action Research is not without its problems. In particular, action researchers struggle with the dilemmas that are embodied in the tension between the intentions of the researchers and the intentions of the members of the host organization that may be collaborating in the project. These tensions inhabit even the basic definitions of the action research method itself. For example, Rapoport (1970, p.499) defines action research as an approach that "aims to contribute *both* to the practical concerns of people in an immediate problematic situation and to the goals of social science by joint collaboration within a mutually acceptable ethical framework".

While this definition draws attention to the collaborative aspect of action research, it also draws out the potential for conflicts that might arise from its use. Researchers and practitioners may not share the same values and they are likely to have different goals. On the one hand, action research is concerned to enlarge the stock of knowledge of the social science community (Clark 1972). On the other hand, action research is also concerned about solving practical problems confronting the organization in which the research is embedded. The "double challenge" of combining both practical action and research potentially leads to conflict where the roles of the collaborative members of the research team are different.

The issues of power in action research are not well understood. Previous studies have focused on the issues in terms of control (Avison, et al., 2001). But control is far too mechanical as an umbrella concept for considering potential conflicts between researchers and practitioners. Control is the exercise of restraining or directing influence. Power is the ability to act or produce an effect. Power is the possession of control, authority or influence over others. Control is the exercise of power. A situation in which the goals of the researchers are in conflict with those of the practitioners in the host organization can give rise to power struggles. Who is empowered in action research projects? If it is the practitioners, then they can control the researchers. If it is the researchers, then they can control the practitioners. If an action research project operates without an understanding of the power distribution, then conflicts between researchers and practitioners may lead to a power struggle as each group seeks to control the project directions.

Such power struggles are deeply embedded in social and cultural factors in the research setting. There may even be basic contradictions between the ethical and ontological assumptions of the researchers and the practitioners. Additionally, there may be power struggles *within* the research team and even more so *within* the organization with respect to goals and value of the project (and not just between the researchers and the representatives of the host organization). The potential for power issues add to the complex situational nature of action research.

In this paper, we draw upon the work of Jasperson et al. (2002), who provide a comprehensive review of the use of power in IT research. They point out that there are multiple conceptualizations of power in the IS research literature. They categories the literature according to various common themes: Authority; Centralization, Decision Rights, Participation in Decision Making; Influence; and Politics. Table 2-1 lists a subset of those particular themes that are particularly relevant to power issues in action research projects.

There are four major sources of power that inhabit these four common themes. First, there is authority. Authority is a source of power derived from formal or institutional structures. Formal structures are exemplified by authority attached to an office or job position while institutional authority is attached to university degrees, training certificates, etc. Second, there are resource rights. This source of power is derived from ownership or control over resources. Resource rights are exemplified by the ability to assign people or office space to an action research project. Third, there is influence. Influence is a source of power derived from social attributes like trust or charisma. Influence is exemplified by an ability of an action researcher to persuade practitioners to take actions even though the researcher has no formal authority. Fourth, there is politics. Politics is a source of power derived from the exercise of strategic processes. Politics is exemplified by the use of creeping commitment as a strategy for drawing cautious practitioners into taking revolutionary actions.

Because of the situational nature of action research and the potential for power issues, each action research project, to some at extent at least, is unique, and it is difficult to draft general *laws* about how to carry out such projects. Different themes and aspects of power will be relevant depending upon the situation. Therefore, rather than attempting to draft general laws that must be applied in every situation, we develop general *guidelines* for diagnosing and resolving problems of power in action research projects in IS. Where such issues arise, action researchers might consider these guidelines, although it is clearly up to IS researchers to interpret and apply the guidelines for themselves.

Table 2-1. Common Themes in Power Conceptualizations (adapted from Jasperson et al., 2002)

Authority	
Institutional Power	Power is mandated from ownership.
Rational Structural	Power that focuses on authority, information, and expertise as bases of power.
Centralization, Decision Rights, Participation in Decision Making	
Disciplinary Power	Power is a mechanism constituted by the multiplicity of power/knowledge relationships between agents. It is associated with bodies of

	knowledge (disciplines) that constitute the dominant view and meaning of things.
Rational	Structural Power that emphasizes rational decision making.
Resource Control	Power that relies heavily on exchange theory and is derived from the ability to control the supply of resources to others.
Zero Sum Power	Power is defined in terms of the control or ownership of resources.
Influence	
Behavioral Power	Focuses on exercise of power in which one actor influences another actor to behave in a manner differently than s/he would have behaved without the influence.
Interpretive	Power that assumes that reality is socially constructed... [and] that the parties involved exert influence by constructing the meaning of what others experience.
Politics	
Organizational Power	Power is derived from how political roles are played; rational views of political interests.
Pluralist	Development, prioritization, and execution of organizational goals are an explicitly political process involving conscious negotiation based on control of resources and information.
Processual Power	Power is part of the decision-making sphere and micro-politics of organizational life. Decisions and priorities involved in negotiation are emergent phenomena. Power lies not in concrete resources but in strategies like coalition-formation and the manipulation of information that protagonists employ in the power game.
Radical	Power and politics are outgrowths of social structures. Political activity, broadly defined, involves either maintaining or undermining (and ultimately overthrowing) existing power structures.
Zero Sum Power	Power is a zero-sum political game in which there is a fight between individuals over an object when one party wins the other loses.

2. POWER AND ACTION RESEARCH PROJECTS: ISSUES OF INITIATION AND AUTHORITY

There is no consensus on the ideal power structures for action research projects. However, there are three key aspects of the action research situation that help to determine what the basic nature of these power structures should be. The first aspect concerns the initiation of the action research project, the second concerns the determination of authority for action in the research project, and the third aspect concerns the degree of formalization of the project.

2.1 The initiation of action research projects

Considering the first aspect, how are action research projects initiated? Action research focuses on addressing a situation where problems exist. Sometimes the action researcher may 'discover' the problems, but in other situations the problems 'discover' the action researcher (Root-Bernstein, 1989).

The former case is research-driven initiation, in that the action researcher might be in possession of a general theoretical approach to addressing problem situations and looking for settings that are characterized by such problems. In this situation, the practitioners may be somewhat dubious or indifferent, particularly if they are unaware that they are in fact confronting serious problems. Sometimes, there is a mixture of the two ways of initiation. It evolves from discussions between researchers and practitioners, possibly following on from consultancy work.

The latter case is problem-driven initiation, in that practitioners might be confronted by a seemingly insurmountable problem and seeking help from theoretical specialists. In this situation, the researchers may have to develop their research program somewhat opportunistically, undertaking a series of research projects that have a broad theoretical span. The researchers attempt to learn from these experiences and draw conclusions which then help to further develop the theory.

The goal of the initiation process among both the practitioners and the researchers is the discovery of a mutual interest in solving the problem at hand. Either of the cases above can lead to success or failure depending on whether this initiation goal is achieved. This failure occurs because the researchers find no prospects for knowledge discovery in the problem setting, or the practitioners find no prospects for solving the immediate problem (or both).

Kock (1997) has shown exactly how this failure unfolds in researcher-driven initiation, identifying three failure forms:

(1) *Iceberg Subjects.* Practitioners do not understand the real opportunities for improvement.
(2) *Irrelevant Subjects.* There are no prospects for generating knowledge in the particular problem setting.
(3) *No Client.* No problem setting can be found that matches the theoretical frames of the action researcher.

2.2 The Determination of Authorities for Action Research Projects

The second aspect of power – the determination of authority for action research projects – is more complex. Once the project has been started the mechanisms by which authority is defined are very important. These mechanisms include the determination of action warrants, power over the structure of the project, and processes for renegotiation and /or cancellation.

Action warrants define the authority under which action may be taken. Rarely will an organization cede ultimate authority for organizational action to an external researcher. This guarded commitment is reasonable since the researcher's motives are divided between research goals and organizational problem-solving goals (Rapoport, 1970). In some cases, the entire action research team, composed of both researchers from a university or other research team (whom we have termed researchers) and internal organizational professionals (whom we have termed practitioners) is consultative, advising decision-makers on recommended actions and possible outcomes. In other cases, a team consisting of researchers and practitioners may be granted final authority for determining organizational action. The form of such a warrant is rarely created by a direct fiat, but rather by appointing internal team members who already possess such authority for action.

The source of the warrants reveals a great deal about the project setting. A warrant established by the CEO in a large enterprise differs qualitatively from one established by an office manager in a small, remote field office of the same enterprise. The decision-maker issuing these warrants defines the actual scope of the project. Importantly, the organizational power held by that decision-maker also defines the potential scope of the project.

The nature of the action warrants has implications for the project. A team which is consultative rather than led by individual decision-makers has more potential for domination by researchers, since ultimate decisions for action are pushed outside of the group, and the practitioners can more easily defer to the researchers, particularly for high-risk action advice. A team with authority-bearing practitioners has more potential for domination by these powerful practitioners, since they will be personally held responsible for the results of the team-determined action. Issues of risk may loom larger in such cases depending on the degree of risk-adversity that characterizes the powerful practitioners. Such a group may be more likely to make changes iteratively, since a series of small organizational experiments will be less risky in most situations than bold, sweeping organizational changes.

2.3 The Degree of Formalization in Action Research Projects

The third aspect of power in an action research project involves the ability to renegotiate action research structures. Formal or informal mechanisms may permit changes in the research team membership and warrants (perhaps thereby redefining the project scope). This renegotiation is likely to be quite informal, representing an evolution of the project as the outcomes from organizational actions emerge. The evolution may change a consultative team into an authority-bearing team, a linear action process into an iterative action process or vice versa. Indeed, the project may be re-initialized, shifting from a researcher-driven mode to a practitioner-driven mode, as the practitioners discover implications of a previously unnoticed problem.

Most action research projects begin with a fairly concrete conceptualization of the determination of their conclusion: a goal-state in which an immediate organizational problem or set of problems have been alleviated. This pre-conceptualization is particularly evident in practitioner-initiated projects. This conceptualization may evolve as a result of changes in the warrants (the scope), but the concluding goal state, whether achieved or not, can often be characterized, at least through later reflection, from the very beginning.

It is sometimes less clear, and an interesting indication of the project setting, how a project may be cancelled. A cancellation midstream by the host organization might be a disaster for the researcher, for example, if part of a PhD program, particularly if the work is a key element of a larger research program or the researcher has invested considerably in developing the theoretical foundations after the problem was discovered (Braa and Vidgen, 1999, look into the suitability of action research as a PhD project). Similarly, a cancellation midstream by the researchers may leave the host organization in a worse condition, relevant to the immediate practical problem, than their original position at the outset of the project. Valuable time and effort may have been wasted while a serious practical problem remains unsolved.

Particularly relevant in such cases will be the degree of formalization, typically defined in written agreements, such as a contract or letter of agreement. If the AR project goes well, there may seem to be no need for such agreements. However, if a project is cancelled, or in danger of being cancelled, then the lack of a formal written agreement might be a cause of problems and disputes (though a formal agreement itself does not preclude the latter). A contract might also specify such aspects of researcher engagement and team composition (and formalities regarding publication, a major concern to researchers). Some potential alternatives for the formalization of action research projects will also be discussed further in the next section.

3.   SEVEN ACTION RESEARCH PROJECTS: THE STRUCTURE OF POWER

We now look at seven action research projects in order to assess their power structures according to the three aspects discussed in section 2: initiation, authority, and formalization. These seven examples were invited for discussion at the 1998 North American Information Systems Action Research Workshop in Atlanta, Georgia, USA. These were selected because of the opportunity afforded in the workshop to discuss the power structures of a variety of information systems action research projects with the researchers who conducted the studies. Of course, not all of the examples fell neatly and tidily into each of these categories, power in real-world research is both complex and subtle, but Table 2-2 emerged from the workshop discussions of the seven examples as being a fairly accurate description of what happened in practice.

Table 2-2. Power aspects of seven IS action research projects

Example	Initiation	Authority	Formalization
Semantic Database Prototypes (Baskerville, 1993)	Client	Client	Formal
Reorganization of the IS of the NCF (Simon, 1998)	Client	Client	Formal
Coping with Systems Risk (Straub and Welke, 1998)	Researcher	Client	Informal
An Action Research Study of Asynchronous Groupware Support (Kock and McQueen, 1998)	Researcher	Staged	Informal

Example	Initiation	Authority	Formalization
Building a Virtual Network (Lau and Hayward, 1998)	Collaborative	Client	Formal
Revealing Complexity in ISD (Chiasson and Dexter, 1998)	Collaborative	Identity	Evolved
IT Requirements to Augment Organizational Sensemaking (Nosek, 1998)	Collaborative	Identity	Informal

3.1   Initiation

Initiation refers to the genesis of the action research project. Did the problem discover the research or vice-versa? There are three forms of initiation found in the seven examples: client initiation, researcher initiation, and collaborative initiation.

Client initiation represents the classic genesis of action research, in which a host organization with a serious immediate problem seeks help from a knowledgeable researcher. While this form of initiation has been characterized as typical, or even characteristic in action research (Schein, 1987), only two of the seven examples seem to fit this type. Baskerville's (1993) study of *Semantic Database Prototypes* involved a search by an organization for an alternative design approach following the failure of two previous projects. Simon's (1998) study on *Reorganization of the Information Systems of the US Naval Construction Forces* involved an invitation to the researcher by the organization. In both these settings, the researcher neither selected the research site nor the research question: the researcher's interest was called upon by the problem organizations. Rather than the researcher defining the research setting, the problem discovered the researcher.

Researcher initiation represents an alternative approach for action research, in which the researcher begins by searching for a host organization as a site for an action research project. This form of action research initiation leads to a project bearing some similarity to a field experiment. While supposedly less common, two of our examples appear to fit this characteristic. The action project underlying Straub and Welke's (1998) study on *Coping with Systems Risk* began as a non-intervention case study with an established theory. The opportunity for intervention arose after the engagement had begun. In Kock and McQueen's (1999) study *An Action*

Research Study of Asynchronous Groupware Support, the researcher sought two host organizations, whose primary concern was business process redesign, which were willing to experiment with groupware as a means to achieve the redesign.

Collaborative initiation represents a setting in which the action research evolved from the interaction between researchers and client. In Nosek's (1998) study *IT Requirements to Augment Organizational Sensemaking*, executives in a special MBA program led by the researcher chose to participate actively by intervening in their own organizations. Similarly, in Lau and Hayward's (1998) study, *Building a Virtual Network*, the research evolved from the interventions of regional health representatives following a seven-week training course that positioned information technology in the restructuring of community health services. In Chiasson and Dexter's (1998) study, *Revealing Complexity in ISD*, the researcher was developing software and infrastructure in two heart clinics, and used this venue as an opportunity to engage the host organization in an 'offshoot' action research project. In these projects, researchers and host organization representatives were originally engaged in one activity, and although not unrelated to the ultimate action research project, both the problem and the research seemed to be interactively discovered by both the client and the host.

3.2   Authority

Authority refers to the issue of 'who is really in charge of the research project'. Elements of this authority include action warrants, processes for renegotiation of the structure of the project, and authority for cancellation discussed in section 2. While action research reports may not explicitly describe the division of power among the stakeholders, it can sometimes be inferred from the way that the research project evolved. As in the initiation characteristic, there are three notable authority patterns in action research projects. However, these are not parallel with the initiation characteristics. These patterns are client domination, staged domination, and identity domination.

In a client dominated action research project, the research team itself does not hold an action warrant. Rather the team recommends and justifies action to organizational managers outside of the team. Once approved, the team may thereafter be intervening, that is, executing the approved action and monitoring the outcomes. This form of authority seems to be quite common in action research practice, despite the preoccupation with collaboration espoused in the general social science action research literature (Whyte, 1991). Three of the examples are characterized by client domination. In Baskerville's (1993) study, the action research team was composed of analysts and programmers without any warrants for action or authority to renegotiate the project structures established between a government department and a consortium of universities. An interagency agreement nested cancellation authority strictly with the client. In Simon's (1998) study, the research team did include three powerful managers (chiefs of staff), however it is explicitly noted that the team's proposals of action must be sanctioned by more senior commanders outside of the team. In Lau and Hayward's (1998) project, the role of the researcher involved suggesting technologies, but the final decisions regarding their use were always left with the organizers, participants, coordinators and support staff.

In Straub and Welke's (1998) study, the power domination profile is much more subtle. The intervention involved inserting concepts and principles of theory-grounded models of security planning into a professional training program and systematically evaluating the outcome. While it is conceivable that this intervention might have been made without notice from upper management in the organization, the researcher continuously met with these senior managers and conceded authority over the intervention to their approval.

Staged domination involves a migration of power domination among the action research stakeholders. For example, a project that begins rather informally regarding a problem that the practitioner organization does not feel is serious, might initially be dominated by the researcher. As the collaborative team develops organizational awareness of the gravity of the problem, the field of action may broaden. The power domination may migrate from the researcher into a form of collaborative power-sharing. A further, wider-scope stage may even migrate power from the collaborative form to a final practitioner-dominated form. This stage pattern may be found in action research projects that grow in scope and field of action. An example of staged domination is found in Kock and McQueen's (1998) study, in which the researcher intervened initially to insert the use of a particular group process methodology into the organizational processes. Further interventions became more collaborative, as the members of the original group dispersed back to their parent organizations and the long-range effects of the original intervention rippled through five organizations.

Identity domination means that the researchers and the practicing organization professionals were the same person (or persons). In other words, one or more of the researchers were internal members of the practitioner organization, and already possessed the action warrant authority necessary to make the interventions. Typically, these persons would also have the authority to renegotiate the scope or cancel the action research project. Two example studies are characterized by identity power domination patterns. In Nosek's (1998) study, executives involved in an executive MBA program became the action investigators. These people were either already participating in making the decisions within the field of action scope, or were able to become involved in these decisions. Four researchers joined together in Chiasson and Dexter's (1998) study to undertake the multi-purpose SoftHeart project. The purposes of this project were varied, with each researcher operating with shared and individual goals that were nevertheless kept explicit.

3.3   Formalization

Formal power structures are typically defined in written agreements, such as a contract or letter of agreement. These agreements may describe the immediate problem situation and the scope of the research. These may also prescribe the mechanisms of researcher entry into the organization (engagement), the collaborative team composition, the warrants for action, mechanisms for renegotiating the agreement, and termination of the project through either cancellation or disengagement (Susman and Evered, 1978). These agreements may also deal with research sponsorship or compensation for the researcher.

Informal power structures are found when no written agreements exist. In some cases, the project may begin with little consensus or understanding by the parties involved over essential aspects of the research. The exact nature of the problem situation may be indeterminate; the scope of the problem may be unseen, and the remaining action research project details equally unpredictable. In such settings, the researcher's first task may be to discover the nature and scope of the problem, and thereby determine the power structures. Here, any formal power structures must emerge after the research commences. The question of formal structures may never be raised, and some action research projects may complete having engaged the researchers and practitioner organizations informally throughout.

A 'pure' formal or informal set of action research power structures may be rare in practice. Depending on the nature of the researcher, the practitioner organization, resource provisions, and the problem setting, some projects may commence with more formal structures than others. There may be some transition as the project emerges, and this transition will not always move from informal to formal power structures. A project that begins with more formal power structures is not likely to become less formal as the project develops. However, informal power structures may evolve into other forms of informal power structures as an action research project emerges. Another possible variation occurs where a written contract is agreed and signed on the basis of 'don't worry about this – it is just a formality', but which might be enforced brutally later if one party is dissatisfied with the outcome. In the past, researchers and research institutions have been particularly prone to suffer from a partner organization's legal department.

Action research power structures can be classified as formal, informal and evolved. Formal power structures are well-defined in written agreements at the project outset. Informal power structures will begin and complete with, at most, only broad and general written agreements. Evolved projects require changes in the power structures as the research scope develops progressively, but not necessarily from informal to formal structures.

The nature of the researcher or research organization is one of the factors that may influence the power structures. If the research is organized through a large or formal research organization, this organization may have policies or common practices that involve formal agreements (often standardized) with research hosts. The researcher's status as an authority in the particular problem setting may affect the demands for initial resource provision, which in turn may require the practitioner to initially increase the formality of the research power structures.

Another factor is the nature of the practitioner organization. Organizational size will affect the formality of allocating resources and policies. Organizations will vary in their policies about involving external expertise, and the organizational element negotiating the action research power structures may have more or less latitude for involving external expertise. The visibility of the problem and the consequent research results to other parts of the organization (or outside the organization) may increase the organization's need for formal research agreements.

The need for resource provision is another factor. The material support for the research must be divided between the practitioner and the researcher organizations or housed entirely in one or the other. Action research often requires a substantial involvement of practitioner organizational staff as well as researchers. Support and clerical staff will also become involved. Where the practitioner organization adopts a philosophy of cost-accounting, the dedication of these resources to the action research project may require formal power structures. The practitioner organization may also provide compensation directly to the researcher in the form of consulting fees, or to the researcher's organization for consulting, research support, or for a secondment package. This may be seen to be the practitioner organization 'buying' power at the expense of that of the researcher and some researchers doing action research refuse to be paid by the practitioner organization for this reason.

The perceived seriousness of the problem may also be a factor affecting the need for more formal power structures. If organizational survival is at stake, the practitioner may seek strong guarantees that the researcher is committed to developing a 'solution'. Likewise, if the researcher or the research institution is struggling, this pressure could lead the researcher to seek increased formality in the power structures.

There are two further factors related to the seriousness of the problem. One is the scope of the perceived problem. A broad scope reaching across the entire organization may be considered more difficult than a narrow scope. The problem history is also a factor. An intractable problem that has endured repeated, expensive attempts at solution may incline the practitioner to seek stronger commitments from the researchers.

These factors may evolve as the action research project develops. A project that was initiated with informal power structures may progressively discover more and more underlying problems with broader scope demanding increasing resources. The formality of the power structures may evolve in concert with these developments.

Two of the examples involved relatively informal power structures throughout the action research project. Executives involved in an executive MBA class became voluntarily involved in the action research interventions and analysis in Nosek's (1998) study. Although there were some formal power structures involved in the MBA course, these were tangential to the research. The action research was conducted without any need for resources, or even a substantial commitment of the participants beyond that normally required for their professional and academic activities. There were no formal agreements between the practitioner organizations and the researcher. In Kock and McQueen's (1998) project, the action research was implemented in the context of an organizational process redesign training program that would have progressed to its practical outcome with or without the overlaying action research infrastructure. Although there were formal power structures regarding the process redesign training, no such structures were agreed between the practitioner organizations and the researcher.

Three of the examples involved relatively formal structures. Baskerville's (1993) study involved an inter-agency agreement between government agencies and a university consortium. Formal letters established the project infrastructure detailing tasks and resource commitments from the researcher and practitioner organizations. The immediate problem was highly visible, somewhat serious, and 'consumed' with history. Similarly, the research power infrastructures underlying Lau and Hayward's (1998) study were established with the sponsorship of a partnership of eighteen health authorities. The action research was a component of a pilot project involving resources from three universities and a funding agency. The action research project underlying Simon's study did not involve a separate research organization, or a written agreement with the researcher (who was a member of the organization). The action research power structures were nevertheless established internally in the practitioner organization with formal power structures (for example, the command staff board). The need for this formal power structure is closely related to the visibility and seriousness of the problem (mission critical system infrastructure).

Changes in the power structures do not always imply an evolution in formalization. Two of the examples exhibit evolutionary power structures, moving among power structures as the project developed. Only one of these evolved in its formalization. The SoftHeart software project underlying Chiasson and Dexter's (1998) study began as an informal collaboration between four researchers, but evolved as the scope of the stakeholder community broadened into the clinic. Problems and communication breakdowns with the clinic increased the need for more formal structures. The power structures in the project underlying Straub and Welke's study (1998) also evolved, with the project progressing in an organic way. Some formality is indicated, for example, the use of non-disclosure agreements. But the relationship with the practitioner organization afforded the latitude for a case study design to emerge into an action research design. While these power structures may have remained more-or-less informal throughout the evolution, structures for controlling an action research project must be quite different from a case study. For example, in a case study the determination of action warrants and authority for cancellation are not typical structures.

4. DISCUSSION

We have suggested that the rigor of action research projects in information systems can be improved if more attention is given to the issue of power. Table 2-3 details the forms and characteristics of the three aspects of power structures discussed above: initiation, authority and formalization. Table 2-4 details the forms and characteristics of the various authority mechanisms discussed above that were implied by the examples. These mechanisms include the determination of action warrants, power over the structure of the project, processes for renegotiation and authority for cancellation. Table 2-5 summarizes the various influence factors that were important in understanding the determination of formalization for action research projects.

The description of the action research power structures indicates how these power structures are interactive to a limited degree. For example, we associated factors like a high visibility problem that involves practitioner organizational survival with power structures like formalization, practitioner initiation and practitioner domination. This interaction implies that the elements in the power groups (Table 2-3) are deterministically associated with the mechanisms and influence factors. This determination is certainly not absolute, but may be considered implicit. We can detail these implications by mapping the influence factors and mechanisms onto the common forms within the power groups. Table 2-6 embodies this mapping.

4.1   Recommendations

The action research power structures make it clear that determining the control of an action research project is beyond the independent power of both the practitioner organization and the researcher. Project control is shared, collaboratively determined and emergent. The researcher is obliged to stay within the realm of applied theory, those theoretical aspects that are relevant to real problems of today's managers. The practitioner within the organization is also obliged to stay within the realm of applied theory, taking those actions that can be reasoned from what is broadly known within the field of information technology.

An explicit discussion of power structures is rarely found in action research reports and yet it is clearly of great importance. In some cases these power structures can be detected as implications of the descriptions of the research project setting. Although ambiguity can often be a helpful 'social glue' and some blurring of power structures may be positive in an action research project, there needs to be some, perhaps brief, explicit reference to power structures in action research reports to help us interpret and validate the study. There may be some cases, for example, where shifts in the power structure of the action research project needs to be reported in order to maintain the validity of the study as findings shift across method variants. Straub and Welke (1998) provide a good example of this as the authors describe how the elements of action research evolved from a case study.

Despite the importance of the power structures for a collaborative activity like an action research project, these structures are sometimes emergent, either highly undefined at the beginning of a project or highly adapted in the later stages of the project. As the examples illustrate, highly defined, formal power structures are not necessary in action research projects. Indeed, they are probably impractical in many action research situations. However, there are some common associations between various influence factors, control mechanisms and forms of action research power.

Our recommendations do not deal so much with exactly how action research power structures ought to be determined for certain research settings, rather, we recommend that researchers and their action research practitioner professionals actively and collaboratively determine these power structures in the early stages of the project. Even if this determination only yields informal structures (for example, an undefined cancellation authority), it is important that these determinations be consciously discussed and preferably decided during the course of the research, rather than ignored. The reason that this is important is based on the possible evolution of the power structures. If these structures are not recognized at the outset, their gradual development may go unnoticed by either the practitioner or the researcher. These changes may signify oncoming important scope shifts, critically important information for both practitioner and researcher, but perhaps more critical to practitioners. These changes may also signify shifts of power between practitioner and researcher. Such power shifts may suggest concerted changes in related power structures.

In order to manage the action research project, power is required. Power depends on an understanding of the project power structures. Action research is collaborative. Without an explicit understanding of the current and past project power structures, either the researcher or the practitioner (or both) can unknowingly lose power and thereby mismanage the project. This reduces the potential of action research as a way to improve a problem situation in organizations and also as a way of increasing our stock of knowledge about information systems.

Table 2-3. Forms and characteristics of the major action research power structures

Power Aspect	Forms	Characteristics
Initiation	Researcher	Field experiment
	Practitioner	Classic action research genesis
	Collaborative	Evolves from existing interaction
Authority	Practitioner	Consultative action warrant
	Staged	Migration of power
	Identity	Practitioner and researcher are the same person
Formalization	Formal	Specific written contract or letter of agreement
	Informal	Broad, perhaps verbal agreements
	Evolved	Informal or formal projects shift into the opposite form

Table 2-4. Forms and characteristics of authority in action research projects

Authority Mechanisms	Forms	Characteristics	Ideal Researcher Power Sources
Action warrants determination	Consultative	Practitioner organization leadership retaining power	Institutional Authority Influence
	Authority-bearing team members	Practitioner organization projecting power into research team	Institutional Authority Influence
	Vested by fiat	Research team assumes responsibility	Institutional Authority Formal Authority Resource Rights Influence Politics
Power over the structure of the project	Researcher dominated	Consultative, low risk, low profile problems	Institutional Authority Formal Authority Resource Rights Influence Politics
	Practitioner dominated	Authority-bearing team membership, high risk	Institutional Authority Influence
Renegotiation processes	Team membership, problem definition	Changing scope of problem	Institutional Authority Influence
	Re-initiate project	Discovery of essentially different underlying problem, scope shifts from researcher-dominated to practitioner-dominated	Institutional Authority Influence
Cancellation authority	Researcher	The practitioner characterizes the problem as minor	Institutional Authority
	Practitioner	Limit practitioner commitment to the research	Institutional Authority Formal Authority Resource Rights Influence Politics
	Undefined	Most common	Institutional Authority Formal Authority Resource Rights Influence Politics

Table 2-5. Action research power structure influence factors

Factor	Forms	Characteristics	Ideal Researcher Power Sources
Nature of the researcher	Formal research organization	Policies may require formal power structures and researcher domination	Institutional Authority Formal Authority
	Researcher status as an authority	Limited availability, may require more resources and researcher domination	Institutional Authority Influence
Nature of the practitioner organization	Organization size	Large organizations often have more formal policies	Formal Authority
	Policies about involving external expertise	Affects latitude to engage researchers informally and limits researcher domination	Institutional Authority
	Visibility of the problem	High visibility increases need for formalization and practitioner domination	Institutional Authority
Need for resource provisions	Substantial involvement of practitioner organizational staff	Formalization affected by tight cost accounting philosophy	Formal Authority
	Compensation to researcher or research organization	Formalization for payment of grants, fees, honorariums, *etc.*	Institutional Authority Formal Authority
Perceived seriousness of the problem	Organizational survival	Great practitioner commitment may increase formalization and practitioner domination	Institutional Authority Formal Authority
	Scope	Broader scope may increase formalization and practitioner domination	Institutional Authority Formal Authority
	Problem history	Intractable, enduring problems may lead to more formalization and practitioner domination.	Institutional Authority Formal Authority

Table 2-6. Associations between action research power structures and research setting factors.

Mechanisms and influence classes	Factor	Forms	Initiation			Domination			Formalization		
			Researcher	Practitioner	Collaborative	Practitioner	Staged	Identity	Formal	Informal	Evolved
Authority mechanisms	Action warrants determination	Consultative	⇔							⇔	
		Authority-bearing team members		⇔		⇔			⇔		
		Vested by fiat		⇔		⇔			⇔		
	Power over the structure of the project	Researcher dominated	⇔				⇔			⇔	⇔
		Practitioner dominated		⇔		⇔					⇔
	Renegotiation processes	Team membership, problem definition			⇔						⇔
		Re-initiate project			⇔						⇔
	Cancellation authority	Researcher	⇔				⇔				
		Practitioner		⇔		⇔			⇔	⇔	
		Undefined				⇔				⇔	
Factors influencing power structures	Nature of the researcher	Formal research organisation		⇔					⇔		
		Researcher status as an authority		⇔			⇔		⇔		
	Nature of the practitioner organisation	Large organisation size							⇔		
		Policies about involving external expertise							⇔		
		Visibility of the problem (Lo. Hi)	Lo	Hi		Hi	Lo		Hi	Lo	
	Need for resource provisions	Substantial involvement of practitioner organisational staff		⇔		⇔			⇔		
		Compensation to researcher or research organisation		⇔					⇔		
	Perceived seriousness of the problem	Organisational survival		⇔		⇔			⇔		
		Scope (N-Narrow, W-Wide)	N	W		W			W	N	
		Long problem history		⇔		⇔			⇔		

5. CONCLUSION

Action research is a qualitative research method that emphasizes collaboration between researchers and practitioners. The action researcher is directly involved in planned organizational change along with the practitioners. A mutually ethical framework is usually assumed or deemed essential for the success of an action research project, yet researchers and practitioners are likely to come from different cultures, may have different values, and different objectives. Tension and consequent power struggles are therefore not unknown in action research. They may come to the surface within the researcher-practitioner team and/or with the host organization and/or academic institution. It is this tension and the way the balance of power can be resolved in an action research project that we have emphasized in this chapter. We suggest general guidelines for discussing, diagnosing and resolving problems of power in action research projects in IS.

Following Jasperson et al. (2002), we discuss power in terms of a number of themes: authority; centralization, decision rights, participation in decision making; influence; and politics. We look at how the four main sources of power: authority; resource rights; influence; and politics inhabit these four themes in an action research project. There are three key aspects of the action research situation that help to determine what the basic nature of these power structures will be. The first aspect concerns the initiation of the action research project, the second concerns the determination of authority for action in the research project, and the third aspect concerns the degree of formalization of the project. A discussion of these shows us how different AR projects can be from each other. Initiation can come from the researcher or from practice and be research driven or problem driven. Authority can come from within the team (researcher or collaborator) or from outside (from the organizational hierarchy or academic funding body), and this list is not exclusive. The degree of formalization can be high with strongly-worded contracts or much weaker and dependent on trust and goodwill and can change during the life of a project.

Given this variance – all action research projects are different – it is not feasible to provide hard and fast rules on how to achieve a balance of power for all situations. However, we have discussed seven action research projects to show how some of the issues were resolved in a number of contexts. In some successful projects control is shared, collaboratively determined and emergent; the allocation of power is informal, indeed 'blurred', and may become clearer by mutual consent as the project develops. This may suggest avoiding discussion of power issues in the early stages of a project. We do not share this view. We argue that it is indeed important to discuss these issues early but this does not imply determining formalized (written and/or authoritarian) agreements. On the contrary, such discussions should lead to understandings about these important issues and become a basis for the collaboration. Tables 2-3, 2-4 and 2-5 (which detail the forms and characteristics of the major action research power structures; the forms and characteristics of authority in action research projects; and action research power structure influence factors respectively) can, we hope, help to inform and drive these discussions. However, this does require that the mutual trust that can be established from these discussions is well founded. We therefore end by re-emphasizing the final phrase of Rapaport's (1970) definition of action research viz. that it can only be successful if the joint collaboration occurs *within a mutually acceptable ethical framework.*

ACKNOWLEDGEMENTS

This chapter is a substantially revised version of an article by the authors published in the 2001 volume (14:1) of *Information Technology and People*.

6.   REFERENCES

Avison, D., Baskerville, R., & Myers, M. (2001). Controlling Action Research Projects. Information Technology and People, **14**(1), pp.28-45.

Avison, D., Lau, F., Neilsen, P. A., and Myers, M. (1999) "Action Research." *Communications of ACM*, **42** (1), 94-97.

Avison, D., and Wood-Harper, A. (1991) "Information systems development research: An exploration of ideas in practice," *The Computer Journal*, **34** (2), 98-112.

Baskerville, R. (1993) "Semantic Database Prototypes." *Journal of Information Systems*, **3** (2), 119-144.

Baburoglu, O.N. and Ravn, I. "Normative Action Research." *Organization Studies* (13:1), 1992, pp. 19-34.

Baskerville, R., and Wood-Harper, A. T. (1996) "A Critical Perspective on Action Research as a Method for Information Systems Research." *Journal of Information Technology*, **11** (3), 235-246.

Braa, K. and Vidgen, R. (1999), Interpretation, intervention and reduction in the organizational laboratory: a framework for in-context information systems research, *Accounting, Management & Information Technology*, **9** (1): 25-47.

Chiasson, M., and Dexter, A. S. (1998) "Revealing Complexity in Information Systems Development During Action Research: Implications for Practice and Research." in *1998 North American Information Systems Action Research Workshop*, (R. Baskerville, ed.), Georgia State University Department of Computer Information Systems, Atlanta, Georgia.

Clark, P. (1972) *Action Research and Organizational Change*, Harper & Row, London.

Jasperson, J.S., Carte, T.A., Saunders, C.S., Butler, B.S., Croes, H.J.P., and Zheng, W. "Review: Power and Information Technology Research: A Metatriangulation Review," *MIS Quarterly* (26:4), 2002, pp. 397-459.

Kock, N. (1997) "Negotiating Mutually Satisfying IS Action Research Topics With Organizations: An Analysis of Rapoport's Initiative Dilemma." *Journal of Workplace Learning*, **9** (7), 253-262.

Kock, N., and McQueen, R. J. (1998) "An Action Research Study of Effects of Asynchronous Groupware Support on Productivity and Outcome Quality of Process Redesign Groups." *Journal of Organizational Computing and Electronic Commerce*, **8** (2), 149-168.

Lau, F. (1997) "A Review On The Use of Action Research in Information Systems Studies." in *Information Systems and Qualitative Research*, (A. Lee, J. Liebenau, and J. DeGross, eds.), Chapman & Hall, London, 31-68.

Lau, F., and Hayward, R. (1998) "Building a Virtual Network in a Community Health Research Training Program." in *1998 North American Information Systems Action Research Workshop*, (R. Baskerville, ed.), Georgia State University Department of Computer Information Systems, Atlanta, Georgia.

Myers, M.D. "Qualitative Research in Information Systems," *MIS Quarterly* (21:2), June 1997, pp. 241-242. *MISQ Discovery*, archival version, June 1997, http://www.misq.org/discovery/MISQD_isworld/. *MISQ Discovery*, updated version, July 2005, www.auckland.ac.nz

Nosek, J. (1998) "Exploring IT Support for Organizational Learning in the Virtual Corporation." David D. Lattanze Center Technical Report, Baltimore, Maryland.

Rapoport, R. (1970) "Three Dilemmas of Action Research." *Human Relations*, **23** (6), 499-513.

Root-Bernstein, R. S. (1989) *Discovering: Inventing and Solving Problems at the Frontiers of Scientific Knowledge*, Harvard University Press, Cambridge, Mass.

Schein, E. (1987) *The Clinical Perspective in Fieldwork*, Sage, Newbury Park, Calf.

Simon, S. J. (1998) "The Reorganization of the Information Systems of the US Naval Construction Forces: An Action Research Project.", Florida International University Working Paper, Miami, Fl.

Straub, D. W., and Welke, R. J. (1998) "Coping with systems risk: Security planning models for management decision-making." *MIS Quarterly*, **22** (4), 441-469.

Susman, G., and Evered, R. (1978) "An Assessment of the Scientific Merits of Action Research." *Administrative Science Quarterly*, **23** (4), 582-603.

Whyte, W. F., Greenwood, D. J., and Lazes, P. (1991) "Participatory Action Research: Through Practice to Science in Social Research." in *Participatory Action Research*, (W. F. Whyte, ed.), Sage, Newbury Park, 19-55.

Chapter 3

ACTION IS AN ARTIFACT:
What Action Research and Design Science Offer to Each Other[1]

Allen S. Lee
Virginia Commonwealth University, USA

Abstract: Both action research and design science provide the means for doing research that is rigorous and relevant. In this essay, I combine the different stages of the action research cycle with the different research activities and research outputs of design science. The result is a framework in which action research and design science are able to complement and strengthen each other.

Key words: design science, action research, dialogical action research, interpretive research, scientific attitude, theoria, natural attitude, praxis

1.   INTRODUCTION

Action research and design science have been enjoying a resurgence of interest from researchers in the academic discipline of information systems.[2] That the resurgence of interest in each one is unfolding at the same time is auspicious. Viewed together, action research and design science exhibit parallels suggestive of how the two may complement and strengthen each another.

---

[1] The ideas in current paper have their genesis in an earlier paper (Susarapu and Lee, 2005). Any problems wrought by the additional ideas or changed ideas in the current paper are entirely my own responsibility.

[2] Special issues on action research have been published by *Information, Technology, and People* (Volume 14, Issue 1, March 2001, guest editors Francis Lau and Ned Kock) and *MIS Quarterly* (Volume 28, Number 3, March 2004, senior editors Richard Baskerville and Michael D. Myers). *MIS Quarterly* has published a major explication of design science in the context of "develop[ing] and communicat[ing] knowledge concerning both the management of information technology and the use of information technology for managerial and organizational purposes" (Hevner, March, Ram, and Park, Volume 28, Number 1, pp. 75-105). Currently, *MIS Quarterly* also has a call for papers for a special issue on design science research (senior editors Salvatore T. March and Veda C. Storey).

Contributing to and being encouraged by the resurgence of interest in action research and design science has been the corresponding resurgence of interest in improving the relevance of information-systems research. In general, a scientific field's relevance refers to the usefulness of its theories for solving problems in the "real world" – problems faced by individuals, organizations, and societies. The academic discipline of information systems has achieved great rigor in its research, but not great relevance. Rigor in research neither automatically nor unproblematically endows it with relevance (Benbasat and Zmud, 1999). One may characterize the problem as a dilemma between rigor and relevance, where there is seemingly an inverse relationship between the rigor and the relevance of research (Kock, Gray, Hoving, Klein, Myers, and Rockart, 2002). In this light, both action research and design science garner interest because they offer ways of resolving the rigor-relevance dilemma.

A *raison d'être* of action research is, by definition, action, where the purpose of such action is to solve an immediate, real-world problem.[3] Action research carries out interventions in natural organizational settings populated by the very people whom the action researcher is studying and intends to directly and immediately benefit. Design science likewise focuses on solving problems and performing tasks encountered in the real world. Design science requires the design of an artifact (such as an information technology) to enable it to address a real-world problem. In explicitly making the solving of practical problems the motivation for its rigorous research, design science also offers an approach to resolving the rigor-relevance dilemma.

The high priority that both action research and design science give to relevance stands in sharp contrast to the secondary or residual attention paid to practical considerations in much information-systems research, which could be properly described as pure or basic research. Basic research does not preclude practical considerations in its development of a theory, but is satisfied in simply assuming that real-world applications for the theory (or subsequent theories that build on it) will occur at some point in the future and that, in the meanwhile, continued basic research will strengthen the foundation of scientific theory required for real-world applications to materialize. One might argue that the resurgence of interest in action

---

[3] A more accurate wording would be: "the purpose of the action is to remedy or solve an immediate problem in the real world, make progress towards achieving a goal in the real world, or perform a task in the real world." In the remainder of this essay, "problem solving" will also connote "achieving a goal" and "performing a task," where such problems, goals, and tasks are those of the practitioner, not the action researcher or design scientist.

research and design science is fueled, at least in part, by some researchers' and practitioners' impatience with the pure-science approach.

In this essay, I construct a framework that infuses the activities of design science into action research, and the stages of action research into design science. The premise is that action research and design science have the potential to bring about greater rigor and greater relevance by acting together than by acting alone. The framework illustrates a way to actualize this potential.

In the next two parts of this essay, I briefly describe action research and design science. After that, I present a framework that combines them. In the last part of the essay, I return to larger issues about action research, design science, and information-systems research in general.

2. ACTION RESEARCH

The concept of action research can be traced back to the work of Kurt Lewin and the Tavistock Institute (Baskerville, 1999). Since that time, action research has developed into many different and sophisticated forms (Lau, 1997). Nevertheless, the different forms all recognize that action research is a cyclical process, where a cycle includes one or another rendering of these stages: diagnosing, action planning, action taking, evaluating, and specifying the learning (Figure 3-1).

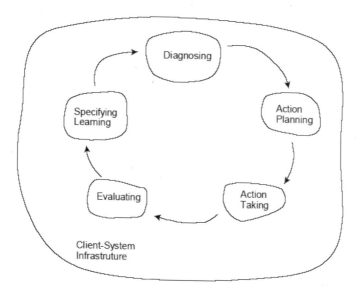

Figure 3-1. The Action Research Cycle

(This diagram is quoted from Baskerville 1999. p. 14)

The form of action research that I use in my framework for combining action research and design science is dialogical action research (Mårtensson and Lee 2004). In this form of action research, an action researcher and a real-world practitioner interact in periodic, one-on-one meetings situated away from the practitioner's setting. In their dialogues, the action researcher uses her own scientific expertise (both explicit and tacit) to perform a diagnosis of the problem in the practitioner's setting and to identify some appropriate actions for ameliorating the problem. To make the diagnosis, the action researcher forms observations of the practitioner's situation by questioning and conversing with the practitioner. When expressing her diagnosis and then proposing some actions for the practitioner to take (**action planning**), the action researcher refrains from "speaking science" and instead deliberately speaks in the practitioner's own everyday language. In the dialogue, the action researcher collaborates with the practitioner in his effort to understand, on his own terms and in his own way, the diagnosis, the proposed actions, and the rationale for the proposed actions. In continuing the dialogue and therefore making more observations about the practitioner's situation, the action researcher may refine her diagnosis and also better specify the actions that she is proposing to him (further **action planning**). In this way, the planned actions are a joint product of the action researcher and the practitioner. Motivating the practitioner's involvement in the dialogue is the fact that, in this form of action research, the practitioner knows that it is he and he alone who will be returning to his organization, taking the action (planned in collaboration with the action researcher) as his own, and taking responsibility for his action's consequences. After the dialogue, the practitioner returns to the organization and implements the action that he and the action researcher planned (**action taking**). In a new, subsequent one-on-one dialogue in the removed setting, the practitioner shares his own evaluation of how successful the action was, and the action researcher again uses the dialogue with the practitioner as a source of observations, this time for the purpose of testing out how well her theory performed in prescribing what action to take (**evaluating**). Then, accounting for any less-than-successful action, the action researcher specifies, for herself, the lessons learned and then improves the theory with which to perform the diagnosis in the next action research cycle (**specifying learning**).

Some additional features of dialogical action research that I will build into the design-science and action-research framework are the scientific attitude, with its companion notion of *theoria*, and the natural attitude, with its companion notion of *praxis*. Mårtensson and Lee (2004) define these terms as follows (pp 513-514):

> The scientific attitude refers to a body of knowledge (academic theory, research literature) and manner of reasoning (research

methods, intuition) that characterize the thinking of Ph.D.-trained social scientists as scientific, whether they subscribe to positivist, interpretive, or critical research approaches. We use the term theoria to refer to this body of knowledge and manner of reasoning. Pure or basic research is an excellent example of theoria. A scientific researcher takes the scientific attitude to make sense of her world of research, which consists of research problems as well as the particular community of action researchers of which she is a member.

...

The natural attitude of everyday life refers to a body of knowledge and manner of reasoning (common sense and tacit knowledge) in use by a member of a naturally occurring (i.e., not created by an outside researcher) organization, society, or other social unit. We use the term praxis to refer to this body of knowledge and manner of reasoning. Theoria is not a more rigorous form of praxis, just as praxis is not a weaker form of theoria. Rather, they are qualitatively different categories of knowledge and reasoning, each category being distinguished by and dependent on its own social context. A practitioner takes the natural attitude to make sense of the world of his organization, to solve problems, and to navigate through the organization's politics. Regarding the natural attitude, dialogical AR [action research] does not require the practitioner to do anything in particular; in his natural state, the practitioner is already taking the natural attitude. However, dialogical AR places the burden on the action researcher to be aware of the presence of the natural attitude, to realize that it is different from her own scientific attitude, and to understand that she can better diagnose the practitioner's organization and its problems by trying to adopt the practitioner's natural attitude.

Not all forms of action research frame the researcher-practitioner relationship according to the strict division of labor and strict division of background that dialogical action research does. However, the division of labor will facilitate our creation of a framework that combines action research and design science.

2.1 Design Science

In its rendering by March and Smith (1995), design science focuses on artifacts useful for individual and social purposes, where this involves four different research activities and four different research outputs. March and Smith refer to Simon (1981), who distinguishes between the study of the human-made and the study of the natural. He gives the former one the name, "sciences of the artificial." Figure 3-2 illustrates the design science research framework advanced by March & Smith (1995).

Research Activities

		Build	Evaluate	Theorize	Justify
	Constructs				
Research Outputs	Model				
	Method				
	Instantiation				

Figure 3-2. Research Framework of Design Science

(This diagram is quoted from March & Smith 1995)

The four columns of the March and Smith (henceforth, M&S) framework designate the four design-science research activities: 1) to build constructs, a model, a method, and an instantiation, 2) to evaluate the quality or validity of what was just built, 3) to theorize about how and why the quality or validity turned out to be, or not to be, satisfactory, and 4) to justify what was just theorized. Corresponding to the four rows are the four design-science research outputs: constructs, a model, a method, and an instantiation. March and Smith define *constructs* as the "vocabulary of a domain" (p. 256) that is used for describing the practitioner-experienced problems; *model*, as a "set of propositions or statements expressing relationships among constructs" (p. 256); *method*, as "a set of steps (algorithms or guidelines) used to perform a task" (p. 257); and *instantiation*, as "the realization of an artifact in its environment" (p. 258). A design scientist builds and evaluates an artifact that, once sufficiently honed, can be used by a practitioner to solve a problem. The success or failure of the artifact in solving the problem provides feedback to the design scientist about whether and how to improve the artifact's design.

Two more features of design science are worth noting. First, design science, like action research, presumes intervention in the real world, while natural science and social science consider intervention as something to be avoided because it contaminates the subject matter and can give the appearance of biasing the analysis so as to lead to favorable findings. Second, natural science and social science are primarily interested in achieving true theories, whereas design science is primarily interested in achieving efficient and effective designs; the difference and relationship between them is akin to the difference and relationship between diagnosis and prescription.

2.2 A Framework Joining Design Science and Action Research

There are likely countless ways to set up design science and action research to work with each other. I join design science and action research to each other by using the M&S design-science framework as a starting point and then adding to it. The result will be a framework with which an action researcher can incorporate design science into the stages of the action research cycle.

First, however, I am pleased to note that the M&S design-science framework seems as if it had been custom designed to accommodate action research. This is because the action in action research is itself an artifact that is 1) built, 2) evaluated and 3) theorized about, where 4) what was theorized is justified, thereby covering all four design-science research activities. In other words, in my extension of the M&S design-science framework, *action is an artifact*. Considering that "artifact" implies "artificial" and that action is literally human-made, the equation of action with artifact is apt. For the purpose of simply illustrating a way to actualize the potential for action research and design science to strengthen each other, where action is an artifact, I proceed with design science in the form presented by March and Smith (as embodied in Figure 3-2) and action research in the form presented by Mårtensson and Lee (dialogical action research, described earlier).

In my effort to create a framework that infuses action research into design science and design science into action research, I attend to four major considerations. The first one is the cyclical nature of action research. I build this into the M&S design-science framework by repeating its set of four research activities (build, evaluate, theorize, and justify) *ad infinitum*, at least in principle. Figure 3-3 indicates this with a single repetition of the four design-science research activities, followed by ellipses (…) in the right-most column. Each such set of design-science activities make up an action-research cycle. The resulting design-science and action-research (henceforth, DSAR) framework, therefore, is literally an extension of the M&S design-science framework.

	Design-Science Research Activities in Action-Research Cycle 1				Design-Science Research Activities in Action-Research Cycle 2				
	Build	Evaluate	Theorize	Justify	Build	Evaluate	Theorize	Justify	⋮
constructs									⋮
model									⋮
method									⋮
instantiation									⋮

Figure 3-3. An Extension of the M&S Design-Science Framework

		Design-Science Research Activities in Action-Research Cycle 1				Design-Science Research Activities in Action-Research Cycle 2				
		build	evaluate	theorize	justify	build	evaluate	theorize	justify	...
Action Researcher (expert advisor to practitioner; takes the scientific attitude; knowledge is in the form of *theoria*)	Design-Science Research Outputs									
	constructs									...
	model									...
	method									...
	instantiation									...
Practitioner (client of action researcher; takes the natural attitude; knowledge is in the form of *praxis*)	Design-Science Research Outputs									
	constructs									...
	model									...
	method									...
	instantiation									...

Figure 3-4. A Design Science and Action Research Framework

The second consideration has to do with the feature of dialogical action research that recognizes a division of labor between the action researcher and the practitioner. The division of labor allows us to account for the difference that their different backgrounds in knowledge and socialization can make to how they participate in action research. As earlier mentioned, the different backgrounds manifest themselves in the form of *theoria* and the scientific attitude for the action researcher and in the form of *praxis* and the natural attitude for the practitioner. I build this into the framework by dedicating one section of the framework for the action researcher and another section for the practitioner. Figure 3-4 shows the resulting DSAR framework, which now also explicitly labels the design-science research outputs.

The third major consideration is that, owing to the division of labor between the action researcher and practitioner, the framework could helpfully show what an action researcher or practitioner does *not* do. In Figure 3-5, I "gray out" the cells where the action researcher or practitioner does not engage in the given design-science research activity for the given design-science research output. I also number the cells (i, ii, ..., xiv) to which I later refer in my illustration of the DSAR framework.

For the practitioner, the rows indicating two of the four design-science research outputs (constructs and model) are completely grayed out because they are research outputs that dialogical action research reserves for the action researcher to create, not the practitioner.

The grayed-out cells in the action researcher's instantiation row and the practitioner's instantiation row reflect two features of dialogical action research. One is that the action researcher does not accompany the practitioner back to his organization and, therefore, does not participate in taking the planned action, hence graying-out cell vii. An evaluation of what a real-world person considers effective and efficient in solving a real-world problem calls for the natural attitude and *praxis*, not the scientific attitude and *theoria*; this grays out the cell viii. The other feature of dialogical action research is that the practitioner does not theorize about how and why his action was or was not effective and efficient. In the DSAR framework, it is the action researcher, not the practitioner, who takes the scientific attitude to theorize about how and why the experimental stimulus or treatment (which the practitioner sees as his action) did or did not elicit the reaction or response anticipated by her theory, hence graying out cell xiii. Furthermore, the research activity of justifying what the researcher theorized likewise calls for the scientific attitude and *theoria*, not the natural attitude and *praxis*. This grays out cell xiv.

		Design-Science Research Activities in Action-Research Cycle 1				Design-Science Research Activities in Action-Research Cycle 2				
		build	evaluate	theorize	justify	build	evaluate	theorize	justify	...
Action Researcher (expert advisor to practitioner; takes the scientific attitude; knowledge is in the form of *theoria*)	constructs	i	ii							...
	model	iii	iv							...
	method	v	vi							...
	instantiation	vii	viii							...
Practitioner (client of action researcher; takes the natural attitude; knowledge is in the form of *praxis*)	constructs									...
	model									...
	method	ix	x	xiii	xiv					...
	instantiation	xi	xii							...

Research Outputs: Design-Science (Action Researcher and Practitioner sections)

Figure 3-5.

With respect to all four rows for the practitioner (not just the instantiation row), all the cells are grayed out in the theorize column and justify column, again for the reason that the DSAR framework reserves these two research activities for the action researcher.

The fourth and last major consideration is that the DSAR framework not only sees the practitioner's action as a design-science artifact, but also places the practitioner's action in the role of the action researcher's experimental stimulus used in testing a theory. In other words, the DSAR framework considers all of the following to be equivalent: 1) what the practitioner sees as an *action* he takes, 2) what the design scientist sees as an *artifact* that instantiates a design, and 3) what the action researcher sees as an experimental *stimulus* or treatment that tests her theory.[4] I will use these terms interchangeably: action, artifact, treatment, and action/artifact/ stimulus.

Having set up the DSAR framework, I can use it to illustrate how design science and action research can contribute to each other. A high-level contribution is that action research may benefit from design science by intentionally striving to perform the four design-science research activities (build, evaluate, theorize, and justify) and to produce the four design-science research outputs (constructs, model, method, and instantiation). It is likely that different forms of action research are already doing some of this. However, the framework offers the advantage of providing a systematic way of identifying and addressing all the activities and all the outputs. Another high-level contribution is that design science may benefit from action research by taking advantage of the action-research requirement that the practitioner be present and participate. This would make a difference to the design-science research activity, evaluate.

Doing a walkthrough of the DSAR framework in Figure 3-5 will provide, at a more nuts-and-bolts level, details of what action research and design science offer to each other.

---

[4] I adopt the general definition of "experiment" provided by Schön (1983, p. 146): "Any deliberate action undertaken with an end in mind is ... an experiment." This general definition covers specific types of experiments that Schön describes: exploratory experiments ("action is undertaken only to see what follows, without accompanying predictions or expectations"), move-testing experiments ("we take action in order to produce an intended change"), and hypothesis-testing experiments ("If, for a given hypothesis, its predicted consequences fit what is observed, and the predictions derived from alternative hypotheses conflict with observation, then we can say that the first hypothesis has been *confirmed* and the others, *disconfirmed*..."). In this essay, "experiment" refers not only to hypothesis-testing experiments, but also to move-testing experiments. Likewise, "experimental design" refers not only to the design of a hypothesis-testing experiment, but also to the planned set-up for a move-testing experiment.

We begin the walkthrough at cells i and ii. Here, an action researcher performs the design-science research activities, build and evaluate, in order to produce the design-science research output, constructs. An action researcher could carry out these two research activities in an explicit and calculated fashion by applying the procedures of Yin's case study research (1994) or Strauss and Corbin's grounded theory (1990, 1998). Yin directly addresses how to collect data to build constructs and how to evaluate construct validity. Strauss and Corbin offer procedures to accomplish what they call "open," "axial," and "selective" coding. A product of the coding is what grounded theory calls "categories," which design science would recognize as constructs. After they are built, the constructs/categories can be evaluated by the action researcher with the help of the grounded-theory criterion that validity is signaled by "saturation," which refers to the point at which the coding no longer yields improved or new categories/constructs. Action researchers who subscribe to positivism have the added option of conceptualizing constructs in the form of independent and dependent variables.

Next, I consider how an action researcher would perform the same two design-science research activities, build and evaluate, but this time for creating a different design-science research output, a model. This takes us to cells iii and iv. Operationally, a model is sometimes illustrated in the form of boxes (constructs) and arrows (the relationships between them). In grounded theory, it can take the form of Strauss and Corbin's "paradigm model" (1990, p. 99). As a collection of constructs (or categories, or variables, or factors, etc.), along with relationships specified between them, a model can also be what natural-science researchers, social-science researchers, and action researchers consider to be a theory, where an action researcher creates and uses such a theory in the diagnosis stage of the action-research cycle. For the action researcher, a theory provides the basis on which to diagnose the ill in the practitioner's situation and to identify plausible remedial actions. Building a theory and evaluating (i.e., empirically testing) a theory are well-covered topics, with many procedures already established and available for an action researcher to use; they even include qualitative-research procedures for building and evaluating a theory in natural, organizational settings (Eisenhardt, 1989; Lee, 1991; Yin, 1994). For action researchers who favor positivism, qualitative procedures for conducting empirical tests of a theory's predictions have likewise already been established (Lee, 1989a, 1989b, 1991; Sarker and Lee, 2002) and are available for an action researcher to use.

Continuing with the two design-science research activities, build and evaluate, I turn our attention to the third design-science research output, method. This refers to cells v, vi, ix, and x. Whereas the term "method" in natural science and social science typically pertains to ways of collecting and analyzing data, the same term in design science pertains to ways of forming something, in the sense of bringing something into being. For instance, a systems development method as applied in an organization could be a set of steps specified for putting together different elements to implement (form) the information system that the organization needs. These steps could be built from concepts offered by a more generic systems development methodology. March and Smith describe data structures as a method (p. 257) insofar as they provide a set of steps for forming the data requested by a user or forming the record to store the data provided by a user. For a natural or social scientist, a particular experimental design is a method insofar as it provides the steps for setting up (forming) a particular experiment in which a stimulus or treatment is applied for the purpose of testing a theory. To build, and then to evaluate the validity of, an experimental design, a social scientist may turn to some well established procedures (e.g., Campbell and Stanley, 1963; Cook and Campbell, 1979). The action-research analogue to the procedures of experimental design would be whatever procedures have been available to action researchers for use in the action-planning stage of the action research cycle. As mentioned previously, the practitioner participates in the action planning (cells ix and x) through his dialogues with the action researcher. For the action researcher, the sophistication of the procedures of experimental design suggests that the rigor of action research can be improved by better formalizing and systematizing the procedures of action planning. Experimental rigor, however, need not push out real-world relevance; Schön endorses the utility of what he calls "move-testing experiments," not just hypothesis-testing experiments, for use in an action context.[5]

As for the fourth and last design-science research output, instantiation, this involves (as described earlier) the practitioner and the practitioner alone, who returns to the organization, makes preparations for the action that he planned with the action researcher, takes the action, accepts the responsibility for the consequences of his action, and then evaluates the extent to which his action did or did not lead to useful results. This refers to cells xi and xii. Because the action researcher is not present for this, cells vii and viii are grayed out.

The parts of the DSAR framework still requiring description are the columns for the design-science research activities, theorize and justify, which the DSAR framework reserves for the action researcher. For the action researcher, I define the design-science research activity, theorize, to refer to formulating an explanation for why a construct, model, method, or instantiation did not perform as expected. I reserve the verb "to theorize" to refer to what, in the build and evaluate activities, might have gone wrong and what might be done differently, which also happens to correspond to the

---

[5] The previous footnote provides definitions of move-testing experiments and hypothesis-testing experiments.

action-research stage of specifying learning; in other words, I do not avoid this term's standard usage, which refers to creating a predictive theory about something in nature (natural science) or society (social science). I define the companion design-science research activity, justify, to refer to establishing the plausibility of the explanation. These two research activities are triggered whenever the action/artifact/stimulus does not achieve the expected results. The unexpected results can prompt the action researcher to look for deficiencies in the four design-science research outputs: the constructs (do we really have construct validity?), model (could the theory simply be flat-out wrong?), method (did we forget to account for something in the experimental design?), and instantiation (maybe the constructs, model, and method are all fine, but might the practitioner have performed the action differently from how we planned?).

In each of these cases, the action researcher could theorize one or another explanation for the deficiency – for instance, perhaps the construct lacks validity because it was not based on multiple sources of evidence; perhaps there is a key variable or relationship that the model or theory overlooked; perhaps there was a source of interference that the experimental design or planned action did not anticipate; or perhaps the constructs, model, method, and instantiation are all fine, but not enough time has yet passed for the action/artifact/stimulus to take effect. Establishing the plausibility of such explanations could involve recognized research practices and standards; one example is that Yin prescribes multiple sources of evidence for construct validity, and another example is that a reformulated theory, like any other theory, would need to be logically consistent, empirically testable, and at least as explanatory as any rival theories. In some cases, the plausibility of the explanation can be demonstrated only subsequently: it would become apparent in the next action research cycle if the construct, model, method, or instantiation, once built, is evaluated favorably.

In all field research, including action research, the great difficulty in or the impossibility of setting up controlled observations (of which laboratory controls and statistical controls are two special cases) can be blamed for unexpected results. For one way to address this problem, we take a cue from statistical researchers who face the same problem. In relying on data already collected (often by government agencies), researchers in economics, finance, and sociology face limited choices in what they can choose to be their variables, including those needed to put statistical controls in place. This limitation does not halt the work of these researchers. The resulting work would not prove their theory to be true (in fact, evidence may, at best, only be consistent with a theory and may *never* prove a theory), but could still usefully identify and rule out theories that are false. For a second way to address this problem, we could rely on natural controls, which refer to controls groups that occur naturally rather than result from experiment-based inducement (Lee, 1989a, 1989b). Although natural controls have been used in the natural sciences and social sciences, they cannot always be counted on to be available. For a third way, the action researcher could formulate (in collaboration with the practitioner) an alternative action/artifact/stimulus that would encounter less interference or less confounding than did the previous action/artifact/stimulus (Kock, 2003).

In summary, the stages of the action-research cycle all appear in the DSAR framework. I locate the diagnosis stage in cells iii and iv; the action-planning stage, in cells v, vi, ix, and x; the action-taking stage, in cells xi and xii; the evaluating stage, in cells ii, iv, vi, x, and xii; and the specifying-learning stage in the two columns for the research activities, theorize and justify.

3.   DISCUSSION

Putting aside the nuts-and-bolts details, the "big picture" is that the DSAR framework illustrates just one possible way in which action research and design science may benefit and strengthen each other. To open up another possibility, consider that the DSAR framework is, in a sense, design science-centric in that it begins with the M&S design-science framework and then instructs an action researcher about what to do. This suggests that we could just as well use, for our starting point, the five stages of the action research cycle instead of the M&S design-science framework. The details we would then add to each stage of the action research cycle would provide a structure of tasks for the design scientist to perform. And just as the structure of the DSAR framework can benefit and strengthen action research, the structure of the corresponding action-research based framework could benefit and strengthen design science.

Not all forms of action research and design science, of course, are suitable to be placed in a framework that combines them, nor is there a necessity for any form of action research to be combined with any form of design science and *vice versa*. Dialogical action research and the M&S design-science framework are suitable for sharing a framework because they share the recognition that action is an artifact.

4.   CONCLUSION

The main conclusion – that design science can benefit from action research and action research can benefit from design science – leads to another conclusion. It has to do with two different groups in the information-systems research community. Members of one group, consisting of technological or technical researchers, are generally inclined towards design science, focus on information technology, and see research in terms of quantitative data and mathematical and other formalisms. Members of the other group, consisting of qualitative researchers, include most action researchers, focus on the behavior of individuals and organizations, and see research in terms of qualitative data and narrative. Ordinarily there is little overlap and interaction between these two groups of information-systems researchers. However, the DSAR framework shows that they have much in common and have much to gain by collaborating with each other.

5. REFERENCES

Baskerville, R. (1999). Investigating information systems with action research. *Communications of the AIS* (2), 2-32.

Benbasat, I. and Zmud, R. (1999). Empirical research in information systems: the practice of relevance. *MIS Quarterly,* **23**(1), 3-16.

Campbell, D.T. and Stanley, J.C. (1963). *Experimental and Quasi-Experimental Designs for Research.* Boston: Houghton Mifflin, 1-33.

Cook, T.D. and Campbell, D.T. (1979). *Quasi-Experimentation: Design & Analysis Issues for Field Settings.* Boston: Houghton Mifflin.

Eisenhardt, K.M. (1989). Building theories from case study research. *Academy of Management Review,* **14**(4), 532-550.

Hevner, A.R., March, S.T., Ram, S., and Park, J.(2004). Design science in information systems research. *MIS Quarterly,* **28** (1), 75-105.

Kock, N. (2003). Action research: Lessons learned from a multi-iteration study of computer-mediated communication in groups. *IEEE Transactions on Professional Communication,* **46** (2), 105-128.

Kock, N., Gray, P., Hoving, R., Klein, H., Myers, M., & Rockart, J. (2002). IS research relevance revisited: subtle accomplishment, unfulfilled promise, or serial hypocrisy? *Communications of the AIS,* **8** (23), 330-346.

Lau, F. (1997). A review on the use of action research in information systems studies. A.S. Lee, J. Liebenau and J.I. DeGross, eds. *Information Systems and Qualitative Research.* London: Chapman and Hall, 31-68.

Lee, A.S. (1989a). A scientific methodology for MIS case studies. *MIS Quarterly,* **13** (1), pp. 33-50.

Lee, A.S. (1989b). Case studies as natural experiments. *Human Relations,* **42** (2), 117-137.

Lee, A.S. (1991). Integrating positivist and interpretive approaches to organizational research. *Organization Science,* **2**(4), 342-365.

March, S.T. and Smith, G.F. (1995). Design and natural science research on information technology. *Decision Support Systems,* (15), 251-266.

Mårtensson, P. and Lee, A.S. (2004). Dialogical action research at Omega Corporation. *MIS Quarterly,* **28** (3), 507-536.

Sarker, S. and Lee, A.S. (2002). Using a positivist case research methodology to test three competing practitioner theories-in-use of business process redesign. *Journal of the Association for Information Systems,* (2), 1-72.

Susarapu, S. and Lee, A.S. (2005). Lessons that action research offers to design science in information systems. *Proceedings of the Eighth Annual Conference of the Southern Association for Information Systems (SAIS),* Savannah, GA, 79-84.

Schön, D.A. (1983). *The reflective practitioner: How professionals think in action.* New York: Basic Books.

Simon, H.A. (1981). *The sciences of the artificial.* Cambridge, MA: MIT Press.

Strauss, A.L. and Corbin, J. (1990). *Basics of qualitative research: Grounded theory procedures and techniques,* Newbury Park, CA: Sage Publications.

Strauss, A.L. and Corbin, J. (1998). *Basics of qualitative research,* Thousand Oaks, CA: Sage Publications, second edition.

Yin, R.K. (1994). *Case Study Research,* Newbury Park, CA: Sage Publications.

Chapter 4

ACTION RESEARCH AND DESIGN IN INFORMATION SYSTEMS
Two Faces of a Single Coin

António Dias de Figueiredo and Paulo Rupino da Cunha
University of Coimbra, Portugal

Abstract: As the production of knowledge moves from a linear innovation model in an explanations-oriented world to a networked innovation model in a solutions-oriented world, the practice of design in engineering and industry and the practice of research in academia are getting closer and closer. This proximity is calling for a renewal of the debates on the nature of academic research, on the epistemology of design, and on the relationship between research and design. This is particularly challenging as we concentrate on the specific field of information systems. It is, also, mostly enlightening as we look into the philosophical groundings of both the design disciplines and action research. This chapter attempts to escort the reader in the examination of these issues. It starts with a brief characterization of the two main modes of knowledge production, followed by a debate on the relationships between research and design. It then puts forward a simple philosophical framework that will be used to put in perspective the designerly ways of knowing, their relationship with action research, and the resulting implications on information systems research. The chapter closes with the re-examination, under this new perspective, of some recent debates on topics such as the rigor *vs* relevance dilemma and the ethical dimension of action research in information systems.

Key words: action research, critical discussion, design, epistemology, ethics, methodology, mode 2, ontology, relevance, rigor, value proposal.

1. INTRODUCTION

The inquiry into the changing relationship between Industry and University has led, in recent years, to the emergence of a variety of research schools concerned with what has become known as "the new modes of knowledge production". One of the earliest books in this movement, *The New Production of Knowledge*, by Gibbons, Limoges, Nowotny, Schwartzman, Scott, & Trow (1994), sparked a wave of debates on science and technology policy and generated multiple research questions on the role of knowledge in society, on the relationship between universities and the economy, and, of course, on the creation of new approaches to scientific research.

The concept of "Mode 2" knowledge production, one of the key notions of the movement, calls the attention of academia to the emerging challenges of a solutions-oriented world where research agendas are driven by economic and social contexts, where theory and practice are mixed together, and where experimental activity follows the principles of industrial, engineering, and architectural design. Paradoxically, this occurs at a time when a significant part of the design researchers' community is declaring the incompatibility between design and science, arguing that the epistemology of science is in disarray, that it has little to offer to an epistemology of design (Cross, 2001a, p.51), and that what the design community needs is to concentrate on the "designerly" ways of knowing, thinking and acting (Cross, 2001b).

This chapter argues that the conciliation between science and design is not only possible but very promising, and that its implications upon the concept of action research are particularly auspicious when action research is to be conducted in knowledge domains where design plays a central role, such as the information systems field. In this sense, it argues for the significance of "designerly action research" as a way to carry out research in information systems and examines, under this perspective, the topics of rigor, relevance, and ethics in information systems research.

The chapter starts with a paragraph on the new modes of knowledge production. It then moves to the challenges of bridging the gap between theory and practice, comments on the scientization of design, and analyses the relationships between design and scientific research. Next, it puts forward a philosophical framework that, in spite of its general applicability, will be used here to discuss the designerly ways of knowing, their relationship with action research, and the resulting implications on information systems. The last paragraph before the conclusions is devoted to the discussion of the use of designerly action research in information systems and of the implications of adopting a designerly approach to action research in this field, namely in what regards its more sensitive dimensions of rigor, relevance, and ethics.

2. THE NEW PRODUCTION OF KNOWLEDGE

Since the publication of *The New Production of Knowledge* (Gibbons et al., 1994), a great deal of attention has been turned to the so-called "new modes of knowledge production". Basically, two radically distinct but mutually related and co-existing modes of knowledge production have been identified by these authors: Mode 1 and Mode 2. In Mode 1 the research agendas are largely governed by the academic interests of a disciplinary community. Research happens predominantly in university environments, carrying a strong distinction between what is fundamental and what is applied. It is typically produced by individuals or homogeneous teams, it is discipline based, its outcomes are primarily shared with fellow researchers, and quality control is maintained mainly through peer reviewing. The social and economic implications of these scientific outcomes, when they are considered, tend to take for granted the linear model of innovation, where the knowledge produced by scientists is placed upstream of its applications to the economic and social realms by practitioners whose contribution to the creation of that knowledge is usually seen as trivial. In Mode 1 knowledge production the quality control criteria reflect the interests and concerns of the discipline and its gatekeepers, implicitly determining who is competent to be judged as a peer, what kinds of research questions are central to the advancement of the discipline, and what research methods shall be used.

In deep contrast with Mode 1, Mode 2 knowledge production is solution-focused and takes place in the context of economic and social applications, the research agendas being determined by the common interests of a variety of stakeholders. Research tends to happen in multiple sites concerned with the applications being explored, and permanent flows occur between the fundamental and the applied, the theoretical and the practical. Research is typically produced by teams integrating scientists, practitioners and many other heterogeneous actors, it is transdisciplinary rather than discipline based, and it is heterogeneous in the skills and experiences it brings in. In general, knowledge is built in the contexts where it is put to use, and its products and results, as they materialize, contribute to further theoretical advances. Inquiry is much more oriented to contextualized results than to first principles, the tacit knowledge of the various partners plays a key role, and the experimental processes tend to follow the principles of design, much more typical of the industrial context than of traditional scientific inquiry.

Although some of the quality control criteria of Mode 1, like peer reviewing, still hold in Mode 2, they are by no means exclusive. Additional criteria, of social, economic and political nature, are called up trough the context of application. A wider, more composite and multi-dimensional, set of criteria is thus put together and the social composition of the review system is broadened, largely transcending the judgments of disciplinary peers. Quality control is more context and use dependent, as well as more concerned with social accountability and reflexivity: social accountability, because the complexity of the problems at hand cannot generally be faced just in scientific and technical terms; reflexivity, because the heterogeneous communities of partners in the various projects, including those traditionally outside the scientific system, need to quickly recognize the broader implications of what they are doing.

Mode 2 success is defined in different terms from Model success, contemplating, not just the traditional dimension of scientific excellence, as judged by disciplinary peers, but also efficiency, usefulness, and the ability to fulfill the expectations of multiple stakeholders, as judged by broad communities of scientists from different backgrounds, practitioners from diverse professional cultures and, even, the general public. This is recognizable today in a substantial proportion of the public funding systems, which, besides the inescapable requirement of scientific excellence, also line up several extra-scientific criteria regarding social and economic priorities. One of the more conspicuous consequences of these different ways of assessing Mode 2 success is that *rigor without relevance becomes meaningless*.

3.   BRIDGING THE THEORY/PRACTICE GAP

Although the tensions between theory and practice – as the tensions between thought and action, or subject and object – pertain to all kinds of research, they are particularly critical in the case of action research, where the two facets of the duality are explicitly called to come together. One way of looking at these tensions is given by the split between science and design. This has been the ground for most fruitful debates in the last eighty years, and its discussion here brings in a number of important elements relating to the epistemology of practice, while establishing the connection to an essential dimension of the information systems discipline: information systems design. In addition, it helps getting the discussion closer to the concept of Mode 2 knowledge production, which, as stressed earlier, is strongly inspired by the design discipline. To give some metaphorical background to this discussion, we will contextualize it in light of Stephen Pepper's metaphysical system (Pepper, 1942), from which the discussion of the scientization of design and of the major differences between design and scientific research will develop.

Stephen Pepper, a philosopher of the pragmatist tradition, formulated a metaphysical system according to which our understanding of the world may happen through four distinct "root metaphors", or "world hypotheses" (Pepper, 1942): formism, mechanism, organicism, and contextualism. When we take a formist view, we try to understand the world through the apprehension of its categories, identifying similarities and differences between things and placing them into categories as our knowledge progresses. If our view is mechanist, we try to understand how things work, looking for causes and consequences and decomposing what is complex into constituent parts. Organicism gives us an organic perspective of the world, concerned with the coherence between the parts and the whole in the creation of integrated visions of processes, abstractions and entities. Contextualism makes us see the world in the complexity of its contexts and in the need to adapt permanently to its unpredictability and contingency.

In a recent analysis of the literature on the social changes brought about by information technologies, Pepper's root metaphors have been used to screen the works published in the last thirty years by a number of representative authors, including Machlup, McLuhan, Bell, Masuda, Naisbitt, Toffler, Negroponte, Castells, Majó, and Fukuyama (Alvarez & Kilbourne, 2002). One of the conclusions of this study was that society is, at present, quietly moving from a world of formist and mechanist visions to a world of organicism and contextualism. Our judgment is that a similar trend can be observed in the advancement of science in general, as well as in the development of the design discipline in particular, namely in the way in which it has evolved from its original nature as a craft to its present standing as a scientifically grounded discipline.

3.1 The scientization of design

If, to keep this chapter within manageable proportions, we restrict to the modern age our understanding of the "scientization" of design, we may follow Nigel Cross's interesting account (Cross, 2001a). In Cross's words, a will to "scientize" design can be traced back to ideas in the twentieth century "modern movement of design", in the early 1920s, which bore the desire to base the products of design on the values of objectivity and rationality, that is, of science (Cross, 2001a, p.49). According to Cross, the renewal of the desire to scientize design emerged again, strongly, in the "design methods movement" of the 1960s, when design methodology started becoming a subject of inquiry and the values of objectivity and rationality started being applied, not just to products, but also to processes (Cross, 2001a, p.49).

Cross then signals what he describes as a backlash, in the 1970s, against design methodology and the rejection of its underlying values (Cross, 2001a, p.50). He recalls Christopher Alexander, who had originated, in the 1960s, a rational method for architecture and planning (Alexander, 1964), declaring in 1971 his total dissociation and disappointment with it all (Alexander, 1971). He also quotes J. Christopher Jones saying: "In the 1970s, I reacted against design methods. I dislike the machine language, the behaviorism, the continual attempt to fix the whole of life into a logical framework" (Jones, 1977).

Our interpretation of this backlash is that it did not mean, at all, a rejection of the scientization of design, but the rejection of a formist and mechanist vision of the principles of science that were being used to support it. In the 1970s, any science denying the formist and mechanist principles would be considered, by the scientific community at large, a phony science. So, Jones' rejection of "machine language", of "behaviorism", of "the continual attempt to fix the whole of life into a logical framework" was, in our view, not the rejection of science but the call for a more organicist and contextualist vision of science. This is confirmed by other texts of the time, such as Rittel and Webber's influential proposal of the concept of "wicked problems", a term describing the problems, generally found in social and organizational environments, which, because of their complexity and close interdependence with organizational factors, cannot be formulated[1] (Rittel & Webber, 1973). This vision of circumstances where the process of solving a problem is identical with the process of understanding its nature, where problem understanding and problem resolution are concomitant, and where the information needed to understand a problem depends on the designer's ideas for solving it (Rittel & Webber, 1973) corresponds to an organicist and contextualist vision of design.

Referring to the scientization of design in the decades that followed, Cross remarks that design methodology continued to develop, especially in engineering and some branches of industrial design (Cross, 2001a). He stresses, however, that design methodologists continued to insist on the essential distinction between design and science (Cross, 2001a). Simon, for instance, argued that the natural sciences are concerned with how things are, while design is concerned with how things ought to be (Simon, 1969, p.114). Archer, an instrumental leader of the designers of his generation, who fought for design as a discipline with its own requirements for systematic research and methodological rigor at all times, insisted, as well, on the distinction between design and science (Archer, 1992). Cross, in turn, emphasized the

---

[1] Is it possible to formulate, for instance, in any reliable terms, the problem of poverty?

need to concentrate on "design as a discipline, but not design as a science" (Cross, 2001a, p.54; 2001b, p.6). In this sense, he distinguished between (Cross, 2001a, pp.52-54):

- **scientific design**, modern design (as distinct from pre-industrial, craft-oriented design), based on scientific knowledge but utilizing a mix of both intuitive and non-intuitive design methods;
- **design science**, an explicitly organized, rational, and wholly systematic approach to design – design as a scientific activity itself – a concept challenged by many designers and design theorists;
- **science of design,** a body of work attempting to improve the understanding of design through "scientific" (i.e., systematic, reliable) methods of investigation; and
- **design as a discipline** of an interdisciplinary nature, studied on its own terms and within its rigorous culture, developing domain-independent approaches to theory and research in design, addressing the human-made world of artifacts, the knowledge inherent in the activity of creating the artifacts, the knowledge inherent in the artifacts, and the knowledge inherent in the processes of manufacturing them.

3.2 Scientific research *vs* design

The extreme skepticism of most prominent design methodologists and researchers on the relevance of a "design science", in its failure to accommodate the richness of the design disciple, as well as their insistence in distinguishing between design and science, suggests two central questions: What are, then, the major differences between science and design? Are those differences definitely irreconcilable?

The major differences between science and design are explicitly addressed by Archer, who favors "a designerly approach, rather than a scientific approach" (1992, p.12). To him, both science and design are processes. "The science process seeks to isolate a phenomenon from the complexities of the situation in which it is embedded, and to abstract generalizable principles from observation and experiment. (...) On the other hand, there is no insistent demand that subjects for scientific enquiry should be confined to particular categories or that findings should be useful. Scientists are entitled to turn their minds to anything so long as they do it scientifically" (Archer, 1992, p.8). Also, "Design is directed towards meeting a particular need, producing a practicable result and embodying a set of technological, economic, marketing, aesthetic, ecological, cultural and ethical values determined by its functional, commercial and social context" (Archer, 1992, p.8). In his view, the activities of design "are justified by their results, rather than their reasons. In contrast to the overriding importance of orthodox methodology in the conduct of science, the conduct of design is validated by its efficacy rather than the rigor of its methods. Designers can, and do, on occasion, seize upon chance information, adopt capricious ideas and exercise untidy methods in the course of a project" (Archer, 1992, p.9).

Cross argues in the same sense. On one hand, he points out the critical distinction concerning method: "method may be vital to the practice of science (where it validates the results), but not to the practice of design (where results do not have to be repeatable, and, in most cases, must *not* be repeated, or copied)" (Cross, 2001a, p.54). He insists that "there are forms of knowledge peculiar to the awareness and ability of a designer" and that "we must concentrate on the 'designerly' ways of knowing, thinking and acting" (Cross, 2001b). This builds on his earlier claim, with other authors (Cross, Naughton, & Walker, 1981), that "the epistemology of science was, in any case, in disarray and, therefore, had little to offer an epistemology of design" (Cross, 2001a, p.51).

Are those differences between science and design irreconcilable? On first impression, they are. If we look more closely, however, we notice that the impossible reconciliation is only between the organicist and contextualist nature of design and the formist and mechanist nature of the vision of science that was being imposed upon design researchers. This is why, instead of fighting for recognition within a "science" that they did not recognize, they opted to create their own discipline, where the richness of designerly knowledge could be fully expressed and theoretically supported and where the validation of results could be established on different, though equally demanding, grounds. This is clear when, in support of his proposal of "design as a discipline", Cross explicitly praises Donald Schön (Schön, 1983), who is described as having "challenged the positivist doctrine underlying much of the 'design science' movement, and offered instead a constructivist paradigm" (Cross, 2001a, p.53). And he goes on: "Schön proposed (…) to search for an epistemology of practice implicit in the artistic, intuitive processes which some practitioners do bring to situations of uncertainty, instability, uniqueness, and value conflict, and which he characterized as 'reflective practice'. Schön appeared to be more prepared than his positivist predecessors to put trust in the abilities displayed by competent practitioners, and to try to explicate those competencies rather than to supplant them" (Cross, 2001a, p.53-54).

4. A PHILOSOPHICAL FRAMEWORK

Excellent frameworks for the classification of philosophical paradigms exist in the literature, covering social research in general (Guba & Lincoln, 1994; Lincoln & Guba, 2000) and information systems in particular (Iivary, 1991; Iivary, Hirscheim, & Klein, 1998; Monod, 2002), as well as other fields of business research (Chua, 1986). Our aim is by no means that of reviving these frameworks here, or of reproducing the paradigmatic debates that were so popular in the information system literature of some years ago: it is, in fact, much more organicist and contextualist than formist and mechanist. We might say, borrowing Wittgenstein's metaphor on the role of language-games in helping to construct meaning (Wittgenstein, 1953), that our aim is that of developing a simple language-game around two of the most relevant philosophical paradigms – positivism and constructivism – so that we can use it to give meaning, later, to the scientific legitimacy of designerly ways of knowing and of action research approaches that build on them.

In order to differentiate between the two paradigms, we will look into the ways they answer four key philosophical questions: the ontological, the epistemological, the methodological, and the ethical questions (Guba & Lincoln, 1994). The ontological question inquires about *what can be known*. The epistemological question looks into *what is knowledge*, or *what knowledge can we get*. The methodological question inquires about *how we can build that knowledge*. The ethical question, which sees ethics in very broad terms, asks *what is the worth, or value, of the knowledge* we build (Piaget, 1967, p.6). The four questions and resulting answers are summarized in Table 4-1. In this exploration, we will be drawing considerably on proposals put forward by LeMoigne (1999) and Figueiredo and Afonso (2006).

4.1 The ontological question

The ontological question – *what can be known?* – is answered by the positivist paradigm with the *realist hypothesis*: the reality we may know is independent from us, it exists before we try to know it, it is potentially knowable, and it is explainable by immutable laws, whatever its complexity. If we wish, for instance, to understand the impacts of a new information system on an organization, the realist hypothesis tells us that we can see the organization as independent from us and founded on stable structures and universal rules, and that we may regard the information system as a technical artifact that is also independent from us (Iivari, 1991). Thus, by inquiring into the structures and rules of the organization, and taking into account the characteristics of the information system as a technical artifact, we will be able to know the impacts with as much rigor and detail as we wish. Also, if the same study is carried out by a different and equally competent expert or team, the realist hypothesis tells us that identical results should be obtained.

The answer of the constructivist paradigm to the ontological question is given by the *phenomenological hypothesis*: we know reality by constructing it through our interactions with the world, in an emergent process that changes knowledge as we keep interacting with the world. If we wish, for instance, to understand the impacts of a new information system on an organization, the phenomenological hypothesis, though accepting that we may depart from some fixed structures and rules, tells us that our perception of the organization and of the information system, understood as making up a complex socio-technical system, will change as we proceed with our effort to know the whole system better. If the same study is carried out by a different and equally competent expert or team, the phenomenological hypothesis tells us that an entirely different result may be obtained, though both results may be equally useful. In other words, there is interdependence between the phenomenon we perceive and the knowledge we build about it, so that, from the representation we get of the phenomenon, we build an active representation that transforms that knowledge, producing a new representation, and so on, recursively (LeMoigne, 1999, p.74). The act of knowing an object is inseparable from the act of knowing ourselves: we do not know the things themselves but the interactions of those things with us and our context (LeMoigne, 1999, p.71).

4.2   The epistemological question

The epistemological question – *What is knowledge? What knowledge can we get?* – also leads to distinct answers from the two paradigms. The positivist answer is given by the *deterministic hypothesis*, for which knowledge is what we can learn by exploring the causes of the problems we face: the only knowledge we can get is that resulting from our inquiries into the causes of the problems. As expressed in 1637 by René Descartes, in his *Discourse on Method*, all realities, even the most complex, can be decomposed in "long chains of reasons, all simple and easy", so that, provided "one always kept to the order necessary to deduce one thing from another, there would not be anything so far distant that one could not finally reach it, nor so hidden that one could not discover it" (Descartes, 1961, p.66). The belief in the deterministic hypothesis expresses, not only the possibility of describing a reality independent from the subject (as postulated by the realist hypothesis), but also the possibility of explaining it in a unique and permanent manner.

According to LeMoigne (1999), constructivism answers the epistemological question with the *teleological hypothesis*. In simple terms, the teleological hypothesis can be described as stating that knowledge is what gets us to an intended result. It is, thus, a natural consequence of the phenomenological hypothesis and of the key role it attaches to the subject in the construction of knowledge.

Further clarification of the distinction between determinist and teleological hypotheses calls for elaboration on the concept of cause. Aristotle proposed, in Physics II, 3 (350 BC), a classification of four kinds of causes: *material causes*, the materials out of which things are made (such as the bronze in which a statue is cast); *formal causes*, the statements of essence (such as the sketches that lead to the statue); *efficient causes*, the agents or forces that produce change (such as the sculptor who makes the statue); and *final causes*, or purposes for which things exist (such as the intent of a statue made to represent justice). The positivist paradigm takes efficient causes as the only capable of producing change and, hence, of explaining reality. From a positivist point of view, final causes are irrelevant.

Contending from the constructivist perspective, and recalling Heinz von Foerster, LeMoigne reminds us that the answer to the question "why?" can have two completely different kinds of answer: "because" and "in order to". As he argues, the intelligence of a cognitive being is often much better activated by the latter than by the former, namely when no clear causes can be found (LeMoigne, 1999, p.77). This should also make a lot of sense to anyone familiar with information systems design. Indeed, it is usually much more powerful to design an information system "in order to" obtain some intended strategic change than to design it "because" this and that specific problem have been identified.

Table 4-1. Positivism and constructivism in light of the four philosophical questions

QUESTIONS	ANSWERS	
	POSITIVISM	**CONSTRUCTIVISM**
ontological question what can be known?	**realist hypothesis** we can know reality, which is external to us, independent from us, and driven by immutable laws	**phenomenological hypothesis** we know the world by interacting with it in an emergent process that changes knowledge as we keep interacting
epistemological question what is knowledge?	**deterministic hypothesis** knowledge is what we learn by exploring the causes of the problems we face	**teleological hypothesis** knowledge is what gets us to an intended result
methodological question how can knowledge be built?	**principle of analytical modeling** to explain reality we must divide each difficulty into as many parts as possible and necessary to resolve it better	**principle of complexity** we build knowledge by recognizing the world as complex and in constant flux, embodying stability, change, chaos, and order, the whole exceeding the sum of parts and the parts interacting in the shared, emergent and largely unpredictable construction of reality
	principle of sufficient reason there is no effect without a cause and no change without a reason for change	**principle of intelligent action** human reason can transform intelligible representations of the dissonances to which it is confronted by creating responses in the form of "intelligent actions" adapted to reduce these dissonances
ethical question what is the value of knowledge?	**principle of value exclusion** values have no role to play in knowledge construction	**principle of value inclusion** values have an essential role to play in the emergent process of knowledge construction
	principle of extrinsic ethics ethical behavior is formally policed by external mechanisms	**principle of intrinsic ethics** ethical behavior is constructed by each researcher in the persistent search for the collective good

4.3 The methodological question

As explained by LeMoigne (1999, p.19), the methodological question – *How can we build knowledge?* – is answered by the positivist paradigm with two principles: the principle of analytical modeling and the principle of sufficient reason. The *principle of analytical modeling*, formulated by Descartes as the second percept of his *Discourse on Method*, states that to explain any reality we must "divide each difficulty (…) into as many parts as possible and necessary to resolve it better" (Descartes, 1961). The *principle of sufficient reason*, formulated by Leibnitz, holds that there is no effect without a cause or no change without a reason for change.

Constructivism also answers the methodological question with two hypotheses, both recognizing (following the teleological hypothesis) that we need knowledge, not just to understand, but also to build the reality we experience: the principle of complexity and the principle of intelligent action. The *principle of complexity* acknowledges that to build knowledge we must see the world as complex and in constant flux, holding characteristics of both stability and change, with the whole being more than the sum of the parts (the parts hardly being knowable without knowing the whole, and vice-versa), chaos living coupled with order, and parts interacting with each other in the shared construction of reality, in an emergent and often unpredictable fashion that is supported, to some extent, by processes of self-organization and co-creation (Figueiredo & Afonso, 2006).

The *principle of intelligent action*, quoted by LeMoigne as contained in Dewey's definition of "intelligent action" (Dewey, 1938) establishes that human reason can, in a reproducing way, elaborate and transform intelligible representations of the phenomena of dissonance to which it is confronted, creating responses in the form of "intelligent actions" adapted to reduce these dissonances (LeMoigne, 1993, p.83). This principle finds one of its more suggestive expressions in the work of Donald Schön (1983) on "reflective action" and "reflection-in-action". In reflective action, which is typical of the work of practitioners, namely designers, work progresses through a trajectory of trial and error, of reformulating problems as they are solved, in a permanent dialogue between the problem solver and the problematic situation being solved, which is influenced and influences the intervention.

4.4 The ethical question

The ethical question – *what is the value of the knowledge we build?* – refers, in broad terms, to the axiological implications of the work of the researcher. Instead of looking at the judgments of fact that characterize science, the ethical question looks at the judgments of value afforded by philosophy. Guba and Lincoln (1994) point out two questions of particular relevance: the role of values and the place of ethics.

The positivist paradigm responds to the question of the role of values with the *principle of value exclusion*: values have no role to play in knowledge construction. In fact, they are "seen as confounding variables that cannot be allowed a role in putatively objective inquiry" (Guba & Lincoln, 1994, p.114). As to the place of ethics in inquiry, the positivist answer is given by what we call the *principle of extrinsic ethics* to describe Guba and Lincoln's statement that in positivist research "ethical behavior is formally policed by external mechanisms, such as professional codes of conduct and human subjects committees" (Lincoln, 1994, p.114-115).

The answer of constructivism to the question of the role of values is given by the *principle of value inclusion*: in agreement with the phenomenological hypothesis, values have an essential role to play in any emergent process of knowledge construction. In fact, it would be hardly tolerable to exclude them, at the risk of letting down the interests of the weaker audiences (Guba & Lincoln, 1994, p.114). On the other hand, the role of the researcher as orchestrator and facilitator could hardly be exercised in the absence of values (Guba & Lincoln, 1994, p.114). The place of ethics in constructivist research is answered by what we call the *principle of intrinsic ethics*: ethical behavior is constructed by each one of us in the persistent search for the common good. As maintained by Varela (1992), the ethics of phenomenology is much closer to the oriental traditions of wisdom, in their inner pursuit of the common good, than to the occidental traditions of obedience to external norms.

5.   DESIGNERLY WAYS OF KNOWING

Our earlier discussion of the scientization of design and of the distinction between design and traditional scientific research will now let us explore the philosophical foundations of the designerly ways of knowing.

5.1   The ontology of designerly ways of knowing

Our previous characterization of designerly knowledge suggests that the ontological question must be answered in phenomenological terms. True enough, on the surface (probably intuitively, but also thanks to the positivist upbringing of our generation), most designers take a realist view of the "external" world they are trying to change. However, their behavior as practitioners shows their products are conceived in an emergent process of interpretation and reconstruction of that world. This process is not just individual, but of eminent social construction. When designers construct a model (graphical, mathematical, or of any other kind) on which they base their progress, this model is a "world" that makes sense to their restricted communities. The ontological nature of engineering and design models is becoming so implicit in the language of the present day that we are witnessing the word "ontology" – *an* ontology – being used, not to refer to the branch of Philosophy we are considering in this chapter, but to "a formal explicit specification of a shared conceptualization" (Gruber, 1993; Gruninger & Lee, 2002).

5.2 The epistemology of designerly ways of knowing

Moving now to the second line of the framework of Table 4-1 – that of the epistemological question – we may say that Archer's statement, quoted above, that design is directed towards meeting a particular need and producing a practicable result (Archer, 1992, p.8) reflects the teleological nature of designerly knowledge from an epistemological point of view. This does not mean, however, that designers can do their jobs without the best possible understanding of the efficient causes of the phenomena they are dealing with. In fact, they cannot. This is why design – be it engineering design, industrial design, architectural design, or design of any other kind – depends so much from the explanatory sciences. The essence of the question is that, although the explanatory sciences are unquestionably necessary for designers to carry out their missions, they are by no means sufficient. To design is not just to apply the explanatory sciences. It is also to get *beyond* the explanatory sciences in the construction of solutions that never existed. The explanatory sciences are essential, but they are essential only in the context of the teleological mission of the designer.

On the other hand, while the discovery of new explanations is sufficient for the explanatory scientist, it is by no means sufficient for the designer. In the paths toward the construction of their solutions, designers can, and often do, discover a lot of original explanations, but their jobs are only completed when the solutions they were supposed to construct are actually constructed and proved to satisfy their teleological purpose. On the other hand, not all the knowledge they build when constructing their solutions can be made explicit. Part of it becomes tacit in the minds of the designers and their teams, another part settles down in their design processes, and still another part appears embedded in the very artifacts that result from their work (Cross

2001b, p.4). This encapsulation of knowledge into artifacts is one of the consequences of the teleological hypothesis: if we asked, again, the question "what is knowledge?" the answer should not forget that part of that knowledge becomes incorporated in the product of the designer's work.

5.3   The methodology of designerly ways of knowing

The third line of the framework deals with the methodological question. The rejection by design methodologists and researchers of the formist and mechanist visions of science, and their opening up to the organicist and contextualist vision of Schön's epistemology of practice (Schön, 1983), suggest that the principles of complexity and intelligent action should be used to answer the question: "how can designerly knowledge be built?". As in the case of the epistemological question, this does not mean that the application of the positivist answers to the methodological question is fully rejected. The positivist principles, if not considered universal, but just pragmatic principles applicable to commensurate realities, continue to make a lot of sense. In fact, the division of a difficulty into as many parts as possible and necessary to resolve it better is extensively used by engineers and designers in general. The constructivist principles of complexity and of intelligent action, seen as accommodating, rather than rejecting, the positivist principles, are, however, the ones capable of dealing with complexity, namely the complexity of social and organizational environments, where difficulties such as those described by Rittel and Webber (1973) as "wicked problems" emerge.

The statement, by Archer, that "designers can, and do, on occasion, seize upon chance information, adopt capricious ideas and exercise untidy methods in the course of a project" (Archer, 1992, p.9) may sound shocking to the scientist used to see rigor coming out, almost exclusively, from the unblemished application of sound scientific methodologies. Some explanation is, therefore, necessary when the methodological question is asked in the context of the design discipline. This takes us to an interesting aspect of designerly knowledge production – that of consistently attempting, mostly with success, to *build comprehensive rigor on top of discrete situations where rigor is impossible to achieve*. A well known example is found in the production of integrated circuits, where the technological unfeasibility of producing passive components with accurate values is overcome through design approaches that balance the various sources of imprecision, thus offsetting their effect. Another suggestive example is given by Tom de Marco, in *Deadline*, a novel about project management, where he introduces the *ithink*™ performance modeling system (HPS, 1994), an approach that lets managers build accurate predictions of reality by departing from their "hunch bases" and, through modeling and peer interaction, develop simulations that increasingly refine rigor by tuning those models against actual results (DeMarco, 1997, pp.95-115).

This is something designers have been doing for ages: to indulge in, or even provoke, creative leaps that have little to do with rigor, only to recover at subsequent stages the rigor that had temporarily been broken. The concept of abduction, as proposed by Charles Peirce, a pragmatist philosopher considered by many the earliest modern times predecessor of action research, is a brilliant way of scientifically accommodating creative leaps and intuition. For Peirce, abduction is the standard form of setting up scientific hypothesis, and can count as the third kind of inference, together with induction and deduction (Mautner, 1996, p.1). To abduct is, for Peirce, to formulate hypotheses in exploratory ways, on the basis of incomplete evidence, before moving on to the confirmation of the hypotheses thus formulated. It just happens that design is considered as eminently abductive: "The more useful concept that has been used by design researchers in explaining the reasoning process of designers is that *design is abductive*" (Cross, 1999, p.29). By resorting to abductive approaches, we can get beyond mere inductive and deductive chains of reasoning and make room for the exploration of creative leaps and intuition. Of course, our main exploratory hypotheses are likely to be inspired by some sort of evidence. However, since their scientific soundness is only to be confirmed later, we can freely start with mere gut feelings, or even with insights induced by chance events, and explore them at length without any risk of blotting scientific rigor.

It is important to recall, in this respect, Popper's arguments, in a lecture at Harvard University, in February 1963, that "theories are steps in our search for better and better solutions of deeper and deeper problems", [that] "scientific problems are preceded (...) by pre-scientific problems, and especially by practical problems", [that] "the growth of knowledge always consists in correcting earlier knowledge", [that] "without understanding the problem situation that gave rise to [a] theory the theory is pointless", [and that] "there is only one way of *learning to understand a problem* that we do not understand – and that is to try to solve it *and to fail*" (Popper 1994, p.154-157). Following this argument, we may say that to fail – to be wrong – may be an essential step in developing a scientific theory. In other words, it can make a lot of sense to "adopt capricious ideas and exercise untidy methods in the course of a project" (Archer, 1992, p.9) provided this is just a step in the construction of the knowledge required for it to succeed, a step containing "practical problems" that may precede "scientific problems". The rigor of the theories developed from these problems may subsequently be granted by what Popper calls *critical discussion*, his systematization of the pre-scientific method of learning from mistakes (Popper, 1994, p.158), which we shall comment in more detail later, in paragraph 7.

5.4   The ethics of designerly ways of knowing

As stressed earlier, the concept of ethics is understood here in a very broad sense. We might even replace it by the concept of axiology, the theory of value, as suggested by Lincoln and Guba (2000, p.163), bearing in mind that it covers not just ethical values, but human values in general. When we walk along the river Seine, in Paris, in a bright day, unhurriedly looking at the scenery and breathing the freshness of the river, when we stroll beside its margins in the mysterious mist of an early morning, or when we watch it in the night, flowing quietly in a haze of soft lights, we immediately notice that the bridges of the Seine have not been built just to get people across. They have been built to become integral parts of the soul of Paris. This is, somehow, what distinguishes artifacts that embody all sorts of human values from artifacts that have been built just for instrumental purposes.

The same kind of concern, as it relates to design, has been delightfully expressed by Christopher Alexander (1979) in *The Timeless Way of Building*, where he talks of the Timeless Way as "a process which brings order out of nothing but ourselves" (Alexander, 1979, p.3), with a quality that "is a subtle kind of freedom from inner contradictions" (Alexander, 1979, p.26). Described as an original approach to the theory and application of Architecture, this book offers, also, a most inspiring model for the development of any complex socio-technical system. The philosophy of The Timeless Way maintains that the process of building "is not a process of addition, in which pre-formed parts are combined to create a whole: but a process of unfolding, like the evolution of an embryo, in which the whole precedes its parts, and actually gives birth to them, by splitting" (Alexander, 1979, p.365). If we recall what we said earlier about the ethical principles of constructivism, we notice that the organic and emergent processes of the Timeless Way of Building, as well as its inner, persistent, search for perfection, has a lot to do with them.

Before we move over to the discussion of designerly action research, it seems appropriate to help the reader visualize the implicit relationships between the most critical concepts introduced so far. This is done in the simplified diagram of Figure 4-1.

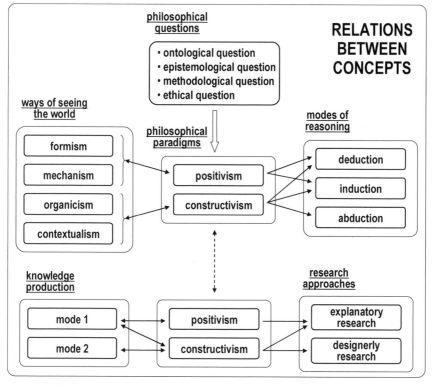

Figure 4-1. Relations between key concepts presented in this chapter

6. ACTION RESEARCH AND THE DESIGNERLY WAYS OF KNOWING

Modern action research has developed from a variety of strands, with its origin almost unanimously said to be located on the work developed by the *Group Dynamics* movement in social psychology, in the 1940s, namely by Kurt Lewin. Similar practices started being used, in the meantime, at the Tavistock Clinic (later the Tavistock Institute), to study psychological and social disorders among veterans of battlefields and prisoner-of-war camps (McKernan, 1991; Baskerville & Wood-Harper, 1996). Authors such as Rapoport (1970) and Reason & Bradbury (2001) identify a multiplicity of other interesting strands. Enid Mumford was possibly one of the first authors to explore the relationship between the essence of action research and information systems design (Mumford, 1983). According to Baskerville (1999), action-research was explicitly introduced to the information systems community, as a pure research methodology, by Wood-Harper (1985). We will be concentrating here on what we see, sometimes, as the domination of the culture of the social sciences in the current practice of action-research within the design disciplines, on the discussion of action-research in light of the philosophical framework presented earlier, and on the debate of the relationships between action research, designerly knowledge and Mode 2 knowledge production.

6.1   Action research and the dominant culture of the social sciences

Some authors have suggested that the prominence of Lewin and related social work in the writing of the history of action research has subsequently led to an unnecessarily skewed vision of its nature (McKernan 1991; Swepson 1998; Whitelaw, Beattie, Balogh, & Watson 2003). Our view of the use of action research in the design disciplines takes us to a similar conclusion: as it is currently practiced, even though in many flavors, action research is often captive of the dominant explanatory culture of the social sciences. In other words, in spite of the eminently constructivist nature of its philosophical roots, it is too often used just to search for efficient causes and scarcely used, if used at all, to construct knowledge while in the pursuit of final causes. In our view, it would be difficult to find a more paradoxical, if not harmful, utilization of a research approach so naturally cut to support knowledge construction in the design disciplines.

We argue here in favor of a vision of action research that can apply to the designerly ways of knowing and still fit the mold of action research. We shall call it *designerly action research*, not to separate it from the existing concept, but, on the contrary, to suggest that it can be used to enrich it. This should be seen as a contribution to strengthen transdisciplinarity, in agreement with the proposals of Gibbons and co-authors for the development of Mode 2 knowledge construction: "Transdisciplinarity arises only if research is based upon a common theoretical understanding and must be accompanied by a mutual interpenetration of disciplinary epistemologies" (Gibbons et al., p.29).

6.2   Steps to a philosophy of designerly action research

The philosophical framework of Table 4-1 will be used here as a tool to help us support our reasoning. We will be hypothesizing, for each one of the four philosophical questions, the existence of a continuum from the extreme of pure positivism to the extreme of pure constructivism. With our camp thus organized, we will explore the legitimacy of talking about "designerly action research". To keep our reasoning within manageable proportions, and because it would not add much to this specific analysis, we will refrain from concentrating on the ethical question.

Positivist researchers answering the ontological question will see themselves acting in a realist world, studying a reality that is external, stable, and independent from them. When they resort to action research, this is the reality they will be inquiring into. When they look from their positivist standpoint to the constructivist camp, some of them, the more radically positivist, will see nothing. For them, there is no continuum at all linking them to constructivism. Some other positivist researchers, however, will see moderate forms of constructible reality. They will not see the whole continuum, but they will admit a variable amount of leeway toward the side of phenomenology.

Constructivist researchers, on the other hand, will see reality as being constructed through their interactions with the world, in an emergent process. The reality they will be studying through action research is not seen as stable, but as changing because of their interactions and those of their partners with it, as well as because of predictable and unpredictable factors that happen in spite of them. The more open-ended or socially complex the action is, the less they can predict the development of their research. However, when they turn their eyes across to the positivist camp, they will very likely see the whole continuum, and they will probably agree that it may, in some cases, make a lot of sense to follow the positivist views. Indeed, if they are acting on simple (but not artificially simplified) worlds that remain unchanged during the time scale of their research, the positivist approaches may be more effective and likely to lead to easier communication within teams that are not used to the phenomenological view. This is by no means negligible when we are talking about action research, which usually involves teams with very heterogeneous compositions that escape our control.

Positivist researchers answering the epistemological question will see themselves looking for efficient causes and analyzing reality to uncover its deterministic principles and predict future behavior. So, for many of them, to *act*, in action research, is to engage, as much as possible, in activities leading to the confirmation of their hypothesis. Acting in the construction of anything that has no visible scientific purpose is not seen by them as the task of researchers, but rather as the task of practitioners: the mission of researchers is to develop explanations and theories to be used by practitioners; when the theories are finished, and scientifically proved correct, they can then be made available to the practitioners, and the epistemological continuum closes there – what the practitioners do with it is hardly relevant. Some other positivist researchers, however, will be interested in looking to the constructivist side of the continuum. They will acknowledge that it makes sense to engage in projects together with the subjects they are studying (for instance, a client company attempting to improve its business processes), and they will be prepared to help these subjects satisfy their aims, provided the experiences generated in the process are rich enough to lead to the development of scientific principles that explain and help predict the behavior of the reality they are concentrating upon. The definition of research questions is, in principle, established beforehand and carried out entirely by the researchers.

Constructivist researchers are likely to be much more driven by the desire to share an economic or social aim with a client. They may depart with some exploratory research questions formulated, generally in a much more open sense than their positivist counterparts. In some cases, they may just establish broad research objectives founded on informed intuitions and prepare to define the research questions in collaboration with their client as the project moves along. Using a metaphor inspired by civil engineering design, we may say that, resting on their knowledge and experience (and on that of their advisors and teams) they may be engaging in the complex design of a large bridge. They know that the project poses many problems, some of them never experienced and solved, requiring hard conciliations between disciplinary fields and stakeholders, mixed with environmental controversies, land related litigations, pressures from powerful lobbies, and many other unexpected issues, both technical and social, that affect the whole design. They feel that some such problems will emerge in connection with the knowledge domains of their interest, and may let them break new ground. However, they cannot tell what those problems will be like. In any case, when they look to the positivist camp, they will see the whole continuum extending before them and they will recognize that if, in the middle of their research, part of the reality they are working on becomes simple enough to suggest the inquiry into efficient causes, they will be prepared to use freely the principles of positivism.

As far as the methodological question is concerned, positivist researchers will be, once again, prepared to look for efficient causes and analyze reality to uncover its deterministic principles and predict future behavior. In addition, and in order to face complexity, they will expect to divide each difficulty in as many parts as possible and necessary to resolve it better. Many of them, when looking to the constructivist camp, will be nonetheless prepared to recognize that part of the continuum makes sense: they will agree with the existence of "ill-structured" problems and with Simon's call for the recognition of "bounded rationality" (Simon, 1973). They will tend to believe, however, that "ill-structured" problems can be analyzed, decomposed, and converted into well structured problems, and this will be, in principle, as far as they are prepared to go in their action research.

Constructivist researchers, on the other hand, will be concerned with the construction of their knowledge in a world of complexity, trying to get "better and better solutions of deeper and deeper problems [knowing that] the growth of knowledge always consists in correcting earlier knowledge [and that] there is only one way of *learning to understand a problem* that we do not understand – and that is to try to solve it *and to fail*" (Popper, 1994, p.154-157). However, when they look to the positivist side of the continuum, and see the principles of analytical modeling and sufficient reason being applied, they are likely to acknowledge them as acceptable, and maybe even preferable, if their aims, and the reality to be studied, or parts of it, are simple enough to let them avoid facing complexity in its entirety.

If we now attempt to grasp the wholeness of the four philosophical questions in the perspective of our research experience, we will have to acknowledge *the excessive emphasis of most research literature, including IS research literature, on the dimension of methodology at the expense of the ontological, epistemological and ethical dimensions* (or, at least, in unjustified isolation from them). This emphasis can attain, in some cases, utterly unthinkable levels, such as when the planning / acting / reflecting "spiral of steps" of action research proposed by Lewin (1946), or the five-stage cyclic process put forward by Susman and Evered (1978), are transformed into mere mechanist algorithms for carrying out research. We would not go as far as Hans-Georg Gadamer (1976) in his insistence on the ontological, rather than methodological, function of philosophical hermeneutics, but we would maintain that an overall balance is desirable.

To illustrate this point in a few words, we shall borrow a metaphor explored in a different context by Jim Highsmith, a well-known software design expert: the metaphor of battlefield commanders planning extensively, but knowing that they succeed by defeating the enemy, not by conforming to a plan. And he adds: "I cannot imagine a battlefield commander saying, 'We lost the battle, but by golly, we were successful because we followed our plan to the letter.'"(Highsmith, 2002, p.4). Translating this metaphor into our concerns, we would say that the questions of methodology are unquestionably important, but we must not lose sight of the kind of reality we are dealing with (ontological question), of the aims we want to attain (epistemological question, answered with the teleological hypothesis), and the value of what we are achieving (ethical question).

6.3   Action research, designerly knowledge, and Mode 2

By placing positivism and constructivism at the extremes of the four –
ontological, epistemological, methodological, and ethical – continua, rather
than seeing them as isolated and incompatible worldviews, the framework of
Table 4-1 attempts to create a coherent whole: its aim is to connect, rather
than separate. Of course, we must acknowledge that the four continua are by
no means perfect, especially when traveled from the positivist to the
constructivist side. We hope, however, that they stress not only the
differences but also the productive complementarities between the two
paradigms. The framework is not unrelated, either, to other paradigms that
are popular in information systems research, such as interpretivism.
Although a proper justification would largely exceed the space available in
this chapter, we may say, in simple terms, that interpretivism satisfies all the
tenets of constructivism, as we describe them here, with the sole exception
of its answer to the epistemological question, which tends to be much more
turned to the inquiry into efficient causes than to the construction of
knowledge in the pursuit of final causes.

This leads us to what we see as *the important distinction between
categories of knowledge in present-day scientific research: the distinction
between explanatory and designerly knowledge*. In our view, the failure to
recognize this distinction may be as detrimental to the progress of scientific
research in a Mode 2 knowledge construction world as the failure to
distinguish between positivism and constructivism. Explanatory knowledge
means, here, the disciplinary knowledge needed in an explanations-oriented
world: the knowledge for analyzing, describing, understanding, explaining,
and predicting. It is, in essence, Mode 1 knowledge. Designerly knowledge
means the knowledge needed in a solutions-oriented world: the knowledge
to design solutions and purposefully change the world. Part of it is
disciplinary knowledge that can be made explicit in research papers, books,
and repositories, so that it can be explored to solve a wide variety of
scientific and practical problems – it is, in essence, again, explanatory, or
Mode1, knowledge. Another part, however, is much more elusive. It
includes tacit knowledge kept in the individual and collective minds of the
people involved in the projects that lead to its generation. Some of it is
encapsulated in metaphors and analogies, in "exemplars", as Kuhn called
them (Khun, 1974, p.306), in stories, in multiple accounts of lessons learned,
in the networks of relationships and communities of practice that develop
during the projects. It also includes the knowledge held in the strategies and
tactics of the design processes (Cross, 2001b, p.4). Finally, it includes

knowledge inscribed in the products that result from the (successful and unsuccessful) projects (Cross, 2001b, p.4) and in the relationships between these artifacts and their social and economic contexts.

Designerly knowledge is transdisciplinary, part of it unstructured and non-generalizable. It embodies, however, a largely untapped power to spark new insights and lead to new solutions, new problems and new knowledge in other (similar and dissimilar) contexts. This is a kind of knowledge that is much less clearly described by its (disciplinary) *object* than by its *project*, that is, by its potential to materialize in the construction of solutions, innovation and change. This is, in essence, Mode 2 knowledge. If we look at action research, not through the lens of traditional research, but through the lens of our philosophical framework, where plenty of room exists for a continuum between positivist and constructivist approaches, we will be able to start talking about *designerly action research* as a natural way of doing action research, namely when dwelling in the design disciplines.

7. DESIGNERLY ACTION RESEARCH IN INFORMATION SYSTEMS

In this paragraph, we will illustrate briefly the evolution of information systems design toward what we have described earlier as the designerly ways of knowing. We will then discuss the implications of adopting a designerly approach to action research in the information systems field, namely in what regards its more sensitive dimensions of rigor, relevance, and ethics.

7.1 Information systems and designerly ways of knowing

The evolution of information systems design, from formist and mechanist worldviews to organicist and contextualist visions, has followed a process that can be described as similar to that followed by the design disciplines in general. Susan Gasson, building on an original categorization by Lanzara (1983), of three models of information systems design, proposes an updated classification (including a fourth model) that gives a suggestive picture of this evolution. She distinguishes between design as functional analysis, design as problem-solving, design as problem-setting, and design as emergent, evolutionary, learning (Gasson, 2004).

Design as functional analysis assumes requirements to be fully available at the outset, so that the designer just needs to analyze the problem and deductively proceed to the solution. Design is seen as a process of rationally selecting the means for achieving clear ends. The goals of design and the criteria for achieving them are predefined, and requirements are assumed to be well known before problem representation is established and the solution implemented.

Design as problem-solving resolves complex, namely organizational, problems by simplifying them to a level where they can still satisfy a minimal set of criteria leading to their rational solution. It is inspired by Simon's concept of "bounded rationality" which, recognizing that human-beings have cognitive limitations that hamper their full understanding of most complex problems, assumes that these problems can be reduced and simplified – bounded – until they become sufficiently well defined to be resolved (Simon, 1973). As argued by Wood and Wood-Harper (1993), those two models are dominated by the rationalistic tradition. They are formist and mechanist.

Design as problem-setting views design as a systemic activity requiring the discovery and possible negotiation of unstated goals, implications, and criteria before a problem can be formulated and, subsequently, solved. It values the focus on the formulation of the problem rather than the mere description of the problem (Wood & Wood-Harper, 1993). It also entails the need to discover new knowledge, namely unstated goals and evaluation criteria, and is particularly concerned with handling problems that cannot be formulated because of their complexity and their interrelatedness with organizational issues ("wicked problems"), requiring their framing or definition in terms of the context before they can be solved (Rittel & Webber, 1973). This is, already, a much organicist and contextualist model.

Design as emergent, evolutionary, learning corresponds to the fourth model, proposed by Gasson (2004), which sees design as the convergence of problem and solution in an emergent process that fulfills a situated action perspective. Design becomes a cyclical process of learning about a situation and then planning short-term partial goals that emerge as the process progresses (Suchman, 1987). Aspects of the solution are thus explored in conjunction with aspects of problem understanding: not only the problem is unclear at the start of the process, but the goals of the design are also ill-defined (Gasson, 2004). Design, now emerging in multiple circular references, linking problem formulation and problem solution, explicitly emphasizes the eminently organicist and contextual nature of this model.

With the evolution of information systems design characterized in this way, in increasing agreement with what we have described earlier as the designerly ways of knowing, we can now shift the core of our debate from the design discipline in general to information systems design in particular, concentrating on the implications the adoption of a designerly approach to action research in information systems may have upon the dimensions of rigor, relevance, and ethics.

7.2 Relevance and the value proposal

For any partnership to be sustainable – be it a marriage, the relationship between research student and advisor, a business partnership, or a project involving thousands of stakeholders – it must fulfill in permanence the interests and motivations of *all* the parts. Otherwise, sooner or later some parts will lose their interest, a number of them will leave, and a few may even oppose to its progress. The clarification of the interests of each one of the parts in a partnership is, thus, an essential preliminary stage in its constitution. We call the result of this stage the *value proposal*. The creation of a value proposal may result from an explicit negotiation process. In most cases, however, the value proposal is completely, or at least partly, implicit, even if tacitly negotiated very toughly.

On the other hand, the interests of the various partners will change as the partnership develops. The mostly implicit nature of the value proposal and the changeable character of the partnership have two important implications: on one hand, the value proposal must keep being negotiated permanently, even if no words are exchanged; on the other hand, each partner must permanently be concerned, not only with the satisfaction of his or her *own* interests, but also with the satisfaction of the interests of *the other* partners. Otherwise, the partnership may collapse, and everyone will lose. We often say that *any genuinely sustainable partnership is an ethical partnership*, in the sense that it naturally requires the fulfillment of Kant's categorical imperative: "Always so act that you are able to will that the maxim of your action be also a universal law" (Kant, 1964).

Any action research project is a partnership. The partners are often described in the literature as being just the researchers and the practitioners engaged in the project, but the network of stakeholders may be, and usually is, very much wider. Our view, supported by countless studies developed within the *Sociology of Scientific Knowledge (SSK)* and the *Science and Technology Studies (STS)* movements since the early 1970s (see e.g. Pickering, 1992; Brey, 1997) is that in our society most stakeholders, even the less visible, such as, in some cases, the general public, may need to be counted as members of a research project. Although the information systems field is not as sensitive as the environmental sciences or biotechnology in the eyes of the general public, it is, conversely, a technological field where the interests of politics and the games of power play a very critical, albeit invisible, role on the development of research projects. The fact that we are living in an increasingly Mode 2 world only reinforces this view.

If we agree that in a Mode 2 world an action research project is a partnership involving a very broad community of partners, including, but far exceeding, the scientists in our disciplinary field, than we must build our value proposal with this in mind (and keep adjusting it as the project develops). With the value proposal made clear, we can then talk about *relevance*: relevance is the pertinence of our project to its stakeholders. Of course, as unanimity between heterogeneous stakeholders is hardly possible, we have to make choices and take risks. What many researchers do is to take no risks and make the obvious choice of molding their projects to the editorial boards of their future publications. However, when the projects come with other requirements attached, besides those of publication, as it happens in Mode 2 contexts where action research is used, the scenario changes significantly.

Part of the question of relevance, in our scientific community, is thus displaced from the hands of the researchers to the hands of journal editors and program committees. At present, it is guided by the tenets of Mode 1 quality control, as we described them at the beginning of this chapter. Our feeling is that, if information systems are to become a relevant scientific discipline in a Mode 2 world, where designerly ways of doing research are becoming more and more relevant, than the editors and program committees of our journals and conferences must take that world into account. In particular, they must be able to attract to their ranks a good range of competent, mature, forward looking, and heterogeneous stakeholders capable of representing that world, while keeping in mind that the criteria for quality control in a Mode 2 world include at least the social and economical dimensions, as well as the concerns with social accountability and reflexivity.

As we have pointed out earlier, in a Mode 2 world rigor without relevance is meaningless. The key issue, thus, becomes, not that of deciding between rigor and relevance, but that of *making sure that all the relevance we create is created with rigor*. We have been arguing in this direction in the previous paragraphs, and we will continue to do so now.

7.3   **Rigor and designerly action research**

It should be no surprise that the dilemma between rigor and relevance should have been raised by Donald Schön, a major early advocate of the scientific legitimacy of designerly ways of knowledge production (Schön, 1983). We shall concentrate here on the rigor of designerly action research, leaving the examination of the relationship between rigor and relevance to the subsequent discussion of its ethical dimension.

Bearing in mind the philosophical framework we have presented earlier in this chapter and the discussion we have conducted about the place occupied by designerly action research in that framework, we may say that the eight tactics that we have compiled elsewhere (Cunha & Figueiredo, 2002) to ensure the rigor of an action-research project still hold. These tactics, by a variety of authors, take into account our discussion, there, of the fallacy of positivist induction as well as our support of Karl Popper's critical rationalism. We reproduce these tactics here, with some adjustments to fit this chapter:

1. A theoretical framework must be set at the beginning of the process. It is in light of this framework that new knowledge arising from the research will be identified.
2. The use of cycles is strongly encouraged. In each cycle the researcher should try to *falsify* the emerging interpretation. Using several short cycles may lead to more opportunities for that. Cycles can be used within cycles, with larger ones spanning whole phases of the research program.
3. Research methodology, as well as the research questions, should be critically analyzed and refined in each cycle.
4. Data collection and interpretation should be a part of each cycle. This lets both be challenged in later cycles.
5. In each cycle, the researcher should focus only on agreements and disagreements, ignoring the idiosyncratic data. Apparent agreements should be tested and apparent disagreements explained.
6. Divergent data should be deliberately sought. This increases the chances that any piece of data or interpretation be challenged. The existing literature can also play an important role in this effort.
7. Multiple sources of information should be sought (or different perspectives concerning the same source) in order to create a dialectical process.
8. Results from change induced into the research situation should be used as an additional source of information for challenging emerging theories (since the planned actions have been grounded on previous data and interpretations).

To reinforce our claim on the rigor of designerly action research, as well as to facilitate the application of the above tactics, it is appropriate to raise here Karl Popper's view of the scientific method, as put in his Harvard lecture of February 1963 we have mentioned earlier (Popper, 1994, p.158-159): "My whole view of the scientific method may be summed up by saying that it consists of these four steps:

1. We select some *problem* – perhaps by stumbling over it.
2. We try to *solve* it by proposing a *theory* as a tentative solution.
3. Through the *critical discussion of our theories* our knowledge grows by the elimination of some of our errors, and in this way we learn to understand our problems, and our theories, and the need for new solutions.
4. The critical discussion of even the best theories always reveals new problems."

And he goes on: "(…) to put these four steps into four words: *problems – theories – criticisms – new problems*. (…) Of these four all-important categories the one which is most characteristic of *science* is that of error-elimination through *criticism*. For what we vaguely call the *objectivity of science*, and the *rationality of science*, are merely aspects of the *critical discussion* of scientific theories." (Popper, 1994, p.159). We believe that it would be hard to find a more expressive legitimation of the emergent, cyclical, nature of designerly action research, in its combination of safe steps with abductive leaps and bonds whose lack of rigor can be recovered subsequently through the rigorous application of *critical discussion*.

7.4   The ethical dimension

Rigor and relevance and their mutual relationship in the context of designerly action research emerge with different shades when the ethical dimension is brought to the foreground. For one basic reason: although a Mode 2 project may have a very high potential for the emergence of novel scientific knowledge, its economic or social aims can be far removed from the researcher's scientific aspirations. Relevance must be seen in light of the overall value proposal, which obviously privileges the interests of the client and those of the main stakeholders. So, if, and when, options are called for, they must favor the economic or social aims initially agreed upon.

What about rigor? In our view, rigor must follow relevance. We argue, however, that it must do it to the highest possible standards. It may be enlightening to recall, in this context, that the motto of Leonardo da Vinci, the greatest master of *disegno* (design) of all times, was: *"ostinato rigore"* (persistent rigor). This is, certainly, a piece of advice we can try to follow when applying Popper's critical discussion.

An additional reason for pursuing rigor to its highest standards has been put very expressively by Rittel and Webber in their characterization of wicked problems: "the planner has no right to be wrong" (Rittel & Webber, 1974, p.280). And they illustrated: "(...) every implemented solution is consequential. It leaves 'traces' that cannot be undone. One cannot build a freeway to see how it works, and then easily correct it after unsatisfactory performance (...). The effects of an experimental curriculum will follow the pupils into their adult lives." (Rittel & Webber, 1974, p.276). Eddie Norman, adapting from Rittel and Webber, put it just as expressively: "(...) a researcher working in a designerly mode has no right to be wrong" (Norman, 1999, p.304).

If we analyze these observations in light of the relationship between rigor and ethics, we notice that they underscore the fact that in a designerly world our judgment about scientific rigor must get far beyond the traditional concept of scientific rigor. Indeed, if we agree that to fail is a natural and often necessary step in the pursuit of scientific rigor, while recognizing that the social and economic interests of the stakeholders must be preserved from our failures, than we have to acknowledge that the pursuit of scientific rigor must include the assessment of the risks involved and of the contexts where the researchers' failures can be allowed to occur.

A final word seems appropriate to close our comments on the ethical dimension of designerly action research, now looking at it from a broader axiological perspective that includes human values of all sorts, and not just the moral ones. Bearing in mind that socio-technical approaches are a major path toward the incorporation of human values in the researcher's work, it is gratifying to notice that information systems research has been an early adopter of that path (Mumford & Weir, 1979; Checkland, 1981; Mumford, 1981; Mumford, 1983; Wood-Harper, Antill & Avison, 1985). In a previous paragraph we mentioned, as an inspiration for the ethics of designerly action research, Christopher Alexander's *The Timeless Way of Building* (Alexander, 1979) and his concern with the inner, persistent, organic, all-encompassing, search for perfection. We might complete it now, in the spirit of Popper's call for relentless critical discussion, with Pindar's (522 BC – 443 BC) famous ethical plea, which is also a plea for rigor and relevance: "Strive not, my soul, for an immortal life, but exhaust the limits of the possible".

8.   CONCLUSIONS

Taking as its background a framework for the clarification of philosophical meanings in scientific research, this chapter has discussed the relationships between the explanations-oriented and solutions-oriented approaches to knowledge construction. From this discussion, it has moved to the debate of the correlations between designerly knowledge and action research, focusing next, more specifically, on the information systems field and on its dimensions of rigor, relevance, and ethics. Following Karl Popper's view of the scientific method (Popper, 1994), we have selected some problems, tried to solve them by proposing theories as tentative solutions, and made attempts at the critical discussion of these theories. The main strands of our theories, in their current formulation, can be synthesized as follows:

- *Explanatory knowledge* and *designerly knowledge* are two fundamentally distinct, though compatible, kinds of knowledge, requiring different ways of production: *explanatory research* and *designerly research.*
- In (disciplinary and transdisciplinary) knowledge domains where design plays a central role, action research should contemplate both the explanations-oriented dimension inherited from its social sciences origins and a solutions-oriented dimension borrowed from the design disciplines.
- Action research should not overemphasize the methodological dimension at the expense of the ontological, epistemological and ethical dimensions, but rather be carried out comprehensively so as to cover them all while harmonizing with the whole.
- The sustainability of an action research project, seen as a partnership between heterogeneous constituents, requires the clarification of a *value proposal*. The relevance of the project and of its results should be assessed taking the value proposal as a reference.
- When action research is used to construct designerly knowledge, rigor has no meaning in the absence of relevance.
- The construction of rigor may be obtained through reasoning and experimentation containing imprecision, error, and abductive leaps of creativity, provided successive cycles of *critical discussion* are subsequently and persistently pursued.
- The eminently ethical nature of action research in knowledge domains where design plays a central role should stress the social dimension of the projects and bear in mind that scientific rigor in designerly worlds largely transcends the meaning attributed to it by traditional science.

To close this chapter, we will keep with Popper's view. Through the critical discussion of our theories, our knowledge has grown by the elimination of some of our errors. We have learned to understand better our problems, our theories, and the need for new solutions. But the critical discussion of any theories, Popper reminds us, always reveals new problems. We thus see this ending as a beginning. We hope that the less conventional views we have put forward in this chapter will inspire our readers in the identification of new problems and in the proposal of new theories.

REFERENCES

Alexander, C. (1964). *Notes on the Synthesis of Form*. Harvard: Harvard University Press.

Alexander, C. (1971). The state of the art in design methods". *DMG Newsletter*. 5(3).

Alexander, C. (1979). *The Timeless Way of Building*. Oxford: Oxford University Press.

Alvarez, I. & Kilbourn, B. (2002). Mapping the information society literature: topics, perspectives and root metaphors. *First Monday*. 7(1).

Archer, B. (1992). The nature of research in design and design education. B. Archer, K. Baynes & P. Roberts, eds. *The Nature of Research into Design and Technology Education: Design Curriculum Matters*. Loughborough: Department of Design and Technology, Loughborough University.

Baskerville, R. L. (1999). Investigating information systems with action research. *Communications of the Association for Information Systems*. 2(19).

Baskerville, R. L., & Wood-Harper, A. T. (1996). A critical perspective on action research as a method for information systems research. *Journal of Information Technology*. 3(11), 235-246.

Boland, R. J., Renkasi, R., & Te'eni, D. (1994). Designing information technology to support distributed cognition. *Organization Science*. 5(3), 456-475.

Brey, P. (1997). Philosophy of technology meets social constructivism. *Journal of the Society for Philosophy and Technology*. 2(3-4).

Checkland, P. B. (1981). *Systems Thinking, Systems Practice*. Chichester: Wiley.

Chua, W.F. (1986). Radical developments in accounting thought. *The Accounting Review*. 61, 601-632.

Cross, N. (1999). Natural intelligence in design. *Design Studies*. 20, 25-39.

Cross, N. (2001a). Designerly ways of knowing: design discipline versus design science. *Design Issues*. 17(3). Massachusetts Institute of Technology.

Cross, N. (2001b). Design/Science/Research: Developing a Discipline. Keynote Speech, 5th Asian Design Conference, Seoul, Korea. Retrieved 08/16/2005, from http://design.open.ac.uk/people/academics/cross/DesignScienceResearch.pdf

Cross, N., Naughton, J., & Walker, D. (1981). Design method and scientific method. In R. Jacques and J. Powell, eds. *Design: Science: Method*, Guildford: Westbury House.

Cunha, P. R., & Figueiredo, A. D. (2002). Action research and critical rationalism: a virtuous marriage. *Proceedings of the 10th European Conference on Information Systems*, ECIS 2002, Gdansk, Poland.

DeMarco, T. (1997). *Deadline: a Novel about Project Management*. New York: Dorset House Publishing.

Descartes, R. (1961). *Discours de la Méthode* (avec introduction et notes par Etienne Gilson). Paris: Librarie Philosophique J. Vrin.

Dewey, J. (1938). *Logic: The Theory of Inquiry*. New York: Henry Holt and Co.

Figueiredo, A. D., & Afonso, A. P. (2006). Context and learning: a philosophical framework. In A. D. Figueiredo & A. P. Afonso, eds. *Managing Learning in Virtual Settings: The Role of Context*, Hershey, PA: Idea Group Publishing, PLC, 2006.

Gadamer, H-G. (1977). *Philosophical Hermeneutics*. Translated by David E. Linge, Berkley: University of California Press.

Gasson, S. (2004). *Organizational 'Problem-solving' and Theories of Social Cognition* (working paper). Last updated 11/01/2004. Retrieved 08/16/05 from http://www.cis.drexel.edu/faculty/gasson/Research/Problem-Solving.html.

Gibbons, M., Limoges, C., Nowotny, H., Schwartzman, S., Scott, P. & Trow, M. (1994). *The New Production of Knowledge: The Dynamics of Science and Research in Contemporary Societies*. London: Sage Publications.

Gruber, T. R. (1993). A translation approach to portable ontologies. *Knowledge Acquisition*. 5(2), 199-220.

Gruninger, M., & Lee, J. (2002). Ontology: applications and design. *Communications of the ACM*. 45(2), 39-41.

Guba, E. G. & Lincoln, Y. S. (1994). Competing paradigms in qualitative research. In K. D. Denzin & Y. S. Lincoln. *Handbook of Qualitative Research*. Thousand Oaks, CA: Sage Publications.

Highsmith, J. (2002). What is agile software development? *Crosstalk*. U. S. Department of Defense.

HPS (1994). *Introduction to Systems Thinking and iThink – iThink Technical Reference Manual*. Hanover, NH, High Performance Systems, Inc.

Iivari, J. (1991). A paradigmatic analysis of contemporary schools of IS development. *European Journal of Information Systems*. Houndmills, UK: Palgrave Macmillan Ltd., 249-272.

Jones, J. C. (1997) How my thoughts about design methods have changed during the years. *Design Methods and Theories*, 11:1.

Kant, I. (1964). *The Groundwork of the Metaphysic of Morals*, New York: H. Paton.

Lanzara, G.F. (1983). The design process: frames, metaphors and games", *in* U. Briefs, C. Ciborra, L. Schneider, eds. *Systems Design For, With and By The Users*. North-Holland Publishing Company.

LeMoigne, J.-L. (1999). *Les Épistémologies Constructivistes*. (2nd ed.) Paris: Presses Universitaires de France.

Lewin, K. (1946). Action research and minority problems. *Journal of Social Issues*, II, pp. 34-46.

Lincoln, Y. (2001). Engaging sympathies: relationships between action research and social constructivism. P. Reason & H. Bradbury, eds. *Action Research: Participative Enquiry and Practice*. London: Sage.

Lincoln, Y. S., & Guba, E. G. (2000). Paradigmatic controversies, contradictions, and emerging confluences. In N. K. Denzin & Y. S. Lincoln, eds. *Handbook of Qualiative Research*, 2nd edition, Thousand Oaks, CA: Sage Publications.

Mautner, T. (1996). *The Penguin Dictionary of Philosophy*. London: Penguin Books.

Mayer, R.E. (1989). Human non-adversary problem-solving. In K. J. Gilhooley, ed. *Human and Machine Problem-Solving*. Plenum Press, New York.

McKernan, J. (1991). Curriculum action research. *A Handbook of Methods and Resources for the Reflective Practitioner*, London: Kogan Page.

Monod, E. (2002). Epistémologie de la recherché en systèmes d'information. In F. Rowe, ed. *Faire de la Recherche en Systèmes d'Information*. Paris: Vuibert.

Mumford, E. (1981). *Values, Work and Technology*. The Hague: Martinus Nijhoff.

Mumford, E. (1983). *Designing Participatively*. Manchester: Manchester Business School Publications.

Mumford, E., & Weir, M. (1979). *Computer Systems in Work Design: the ETHICS Method*, NY: John Wiley.

Norman, E. (1999). Action research concerning technology and associated pedagogy, *Educational Action Research*. 7(2), 297-308.

Pepper, S. C. (1942). *World Hypothesis: A Study in Evidence*. Berkeley: University of California Press, 1942.

Pickering, A. (1992). (Ed.) *Science as Practice and Culture*. Chicago: The University of Chicago Press.

Popper, K. (1994). Models, instruments and truth: the status of the rationality principle in the social sciences". In *The Myth of the Framework: In Defense of Science and Rationality*. London: Routledge, 154- 184.

Rapoport, R. N. (1970). Three dilemmas in action research. *Human Relations*. 23, 499-513.

Reason, P., & Bradbury, H. (2001). Preface in P. Reason & H. Bradbury, eds. *Handbook of Action Research: Participative Inquiry and Practice*. London: Sage.

Rittel, H., & Webber, M. (1973). Dilemmas in a general theory of planning. *Policy Sciences*. 4 (1973), 155-69.

Schön, D. (1983). *The Reflective Practitioner: How Professionals Think in Action*. New York: Basic Books.

Simon, H. A. (1969). *The Sciences of the Artificial*. Cambridge, MA: MIT Press.

Simon, H. A. (1973). The structure of ill-structured problems. *Artificial Intelligence*. 4, 181-201.

Suchman, L. (1987). *Plans and Situated Action*. Cambridge, MA: Cambridge University Press.

Susman, G., & Evered, R. (1978). An assessment of the scientific merits of action research. *Administrative Science Quarterly*, 23 (December), 582-603.

Swepson, P. (1998). Separating the ideals of research from the methodology of research, either action research or science, can lead to better research. *Action Research International*, Paper 1. Retrieved 08/16/2005, from http://www.scu.edu.au/schools/gcm/ar/ari/p-pswepson98.html

Varela, F. (1992). *Un Know-How per l'Ética*. Roma-Bari: Gius, Laterza & Figli Spa.

Whitelaw, S., Beattie, A., Balogh, R., & Watson, J. (2003). *A Review of the Nature of Action Research*. SHARP. Crown Copyright.

Wittgenstein, L. (1953). *Philosophical Investigations*. Translated by G.E.M. Ascombe. New York: Macmillan Publishing, Co., Inc.

Wood, J.R.G., & Wood-Harper, A.T. (1993). Information technology in support of individual decision-making. *Journal of Information Systems*. 3, 85–101.

Wood-Harper, A. T., Antill, L., & Avison, D. E. (1985). *Information Systems Definition: a Multiview Approach*. Oxford: Blackwell Scientific Publications.

Wood-Harper, A. T. (1985) Research methods in information systems: using action research. In *Research Methods in Information Systems*. E. Mumford, R. Hirschheim, G. Fitzgerald & A. T. Wood-Harper, eds. Amesterdam: North-Holland, 169-191.

Chapter 5

THE THREE THREATS OF ORGANIZATIONAL ACTION RESEARCH
Their nature and related antidotes

Ned Kock
Texas A&M International University, USA

Abstract: This chapter presents and discusses three main threats inherent in organizational action research, called "uncontrollability", "contingency", and "subjectivity"; and three methodological countermeasures (or "antidotes") to deal with these three action research threats, called "unit of analysis", "grounded theory", and "multiple iterations". Both the threats and the antidotes are discussed in the context of a real information systems action research study that investigated the impact of computer support on the success of group-based business process improvement attempts.

Key words: action research; grounded theory; information systems; computer-mediated communications; email; business process improvement

1.   INTRODUCTION

The emergence of organizational action research (AR) and its later use in the information systems (IS) field (Avison et al., 1999; Baskerville, 1999) has been motivated by the recognition that an organization can be more deeply understood if the researcher is part of it, which can be achieved by the researcher facilitating improvement-oriented change in the organization (Argyris et al., 1985; Bunning, 1995; Checkland, 1991; Elden and Chisholm, 1993; Ketchum and Trist, 1992; Lewin, 1948). This type of involvement is also believed to foster cooperation between researcher and those who are being studied, information exchange, and commitment towards both generating valid research conclusions and desirable organizational changes (Fox, 1990; Kock, 1997; Kock and Lau, 2001; Lau, 1997).

Conducting organizational AR involves helping an organization solve its problems and become "better" in terms of some of its key attributes such as productivity, the quality of their products and/or services, and working conditions. At the same time, AR involves collecting, analyzing, and drawing conceptual and theoretical conclusions from organizational research data. This combination of "action" and "research" in organizational settings is perhaps the most appealing aspect of organizational AR (Checkland, 1991; Sommer, 1994; Sommer and Sommer, 1991). In spite of the advantages that this combination of "action" and "research" can bring about, the use of AR in organizational research and, more specifically, in IS research, has been very limited (Lau, 1997; Ledford and Mohrman, 1993b; Orlikowski and Baroudi, 1991). This is surprising, particularly given AR's potential for generating outcomes that are relevant to industry practitioners pointed out by Truex (2001) and highlighted by the guest-editors of a recently published special issue on IS AR of the journal *Information Technology & People* (Kock and Lau, 2001).

Obviously, there must be reasons why AR is underrepresented. A review of the research literature suggests that AR poses unique "threats" to research success (Galliers, 1992; 1992b; Mumford, 2001; Rapoport, 1970), which can potentially lead to a high proportion of failures in the conduct of AR and scare away potential adopters of AR as an approach for organizational research. This chapter addresses this problem by presenting and discussing three fundamental "threats" posed by AR to researchers, as well as three methodological "antidotes" for the threats. Both the threats and the antidotes are discussed in the context of a real IS AR study that investigated the impact of computer support on the success of group-based business process improvement (BPI) attempts.

2.   ACTION RESEARCH AND ITS USE IN INFORMATION SYSTEMS

Although there is controversy about its origins, AR seems to have been independently pioneered in the US and Great Britain in the early 1940s. Kurt Lewin is generally regarded as one of its pioneers (Argyris et al., 1985; Checkland, 1981) through his work on group dynamics in the US. He is also believed to have been the first person to use the term "action research" (Lewin, 1948). Lewin (1946) defined AR as a specific research approach in which the researcher generates new social knowledge about a social system, while at the same time attempts to change it (Cartwright, 1951; Lewin, 1946; Peters and Robinson, 1984). A distinctive thrust of AR has also developed after World War II in Great Britain at the Tavistock Institute of Human

Relations in London. There, AR was used as an innovative method to deal with sociological and psychological disorders arising from prison camps and war battlefields (Rapoport, 1970; Fox, 1990).

In AR, "action" and "research" are combined into a structured process usually referred to as the AR cycle (Davison, 2001), of which variations exist (McKay and Marshall, 2001). Perhaps the most widely accepted view of the AR cycle is that provided by Susman and Evered (1978) in what is believed to be a seminal article that laid the foundations of modern organizational AR. Susman and Evered's (1978) AR cycle comprises five stages: *Diagnosing, action planning, action taking, evaluating,* and *specifying learning*. The *diagnosing* stage involves the identification by the researcher of an improvement opportunity at a prospective client organization that is likely to lead to the development of relevant knowledge. *Action planning* involves the joint development and consideration of alternative courses of action to attain the improvement identified and knowledge development. *Action taking* involves the selection and implementation of one of the courses of action considered in the previous stage. *Evaluating* involves the study of the outcomes of the selected course of action. Finally, *specifying learning* involves assessing the outcomes of the *evaluating* stage and, based on this assessment, knowledge generation in the form of a conceptual or theoretical model describing the situation under study.

While AR has been used in IS research since the 1980s (Baskerville, 1997), independent surveys conducted during the early and late 1990s lead to the conclusion that AR's representation in the field of IS has been very small (Lau, 1997; Orlikowski and Baroudi, 1991). Given AR's potential advantages for the conduct of IS research, particularly the likelihood that it will lead to outcomes that are relevant to industry practitioners (Kock and Lau, 2001; Truex, 2001) since AR often begins with the identification of problems faced by industry practitioners, the small representation of published AR studies in the field of IS comes as a surprise. The literature on IS research methods suggests that three approaches have accounted for most of the published investigations in the field: experimental, survey, and case research (Cash and Lawrence, 1989; Galliers, 1992b; Orlikowski and Baroudi, 1991).

The lack of AR representation in the IS literature becomes more understandable when some of AR's potential "threats" to research success and publication are investigated. This investigation is conducted next, with an emphasis on three threats that have been widely recognized not only by detractors of AR, but also by those who subscribe to and practice AR.

3.   THE THREE THREATS OF ACTION RESEARCH

An investigation of the research methods literature, and in particular the AR literature, suggests the existence of AR threats that have been repeatedly reported and that seem to require particular attention in the development of methodological tools for improving AR in general and ensure that its use in the field of IS will lead to successful research outcomes (Avison et al., 1999; 2001; Davison, 2001; Elden and Chisholm, 1993; Galliers, 1984; 1991; 1992, 1992; Gustavsen, 1993; Jonsonn, 1991; Karlsen, 1991; Kock et al., 1997; Ledford and Mohrman, 1993; 1993b; McTaggart, 1991; Mumford, 2001; Reason, 1988; 1993; Susman and Evered, 1978). These threats, which are referred to here as *uncontrollability, contingency*, and *subjectivity* threats, seem to be associated with the "emergent" nature of most AR investigations (Galliers, 1992; 1992b), where a theoretical model emerges from the research data rather than being defined a priori and tested against that data (Glaser, 1992). This epistemological characteristic, present in the vast majority of AR investigations, and its associated problems have also been addressed by Orlikowski and Baroudi's (1991) methodological and epistemological discussion of IS research, and by Phillips and Pugh (2000) in their comparative study of doctoral programs and approaches. Orlikowski and Baroudi's (1991) widely cited article identifies similar threats as associated with research that does not conform closely with positivist research traditions, particularly research where the researcher interacts with the environment and the subjects being studied, and where theoretical models emerge from the research data rather than being tested against that data.

3.1   The uncontrollability threat

Even though in AR the researcher attempts to change the environment being studied, he or she does not usually have full control over that environment (Avison et al., 1999; Davison, 2001; Gustavsen, 1993; Jonsonn, 1991; Kock et al., 1997). While this characteristic of AR facilitates the emergence of theoretical models from the research data (Glaser, 1992; Susman and Evered, 1978), it also creates problems for the researcher. The uncontrollability threat of AR comes from the fact that the researcher's degree of control over the environment being studied and the research subjects is always incomplete, even less so when the relationship between researcher and subjects begins with the AR study and has no prior history. In this respect, Avison et al. (2001, p. 30) correctly point out that: "Rarely will an organization cede ultimate authority for organizational action to an external researcher. This guarded commitment is reasonable since the researcher's motives are divided between research goals and organizational problem-solving goals."

The essence of the uncontrollability threat is that while the environment being studied will often change in ways that have been predicted by the researcher, sometimes change will happen in ways that are completely unexpected (Mumford, 2001). The change may in some cases force the researcher to revisit his or her methods, theoretical assumptions, and even his or her research topic before a single iteration of the AR cycle is completed. Also, the researcher may be forced to abandon the research site before the study is completed due to events that are outside of his or her sphere of control (Kock et al., 1997; Mumford, 2001).

3.2   The contingency threat

In addition to not usually having full control over the environment being studied and study subjects, playing the role of an agent of change usually grants the researcher access to a considerably large body of data (McTaggart, 1991; Rapoport, 1970; Reason, 1988), often more than he or she can handle (Kock et al., 1999; Susman and Evered, 1978). The problem is that this body of data is usually "broad and shallow", rather than "narrow and deep" like the bodies of data collected through, for example, experimental research (Jonsonn, 1991; Karlsen, 1991; Kock et al., 1997; Lacity and Janson, 1994). The vast body of "shallow" data collected through AR studies seldom provides cumulative evidence that points to a particular effect or refers to a particular construct, and is often difficult to analyze because the rich context in which it is collected makes it difficult to separate out different components that refer to particular effects or constructs (Ledford and Mohrman, 1993; 1993b; Kock et al., 1997; Rapoport, 1970).

The contingency threat comes from AR's inherent obstacles to isolation of evidence related to particular effects and constructs from the contextual "glue" in which they are naturally found. "Contingency" here is used as synonymous with difficulty to generalize research findings, or difficulty to apply the research findings in contexts different from the one in which they were generated. That is, highly contingent findings carry little external validity (Berkowitz and Donnerstein, 1982; Cook and Campbell, 1976). Regarding the degree of difficulty associated with the isolation and analysis of "units" of research data, AR could be seen as being at the high end of a scale of difficulty of effect and construct isolation, whereas experimental research could be seen as being at the low end of the scale (Elden and Chisholm, 1993; Kock et al., 1997; Reason, 1988; 1993). In experimental research, the effect of one particular variable on another can be easily isolated through experimental controls. This is not possible in AR without making it lose some of the elements that characterize it as such - i.e., given

AR's own definition, if an AR project employs control groups it can no longer be called AR, and should be seen as a field experiment (Galliers, 1992; 1995; Heller, 1993; Kock et al., 1997; Reason, 1988; 1993).

3.3   The subjectivity threat

The deep involvement of researchers with client organizations in AR studies may hinder good research by introducing personal biases in the conclusions (Francis, 1991). This is particularly true in situations involving a conflict of interests. With respect to this, Galliers (1992, p. 152) points out that AR "... places a considerable responsibility on the researcher when objectives are at odds with other groupings." While deep personal involvement from the part of the researcher has the potential to bias research results, it is inherent in AR because it is impossible for a researcher to both be in a detached position and at the same time exert positive intervention on the environment and subjects being studied. This is particularly true when the number of situations experienced by the researcher is small and the emotional intensity of this involvement is high. Research on human cognition has shown not only that human beings rely mostly on experiential learning for the acquisition of knowledge, but also that those experiences that are accompanied by intense emotional discharges (e.g. anger, fear) are remembered more vividly than those in which there is little emotion involved (Gioia and Sims, 1986; Schacter, 2001). The downside of this phenomenon is that it is also likely to distort the way in which people in general, and AR practitioners in particular, may perceive events and situations where there is a high degree of personal involvement, especially when these situations involve conflict, stress, or any events that may lead to an emotional response.

The subjectivity threat hinges on the fact that, in AR, the personal involvement of the researcher is likely to push him or her into interpreting the research data in particular and potentially subjective ways, and that, as a result, some of these interpretations may end up being completely wrong. Some common interpretation biases have been identified by the literature (Argyris, 1977; 1992; Dobzhansky, 1971; Woofford, 1994), one of which is particularly relevant in the context of AR. That is the "externalization" bias, whereby an individual has difficulty assigning blame for "negative" outcomes of his or her own actions (e.g., dissatisfaction or frustration by his or her peers) to himself, instead trying to find ways to explain those "negative" outcomes based on factors that are external to him or her (Argyris, 1964; 1992; Dobzhansky, 1971). In IS AR, for example, this could lead to the wrong interpretation that certain "negative" behavioral patterns associated with dissatisfaction or frustration observed in research subjects are reactions to an information technology when in reality those behavioral patterns may be primarily motivated by the researcher himself and his or her own actions.

4. DEALING WITH THE ACTION RESEARCH THREATS: A DISCUSSION OF THREE METHODOLOGICAL ANTIDOTES

In this section, principles are developed to address the three AR threats reviewed above. These principles are referred to as methodological "antidotes". Three methodological antidotes are proposed and individually discussed below. They are referred to as *unit of analysis, grounded theory*, and *multiple iterations* antidotes, and are based on three main methodological "tools". The first methodological tool is the unit of analysis method (Creswell, 1994; Drew and Hardman, 1985; Yin, 1981; 1989; 1994). The second methodological tool is Glaser and Strauss's (1967) grounded theory methodology (see also Glaser, 1978; Glaser, 1992; Strauss and Corbin, 1990; 1998). The third methodological tool is the multiple AR cycle iteration method (Ketchum and Trist, 1992; Kock at al., 1997; Susman and Evered, 1978).

4.1 The unit of analysis antidote

The unit of analysis antidote is based on the use of the unit of analysis method (Creswell, 1994; Drew and Hardman, 1985; Yin, 1981; 1989; 1994), which prescribes that research data collection and analysis should be centered on *units of analysis* identified prior to the beginning of the research study. For example, units of analysis in IS AR research may be the "individual" user of information technology, or the "group" engaged in the use of a collaboration technology.

Usually, the more instances of a unit of analysis are studied in different contexts, the higher the external validity of findings relating patterns that are observed in different instances of the unit of analysis. Moreover, the more instances of a unit of analysis for which research data can be obtained, the more likely it is that statistical analysis techniques can be used to ascertain whether an observed trend (e.g., a particular behavior observed in many instances of the unit of analysis) is or is not due to chance (Creswell, 1994; Drew and Hardman, 1985; Gregory and Ward, 1974). And, ascertaining whether an observed trend is or is not due to chance is very important when the frequency distribution of the observed trend is scattered (i.e., the trend is not observed in all instances), which is often the case in AR (Sommer and Sommer, 1991).

The unit of analysis antidote counteracts the negative effects of all three AR threats when used in combination with the other methodological antidotes (this is discussed in the following sections), and particularly of the contingency threat, as it provides the basis on which to increase the external validity of research findings that refer to observable patterns in different instances of one or more units of analysis (Berkowitz and Donnerstein, 1982; Cook and Campbell, 1976). While this may seem obvious, the unit of analysis method has seldom been explicitly used in AR (Heller, 1993; Kock et al., 1997; Ledford and Mohrman, 1993b).

4.2   The grounded theory antidote

The grounded theory antidote is based on the use of an adaptation of Glaser and Strauss's (1967) grounded theory methodology. At the core of the grounded theory methodology is a three-step coding process, which is conducted in an iterative fashion and is aimed at increasing the reliability (Carmines and Zeller, 1979) of the analysis of large bodies of unstructured research data. That is, the coding process tries to foster objective data analysis and ensure that different coders, regardless of their level of involvement with the environment and subjects being studied, will produce the same final data analysis results. The first step, *open coding*, involves the identification of emerging categories in textual data. The second step, *axial coding*, involves the identification of relationships between the categories identified through open coding. The third and final step, *selective coding*, involves the grouping of interrelated categories into theoretical models (Glaser, 1978; 1992; Glaser and Strauss, 1967; Strauss and Corbin, 1990; 1998). The adaptation of this three-step coding process is necessary here because it has been originally proposed in a very generic format to allow for its adaptation to specific research needs and goals (Glaser, 1992; Strauss and Corbin, 1990; 1998).

In the adapted version proposed here for the specific needs of AR, grounded theory is used for the summarization of findings into causal models (Bagozzi, 1980; Davis, 1985) linking independent, moderating, intervening, and dependent variables derived from the study (Arnold, 1982; Baron and Kenny, 1986; Creswell, 1994; Drew and Hardman, 1985). In addition, in the adapted version proposed here, open coding involves the identification of *new* variables in any of the stages of the AR cycle, in addition to the variables related to units of analysis identified *before* the AR study begins based on theory (Becker, 1993). Each variable is defined as an attribute of a unit of analysis that can vary on a numeric or non-numeric scale (Drew and Hardman, 1985; Gregory and Ward, 1974; Pervan and Klass, 1992). For example, the variable "cognitive effort", which may be associated with the use of a particular information technology, is an attribute of the unit of analysis "individual" that can vary along an ordinal scale containing the values "high", "medium" and "low". Similarly, the variable "cost" may be associated to a group's use of a particular collaboration technology, is an attribute of the unit of analysis "group", which can vary along a numeric scale. While open coding is used for the identification of additional variables (in addition to the ones identified prior to the beginning of the research study), axial coding becomes then the identification of links between variables, and selective coding becomes the identification of dependent variables, which act as "anchor" variables to which a set of interrelated variables and effects is associated. This process relies heavily on data tabulation (Miles and Huberman, 1994) and to some extent on statistical analysis techniques (e.g., Chi-Square analysis), which will be illustrated later in this chapter through the description of a real IS AR study.

Neither the intermediate steps taken in grounded theory development, nor the causal models generated through them necessarily have to be included in all reports, articles or papers on the AR study. The causal models generated are the highest level of abstraction regarding the findings of the study and serve as both a high-level representation of the main findings of the study, and an "index" against which different pieces of the intermediate research data can be found (Glaser, 1992). Since the coding of grounded theory is "directional", in that it takes the researcher from raw data to summarized data (often in tables) and finally to causal models, it becomes easy for an organized researcher (i.e., one who keeps organized records of the intermediate coding stages) to go back to the intermediate data that led to a particular causal link identified through selective coding (Strauss and Corbin, 1990; 1998). Those intermediate data can then be shown as supporting evidence in a publication that focuses on a particular aspect of the AR study. Grounded theory development is a laborious process that is often "hidden" in the background and not explicitly referred to in publications beyond their "research method" sections (Glaser and Strauss, 1967; Strauss and Corbin, 1990; 1998).

The grounded theory antidote counteracts the negative effects of all three AR threats when used in combination with the other methodological antidotes, and particularly those associated with the subjectivity threat, as it provides the basis on which to remove the subjectivity of the analysis of large bodies of data by fostering inter-coder reliability (Carmines and Zeller, 1979). While grounded theory methodology has been extensively used in qualitative research in general (Strauss and Corbin, 1990; 1998), explicit examples of its use in AR are difficult to find. For example, none of the papers in the two 1993 special *Human Relations* issues on AR explicitly employed it (Elden and Chisholm, 1993), nor did any of the papers in the

2001 special *Information Technology & People* issue on IS AR (Kock and Lau, 2001).

4.3   The multiple iterations antidote

The multiple iterations antidote is based on the conduct of multiple iterations of Susman and Evered's (1978) AR cycle. One of the reasons for conducting multiple iterations of the AR cycle is the opportunity that it allows for collecting cumulative research data about specific units of analysis in different contexts and thus strengthening research findings by building on evidence gathered from previous iterations in the AR cycle. Ketchum and Trist (1992) see the frequency of the iterations in the AR cycle as likely to decrease as the match improves between the researcher's conception of the phenomenon being studied, expressed in the causal models comprising the research findings, and that found as a result of the specifying learning stage in each subsequent AR cycle.

Multiple iterations of the AR cycle should expand the research scope, e.g., the areas of the client organization involved in the research, and build up the generality of the results through the identification of invariable patterns. The observation of invariable patterns in different contexts is a precondition for claiming external validity of research findings (Berkowitz and Donnerstein, 1982; Carmines and Zeller, 1979; Cook and Campbell, 1976).

The multiple iterations antidote counteracts the negative effects of all three AR threats when used in combination with the other methodological antidotes, and particularly those associated with the contingency and uncontrollability threats. Multiple iterations counter the negative effects of the contingency threat by allowing for the observation of invariable patterns in different contexts, for which a degree of external validity can be claimed (Berkowitz and Donnerstein, 1982; Carmines and Zeller, 1979; Cook and Campbell, 1976). The contribution of the multiple iterations antidote to counteract the uncontrollability threat comes from the lower reliance of the research on single iterations that it fosters, and the higher likelihood of success in subsequent iterations enabled by the cumulative experience gained by the researcher as the AR study progresses. In a single iteration study (i.e., one in which a single iteration of the AR cycle is conducted) problems can occur that are outside the sphere of control of the researcher and that can undermine the data collection and analysis. For example, with multiple iterations being conducted, the early termination of an iteration will not have as harmful an effect as if the entire AR study had been conducted as a single iteration study. Moreover, in a multi-iteration study, the experience gained in previous iterations helps the researcher avoid situations that may jeopardize the AR study and come across to the client as more knowledgeable about the topic being studied and thus more worthy of the client's trust. While it seems that multiple iterations of Susman and Evered's (1978) AR cycle are advisable, explicit examples of AR conducted through multiple iterations of the AR cycle are difficult to come by, as most AR studies seem to traverse the AR cycle only once (Elden and Chisholm, 1993; Kock and Lau, 2001).

5. SPOTTING THE THREATS: A LOOK AT A REAL INFORMATION SYSTEMS ACTION RESEARCH STUDY

In this section, I use an IS AR study in which I was the principal investigator to illustrate the occurrence of the three threats. The use of the antidotes is discussed in the following section. The study was conducted through four iterations of Susman and Evered's (1978) AR cycle that lasted approximately four years and four months. One of the iterations, the first, was conducted in Brazil. The other iterations were conducted in New Zealand. The focus of the study was on business process improvement (BPI) groups supported by Internet-based email conferencing systems, particularly regarding the impact of the technology on group success.

Key criteria used for selecting client organizations for the AR study included commitment to process improvement, demonstrated by the existence of at least one formal organization-wide BPI program, and initial absence of electronic communication support for BPI activities. I expected interviews with BPI group members to be one of the main sources of research evidence. Therefore, these client organization selection criteria were aimed at ensuring that BPI group participants had a basis for comparison of "electronic" BPI groups with face-to-face ones, grounded on past participation in face-to-face BPI groups.

The first iteration of the AR cycle involved EventsInc (this and the other organizations are referred to by pseudonyms in this chapter) a service firm in Brazil whose revenues came chiefly from the organization of large professional and trade events (e.g., exhibitions and conferences). The company had 70 employees and yearly revenues of US$ 3.5 million. The second and fourth iterations of the AR cycle were conducted at CollegeOrg, a comprehensive university in New Zealand with 550 faculty and 750 staff and yearly revenues of approximately US$ 83.3 million. The third iteration of the AR cycle was conducted at GovernOrg, a branch of the Ministry of Agriculture and Fisheries of New Zealand employing approximately 2,500 people at a number of offices throughout New Zealand. GovernOrg's yearly revenues were US$ 105 million.

5.1   Motivation and theoretical background

The research topic emerged from my work as a consultant, which gravitated around facilitating business process improvement (BPI) groups in a variety of companies and helping them implement new improved business processes with information technologies. Most BPI groups I had facilitated involved members from different departments who discussed and tried to solve problems related to a business process whose component activities they had to routinely perform as part of their job. A business process can be defined as a set of interrelated activities, usually jointly carried out by people with different types of expertise (Davenport and Beers, 1995; Kettinger and Grover, 1995). Examples of business processes are "fulfilling an order for a batch of exhaust pipes" or "preparing a budget for the construction of a three-story building". The individuals involved in carrying out a process are often referred to as members of a process team (Davenport, 1993).

One of the problems faced by most organizations I worked with was that participation in face-to-face BPI groups was very disruptive for their members, since very often they were not co-located. Given this, it seemed that BPI groups could benefit from the use of computer-mediated communication systems that allowed their members to interact in a distributed and asynchronous manner. When this study began, several technologies incorporated support for distributed and asynchronous electronic communication. One such technology was Internet-based email conferencing (IEC). IEC seemed particularly appropriate to support BPI groups because it relied on an underlying technology, Internet email, which was ubiquitous enough to enable seamless inter-organizational communication.

Most of the empirical evidence from the literature suggested grim expectations regarding the effect of IEC support on BPI groups, as electronic communication media have consistently been seen as less appropriate than the face-to-face medium to support the type of complex and knowledge-ridden communication that usually takes place in BPI groups (Ackerman, 1994; Neilson, 1997; Orlikowski, 1992; 1993; Riggs et al., 1996; Tan et al., 2000), even though some empirical studies reported increases in group efficiency (but not outcome quality) in connection with the use of electronic communication media created by group decision support systems (Dennis et al., 1993; 1999). This empirical evidence was consistent with a few influential theories of organizational communication, such as social presence theory (Short at al., 1976), and media richness theory (Daft and Lengel, 1986). These theories led to the conclusion that for group tasks as complex (or "equivocal", in media richness theory terminology) as BPI, asynchronous computer mediation would lead to outcomes that would be "worse" than those likely to be achieved by BPI groups interacting face-to-face (Markus,

1994). That, in turn, would lead computer mediation to be seen by users as inadequate for BPI, which should be confirmed by related observable patterns of behavior by BPI group members, as well as evidence regarding BPI success. On the other hand, another influential theoretical model, the social influence model (Fulk et al., 1990; Markus, 1994), argued that social influences could strongly shape individual behavior toward technology in ways that are relatively independent of technology traits. The social influence model suggested that certain social influences (e.g., perceived group mandate, peer expectations of individual behavior) could lead BPI members to adapt their use of technology in ways that were inconsistent with predictions based on the social presence and media richness theories, and achieve successful results. Therefore, a detailed investigation of IEC-supported BPI groups, focusing on the impact of IEC support on the success of the groups, seemed to combine practical relevance with the potential to contribute to a better understanding of these theoretical contradictions.

5.2   The business process improvement groups

Many view BPI as one of the underlying ideas of widely practiced and researched management movements (Burke and Peppard, 1995; Kock and McQueen, 1996). Some representative examples are total quality management, which emphasizes incremental and local BPI (Deming, 1986), and business process re-engineering, whose emphasis is on radical and cross-departmental BPI (Hammer and Champy, 1993; Davenport, 1993). One of BPI's key characteristics is its group basis (Hammer, 1996; Ishikawa, 1986; Soles, 1994; Walton, 1991). That is, business process change proposals aimed at BPI usually emerge from a group specifically formed to generate such proposals (Davenport and Stoddard, 1994; Deming, 1986; Hammer and Champy, 1993). This generic type of group is referred to, here, as the BPI group. A BPI group typically has a finite and relatively short lifetime, during which its members define, analyze, and search for alternatives to improve one or a few organizational processes (Choi, 1995; Choi and Liker, 1995; Hammer and Stanton, 1995). The literature suggests that BPI groups usually conduct their activities along three main conceptual stages, namely *definition*, *analysis*, and *redesign* (Deming, 1986; Hammer, 1996; Hammer and Champy, 1993; Ishikawa, 1986; Soles, 1994; Walton, 1991). In the definition stage, the BPI group selects a business process for redesign. In the analysis stage, the group studies the business process in detail. Finally, in the redesign stage, the group proposes redesign modifications to be incorporated into the business process. The groups described here followed these same general stages. These stages are followed by the implementation of the modifications, which is the real test of the quality of the outcomes (process redesign recommendations) produced by the BPI group. A successful BPI group will be followed by the implementation of its business process redesign recommendations, which in turn will lead to positive organizational results (e.g., observable reduction in process cycle time, increase in revenues).

BPI group members communicated electronically using IEC list servers developed based on X-Post (Lantec Corp.) at EventsInc, and Novell Groupwise (Novell Corp.) at CollegeOrg and GovernOrg. In all cases electronic mailboxes were created to allow BPI group members to post and read electronic messages and file attachments among themselves. Spreadsheets, flow charts, presentations, and graphs could be attached as files to electronic messages, and read by recipients. Attachments could be easily read by clicking on icons representing the attached files on the computer screen.

5.3   Data collection and analysis

The 1st iteration of the AR cycle provided anecdotal data about the potentially positive benefit of IEC support for BPI groups. This was confirmed based on a more focused data collection and analysis conducted in the 2nd, 3rd and 4th iterations of the AR cycle. In those iterations, perception frequency-based analyses of interviews triangulated with participant observation notes, electronic postings and other documents suggested that while BPI group members perceived IEC as a poor medium for BPI-related communication, IEC support caused a reduction in BPI group cost, an increase in the quality of the process redesign recommendations generated by BPI groups, and an increase in the rate of success of BPI groups.

Interviews were conducted with process improvement group members and addressed perceived differences between face-to-face and IEC groups they had participated in. To avoid perception bias, interview answers were probed deeply for rationale, personal motivations and other factors that could bias perceptions, as well as triangulated with other sources of data. Sixty-two structured and over one hundred unstructured interviews were conducted. The structured interviews, the core source of evidence in this study, were taped and later transcribed. They employed an "in-depth interviewing" method proposed by Sommer and Sommer (1991), lasted from 45 minutes to 2.5 hours each, and were based on open-ended questions. The open-ended questions used in structured interviews were worded in a neutral way so as not to induce any specific answer. Each question was accompanied by the follow up question "Why?" and other related questions to clarify the interviewees' motivations for their answers, allow for the screening and elimination of ambiguous answers, and generate perception-related qualitative data that could be used for content analysis. The frequency distributions of interview answers were tested for statistical significance using the Chi-Square technique. The Chi-Square tests excluded ambiguous and "I don't know" answers (both placed in the "I don't know" category when frequency distributions were calculated), which added robustness to the results. The frequency distributions of answers in interviews were similar for CollegeOrg and GovernOrg (Cronbach Alpha = .72).

Approximately 89 percent of the participants felt that IEC support decreased group cost. The perception trend toward a decrease in group cost due to IEC support was very skewed and statistically significant (Chi-Square > 100, P < .01). Most of the respondents described the reduction in cost as being "drastic", and as being caused by a virtual elimination of travel and accommodation costs, a reduction in the total amount of time required from them to participate in group discussions, and a reduction in the costs associated with disruption of normal activities normally caused by face-to-face meetings. Only one process improvement group member was of the opinion that IEC support increased group cost. That member had spent a significant amount of time contributing electronic postings to a group that eventually failed to produce process change recommendations and thus explained his perception by noting that a face-to-face discussion would have led to better outcomes and thus his time would not have been completely wasted. He blamed the failure on communication problems associated with the electronic medium, which he saw as too "dry" for BPI discussions.

Group outcome quality, or the quality of the process redesign recommendations generated by BPI groups, was perceived by 43.5 percent of the participants as having been increased by IEC support. The perception trend toward an increase in group outcome quality was statistically significant (Chi-Square = 5.84, P < .05). The two main reasons independently provided by BPI group members to explain why they thought IEC support had increased group outcome quality were a better quality of individual contributions and a higher departmental heterogeneity than in similar face-to-face process improvement initiatives, both seen as fostered by IEC support. On the other hand, 21 percent of the BPI group members perceived a decrease in quality associated with the IEC support. The main and virtually only reason provided to explain this perception was that the IEC medium was not as "good", "rich", or "appropriate" as the face-to-face medium for BPI group discussions, increasing the level of ambiguity in them. Compilations of electronic postings suggest that, in most cases, those who perceived a decrease in group outcome quality due to IEC support had not participated actively in the BPI group discussions, in some cases having completely withdrawn from the discussions right after their start. Also, most of those members were from BPI groups that failed.

The evidence suggests that 4 out of the 6 process improvement groups conducted at CollegeOrg, as well as 4 out of the 6 BPI groups conducted at GovernOrg, were successful. The criteria for success used were derived from the BPI literature – BPI attempts are considered successful if the recommended process changes are implemented fully or partially and lead to positive observable results (Burke and Peppard, 1995; Champy, 1995; Choi and Behling, 1997; Davenport, 1993; Hammer and Champy, 1993). Overall, 8 out of 12 groups were successful, which yields a total success rate of 67 percent. This success rate is over twice the success rate of BPI attempts based on total quality management and business process re-engineering principles, which the literature suggests to be around 30 percent or less (Champy, 1995; Choi and Behling, 1997). That is, the rate of success of the IEC-supported BPI groups studied was significantly higher than the average suggested by the literature.

In summary, the results above suggest a reduction in BPI group cost, an increase in BPI group outcome quality, and an increase in success rate of BPI groups, as associated with IEC support. The results partially support and, at the same time, contradict the social presence (Short at al., 1976) and media richness (Daft and Lengel, 1986) theories. While the evidence suggesting that IEC was consistently perceived as a poor medium for BPI-related communication partially supports the theories, the increase in the quality of the process redesign recommendations generated by the groups and in their success rate contradicts expectations based on the theories. Fulk et al.'s (1994) social influence model provides a explanation for these contradictory results, by showing that social influences (e.g., perceived group mandate, peer expectations of individual behavior) could lead BPI members to *adapt* their use of technology in ways that are inconsistent with predictions based on the social presence and media richness theories, and achieve successful results by compensating for the obstacles posed by a medium of low social presence and richness. This is what seems to have happened, as indicated by one of the two key explanations provided by BPI group members who perceived an increase in group outcome quality, which was a perceived increase in the quality of individual contributions fostered by the IEC medium. Therefore, the combination of the social presence and media richness theories with the social influence model provides a solid basis on which to fully understand the results summarized above.

From an empirical perspective, the findings contradict most of the empirical literature on distributed group support systems (Ackerman, 1994; Neilson, 1997; Orlikowski, 1992; 1993; Riggs et al., 1996; Tan et al., 2000), and provide the basis on which to argue that rational choice (Short et al.,

1976; Daft and Lengel, 1986) and social theories (Fulk et al., 1994) of organizational communication can be combined to understand the behavior of complex and knowledge-intensive groups in real organizational situations. Previously, these types theories had often been pitted against each other and presented as incompatible.

Below, a description of each of the iterations of the AR cycle is provided. These iterations led to the results summarized above. Their description highlights the three threats of AR, which are discussed at the points they emerged within the iterations. A discussion of how the methodological antidotes were employed to deal with the threats is provided in the section following the sections describing the four iterations of the AR cycle below.

5.4   The 1st iteration of action research cycle: EventsInc in Brazil

The first iteration of the AR cycle was perhaps the one that I was the most excited about, but nevertheless was a rude awakening to me, as it showed my lack of preparation to deal with the many challenges posed by field research in general and AR in particular.

Diagnosing. EventsInc's local area network of computers was not working properly, which prevented the full deployment of an email package they had purchased a while ago. Since I was interested on the impact of IEC support on BPI groups, which required a working email system, and had some local area network installation and set up skills, EventsInc saw this as an opportunity to have their technical networking problems solved.

Action planning. We planned to conduct the iteration of the AR cycle over approximately one year, starting with the solution of the networking problems and then moving on to the running of IEC-supported BPI groups.

Action taking. The computer networking problems were fixed and the email conferencing system was installed without any major problems, but a little later than originally planned. The system allowed BPI groups to post electronic messages onto mailboxes created for each group discussion. Twenty-six BPI groups were conducted. The first eleven of those BPI groups interacted only face-to-face because the email conferencing system was not yet available; the others conducted most of the discussions via the IEC system. Most of the groups generated BPI proposals in no more than 40 days, which were in most cases implemented immediately after the completion of the BPI groups.

At the end of the "action taking" stage in the first iteration of the AR cycle, a bizarre turn of events (described in the sidebar below) took place. This turn of events provides a good illustration of the uncontrollability threat.

The uncontrollability threat

The shocking truth about EventInc's management's real intentions

I expected EventsInc's management to want competitors to be as far away as possible from the company's premises so they would not be able to copy EventsInc's new approach to BPI. Nevertheless, in several occasions, the chief executive officer invited the owners of a competing company to see the intermediate results of the project. The visitors, who were introduced to me as "*some friends*" by the chief executive officer, usually asked me (repeatedly) questions about the impact of BPI groups on EventsInc's bottom line (e.g., sustained increases in sales, profitability etc.).

Approximately 9 months into the project, I heard from one irate executive that EventsInc was undergoing the first stages of an amicable acquisition by a competitor, who turned out to be the one whose representatives had been visiting EventsInc and asking me questions. The AR iteration was discontinued and I was asked to conduct an analysis of the project and summarize it in a report for the acquiring company.

As soon as the news about the acquisition became public, key employees left the company in disgust. Conversations with management and employees suggested that the general feeling was that the BPI project had been used to "add market value" to the company. Some viewed me as an "evil consultant" and others as an "idiot fool" (in the words of one manager) who had been manipulated by the chief executive officer. The latter perception was probably more accurate, as it had not been clear to me what was going on until late in the project.

This happened at a time when it became clear to me that I needed more specific data from the participants to reach valid conclusions about the impact of IEC support on BPI groups. The resulting unwillingness of the employees to further collaborate with me made it impossible to obtain the additional research data that I needed.

Evaluating. Given the turn of events described above, there was urgency to analyze the data for the report to the acquiring company. Anecdotal evidence from interviews triangulated with participant observation notes, electronic postings and other documents suggested that the project had been very successful from an organization-wide perspective, even though its final outcome had been less than positive in the eyes of several of its key members. Significant efficiency gains in local processes due to the decentralization of access to information, a major simplification of the organization's departmental structure, and an increase in revenues were the main bottom-line results of the changes brought about by the BPI groups.

Specifying learning. Having just left the research site, I found myself overwhelmed not only by the large body of data to be analyzed but also by important decisions that I had to make in order to be able to produce what I saw as "relevant knowledge". Producing such knowledge is the main goal of the "specifying learning" stage of the AR cycle (Susman and Evered, 1978).

At this point, it became clear that my broad and unfocused data collection had led me to fall prey to AR's contingency threat, which is discussed in the sidebar below. I had not been able to collect enough data to reach valid conclusions about the impact of technology on BPI groups, and the turn of events since the announcement of the acquisition prevented me from collecting any additional data.

The contingency threat

The broad and unfocused data collection led to very context-specific lessons

Every observable event, comment by a BPI group member, printed document, electronic posting etc. had been a data point for me, which led me to observe a number of effects that could have influenced BPI group success. The combination of this abundance of data with the company sell-out made me lose focus and consider research questions that had nothing to do with my initial theoretical motivations. For example, should the use of groupware-supported BPI by management as a means of (in my view, unethically) adding value to a soon-to-be-sold company be the main focus of my analysis, or should the target of my analysis be the impact of groupware on BPI groups?

I eventually decided to use the data that I had at hand to try to reach some conclusions about the impact of IEC support at the group level. My unfocused data collection led me to reach conclusions that were very tentative and accompanied by several caveats and limitations. No theoretical conclusions were possible. Disappointed with the results of my first iteration of the AR cycle, I summarized this phase of the research in a very descriptive paper. The paper, which was later accepted for publication and presentation at a large conference in Australia, described an interesting story, but the lessons were so context-specific that I myself doubted they could be applied in different organizations under different circumstances, even if these organizations were in the same industry as EventsInc.

Interestingly, the paper above received the "best conference paper award" at the conference. Frankly, I am unsure as to whether it really deserved the award. I viewed the award primarily as a sign of AR's appeal in the field of IS, where seldom researchers tried to bridge the gap between them and the practitioners they studied (Orlikowski and Baroudi, 1991; Lau, 1997; 1999).

5.5   The 2nd iteration of the action research cycle: CollegeOrg in New Zealand

Soon after the 1st iteration was completed, I migrated to New Zealand (something that I had planned to do, for personal reasons), and was determined to continue my research on IEC-supported BPI groups there. The second iteration of the AR cycle, carried out at CollegeOrg, was narrow is scope, and helped me get familiarized with the New Zealand culture as well as establish a solid basis for further iterations in that country.

Diagnosing. CollegeOrg had recently developed a hands-on introductory computing course covering a number of software applications, including email, group decision support systems, Internet Web browsers, word processors, spreadsheets and data base management systems. While attracting much interest from students, with about 100 enrolments per semester, the course had recently been the focus of an "avalanche" of student complaints related to course design, level of work required, computer lab scheduling and other related issues. One of the instructors involved in teaching the course thought that an IEC-supported BPI group could help solve these problems in a more expedited fashion than a face-to-face group.

Action planning. I quickly designed and implemented an IEC system similar to the one I had developed at EventsInc. The instructor mentioned above invited several other people to participate in the BPI group. The instructor planned to address the course problems through an IEC-supported BPI group discussion lasting no more than three months so that the agreed upon changes in the process (i.e., the process of teaching the course) could be implemented in time for the following semester.

Action taking. The BPI group lasted 33 days and comprised 7 members from a computer support area and one academic department. The interaction in the group comprised 21 postings, and a number of one-on-one phone and face-to-face conversations. According to estimates provided by group members, the vast majority of the time spent by group members in the group discussion was in interactions through the IEC system, with a small amount of time spent in oral one-on-one interactions. The group was completed in time for the implementation of the process changes to be assessed in the following semester. The impact of the process changes was assessed through a survey of student perceptions about the course. The survey covered most of the points targeted by the BPI group. It indicated a remarkable improvement in the quality of the course, when compared with a previous survey performed in the previous semester.

Evaluating. Perception frequency analyses of interviews triangulated with participant observation notes, electronic postings and other documents suggested that, while BPI group members perceived IEC as a poor medium for BPI-related communication, BPI group cost had been reduced (due to a reduction in the total amount of time required from members to participate in group discussions) and the quality of the process redesign recommendations generated by the group had been increased by IEC support. These effects, when combined, suggested that IEC support could increase the success of BPI groups, but it was clear that more evidence was needed to assess the validity of this conclusion.

Specifying learning. The results from the "evaluating" stage both supported and contradicted the social presence (Short at al., 1976) and media richness (Daft and Lengel, 1986) theories. The majority perception that IEC was a poor medium for BPI-related communication partially supported the theories. However, the apparent increase in the quality of the process redesign recommendations generated by the group contradicted the theories. As predicted, Fulk et al.'s (1994) social influence model provided an explanation for these contradictory results.

5.6   The 3rd iteration of the action research cycle: GovernOrg in New Zealand

The third iteration of the AR cycle involved circumstances close to ideal for the evaluation of the impact of IEC on BPI groups. Not only did GovernOrg conduct BPI groups before, primarily face-to-face and without the support of electronic communication tools, but it also presented a very geographically fragmented office distribution in New Zealand, which rendered it a prime client for an AR project involving IEC-supported BPI groups. However, this iteration also gave me a taste of AR's subjectivity threat.

Diagnosing. GovernOrg's chief executive officer had recently issued a warning about the prospect of imminent deregulation of New Zealand's food production sector, whose government-mandated quality standards were inspected by GovernOrg, and the consequent privatization of GovernOrg, which would then become an independent auditing and consulting firm. GovernOrg's management viewed IEC-supported BPI groups as an opportunity to improve several of GovernOrg's processes in time so it could be prepared for the transition from a government branch to a private firm.

Action planning. I quickly implemented an IEC system similar to the one that had been used at CollegeOrg in the previous iteration of the AR cycle, a task that was made easier by the fact that both CollegeOrg and GovernOrg used the same email server software - Novell Groupwise (Novell Corp.). It was decided that the availability of the IEC system for the conduct of BPI groups, as well as my technical facilitation, would be announced to managers and employees, who would also be invited to voluntarily form and conduct BPI groups using the IEC system with my technical facilitation.

Action taking. Six BPI groups were conducted. The groups lasted from 10 to 29 days, had from 5 to 15 members, and altogether involved 47 managers and employees from 18 different office sites spread throughout New Zealand. Each office site typically supplied a number of services to customers in a town or city and vicinities. In most BPI groups, the process redesign recommendations were implemented with observable increases in process efficiency and/or solution of quality-related problems.

Evaluating. Perception frequency analyses of interviews triangulated with participant observation notes, electronic postings and other documents again suggested that BPI group members perceived IEC as a poor medium for BPI-related communication. Also, the data again suggested a reduction in BPI group cost and an increase in the quality of the process redesign recommendations generated by the group. According to success criteria proposed by the BPI literature, the rate of success of the BPI groups conducted at GovernOrg had been approximately 67 percent, which was over twice the approximately 30 percent success rate reported in the BPI literature for BPI groups in general. That is, the evidence in this iteration was very similar to that obtained in the previous iteration and pointed at the same technology effects.

At the beginning of the "specifying learning" stage in the third iteration of the AR cycle, a conflict erupted between a senior manager from GovernOrg and myself, which is described in the sidebar below. This conflict and its consequent biasing effect on my interpretation of part of the research data, provide a good illustration of AR's subjectivity threat.

The subjectivity threat

A conflict with a senior manager biased my interpretation of the evidence

At GovernOrg, two senior executives who reported directly to the chief executive officer had sanctioned the AR iteration to be conducted in their divisions. It became clear as the research progressed that these two senior executives had very different personalities and management styles. Among the differences was that one adopted a very democratic and consultative management style, whereas the other adopted a much more autocratic style. While the democratic manager rarely did so, the autocratic manager often made key organizational decisions alone. Their perceptions of IEC-supported BPI groups were equally distinct. After four BPI groups had been conducted, involving employees from both divisions, a clear divergence could be observed. The democratic manager's view of IEC-supported BPI groups was very positive. He believed that a national program should be instituted to use IEC-supported BPI groups to improve business processes throughout the Ministry of Agriculture and Fisheries (of which GovernOrg was a branch). The autocratic manager, on the other hand, felt that IEC-supported BPI groups were "a big waste of time", as well as an "obstacle" to swift senior management decisions. From the fifth BPI group on, the autocratic manager became openly hostile toward me.

I had not been given an office at GovernOrg. Therefore, I usually conducted my interviews in either the interviewee's office or the local cafeteria. In the middle of one of these interviews, at one of the tables in the cafeteria, the autocratic manager approached me and said, screaming: "*You have a very cushy lifestyle, huh? Every time I see you here, you're in the cafeteria taking a break! What makes you believe that you can drag my people into this kind of lifestyle too? We have work to do here! You know?*" He continued his public reprimand for a few more minutes and eventually told me that both my interview and my research at GovernOrg were over. A few days later, the autocratic manager called me on the phone and apologized for his actions. In his own words, "*...you made some mistakes, but did not deserve that much.*" I accepted his apology and asked to facilitate one more BPI group involving employees from his division. He reluctantly agreed.

I was obviously offended by what had happened. Why did the manager treat me like that? Obviously, I thought, I had done nothing wrong. My self-pity and pride led me to explain the incident based on the notion that electronic communication empowers employees (Clement, 1994) and that "stupid" and autocratic managers, like the one who had just given me such a hard time, do not know how to deal with that empowerment very well. However, while coding data from an interview with the autocratic manager, conducted after the incident at the cafeteria, and comparing it with my participant observation notes, it became clear that one of my actions at the beginning of the research iteration had had a much stronger impact than technology itself on how he perceived me and anything that had to do with me, including the IEC-supported BPI groups I was facilitating. Early in the third iteration of the AR cycle, I had conducted a simple quality and productivity audit at GovernOrg. That audit revealed that the productivity (assessed by standard metrics such as "revenues per employee") of the democratic manager's division was higher than that of the autocratic manager's division.

It was clear that my audit, and my lack of "tact" when informing the autocratic manager about its results, had played a major role in triggering his reactions toward the IEC-supported BPI groups and anything else that had to do with me. I could not ignore this source of "noise", which eventually prevented me from making unequivocal conclusions about technology effects on management behavior that would otherwise support previous empirical research on the topic (Clement, 1994). This highlights one important aspect of AR, which is that the researcher's deep involvement often works "against" him or her, so to speak, as he or she may be pushed into making subjective conclusions based on the research evidence that may not only be wrong but also likely to bias the interpretation of other evidence and potentially damage the whole research study.

Specifying learning. As with the previous iteration of the AR cycle, the results of the "evaluating" stage in this iteration of the AR cycle supported and, at the same time, contradicted the social presence (Short at al., 1976) and media richness (Daft and Lengel, 1986) theories. Again, as in the previous iteration of the AR cycle, Fulk et al.'s (1994) social influence model seemed to provide a complementary explanation for these contradictory results.

5.7   The 4th iteration of the action research cycle: CollegeOrg in New Zealand

The similarity between the findings of the second and third iterations of the AR cycle suggested, according to the "saturation" criterion proposed by Ketchum and Trist (1992), that the AR study could be concluded after the third iteration. However, I felt that I should go back to CollegeOrg and collect more BPI group data to ensure that the findings of the second iteration were not idiosyncratic. I did this in my 4th iteration of the AR cycle.

Diagnosing. After my second iteration of the AR cycle was concluded, CollegeOrg's president had launched an organization-wide initiative to enhance CollegeOrg's image as a top-quality tertiary education institution. A number of process efficiency and quality gaps were identified as a result of this initiative. Since I had been discussing my AR study with several of CollegeOrg's faculty and staff while conducting the 3rd iteration of the AR cycle at GovernOrg, many of them saw IEC-supported BPI groups as a way to deal with the productivity and quality gaps identified as a result of CollegeOrg's president's initiative.

Action planning. Several interested faculty and staff approached me to provide technical facilitation for voluntary BPI groups using the IEC system employed at CollegeOrg in the 2nd iteration of the AR cycle. It was decided that five BPI groups, whose membership and general problems to be addressed had been agreed upon in advance, would be conducted with my technical facilitation. This would also allow me to collect data about the same number of groups, i.e., six, in CollegeOrg and GovernOrg, which provided some balance of data sources to my AR study.

Action taking. As planned, five BPI groups were conducted. The groups lasted from 32 to 54 days, had from 7 to 13 members, and altogether involved 48 faculty and staff from 15 different departments. In most BPI groups the process redesign recommendations were implemented with observable increases in process efficiency and/or solution of quality-related problems.

Evaluating. Perception frequency analyses of interviews triangulated with participant observation notes, electronic postings and other documents again suggested that BPI group members perceived IEC as a poor medium for BPI-related communication. Also, the data again suggested a reduction in BPI group cost and an increase in the quality of the process redesign recommendations generated by the group. Again, according to success criteria proposed by the BPI literature, the rate of success of the BPI groups conducted at CollegeOrg was over twice the average reported in the BPI literature. That is, the evidence in this iteration was very similar to that obtained in the two previous iterations and pointed at the same technology effects.

Specifying learning. As with the two previous iterations of the AR cycle, the results of the "evaluating" stage in this iteration of the AR cycle supported and, at the same time, contradicted the social presence (Short at al., 1976) and media richness (Daft and Lengel, 1986) theories. Again, as in the two previous iterations of the AR cycle, Fulk et al.'s (1994) social influence model provided a plausible explanation for these contradictory results.

6. APPLYING THE METHODOLOGICAL ANTIDOTES

As mentioned before, the combined use of the three methodological antidotes - *unit of analysis, grounded theory,* and *multiple iterations* - counteracts the negative effects of all three AR threats - *uncontrollability, contingency* and *subjectivity.* The *unit of analysis* antidote drives the cumulative collection and analysis of data about the same unit of analysis in different contexts, which counteracts the *contingency* threat by reducing the context-specificity of the research findings regarding units of analysis about which cumulative data was collected and analyzed. The *grounded theory* antidote entails the use of a reliable research data coding method that makes data analysis more objective, which counteracts the *subjectivity* threat. The *multiple iterations* antidote entails the conduct of AR through multiple iterations of the AR cycle, which counteracts the *uncontrollability* threat by reducing the impact that events outside the sphere of control of the researcher, such as the early termination of one single iteration, have on the AR study as a whole.

My decision to conduct the study through multiple iterations of the AR cycle, which is the essence of the *multiple iterations* antidote, led me to use the experience obtained in previous iterations to avoid problems that characterize the *uncontrollability* threat of AR. For example, it led me to turn down an invitation from a chief executive officer of a New Zealand company who seemed to view the AR study as an opportunity to impose a BPI program on his employees in order to obtain a quality certification; an invitation that took place in between the 1st and the 2nd iterations of the AR cycle. Moreover, the use of multiple iterations prevented the early, and relatively "traumatic", termination of the 1st iteration of the AR cycle from compromising my AR study as a whole.

My decision to focus my data collection and analysis on a specific unit of analysis, which is the essence of the *unit of analysis* antidote, in and after the 2nd iteration of the AR cycle, led me to generate findings with potentially high external validity (Berkowitz and Donnerstein, 1982; Carmines and Zeller, 1979; Cook and Campbell, 1976), and thus avoid the *contingency* threat. It did so by allowing me to observe patterns related to the same unit of analysis, the "BPI group", which repeated themselves in different contexts. Among these patterns were a reduction in group cost, an increase in group outcome quality, and an increase in group success, in connection with the use of the IEC system by group members.

Finally, my decision to employ the three-stage coding process prescribed by Glaser and Strauss's (1967) grounded theory methodology, which is the essence of the *grounded theory* antidote, in and after the 2nd iteration of the AR cycle, helped me counter the *subjectivity* threat by allowing me to analyze the research data in a more objective way, thus preventing my personal biases from clouding my research conclusions. The systematic coding and summarization of data that characterizes grounded theory methodology led me to evidence that forced me to review my technology-based explanation for the autocratic manager's hostility toward me at the end of the 3rd iteration of the AR cycle, and consider the alternative explanation that my own previous actions had triggered that hostility.

7.   CONCLUSION

The discussion of threats and antidotes, conducted in this chapter, illustrates an area of methodological inquiry that has met with some resistance in certain AR circles in the past (Heller, 1993; Reason, 1988; 1993), but that can potentially lead to highly desirable outcomes, which is the adaptation and use of established research methods and techniques in the context of AR. The resistance has been motivated by the assumption held in some AR circles that AR is somehow opposed to positivism, and thus should not adhere to positivist research methods and techniques (Kock et al., 1997; Reason, 1993). This creates problems, since a large number of very useful research methods, techniques, and notions, have been developed in the context of positivist research, including the unit of analysis method (Creswell, 1994; Drew and Hardman, 1985; Yin, 1981; 1989; 1994) and the notion that external validity is a desirable research outcome (Berkowitz and Donnerstein, 1982; Cook and Campbell, 1976), both employed and espoused, respectively, in this chapter.

This chapter looks beyond the "AR versus positivism" debate, and it does so for a reason. The reason is the argument made by Kock and Lau (2001) that AR and positivism can hardly be placed in the same conceptual category. Arguably, AR is a research approach, like experimental research, not an epistemology, like positivism or interpretivism (Hirschheim, 1985; Orlikowski and Baroudi, 1991; Teichman and Evans, 1995). Thus, comparing AR with positivism is equivalent to comparing a "painting technique" (e.g., oil painting) with a "school of painting" (e.g., impressionism). That is, in the same way that oil painting cannot be directly compared with impressionism, AR cannot be directly compared with positivism. Thus AR cannot be opposed to positivism, even though it may not be the most appropriate research approach for traditional positivist inquiry (Kock and Lau, 2001). Once this notion is more widely accepted by those who practice AR, the debate between them and those who subscribe to other research approaches that fall into the broad category of "positivist research" will be replaced by cooperation in the search for solutions to longstanding methodological challenges.

8. ACKNOWLEDGEMENTS

This chapter is a revised version of an article by the author published in 2004 in the journal *Decision Support Systems*. The author would like to thank the individuals and organizations that participated in the several iterations of his action research study for their time and support. Thanks are also due to the reviewers for their comments and suggestions.

9. REFERENCES

Ackerman, M. (1994). Augmenting the organizational memory: A field study of Answer Garden. R. Furuta, & C. Neuwirth, eds. *Proceedings of CSCW'94 Conference*. New York, NY: The Association for Computing Machinery, 243-252.

Alavi, M. (1993). An assessment of electronic meeting systems in a corporate setting. *Information & Management*, 25(4), 175-182.

Argyris, C. (1964), *Integrating the Individual and the Organization*, John Wiley & Sons, New York, NY.

Argyris, C. (1977), Double Loop Learning Organizations, *Harvard Business Review*, V,55, No.5, pp. 115-125.

Argyris, C. (1992). *On Organizational Learning*. Cambridge, MA: Blackwell.

Argyris, C., Putnam, R. & Smith, D.M. (1985). *Action Science*. San Francisco, CA: Jossey-Bass.

Arnold, H.J. (1982). Moderator variables: A clarification of conceptual, analytic, and psychometric issues. *Organization Behaviour and Human Performance*, 29(4), 143-174.

Avison, D., Lau, F., Myers, M.D. & Nielsen, P. (1999). Action research. *Communications of the ACM*, 42(1), 94-97.

Avison, D., Baskerville, R. & Myers, M. (2001). Controlling action research projects. *Information Technology & People*, 14(1), 28-45.

Bagozzi, R.P. (1980). *Causal Models in Marketing*. New York, NY: John Wiley & Sons.

Barley, S.R. (1989). Images of imaging: Notes on doing longitudinal field work. *Organization Science*, 1(3), 220-247.

Baron, R.M. & Kenny, D.A. (1986). The moderator-mediator variable distinction in social psychological research: Conceptual, strategic, and statistical considerations. *Journal of Personality and Social Psychology*, 51(6), 1173-1182.

Baskerville, R. (1997). Distinguishing action research from participative case studies. *Journal of Systems and Information Technology*, 1(1), 25-45.

Baskerville, R. (1999). Investigating information systems with action research. *Communications of the AIS*, 2(19), 1-25.

Bunning, C. (1995). *Placing Action Learning and Action Research in Context*. Brisbane, Australia: International Management Centre.

Becker, H.S. (1993). Theory: The necessary evil. D.J. Flinders & G.E. Mills, eds. *Theory and Concepts in Qualitative Research: Perspectives from the Field*. New York, NY: Teachers College Press, 218-229.

Berkowitz, L. & Donnerstein, E. (1982). External validity is more than skin deep: Some answers to criticisms of laboratory experiments. *American Psychologist*, 37(3), 245-257.

Brynjolfsson, E. & Hitt, L. (1993). Is information systems spending productive? New evidence and new results. J.I. Degross, R.P. Bostrom, & D. Robey, eds. *Proceedings of the 14th International Conference on Information Systems*. New York, NY: The Association for Computing Machinery, 47-64.

Burke, G. and Peppard, J. (1995). Business process re-engineering: Research directions. G. Burke, & J. Peppard, eds. *Examining Business Process Re-engineering*. London, England: Kogan Page, 25-37.

Candlin, D.B. & Wright, S. (1991). Managing the introduction of expert systems. *International Journal of Operations & Production Management*, 12(1), 46-59.

Carmines, E.G. & Zeller, R.A. (1979). *Reliability and Validity Assessment*. Beverly Hills, CA: Sage.

Cartwright, D. (Ed) (1951). *Field Theory in Social Science*. New York, NY: Harper & Row.

Cash Jr, J.I. & Lawrence, P.R. (Eds) (1989). *The Information Systems Research Challenge: Qualitative Research Methods*. Boston, MA: Harvard Business School.

Champy, J. (1995). *Reengineering Management*. New York, NY: Harper Business.

Checkland, P. (1981). *Systems Thinking, Systems Practice*. New York, NY: John Wiley & Sons.

Checkland, P. (1991). From framework through experience to learning: The essential nature of action research. H. Nissen, H.K. Klein, & R. Hirschheim, eds. *Information Systems Research: Contemporary Approaches and Emergent Traditions*. New York, NY: North-Holland, 397-403.

Chidambaram, L. & Jones, B. (1993). Impact of communication medium and computer support on group perceptions and performance: A comparison of face-to-face and dispersed meetings. *MIS Quarterly*, 17(4), 465-491.

Choi, T.Y. (1995). Conceptualizing continuous improvement: Implications for organizational change. *Omega*, 23(6), 607-624.

Choi, T.Y. & Behling, O.C. (1997). Top managers and TQM success: One more look after all these years. *The Academy of Management Executive*, 11(1), 37-47.

Choi, T.Y. & Liker, J.K. (1995). Bringing Japanese continuous improvement approaches to U.S. manufacturing: The roles of process orientation and communications. *Decision Sciences*, 26(5), 589-620.

Clement, A. (1994). Computing at work: Empowering action by low-level users. *Communications of ACM*, 37(1), 53-63.

Cook, T.D. & Campbell, D.T. (1976). Four kinds of validity. M.D. Dunnette, ed. *Handbook of Industrial and Organizational Psychology*, Chicago, IL: Rand McNally, 224-246.

Creswell, J.W. (1994). *Research Design: Qualitative and Quantitative Approaches*. Thousand Oaks, CA: Sage.

Daft, R.L. & Lengel, R.H. (1986). Organizational information requirements, media richness and structural design. *Management Science*, 32(5), 554-571.

Davenport, T.H. (1993). *Process Innovation*. Boston, MA: Harvard Business Press.

Davenport, T.H. & Beers, M.C. (1995). Managing information about processes. *Journal of Management Information Systems*, 12(1), 57-80.

Davenport, T.H. & Stoddard, D.B. (1994). Reengineering: Business change of mythic proportions? *MIS Quarterly*, 18(2), 121-127.

Davis, J.A. (1985). *The Logic of Causal Order*. London, England: Sage.

Davison, R. (2001). GSS and action research in the Hong Kong Police. *Information Technology & People*, 14(1), 60-78.

Deming, W.E. (1986). *Out of The Crisis*. Cambridge, MA: Center for Advanced Engineering Study, Massachusetts Institute of Technology.

Dennis, A.R., Daniels, R.M., Jr, Hayes, G. & Nunamaker, J.F., Jr. (1993). Methodology-driven use of automated support in business process re-engineering. *Journal of Management Information Systems*, 10(3), 117-138.

Dennis A.R., Hayes G.S., & Daniels, R.M., Jr. (1999). Business process modeling with group support systems. *Journal of Management Information Systems*, 15(4), 115-142.

Dobzhansky, T. (1971). *Mankind Evolving: The Evolution of the Human Species*. New Haven, CN: Yale University Press.

Drew, C.J. & Hardman, M.L. (1985). *Designing and Conducting Behavioral Research*. New York, NY: Pergamon Press.

Elden, M. & Chisholm, R.F. (1993). Emerging varieties of action research. *Human Relations*, 46(2), 121-141.

Forman, J. & Rymer, J. (1999). The genre system of the Harvard Case Method. *Journal of Business and Technical Communication*, 13(4), 373-400.

Fox, W.M. (1990). An interview with Eric Trist, father of the sociotechnical systems approach. *The Journal of Applied Behavioural Science*. 26(2), 259-279.

Francis, D. (1991). Moving from non-interventionist research to participatory action. C. Collins & P. Chippendale, eds. *Proceedings of The First World Congress on Action Research, V.2*. Sunnybank Hills, Australia: Acorn, 31-42.

Fulk, J., Schmitz, J. & Steinfield, C.W. (1990). A social influence model of technology use. J. Fulk, & C. Steinfield, eds. *Organizations and Communication Technology*. Newbury Park, CA: Sage, 117-140.

Galliers, R.D. (1984). In search of a paradigm for information systems research. E. Mumford, Ed. *Research Methods in Information Systems*. New York, NY: North-Holland, 281-297.

Galliers, R.D. (1991). Choosing appropriate information system research approaches: A revised taxonomy. H. Nissen, H.K. Klein, & R. Hirschheim, eds. *Information Systems Research: Contemporary Approaches and Emergent Traditions*. New York, NY: North-Holland, 327-345.

Galliers, R.D. (1992). Choosing information systems research approaches. R. Galliers, Ed. *Information Systems Research: Issues, Methods and Practical Guidelines*. Boston, MA: Blackwell Scientific Publications, 144-162.

Galliers, R.D. (Ed) (1992b). *Information Systems Research: Issues, Methods and Practical Guidelines*. Boston, MA: Blackwell Scientific Publications.

Galliers, R.D. (1995). A manifesto for information management research. *British Journal of Management*, 6(4), 45-52.

Gallupe, R.B., Cooper, W.H., Grise, M. & Bastianutti, L.M. (1994). Blocking electronic brainstorms. *Journal of Applied Psychology*, 79(1), 77-86.

Glaser, B.G. (1978). *Theoretical Sensitivity: Advances in the Methodology of Grounded Theory*. Mill Valley, CA: Sociology Press.

Glaser, B.G. (1992). *Emergency versus Forcing: Basics of Grounded Theory Analysis*. Mill Valley, CA: Sociology Press.

Glaser, B.G. & Strauss, A.L. (1967). *The Discovery of Grounded Theory: Strategies for Qualitative Research*. Chicago, IL: Aldine Publishing.

Gregory, D. & Ward, H. (1974). *Statistics for Business Studies*, London, England: McGraw-Hill.

Gustavsen, B. (1993). Action research and the generation of knowledge. *Human Relations*, 46(11), 1361-1365.

Hammer, M. & Champy, J. (1993). *Reengineering the Corporation*. New York, NY: Harper Business.

Hammer, M. & Stanton, S.A. (1995). *The Reengineering Revolution*. New York, NY: HarperCollins.

Harrington, H.J. (1991). *Business Process Improvement*. New York, NY: McGraw-Hill.

Heller, F. (1993). Another look at action research. *Human Relations*, 46(10), 1235-1242.

Heller, F., Pusic, E., Strauss, G. & Wilpert, B. (1998). *Organizational Participation: Myth and Reality*. Oxford, England: Oxford University Press.

Hirschheim, R.A. (1985). Information systems epistemology: A historical perspective. E. Mumford, Ed. *Research Methods in Information Systems*. New York, NY: North-Holland, 13-35.

Ishikawa, K. (1986). *Guide to Quality Control*. Tokyo, Japan: Asian Productivity Organisation.

Jick, T.D. (1979). Mixing qualitative and quantitative methods: Triangulation in action. *Administrative Science Quarterly*, 24(4), 602-611.

Jonsonn, S. (1991). Action research. H. Nissen, H.K. Klein, & R. Hirschheim, eds. *Information Systems Research: Contemporary Approaches and Emergent Traditions*. New York, NY: North-Holland, 371-396.

Juran, J. (1989). *Juran on Leadership for Quality*. New York, NY: The Free Press.

Karlsen, J.I. (1991). Action research as a method. W.F. Whyte, ed. *Participatory Action Research*. Newbury Park, CA: Sage, 143-158.

Ketchum, L.D. & Trist, E. (1992). *All Teams are not Created Equal*. Newbury Park, CA: Sage.

Kettinger, W.J. & Grover, V. (1995). Toward a theory of business change management. *Journal of Management Information Systems*, 12(1), 9-30.

Klein, H.K. & Myers, M.D. (1999). A set of principles for conducting and evaluating interpretive field studies in information systems. *MIS Quarterly*, 23(1), 67-93.

Kock, N. (1997). Negotiating mutually satisfying IS action research topics with organizations: An analysis of Rapoport's initiative dilemma. *Journal of Workplace Learning*, 9(7), 253-262.

Kock, N. & Lau, F. (2001). Information systems action research: Serving two demanding masters. *Information Technology & People*, 14(1), 6-12.

Kock, N. & McQueen, R.J. (1996). Product flow, breadth and complexity of business processes: An empirical study of fifteen business processes in three organizations. *Business Process Re-engineering & Management*, 2(2), 8-22.

Kock, N., Avison, D., Baskerville, R., Myers, M. & Wood-Harper, T. (1999). IS action research: Can we serve two masters? P. De, & J. DeGross, eds. *Proceedings of the 20th International Conference on Information Systems*. New York, NY: The Association for Computing Machinery, 582-585.

Kock, N., McQueen, R.J. & Scott, J.L. (1997). Can action research be made more rigorous in a positivist sense? The contribution of an iterative approach. *Journal of Systems and Information Technology*, 1(1), 1-24.

Lacity, M.C. & Janson, M.A. (1994). Understanding qualitative data: A framework of text analysis methods. *Journal of Management Information Systems*, 11(2), 137-155.

Lau, F. (1997). A review on the use of action research in information systems studies. A.S. Lee, J. Liebenau & J.I. DeGross, eds. *Information Systems and Qualitative Research*. London, England: Chapman & Hall, 31-68.

Lau, F. (1999). Toward a framework for action research in information systems studies. *Information Technology & People*, 12(2), 148-175.

Ledford, G.E. & Mohrman, S.A. (1993). Self-design for high involvement: A large-scale organizational change. *Human Relations*, 46(2), 143-173.

Ledford, G.E. & Mohrman, S.A. (1993b). Looking backward and forward at action research. *Human Relations*, 46(11), 1349-1359.

Lewin, K. (1946), Action Research and Minority Problems, *Resolving Social Conflicts*, Lewin, G.W. (Ed), Harper & Row, New York, pp. 201-216.

Lewin, G.W. (Ed) (1948). *Resolving Social Conflicts*. New York, NY: Harper & Row.

Markus, M.L. (1994). Electronic mail as the medium of managerial choice. *Organization Science*, 5(4), 502-527.

McKay, J. & Marshall, P. (2001). The dual imperatives of action research. *Information Technology & People*, 14(1), 46-60.

McTaggart, R. (1991). Principles for participatory action research. *Adult Education Quarterly*, 41(3), 168-187.

Miles, M.B. & Huberman, A.M. (1994). *Qualitative Data Analysis: An Expanded Sourcebook*. London, England: Sage.

Mumford, E. (2001). Advice for an action researcher. *Information Technology & People*, 14(1), 12-27.

Neilson, R.E. (1997). *Collaborative Technologies and Organizational Learning*. Hershey, PA: Idea Group Publishing.

Orlikowski, W.J. (1992). Learning from notes: Organizational issues in groupware implementation. J. Turner, & R. Kraut, eds. *Proceedings of CSCW'92 Conference*. New York, NY: The Association for Computing Machinery, 362-369.

Orlikowski, W.J. (1993). Learning from notes: Organizational issues in groupware implementation. *Information Society*, 9(3), 237-251.

Orlikowski, W.J. & Baroudi, J.J. (1991). Studying information technology in organizations: Research approaches and assumptions. *Information Systems Research*, 2(1), 1-28.

Pervan, G.P. & Klass, D.J. (1992). The use and misuse of statistical methods in information systems research. R. Galliers, ed. *Information Systems Research: Issues, Methods and Practical Guidelines*. Boston, MA: Blackwell Scientific Publications, 208-229.

Peters, M. and Robinson, V. (1984). The origins and status of action research. *The Journal of Applied Behavioral Science*, 20(2), 113-124.

Phillips, E.M. & Pugh, D.S. (2000), *How to Get a Phd : A Handbook for Students and Their Supervisors*. Bristol, PA: Open University Press.

Rapoport, R.N. (1970). Three dilemmas in action research. *Human Relations*, 23(6), 499-513.

Reason, P. (Ed) (1988), *Human Inquiry in Action*, Sage, Newbury Park, CA.

Reason, P. (1988a), The Co-operative Inquiry Group, *Human Inquiry in Action*, Reason, P. (Ed), Sage, Newbury Park, California, pp. 18-39.

Reason, P. (1993). Sitting between appreciation and disappointment: A critique of the special edition of human relations on action research. *Human Relations*, 46(10), 1253-1270.

Riggs, W.M., Bellinger, W.H., & Krieger, D.B. (1996). The impact of groupware: Work process automation and organizational learning. *Technology Analysis & Strategic Management*, 8(3), 271-283.

Schacter, D.L. (2001). *The Seven Sins of Memory: How the Mind Forgets and Remembers*. New York, NY: Houghton Mifflin.

Semler, R. (1989). Managing without managers. *Harvard Business Review*, 67(5), 76-84.

Short, J., Williams, E., & Christie, B. (1976). *The Social Psychology of Telecommunications*. London, England: John Wiley.

Soles, S. (1994). Work reengineering and workflows: Comparative methods. E. White, & L. Fischer, eds. *The Workflow Paradigm*. Alameda, CA: Future Strategies, 70-104.

Sommer, R. (1994). Serving two masters. *The Journal of Consumer Affairs*, 28(1), 170-187.

Sommer, B. & Sommer, R. (1991). *A Practical Guide to Behavioral Research*. New York, NY: Oxford University Press.

Strauss, A.L. & Corbin, J.M. (1990). *Basics of Qualitative Research: Grounded Theory Procedures and Techniques*. Newbury Park, CA: Sage.

Strauss, A.L & Corbin, J.M. (1998). *Basics of Qualitative Research: Techniques and Procedures for Developing Grounded Theory*. Newbury Park, CA: Sage.

Susman G.I. & Evered, R.D. (1978). An assessment of the scientific merits of action research. *Administrative Science Quarterly*, 23(4), 582-603.

Tan, B.C.Y., Wei, K., Huang, W.W., & Ng, G. (2000). A dialogue technique to enhance electronic communication in virtual teams. *IEEE Transactions on Professional Communication*, 43(2), 153-165.

Teichman, J. & Evans, K.C. (1995). *Philosophy: A Beginner's Guide*. Oxford, UK: Blackwell.

Trauth, E.M. & O'Connor, B. (1991). A study of the interaction between information technology and society: An illustration of combined qualitative research methods. H. Nissen, H.K. Klein, & R. Hirschheim, eds. *Information Systems Research: Contemporary Approaches and Emergent Traditions*. New York, NY: North-Holland, 131-143.

Truex, D.P., III (2001). Three issues concerning relevance in IS research: Epistemology, audience, and method, *Communications of the AIS*, 6(24), 1-11.

Walton, M. (1991). *Deming Management at Work*. London, England: Mercury.

Winter, S.J. (1993). The symbolic potential of computer technology: Differences among white-collar workers. J.I. Degross, R.P. Bostrom, & D. Robey, eds. *Proceedings of 14th International Conference on Information Systems*. New York, NY: The Association for Computing Machinery, 331-344.

Woofford, J.C. (1994). Getting inside the leader's head: A cognitive processes approach to leadership. *SAM Advanced Management Journal*, 59(3), 4-9.

Yin, R.K. (1981). The case study crisis: Some answers. *Administrative Science Quarterly*, 26(1), 58-65.

Yin, R.K. (1989). Research design issues in using the case study method to study management information systems. J.I. Cash, & P.R. Lawrence, eds. *The Information Systems Research Challenge: Qualitative Research Methods*. Boston, MA: Harvard Business School, 1-6.

Yin, R.K. (1994). *Case Study Research*. Newbury Park, CA: Sage.

Chapter 6

DRIVEN BY TWO MASTERS, SERVING BOTH
The Interplay of Problem Solving and Research in Information Systems Action Research Projects

Judy McKay[1] and Peter Marshall[2]
[1]*Swinburne University of Technology, Australia;* [2]*University of Tasmania, Australia*

Abstract: One of the challenges of action research is the need simultaneously to serve two 'masters': as researchers, we need to produce rigorous, relevant research to advance our understanding and knowledge of our discipline. However, there is also a responsibility to intervene in organisational contexts and improve or ameliorate situations or issues perceived to be problematic, and thus, action researchers need also to be problem solvers and change agents. This chapter will discuss this duality of purpose, and discuss ways in which action researchers can successfully manage to address both the research imperative and the problem solving imperative in real world organisational contexts. An argument will be made to suggest that given both the research and action-oriented nature of action research, it is essential that IS action researchers have a sound appreciation of the nature of organisational contexts and of the information systems implemented in response to environmental problems, challenges and opportunities. The chapter will approach the need to serve two masters by suggesting a conceptualization which might support this, and will relate an action research case to this conceptual frame.

Key words: Action Research, Nature of Information Systems, Research Method

1. INTRODUCTION

The archetypal textbook definition of an Information System (IS) typically lists components (such as hardware, software, databases, communications technologies, procedures and people), and may also state that these components can be configured to gather, process and store data (see Stair and Reynolds 2003, for example). Presumably then, IS as a discipline is concerned with these components, and IS research attempts to improve knowledge with respect to the utilisation by humans in organisational contexts of these system artifacts. The IS discipline could thus be viewed as concerning itself with an increasingly complex 'web' of relationships and interactions between the elements listed above. Cognisance also needs to be paid to the view that information systems, considered holistically, are historically and contextually situated (Mitev 2003), in the sense that they are developed and acquired in a context with social, cultural and political dimensions that are inextricably linked into the history of that context and actors in the context. It is thus a source of consternation and contradiction that examination of the majority of IS introductory textbooks perpetuate rational and mechanistic views of and assumptions about organisations, people, information and technology. We tend to decontextualise, sanitise, and deconstruct into simple, digestible component parts but in so doing, the question may fairly be posed as to whether we end up 'teaching', talking about or referring to information systems at all. We strip away the social, the cultural, the political and the historic, to focus on the rational, the technical and the linear. Yet, in an IS context, what is the interest in the technical without the organisational contribution?

This somewhat techno-centric view pervades despite concerns expressed about the high rates of failure and disappointment with implemented systems in organisations (Monteleagre and Keil 2000), and identification of contradictory and at times antagonistic goals enshrined in information systems artifacts in organisations (Ngwenyama and Nielsen 2003). It also pervades despite a wealth of persuasive and cogently argued postmodern and social constructionist publications over the last twenty years (Alvesson 2002). Indeed this segmentation into components together with a rationalistic and mechanical viewpoint continues to pervade even the latest fashions and debates in IS (McKay and Marshall 2005). While it might be argued that it is pedagogically helpful and sometimes necessary to segment and compartmentalize IS in this way, we are concerned that what we regard as such impoverished and excessively narrow views of IS potentially being enshrined in our IS education, hence in our graduates, and in our research agendas.

We would argue rather that IS research and the body of knowledge about theory and practice that it aims to build must acknowledge that IS is fundamentally about human activity systems which are usually technologically enabled. This implies that the context of design and use is critical, and that context has a history that shapes and bounds current possibilities (Mitev 2003). We would argue that research paradigms, practices and activities must embrace such a worldview. We reject any notion that in IS one can separate the technological artifact from the people and the organisational context for which it is being designed, and thus cannot support some researchers' calls for attention and prominence to be given to the IT artifact (Weber 1987) if their intention is to decontextualise, then research, that technical artifact. As our focus in this chapter is on research rather than teaching, it is important to reflect on the impact that such rationalistic and mechanistic views have on IS research agendas and activities.

2. SETTING THE CONTEXT OF IS RESEARCH

The functionalist paradigm has long dominated research and thinking in the IS discipline. Despite calls for broader perspectives (Lee 1999) and more industry-relevant research to be undertaken (Applegate 1999), and suggestions that IS is inclusive of a variety of research traditions and approaches (Boland and Lyytinen 2004), the positivist grip remains fairly compelling (Chen and Hirschheim 2004). A number of early scholarly debates in IS often expressed paradigmatic indignation and called for a softening of the positivist grip on IS research (Fitzgerald et al. 1985), and an acceptance of pluralism in IS research (Landry and Banville 1992). These debates were often accompanied by discussion of how legitimate IS research could and should be conducted, and thus, on research methods appropriate to advance the knowledge base of the discipline (Galliers 1991). Boland and Lyytinen (2004) note that the polarization around paradigms has largely diminished, with the discipline now challenged and possibly struggling with the diversity of perspectives, modes of enquiry and approaches to data collection and analysis. Boland and Lyytinen (2004) assert that such diversity results in a loss of identity or certainty as to what exactly constitutes IS as a discipline. This is evidenced in the more recent interest in defining the core of IS (Rowe et al. 2004), and concerns about the lack of a unifying theory of IS (Hamilton 2004).

The perspective adopted in this chapter is that as IS researchers, our research is informed by a determination to clearly embed or situate the IS artifact into its surrounding context, and acknowledgement of the 'irremovability' of that context. Furthermore we support the perspective that rejects the existence of, and hence true and certain knowledge of, an independent and objective social reality 'out there' awaiting discovery and measurement and from this, prediction and control through the formulation of grand theories (Alvesson 2002, Alvesson and Skoldberg 2000, Burr 2003, Marshall et al. 2005). We also support those proponents of the view that IS is a sociotechnical discipline (Hirschheim 1985), and feel discomfort when this is conveniently subdivided into two separate components, a knowledge of machines or technology or artifacts separate from a knowledge of organisations or human societies and behaviour, with the notion that IS is somehow at the 'intersection' of these two domains of knowledge (Gregor

2002). Surely what separates IS from say, computer science (which sits firmly in the machine domain), and psychology (which sits firmly in the human behaviour domain) is the 'situatedness' of the machine in the sociocultural organisational system. Further, given the commoditization of IT witnessed by the utilization of highly reliable, easy to use PCs accessing standard software packages running on organisational computer networks, the focus of research interest, the authors believe, should be shifting quite naturally ever more so to the organisational context, while the IT artifact becomes more like the IT black box. That is the IT artifact, quite naturally, given developments in contemporary business and IT, is quite appropriately represented by a set of informational and transactional processes that become instantiated in the organisation as business processes. With this in mind regarding the "physical artifacts", our research needs to attend to *"interlocking elements of physical artifacts, institutions and their environments"* (Mitev 2003). It may be conceptually handy to pull these domains apart and examine each bit in isolation, but we would assert that the essence of IS lies in the contextualisation of the machine in the social system, and acknowledgement that different actors within that social system will hold different perspectives and hence attribute different meanings to IS in their contexts.

If it is agreed that IS is a sociotechnical discipline, and thus differentiated from computer science and software engineering (for example) through a focus on sociotechnical (or system) artifacts, this encourages us to consider and research not just the technical artifact, but the system artifact and its situated utilisation in a particular wider sociotechnical context, shaped by a particular history. Arguably then, the task of IS researchers is not to seek ultimate truths or grand theories or universal laws, but to recognise, understand and elucidate practices with respect to transforming situations (by the responsible application of artifacts) into more desired states, taking account of context and the uses for which people may appropriate such systems. IS research therefore, is conducted in sociotechnical contexts, and thus needs to elucidate the contextual interplay between the social and the technical. It implies a need to acknowledge that within our research domain, there exists multiple perspectives of both the technical or other elements deemed to be of interest and relevance to the researcher and multiple perspectives as to what might constitute an improvement in this situation. Such perspectives and objectives may well be in conflict, and there may exist considerable complexity and ambiguity in seeking insights and understanding of the phenomenon of interest, with a view to developing and building theory (Alvesson 2002, Alvesson and Skoldberg 2000, Rosenhead and Mingers 2001).

3.   CONSIDERATIONS OF THE IS RESEARCH CONTEXT IN ORGANISATIONS

From the preceding discussion on the essence of information systems, and hence the nature of IS research and practice, we offer Figure 6-1 below as a preliminary consideration of the context of IS activity. Situated within a particular sociocultural organisational context are people playing roles (analysts, users, managers, etc.), each with their constructed and idiosyncratic worldview (W), frameworks of ideas and beliefs, and the like, by which they perceive, interpret and construe events and behaviours occurring around them.   Such ideas and beliefs are important and have practical consequences, since *"if men define situations as real, they are real in their consequences"* (Thomas and Thomas 1928).   Thus these actors are both shaped by the contexts in which they operate, and in turn, shape, structure and organise occurrences in that context.   Their perceptions, interpretations, judgments and decisions determine actions that are taken within the context, presumably aimed at improving or ameliorating or impacting on the situation of interest.

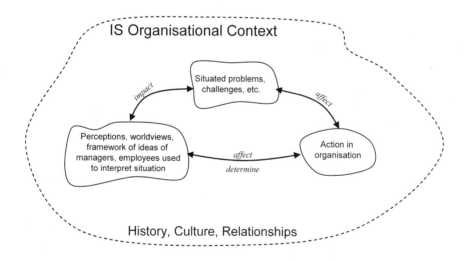

Figure 6-1. Organisational context of IS

If our attention is then turned to the research process, taking an IS perspective as previously discussed, we would argue that the process is characterised by a researcher with both implicit and explicit Ws, theoretical orientations and biases, using a variety of methods, tools and techniques to collect a wealth of data in a real world context. Such data is subsequently structured and organised in some way according to the theoretical orientation of the researcher, producing logical, coherent outcomes and findings (see Figure 6-2 below).

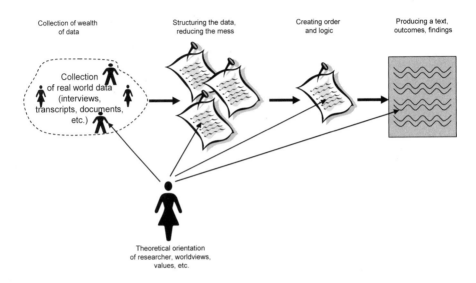

Figure 6-2. The IS research process (from Alvesson 2002)

If, as we argued, the research process needs to be organizationally situated, then Figure 6-3 below depicts the organisational context of IS research. Thus the researcher engages with actors in an organisational context, gathers data, and derives outcomes, which in this idealised model, impact positively on that context by improving understandings, improving knowledge of the intervention, and improving outcomes for organisational members. The situation is made more complex for the researcher as they must not only acknowledge and 'manage' their own Ws, perceptions and interpretations, but they must also be mindful of the fact that their research interest intersects with the Ws, perceptions and interpretations of one or more organisational actors.

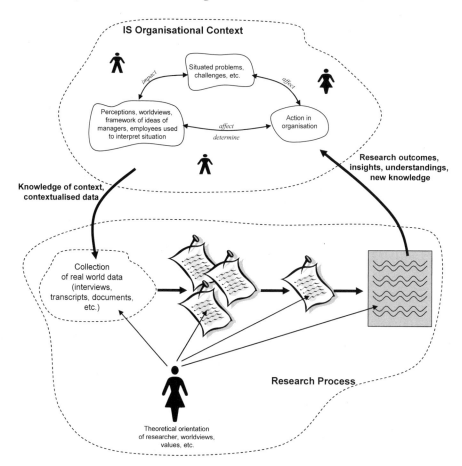

Figure 6-3. Research in IS: organisational context of IS enquiry

Figure 6-3's strong lines linking the organisational context and the research process suggest at a conceptual level a certain degree of confidence in the unimpeded flows from the organisational context to the researcher, and from the researcher back to the organisation. This does not always reflect the reality facing IS researchers, where political and cultural forces may shape and filter the data accessible to the researcher, and different priorities and drivers may limit or impede the flow of research findings into practice in the real world. This second issue has been the subject of much debate in the IS academic community, where researchers are concerned with the limited impact of their research activities on practice in the IS community (Benbasat and Zmud 1999, Davenport and Markus 1999), and the relevance of much IS research has been questioned (Lee 1999, Benbasat and Zmud 1999). If IS research is to reflect the situatedness argued in this chapter to be a defining feature of the IS discipline, then approaches to enquiry need to both reflect and be able to cope with this phenomena. There are a number of possible research approaches that could be employed that allow for organisationally-situated study of IS as sociotechnical artifacts, of which action research is just one. Longitudinal Process Research (LPR) for example, has been employed by IS researchers and allows for both the study of the dynamics of change over time within an organisational setting (Newman and Robey 1992), where both the context and the process under scrutiny are viewed as socially constructed (Ngwenyama 1998) and hence the interplay between actors, context, actions and process are of interest to the researcher (Pettigrew 1997). In the section that follows however, action research will be scrutinised as an appropriate method by which closer links emerge between the interests and activities of researchers and the problems and challenges of real world contexts.

4.   ACTION RESEARCH AS A WAY OF PROGRESSING IS ORGANISATIONAL ENQUIRY

As its name implies, action research involves a simultaneous preoccupation with both taking action to improve a problematic situation, and with researching into and learning from the attempt at problem resolution or improvement. Thus, action research involves both organizing and acting in ways that permit learning and gaining knowledge from attempts to change and improve organisational contexts that are perceived as problematic or challenging, and recognised as being in need of change (Elden & Chisholm 1993, Avison et al. 1999). Rapoport (1970:499) defines action research as aiming *"to contribute both to the practical concerns of people in an immediate problematic situation and to the goals of social science by joint collaboration within a mutually acceptable ethical framework"*. Reason and Bradbury (2001:1) note that action research is a *"process concerned with developing practical knowledge in the pursuit of worthwhile human purposes...It seeks to bring together action and reflection, theory and practice, in participation with others, in the pursuit of practical solutions to issues of pressing concern to people"*. Three characteristics can be added to those definitions, suggesting that action research is firstly identifiable by the direct involvement of the researcher in the problem solving activity (Ladkin 2005), and secondly, by the intention and willingness of both parties to be involved in change (Reason 2003). The third defining characteristic requires that action research should have a clear conceptual framework or theoretical position driving the research aspects of the intervention (Checkland 1991, Eden and Huxham 1996, McKay and Marshall 2001).

Central to the IS discipline is the complex interplay of people, technology, business processes and socio-cultural context. Action research, with its focus on real-world problem solving retains relevance to this rich interplay, since the "laboratory" of action research is the actual organisational context itself. Other research approaches such as laboratory experiments risk losing this immediacy of context and succumbing to the separation of research and practice that typifies many IS research efforts (Susman & Evered 1978, Avison & Wood-Harper 1991, Baskerville & Wood-Harper 1996). A strength of action research then is its recognition that research and practice are *"inherently intertwined in real life"* (Chandler and Torbert 2003:134). Indeed, it could be argued that in applied disciplines such as IS, action research appropriately establishes action and practice as being the prime focus of research efforts, and not a *"bolt-on addition"* to research (Denscombe 1998:59). This point is clearly expanded by Somekh (1995:340), who in characterising action research writes that it rejects *"the concept of a two-stage process in which research is carried out first by researchers and then in a separate second stage the knowledge generated from the research is applied by practitioners. Instead the two processes of research and action are integrated"*. This close integration of research and its application in action research means that it is an ideal research method for identifying how practice can be improved within the context and value system of the owner (Avison 1993). Furthermore, action research acknowledges the influence of past events on present phenomena, on dynamic social and sociotechnical interactions, and encourages the joint design of the future based on values and intentions (Chandler and Torbert 2003). Indeed, it could be argued that the most compelling justification offered for the use of action research is to counter the dubious reliability of research in which subjects have not had to commit to action in the real world and to the creation of a future that will impact directly upon them (Eden 1995).

If it is well planned and executed, action research, with its dual aim of improving actual organisational problem situations and generating and testing theory, leads to a win-win scenario for both organisational practitioners and researchers (Elden and Chisholm 1993. Action research also leads to increased knowledge and skills for both practitioners and researchers (Hult and Lennung 1980). Further, action research also promotes a holistic understanding of organisational phenomena, since the research context comprises an intervention in an actual organisational situation, and is focused, not simply on observing particular details of organisational life, but on fundamentally changing the situation for organisational actors (Hult and Lennung 1980). Thus we argue that adopting action research as one suitable vehicle to drive organizationally-based IS research enables us to reconceptualise Figure 6-3, arguing that the idealised action research model helps to blend the IS organisational context of enquiry with the research process and activity (see Figure 6-4 below).

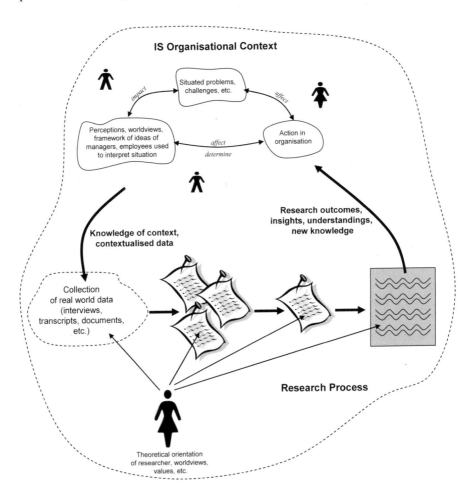

Figure 6-4. Blending the contexts of research and practice

In the section that follows, arguments will be developed to demonstrate more precisely how action researchers can undertake organisationally-based research while simultaneously working with organisational members to achieve improved outcomes in their particular contexts.

5. DUAL IMPERATIVES OF ACTION RESEARCH

Emerging from the preceding discussions are the dual imperatives of action research: that is, its interest in and commitment to organisational problem solving, and its interest in and commitment to research, and the production of new insights and knowledge (McKay and Marshall 2001). Action research is a cyclical approach to enquiry, and the dual parallel interests in action research require researchers to conceptualise action research as being composed of two interlocking cycles of interest. The problem solving interest implies a need for the action researcher to identify a real world problem of interest. Once a problem is identified, there follows a period of organisational reconnaissance and fact finding during which the nature and scope of the problem are determined. In this phase of the problem solving activity, a picture of the problem situation is constructed which includes, among other things, an analysis of the history of the problem, and the social, cultural and political elements of the problem situation. It also includes an analysis of the various stakeholders and their particular perspectives on the problem. When a reasonable picture of the problem situation has been developed, a plan for the problem solving activity is prepared and then implemented. These are then monitored and evaluated, and following this, if a satisfactory situation has been achieved, the researcher exits the problem situation which has now been improved. If, of course, the problem amelioration activity does not prove successful, a period of review takes place, following which a new action plan is prepared and another action research cycle of action, monitoring and review is begun (McKay and Marshall 2001).

However, the action researcher must also be interested in generating new knowledge through this enquiry in the real world, leading to the identification of a research area of interest. The action researcher should then engage with the relevant literature and develop a clear picture of the state of knowledge in this area. This engagement will involve, among other things, investigating and clarifying major issues and challenges in the research area interest, as well as determining helpful perspectives and frameworks that are relevant to the area. The engagement leads to formulation of a research question, or perhaps several related research questions that define the objectives and focus of the research. At this point a theoretical framework should be adopted as a lens or backdrop through which the research question can be examined and elucidated. A research plan and design are then developed, the plan and design being guided by the need to answer the research question(s). Action is then taken in the organisational situation of concern. This action is monitored and evaluated in terms of the research interest, and in particular, in terms of the progress made in illuminating and answering the research question(s). If as a result of the action, its consequences and their evaluation, there are satisfactory research outcomes in terms of the research question(s), then the researcher will exit from the research aspect of the action research. If this is not the case and research outcomes are not satisfactory, the researcher will amend the research, the research plan and design appropriately, and then seek further explanations in another action research cycle (McKay and Marshall 2001).

. These dual imperatives are depicted below in Figure 6-5.

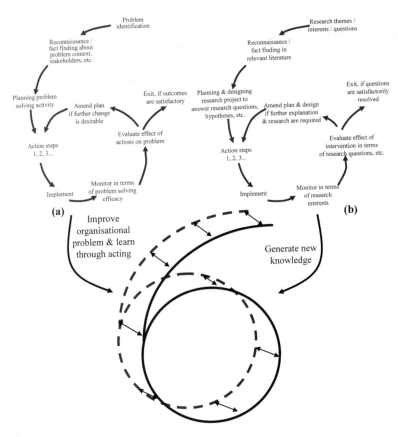

Figure 6-5. The Dual Imperatives of Action Research

In the field of information systems, Checkland's work on action research (Checkland 1991, Hindle et al. 1995) has been pivotal in developing a model to guide the activities of researchers. According to Checkland (1991), any piece of research will consist of a framework of ideas (F), which are employed via a methodology (M) to investigate an area of interest (A). As a result of the research, learning will take place about F, and/or M and/or A. This is illustrated in Figure 6-6 below:

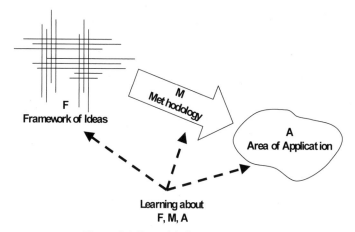

Figure 6-6. Essential elements in research

(Checkland 1991)

In terms of action research, Checkland (1991) argued that the researcher should be guided by an explicit framework of ideas (F), and should identify a number of relevant research themes. The researcher will then select an appropriate real-world problem situation (A), and guided by an appropriate methodology (M), will thus initiate actions to bring about improvements in the situation. Reflections on the changes in A based on F and M will lead to learning about F, and/or M, and/or A, and it is this learning which will generate new insights, new understandings, and new knowledge. This cycle is illustrated in Figure 6-7 below.

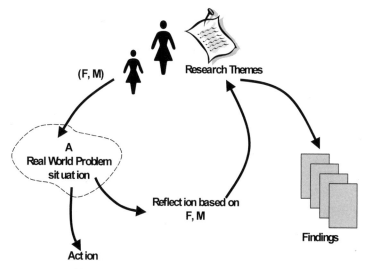

Figure 6-7. Checkland's Action Research Cycle

(Checkland 1991)

Checkland's (1991) FMA framework (see Figures 6-6 and 6-7 above) acknowledges only a single cycle, and we again argue that this can and does result in confusion between the problem solving interest and the research interest. However, reconceptualising action research as being composed of two interlocking cycles, requires Checkland's (1991) FMA framework to be extended to include two Ms (the problem solving method (M_{PS}) and the research method (M_R)), and in addition to the area of interest to the researcher (A), a problem in the real world (P) which allows for enquiry into A (see Figure 6-8 below).

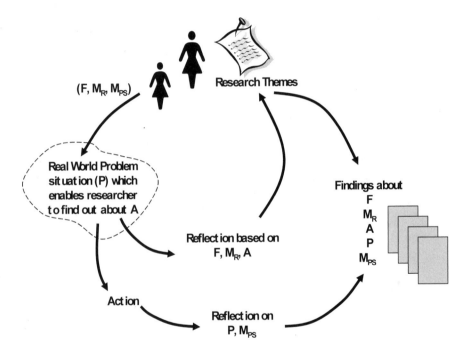

Figure 6-8. The Revised Action Research Framework

(McKay and Marshall 2001)

The implications of doing this become clearer upon closer examination of some of Checkland's own work (Checkland 1991, Hindle et al. 1995) in which the confusion alluded to previously is actually manifest.   In Checkland (1991), the FMA framework is elucidated using an example from science as follows:

Table 6-1. An Example of F, M, and A from Science

F	Plate tectonics
M	Experiment (testing hypotheses to destruction)
A	Earthquakes and vulcanicity

(from Checkland 1991)

Checkland then applies the F, M, and A concept to his own work, where over time the following evolution took place:

Table 6-2. The evolution of F, M, and A in Checkland's work

Checkland's work evolved from:	
F	Ideas of Systems Engineering
M	Systems Engineering
A	Management problems
Checkland's work evolved to:	
F	Systems thinking, Human Activity Systems and Welatanschauung
M	Soft Systems Methodology
A	Management and IS problems

(from Checkland 1991)

Checkland (1991:398) offers the following descriptions of F, M, and A: *"A particular set of ideas, F, are used in a methodology M to investigate some area of investigation A"*. Subsequently in his paper, however, A becomes a *"real-world problem situation"*, and M takes on the additional requirement of needing to *"embody"* the framework of ideas declared in F (Checkland 1991: 400-401). However, these 'redefinitions' of M and A are clearly inconsistent with his first example, drawn from science (and presented in Table 6-1 above). It cannot be argued, for example, that the M (the experiment) embodies the framework of ideas or theory of plate tectonics. It obviously does not. Nor can it be asserted that earthquakes and vulcanicity are themselves real-world problem situations: they become problematic when there is a specific instance or occurrence of these phenomena, such as the recent earthquake in Pakistan in October 2005, or the eruption of Sierra Negra on the Galapagos Islands in October 2005. Thus, if we revisit the Checkland examples, we can add the nomenclature that we would apply.

Table 6-3. Reassessing Checkland's F, M, and A

Checkland's label		Our label
F	Plate tectonics	F
M	Experiment (testing hypotheses to destruction)	M_R
A	Earthquakes and vulcanicity	A
Checkland's work evolved from:		
F	Ideas of Systems Engineering	F
M	Systems Engineering	M_{PS}
A	Management problems	A
Checkland's work evolved to:		
F	Systems thinking, Human Activity Systems and Weltanschauung	F
M	Soft Systems Methodology	M_{PS}
A	Management and IS problems	A

If we now consider the Hindle et al. (1995) paper, F is defined as *"the framework of supporting concepts, theories and models"* (p455), A as *"a real-world problem situation"* (p455), and M is not formally defined other than to say it must be declared, and that it *"defines the nature of the research intervention"* (p455). Given these words, it is not clear whether M_{PS} or M_R is being discussed. The specific examples used in Hindle et al. (1995) can be summarised as follows:

Table 6-4. Articulating the F, M, and A from Hindle et al. (1995)

F	Transaction cost economics, organisational learning, purposeful activity modelling, decision analysis, etc.
M	Soft Systems Methodology
A	Health Services Contracting

According to our thinking, the following labels should be applied:

Table 6-5. Re-labelling the F, M, and A from Hindle et al. (1995)

Checkland's label		Our label
F	Transaction cost economics, organisational learning, purposeful activity modelling, decision analysis, etc.	F
M	Soft Systems Methodology	M_{PS}
A	Health Services Contracting	A

The dual cycle concept introduced here would clearly help to avoid some of the confusion that emerges in the two papers discussed, namely Checkland (1991) and Hindle et al. (1995). Conceptualising action research as a dual cycle can help clarify our thinking. For example, it may be important to separate the area of application or investigation, A, from the real world problem situation, P. It may often be the case that P is a specific, real-world manifestation of A, a more general area of interest. However, it also allows for cases when A and P are not totally similar, but where P does allow for the researcher to find out about A. Likewise, separating M_{PS} and M_R can add clarity to thinking. There may or may not be an explicitly stated M_{PS}. Sometimes that M_{PS} may also overlap with A. But being able to conceptually separate the problem solving interest and the research interest may actually make clearer the nature and the requirements of any action research intervention.

A word of caution needs to be expressed at this juncture. In urging researchers to acknowledge the dual imperatives of action research, it must be remembered that this distinction between action and research is drawn at a conceptual or analytical level. At the practical level, researchers and participants engage in making changes to systems of human activity in all their richness and complexity, and thus, action and research become inextricably intertwined (Bannister et al. 1994).

What is being put forward here is *not* a model of how to proceed with an action research study. This is *not* a performance model. Rather it is a conceptual model, aimed at helping a researcher 'sort out' their thinking about some of the complexities and the interacting elements, and their requirements and implications, inherent in an action research study prior to embarking on the investigation. An example of how the concept of these dual cycles may be used follows in section 6 (see 6.1 and 6.2 specifically). However, in more general terms, we are advocating that action researchers attempt to clarify the nature of the problem at hand, that they plan their intervention in that problem solving context, and then monitor closely the impacts of actions taken and resultant change, mindful of their responsibilities to the problem owners and organisational members to bring about improvement in their shared situation. At the same time, if quality and rigorous knowledge is to be generated through the action research intervention, thinking through issues pertaining to the theoretical framework to be adopted, the sorts of research questions that might be formulated, how data can be collected and analysed so that rigorous research outcomes are derived, all need to be considered. In these real world contexts, perfectly and immutably planning both problem solving and research interventions is unlikely. However the dual imperatives approach encourages researchers to be much more cognisant of the needs of both problem solving and research, and thus to be much more mindful in our decision making and action taking preceding, during and following the action research intervention.

6. EMPIRICAL APPLICATION OF THE DUAL IMPERATIVES OF ACTION RESEARCH

The study to be reported on here from a process perspective is an exemplar of what could be described as 'research-led' action research (see Figure 6-9 below). In this study, the research interest preceded, and indeed initiated, the search for an occurrence of a real-world problem. Once a suitable problem has been identified, and hence a site selected, the researchers and participants collaborated, defining and/or clarifying roles, responsibilities, objectives, expectations, and the scope of the intervention wherever practicable. Through informed action (action guided by a suitable conceptual framework) and reflection, satisfactory problem solving and research outcomes were achieved. The action research cycle was completed by lodging the research outcomes and new insights into the public domain for criticism (McNiff et al. 1996).

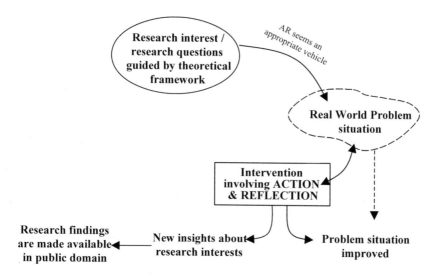

Figure 6-9. 'Research-led' Action Research

From the researchers' perspective, the process of enquiry was easier to manage through conceptually separating the process into two cycles of activity and concern. These will each be briefly described separately below, but it needs to be emphasised that this description refers to the conceptualization and management of the study, and hence does not capture the full richness and complexity of the day-to-day, on-site intervention that occurred.

6.1   The Research Interest

The researchers had conducted an extensive review of the literature on information requirements determination (IRD) and IS failures, and had identified a number of recurrent themes of interest related to IRD that were apparently associated with less than successful outcomes in the finished, implemented system. Through exploration of the soft management science/operational research (MS/OR) literature, where similar sorts of concerns had confronted researchers and practitioners, a view was formed that the approach Strategic Options Development and Analysis (SODA) (Eden and Ackerman 1998) and its associated technique, cognitive mapping (Eden 2004), were ideally suited to application to the IS domain for IRD. As a result of the literature review, the following overarching research aim was formulated:

To establish whether the SODA methodology and its accompanying technique of cognitive mapping are effective for the Information Requirements Determination phase of Information Systems Development.

In addition, four subordinate questions, all related to the efficacy of SODA and cognitive mapping for supporting aspects of the IRD process were articulated. There followed a detailed research planning process where a range of issues associated with data collection and analysis (What data do we need to collect, and how should we analyse it in order to answer our research questions and achieve our research objective?) were discussed and addressed.

The project commenced, and as researchers we endeavoured to keep extensive field notes. In addition, we were careful to maintain each iteration of the cognitive maps, noting what changes were made to the cognitive maps and also, what seemed to have contributed to changes being made to the cognitive maps (CMs), and the like. Some preliminary manipulation and analysis of the cognitive maps was conducted (and note this contributed substantially to progressing the problem solving interest (see section 6.2 below)). As the initial action research cycle was completed, participants were interviewed as to their perceptions and experiences of the process we had all been involved in, and these perceptions compared against the reflections of the researchers. In addition, a short questionnaire, developed to assess satisfaction with an IRD process and outcomes (Limayem and Wanninger 1993) was administered. At the request of the problem owners, the researchers then commenced work with a second cohort of participants on a related problem that had emerged as a priority in the first cycle. The second study was also used for data collection and analysis, and thus also served to provide insights into the research questions and objective (see Figure 6-10 below).

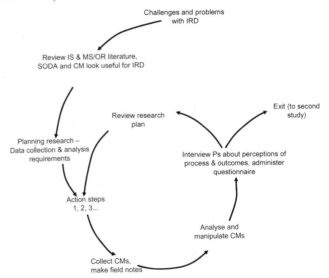

Figure 6-10. The research interest in this Action Research study

6.2 The Problem Solving Interest

Figure 6-11 below illustrates the essence of the problem solving interest in this study. Having previously identified their research objectives, the researchers found an organisation (a semi-autonomous government Port Authority) with a problem that seemed appropriate to allow us to pursue our research but also which seemed appropriate to investigate collaboratively using a particular problem solving approach (SODA and cognitive mapping). Participants and problem owners had recognised problems with their existing Workers' Compensation Systems (WCS), and wanted our help in identifying requirements for a new WCS. Background information on the organisation and this particular problem were obtained. In a series of meetings with the problem owners and participants, the scope of the project was defined, respective roles, responsibilities, expectations and requirements were articulated and agreed upon. Detailed planning of the intervention was then undertaken. Actions to help participants resolve their problem were taken and over time, and both the process followed and the progress towards resolving their problem with the WCS were monitored. When it become clear that a second, related, but to them much more significant problem emerged, we jointly evaluated our progress to that point. Outside the issues of the WCS improvement, the need for a new and independent system encompassing safety management emerged. Problem owners made the decision that an in-house systems analyst could fix the minor errors with the existing WCS, while the researchers were requested to work with the participants to identify requirements for what became known as the safety management systems (SMS).

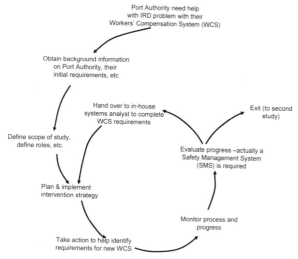

Figure 6-11. The problem solving interest in this Action Research study

6.3   Discussion

The reality of the real world intervention was not as clear cut as the conceptual separation into two cycles of interest may imply. But dealing with that complexity was made much easier as both researchers were very clear in their overall briefs: we were keenly aware of our responsibilities in terms of working with problem owners and participants to help them resolve a problem of concern to them, and acknowledged the desire for all to learn throughout this process. We were keen to leverage their knowledge and experience of the context and our knowledge of the problem solving process to achieve good outcomes within the constraints of the context. By thinking through the problem solving interest cycle, we were able to ensure that the integrity of that process was not compromised by inadvertently putting our research interests to the fore. It helped us to recognise that we were not researchers manipulating entities in a context, but that we needed to work with people in their context to help them achieve their objectives. However, by thinking through the research interest, we were also keenly aware of what was required to meet our research interests. This was particularly important as daily micro-decisions were made, such decisions could be made from an informed position, and thus care taken that the research interests were not inadvertently compromised, nor problem solving interests prejudiced in favour of conducting research.

In our view, these are not insignificant issues, as action researchers are constantly involved in making small decisions, each of which may seem inconsequential, but which cumulatively have impacts, possibly negative impacts on research efforts, for example. An inexperienced researcher looking at many diagrams of action research would be left with a quite unrealistic view of the action research intervention. The reality we were confronted with was one in which it seemed as though we were constantly monitoring, reflecting and evaluating what we were doing, the progress we were making, the issues we were facing, and so on. Thus, there were "mini-cycles" within the cycle, which were significant, we believe, in that they altered the course we took and the overall trajectory of the intervention somewhat, and must therefore have had some impact on the final outcome. This idea is illustrated in Figure 6-12 below.

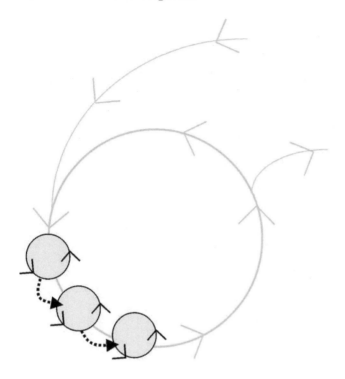

Figure 6-12. Constant, iterative decision making in Action Research

For example, from a research perspective, we had planned to tape record all conversations, and to use these tapes in drawing cognitive maps. This quickly proved impractical because of the time involved in such a process and the relatively minor benefits from this activity, and so we decided to abandon this idea. What was the process involved here? We would argue we were going through a "mini cycle", captured below in Figure 6-13.

When we consider these previous action research interventions, it seems that there was a nearly continual process of doing, reflecting, evaluating, modifying, and so on, and thus our conviction that Figure 6-12 provides a more accurate reflection of the process that we experienced in undertaking this action research project. The number and frequency of these mini-cycles may well be contextually determined. To some extent, it may also be a function of the cognitive style of the action researcher. But our strong conviction is that the practice of action research may well improve if the models we use to talk about this approach avoid oversimplification of complex and subtle behaviours and interactions that typify action research.

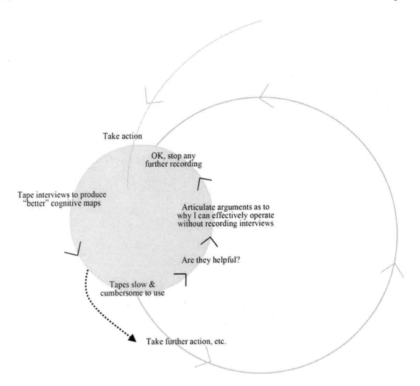

Figure 6-13. An Example of a mini-cycle within the Action Research process

Secondly, conceptualising action research as being comprised of two, interlocking cycles helps to overcome a criticism of action research, that it lacks scientific rigour, a point noted by a number of writers (Galliers 1991, Baskerville 1999). What emerges from our perspective is that notions such as rigour and quality of research apply to the research interest cycle only, and do not impact directly on the problem solving interest cycle. In saying this, there is no implication that quality is not also an important aspect of problem solving. It clearly is, but when we, as researchers, talk about quality and rigour of research, then it must be research that is being evaluated. This will help clarify for the researcher such issues as how to ensure rigour in the design and implementation of an action research intervention from the research interest perspective.

Thirdly, research findings and reflections can be made over a broader and richer range of concepts. As suggested by Figure 6-8, reflections, findings and learning can now be legitimately claimed about the theoretical framework (F), the problem solving method (M_{PS}), the research method (M_R), the area of interest (A), and the specific, real world problem and its context (P). These differences for the study discussed in this chapter are captured below in Table 6-6:

Table 6-6. Elements of an Action Research intervention

F	Cognitive Mapping and SODA have characteristics that would render them effective for application to IRD
M_R	Action Research
M_{PS}	SODA and Cognitive Mapping
A	Issues and challenges in effectively determining information requirements in organisations
P	Identifying information requirements for a new WCS at the government agency

7. CONCLUSION

This chapter has focussed on arguing that the conduct of action research may be enhanced through conceptualising action research as being comprised of two interconnected cycles of interest: a problem solving interest, in which researchers and participants collaborate to ameliorate and change a situation of concern, and in so doing, hopefully learn about the problem, and the problem solving process, and a research interest, in which researchers adopting a particular theoretical stance clarify their objectives and required actions in terms of building understanding and advancing knowledge within a domain of interest. An empirical example was used to illustrate how conceptually separating this commitment to real life problem solving from interest in research can help ensure that both requirements can effectively be realised simultaneously through intervention in the real world. Because of this very fact, action research thus becomes an ideal vehicle for the conduct of IS research given its ability to connect research interest and activity to real world organisational contexts. This is of particular concern if a definition of IS is adopted which recognises the primacy of the contextualization and situatedness of IS in sociotechnical organisational settings comprised of history, culture and relationships which impact and bound what is possible and hence what can be achieved. This makes research activity and the research process more challenging, but avoids the limitations of conceptualising IS as a suite of rational, compartmentalized components.

8. BIBLIOGRAPHY

Alvesson, M. & Skoldberg, K. (2000) *Reflexive Methodology: New Vistas for Qualitative Research.* Sage Publications, London.

Alvesson, M. (2002) *Postmodernism and Social Research.* Open University Press, Buckingham.

Applegate, L.M. (1999) Rigor and relevance in MIS research. *MIS Quarterly*, 23(1), 1-2.

Avison, D.E. (1993) Research in information systems development and the discipline of information systems. *Proceedings of the Fourth Australasian Conference on Information Systems*: 1-27. University of Queensland, Brisbane, 28-30 September.

Avison, D., Lau, F., Myers, M. & Nielsen, P.A. (1999) Action research. *Communications of the ACM* 42 (1), 94-97.

Avison, D.E. & Wood-Harper, A.T. (1991) Conclusions from action research: the Multiview experience. In M.C. Jackson et al. (eds.) *Systems Thinking in Europe.* Plenum Press, New York.

Bannister, P., Burman, E., Parker, I., Taylor, M. & Tindall, C. (1994) *Qualitative Methods in Psychology: A Research Guide.* Open University Press, Buckingham.

Baskerville, R. (1999) Investigating information systems with action research. *Communications of the AIS*, 2(19), October 1999.

Baskerville, R.L. & Wood-Harper, A.T. (1996) A critical perspective on action research as a method for information systems research. *Journal of Information Technology,* 11(1996), 235-246.

Benbasat, I. & Zmud, R.W. (1999) Empirical research in information systems: the practice of relevance. *MIS Quarterly*, 23(1), 3-16.

Boland, R.J. & Lyytinen, K. (2004) Information systems research as design: identity, process and narrative. In Kaplan, B. at el. (eds.) *Information Systems Research: Relevant Theory and Informed Practice.* Kluwer Academic Publishers, Boston.

Burr, V. (2003) *Social Constructionism.* Routledge, London.

Chandler, D. & Torbert, B. (2003) Transforming inquiry and action: interweaving 27 flavors of action research. *Action Research*, 1(2), 133-152.

Checkland, P. (1991) From framework through experience to learning: the essential nature of action research. In H.E. Nissen et al. (eds.) *Information Systems Research: Contemporary Approaches and Emergent Traditions.* Elsevier, Amsterdam.

Chen, W. & Hirschheim, R. (2004) A paradigmatic and methodological examination of information systems research from 1991 to 2001. *Information Systems Journal*, 14 (3), 197 – 235.

Davenport, T.H. & Markus, M.L. (1999) Rigor vs. relevance revisited: response to Benbasat and Zmud. *MIS Quarterly*, 23(1), 19-23.

Denscombe, M. (1998) *The good research guide.* Open University Press, Buckingham, UK.

Eden, C. (1995) On evaluating the performance of 'wide-band' GDSS's. *European Journal of Operational Research*, 81 (1995), 302-311.

Eden, C. (2004) Analyzing cognitive maps to help structure issues or problems. *European Journal of Operational Research*, 159(2004), 673-686.

Eden, C. & Ackerman, F. (1998) *Making Strategy: The Journal of Strategic Management.* Sage, London.

Eden, C. & Huxham, C. (1996) Action research for management research. *British Journal of Management*, 7(1), 75-86.

Elden, M. & Chisholm, R.F. (1993) Emerging varieties of action research: introduction to the special issue. *Human Relations*, 46(2), 121-142.

Fitzgerald, G., Hirschheim, R., Mumford, E. & Wood-Harper, A.T. (1985) Information systems research methodology: an introduction to the debate. In Mumford, E. et al. (eds.) *Research Methods in Information Systems*, Elsevier Science Publishers, Amsterdam.

Galliers, R.D. (1991) Choosing appropriate information systems research approaches: a revised taxonomy. In H.E. Nissen, H.K. Klein and R. Hirschheim (eds.) *Information Systems Research: Contemporary Approaches and Emergent Traditions*. Elsevier Science Publishers, North Holland.

Gregor, S. (2002) Design theory in information systems. *Australian Journal of Information Systems*, Special Issue December 2002, 14-22.

Hamilton, D. (2004) The social and academic standing of the information systems discipline. *JITTA: Journal of Information Technology Theory and Applications*, 6(2), 1-12.

Hindle, T., Checkland, P., Mumford, M. & Worthington, D. (1995) Developing a methodology for multidisciplinary action research: a case study. *Journal of the Operational Research Society*, 46(1995), 453-464.

Hirschheim, R. (1985) Information systems epistemology: an historical perspective. In Mumford, E. et al. (eds.) *Research Methods in Information Systems*, Elsevier Science Publishers, Amsterdam.

Hult, M. & Lennung, S. (1980) Towards a definition of action research: a note and a bibliography. *Journal of Management Studies*, 17(2), 241-250.

Ladkin, D. (2005) The enigma of subjectivity: how might phenomenology help action researchers negotiate the relationship between 'self', 'other' and 'truth'? *Action Research*, 3(1): 108-126.

Landry, M. & Banville, C. (1992) A disciplined methodological pluralism for MIS research. *Accounting, Management and Information Technologies*, 2(2), 77-98.

Lee, A.S. (1999) Rigor and relevance in MIS research: beyond the approach of positivism alone. *MIS Quarterly*, 23(10), 29-34.

Limayem, M. & Wanninger, L.A. (1993) The use of a group CASE tool to improve information requirements determination. *Document de Travail 93-33*, Université Laval, Quebec, Canada.

Marshall, P., Kelder, J. & Perry, A. (2005) Social constructionism with a twist of pragmatism: a suitable cocktail for information systems research. *Proceedings of the 16th Annual Australasian Conference on Information Systems, Manly, Sydney, Australia.*

McKay, J. & Marshall, P. (2005) A review of design science in information systems. *Proceedings of the 16th Annual Australasian Conference on Information Systems, Manly, Sydney, Australia.*

McKay, J. & Marshall, P. (2001) The dual imperatives of action research. *Information Technology and People*, 14(1), 46-59.

McNiff, J. Lomax, P. & Whitehead, J. *You and Your Action Research Project*. Routledge, London, 1996.

Mitev, N.N. (2003) Constructivist and critical approaches to an IS failure case study: symmetry, translation and power. *Department of Information Systems Working Paper 127*, London School of Economics and Political Science, London.

Montealegre, R. & Keil, M. De-escalating information technology projects: lessons from Denver International Airport. *MIS Quarterly*, 24(3), 417-447.

Newman, M. & Robey, D. (1992) A social process model of user-analyst relationships. *MIS Quarterly*, 16(2), 249-266.

Ngwenyama, O.K. (1998) Groupware, social action and organizational emergence: on the process dynamics of computer mediated distributed work. *Accounting, Management and Information Technology*, 8(1998), 127-146.

Ngwenyama, O. & Nielsen, P.A. (2003) Competing values in software process improvement: an assumption analysis of CMM from an organizational culture perspective. *IEEE Transactions on Engineering Management*, 50(1), 100-112.

Pettigrew, A.M. (1997) What is processual analysis? *Scandinavian Journal of Management*, 13(4), 337-348.

Rapoport, R.N. (1970) Three dilemmas in action research. *Human Relations*, 23(6), 499-513.

Reason, P. (2003) Pragmatist philosophy and action research: readings and conversation with Richard Rorty. *Action Research* 1(1), 103-123.

Reason, P. & Bradbury, H. (eds.) (2001) *Handbook of Action Research*. Sage, London.

Rosenhead, J. & Mingers, J. (2001) A new paradigm of analysis. In Rosenhead, J. & Mingers, J. (eds.) *Rational Analysis for a Problematic World Revisited*. Wiley, Chichester.

Rowe, F., Truex III, D.P. & Kvasny, L. (2004) Cores and definitions: building the cognitive legitimacy of the information systems discipline across the Atlantic. In Kaplan, B. at el. (eds.) *Information Systems Research: Relevant Theory and Informed Practice*. Kluwer Academic Publishers, Boston.

Somekh, B. (1995) The contribution of action research to development in social endeavours: a position paper on action research methodology. *British Educational Research Journal*, 21(3), 339-355.

Stair, R.M. & Reynolds, G.W. (2003) *Fundamentals of Information Systems 2nd ed.* Thomson Course Technology, Boston, USA.

Susman, G.I. & Evered, R.D.(1978) An assessment of the scientific merits of action research. *Administrative Science Quarterly*, 23(4), 582-603.

Thomas, W.I.& Thomas, D.S. (1928) *The Child in America: Behaviour Problems and Programs*. Knopf, New York.

Weber, R. (1987) Towards a theory of artifacts: a paradigmatic base for information systems research. *Journal of Information Systems*, 1(2), 3-19.

Part II. IS Action Research in Practice

Chapter 7

STORY TELLING IN ACTION RESEARCH PROJECTS
Malta, Bangladesh, Lebanon and Slovenia

Dr. Simon Bell[1] and Professor Trevor Wood-Harper[2]
[1] The Open University, UK; [2] University of Manchester, UK

Abstract: This paper sets out the two multi-methodologies applied in Action Research form in projects specifically in Malta, Bangladesh, Lebanon and Slovenia, and the manner in which the first steps of adapted Multiview and Imagine/SPSA methodologies were applied. This chapter attempts to answer the question: could multi-methodologies like Multiview and Imagine yield substantial, and appropriate benefits for local people and could the approaches be adapted and adopted by local people or would they remain the specialised property of an expatriate analyst providing that analyst with a privileged understanding not available to local people? The chapter describes how the early stages of the multi-methodologies were applied and in some cases adapted to meet the needs of the specific contexts under consideration. Arising from the research emerge issues of cultural relevance of such Action Research-based multi-methodologies, the role of researchers and the sustainability of such projects.

Key words: multi-methodology, sustainable development, participation, story telling

1.   THE RESEARCH QUESTION TO BE ADDRESSED BY THIS CHAPTER

The authors of this chapter have a long standing interest in the value and applicability of multi-perspective approaches to a range of projects in various cultural contexts (see, for example the three cases described in Bell 1996). In what follows, the authors describe the Action Research (AR) application of the early stages of the multi-methodologies - Multiview and

Imagine/ SPSA[1] (Avison and Wood-Harper 1990; Avison and Wood-Harper 1997; Bell and Morse 1999; Bell and Morse 2003). The chapter sets out how these two related yet discreet approaches were applied in a range of specific organisational/ cultural context in Bangladesh, Malta, Lebanon and Slovenia and analyse outcomes from the action research. The chapter addresses the questions:

- could these approaches yield substantial, and appropriate benefits for local people and
- could the approaches be adapted and adopted by local people or
- would they remain the specialised property of an expatriate analyst providing that analyst with a privileged understanding not available to local people?

A series of issues emerge but, more specifically, the chapter discusses emerging issues relating to the project appropriateness of Action Research (AR) application of multi-methodology, the role of external researchers/ consultants on such projects and the sustainability of such projects

2.   BACKGROUND TO THE RESEARCH DESCRIBED IN THIS CHAPTER

This chapter deals with a range of projects: one applying the Multiview multi-methodology in Bangladesh and three applying Imagine in Malta, Lebanon and Slovenia. In all cases, the Information Systems[2] projects were intended to provide improved local capacity in information awareness and handling for decision making purposes. In the Bangladesh case, a specific Non-Governmental Organisation (NGO) was involved. The NGO had a mission to remove poverty from the country. It focused its attention on training, education, and action. As an organisation the NGO sought to realise the vision of poverty eradication through social mobilisation in small groups, by providing micro-finance, skills and assistance. The essential operating method of the NGO was to form local communities into groups which then

---

[1] Systemic and Prospective Sustainability Analysis – Imagine/ SPSA is abbreviated from this point as Imagine.

[2] In this paper, we refer to all four projects as 'Information Systems' projects. It should be noted that our use of the term Information Systems' is as broad in definition as that provided by authors such as Peter Checkland and Sue Holwell Checkland, P. and S. Holwell (1998). Information, Systems and Information Systems: Making sense of the field. Chichester, Wiley. and includes all aspects of organization, information and technology, rather than the more conventional technology focused definition

co-operate in gaining access to resources and share in the proceeds of improved practices.

In the case of Malta, Lebanon and Slovenia, The projects described here are part of the Mediterranean Action Plan (MAP) and the series of Coastal Area Management Programmes (CAMPs) undertaken by a range of agencies and organisations. The lead organization in all cases described is Blue Plan. The Blue Plan regional activity centre is located on the French Riviera in Sophia-Antipolis, near Nice, and works with local agencies to plan Sustainable Development (SD) projects in the Mediterranean (see the website www.planbleu.org/indexa.htm for more details).

In Malta, Lebanon and Slovenia the Imagine methodology was applied as a means for deriving Sustainability Indicators at a local level. The intention behind the use of Imagine was to develop local awareness of sustainability issues – and the development of a concomitant capacity for local stakeholders to gather, present and apply sustainability indicators.

In terms of sequence, the Malta project was the first to be undertaken. Bangladesh, Lebanon and Slovenia followed. The time period under discussion here is from 1999 – 2005.

In many ways each project acted as a test-bed of the development of the underlying conditionalities of both the Multiview and Imagine multi-methodologies[3]. Both approaches are designed and intended to be used in an AR context, with local buy in to all stages of the various processes involved.

Imagine is more fully described elsewhere (Bell and Morse 1999; Bell and Morse 2003; Planbleu 2004) and can be seen as involving two existing Problem Solving Methods (PSMs):

Soft System Methodology – SSM - (Checkland 1981; Checkland and Scholes 1990; Checkland and Holwell 1998)

Scenario planning (Matzdorf and Ramage 1999; Matzdorf and Ramage 2000) or Prospective (Godet, Monti et al. 1999; Godet 2000; Godet 2000)

Mutlivew shares with Imagine the use of SSM, but contains a variety of approaches – including socio-technical systems analysis and interface design. Both Imagine and Mutiview as applied in these contexts include a toolkit of tools and techniques including Logical Framework (Coleman 1987; Gasper 1997; Gasper 2000), Active listening (Gordon 1970), risk analysis (Hughes and Cotterell 1999) and focus groups.

Both Multivew and Imagine are envisioned as processes to assist communities of stakeholders to structure, understand, measure and promote information in their context - chiefly by providing them with information

---

[3] Both are described in more detail in section 4 below

products, primarily indicators whereby agreed views of the current situation can be discussed and analysed, past conditions thought about and 'visions' for possible, sustainable futures compared.

In the Bangladesh study Technical Assistance (TA) provided by the project in question operated across a range of activities, however the element of key focus for this chapter is the provision of assistance in the development of Management Information Systems (MIS) for the Impact Monitoring Agency (IMA) of the NGO. Clearly, this sub-component is narrowly focused, however from the outset it was recognised that the MIS aspect had a capacity to achieve wider aims than those of narrowly improving impact monitoring. Therefore, the MIS component had several objectives from inception:

Primarily, to assist staff from IMA and related internal agencies to develop a computerised MIS for impact monitoring

Secondly, to review the overall data structure of the NGO in order to gain an overview of the effectiveness of the data and information processing processes as they stand at present

Thirdly, implicitly, and as a virtuous outcome of the first two, to seek to improve information handling within the management of the NGO.

An overview of the conventional components of the Multiview approach is shown in overview in Figure 7-1.

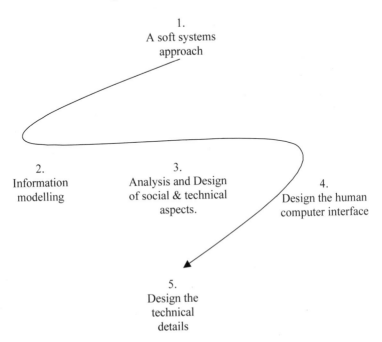

Figure 7-1. A diagrammatic presentation of Multiview

In the Maltese, Lebanese and Slovenian studies the Imagine approach was applied and developed. Overall, it was broadly divided into five stages:

(1) An initial overview of the current situation with regards to sustainable development in the coastal area.
(2) The identification of local agreed and assessed sustainability indicators
(3) The development of amoeba diagrams presenting an holistic overview of the present situation and some specific scenarios of potential futures
(4) Agreement of meta-scenarios for the coastal area as a whole
(5) An analysis of policy options and setting out a framework for future development and use of indicators.

The overall Imagine approach is set out in Figure 7-2.

The outcomes of the first stage of Imagine were rich pictures of the participants' perspective of the current situation, root definitions or visions for the way forward, conceptual or activity models of how to get there. In one case, Logical Frameworks for the setting of indicators emerged from this process.

The second stage of Imagine was centered on agreeing a set of sustainability indicators and then, subsequently, meetings with the wider stakeholder community so as to discuss the project outcomes so far achieved, explain the nature of the Imagine process and seek ideas and questions from the wider stakeholder group. At this time the wider community is asked to comment on and attempt to improve upon the indicators and reference conditions - what values of the indicators are needed for sustainability?

The third workshop was concentrated on using the indicators collected so far to make amoeba diagrams – providing an holistic overview of the current and historic situation.

The fourth workshop reviewed different assumptions and applied these in group work attempting to imagine various visions of future scenarios. In the original version of Imagine this issue of futurity and scenario investigation was included but no specific methodology was required. In the case of the Malta project this was modified, making use of the 'Prospective' approach as previously applied by Blue Plan (Godet et al. 1999; Godet, 2000, 2001). At this time the wider stakeholder views were again assessed, and teams were asked to think about how they might engage the public more actively in the use of indicators.

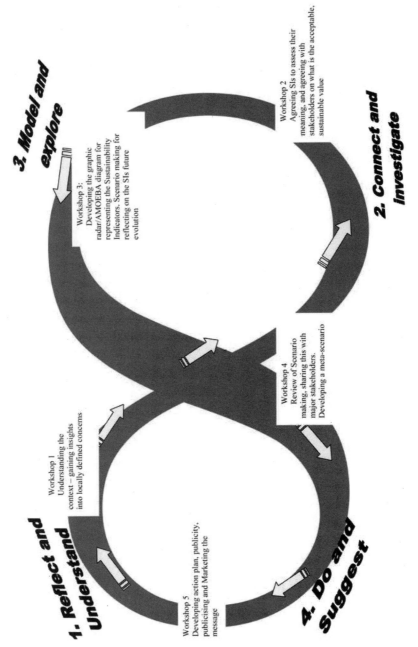

Figure 7-2. The Imagine approach

Finally, the fifth workshop seeks to make use of the indicators and scenarios, applying them to tell a story of how the situation may develop and on how the project messages can be told to influence policy makers.

Imagine and Multiview have, in the experience of the authors in conversation with stakeholder, and in limited questionnaire surveys of stakeholder opinion (See, for example the results reported in: Bell and Morse 2005), been seen to have produced useful outcomes by the actors involved in the projects. The feedback from those involved in the various project activities includes comment that the approaches:

- Encourage 'whole project' activity – this refers to providing the space and capacity for specialists to participate outside their narrow area of expertise and involving them in thinking about the nature of the project as a whole
- Assist in project participation by local people. In the wider stakeholder workshops, wide-ranging debates about the meaning and costs of information took place.
- Provide a forum for whole project thinking to occur
- Assist all project activists to question and review project assumptions.

In each case – Malta, Bangladesh, Lebanon, and Slovenia – there were critical differences in the manner and format which Multiview and Imagine multi-methodologies were involved. For example, the Maltese context was that of a small island and focus was on the sustainability of the environment and uniqueness of the North West. In Bangladesh, the primary interest was on the work of an NGO across the country. In Lebanon, the project site was the area of coast south of Beirut, whereas in Slovenia the project was concerned with a small geographic area – but it included coast and inland 'karst' regions. Similarly, each expression of Multiview and Imagine involved different timescales for project activities and different thematic teams to engage. In each case the outputs first seen in Malta, of: encouraging whole project thinking, participation, a forum for questioning and questioning assumptions were sustained. Given this commonality in underlying purpose as well as inherent diversity, the projects provided an ideal opportunity to test the assumptions behind research question set out in this chapter.

3.   BACKGROUND THEORY, LITERATURE AND EMERGENT METHODOLOGY FOR THE STUDY

Historically, claims for the likely success, capacity to be integrated and ability to produce short and long term benefits of information and information systems in public and private agencies in countries of widely different culture have ranged from the highly optimistic (e.g. seeWoherem 1993) to the candidly cautious (Walsham 2001). Walsham in particular has undertaken extensive studies on the cultural interpretation of different types of IS. Walsham concludes:

- knowledge is understood differently in different cultures
- western style IS needs to be understood within the context of alternative mindsets
- cross cultural collaboration is possible.

Keeping Walsham's findings in mind, the projects described here were undertaken seeking collaboration – this was a feature of the terms of reference of the work and a requirement consistent with AR process. However, the collaboration took place with explicit awareness that cultural factors – in terms of the various understandings of what constitutes knowledge, the different appreciation of what western developed multi-methodology might imply – might lead to the initiative being appreciated negatively. A note from one of the author's practitioner diaries at the outset of the Bangladesh project is illustrative of this issue:

"At this point, as I was beginning the project, I was keenly aware that my previous experience in MIS development in Asia, Africa and South East Asia did not necessarily provide me with a working model for engaging in Bangladesh. I was very aware from the first minute of my touch down in Dhaka that Bangladesh is a unique context and has a rich a complex history and tradition. My task from day 1 was to engage with this perceived complexity and attempt to understand it. My route for this was to engage and understand through the ideas and concepts of my local colleagues".

It should also be noted here that, it was not assumed that the cultural context might not be the main, defining issue. In the Bangladesh case, the culture of the NGO itself, and of its senior management group was likely to be as, if not more determining to the projects success. In Malta and Slovenia a north European cultural approach to projects of all kinds pervaded the overall process, whereas in Lebanon the project was, whilst not unusual in the Lebanese cultural context, it was a significant novelty to many of the stakeholders involved.

Many authors have commented on the development of IS making use of wide ranging methodologies (Midgley, Gu et al. 2000; Midgley and Wilby 2000; Molinari 2000; Munro and Mingers 2000; Taylor 2000) and the relative value and impact of multi-methodology has also been closely considered and categorised (Mingers and Brocklesby 1996). A key lesson drawn from this literature is the capacity of multi-methodology to deal with the richness of the real world. Both Multiview and Imagine qualify as multi-methodology, although they are unusual in that they defy the tendency for such approaches to be either 'soft' or 'hard' (Munro and Mingers 2000), containing combinations of each. Munro and Mingers argued that such approaches tended to be multidisciplinary (Munro and Mingers 2000), however, Multiview and Imagine, in theory and practice, are evidently transdisciplinary according to the typography of Scholz, et al. (Scholz, Lang et al. 2005).

Lewin set out the original basis for AR (Lewin 1947). Bottral provided guidance on the application of action research (AR) as one means to achieve transparency and inclusion in development practice (Bottrall 1982). Bottral's early work has been extended and discussed in many potential fields – often related to IS issues (Stowell, West et al. 1997; Baskerville and Wood-Harper 1998; Checkland and Holwell 1998; Lousberg and Soler 1998; Paton 2001). Baskerville and Wood-Harper have provided an overview of action research typographies (Baskerville and Wood-Harper 1998) and an overview of winning strategies in the approach (Baskerville and Wood-Harper 1996). More recently, the action research approach has been tied into issues of self-reflection, vulnerability and learning from outcomes by Bell (Bell 1998; Bell, Coleman et al. 2000). Also, AR has been argued to be a viable means to deal with conflicts and competing stakeholder requirements (Johnsen and Normann 2004) – this was assessed by the research team as being a potentially important power of the approaches in contexts where local and international perspectives may be at variance. As already argued in the first section of this chapter, cultural responses to IS do vary across nationalities and across organisations (see, for example, Gamila 2003; Puri and Sahay 2003). Action Research has the potential to bring out the understandings of those presenting different perspectives. Wadsworth, addressing the place of interpretivist approaches such as AR to problems solving argues:

"If conventional science wanted to give a group of people the power to determine 'truth' for and on behalf of others, the new science arose from a world of multiple and competing versions of truth and reality as a way of assisting people both to come to the truth of their own reality, and also to embrace that of others". (Wadsworth 1998)

The Multiview and Imagine approaches are interpreted in the cases described in this chapter as multi-methodologies which can be undertaken as part of an interpretivist / AR approach. As Baskerville and Wood-Haper argue:

"Multiview is included among the action research forms because Checkland's soft systems methodology strongly influences the human activity analysis stage of Multiview, and no alternative tools for this stage are suggested".

(Baskerville and Wood-Harper 1998, page 99)

Although Imagine and Multiview might be argued to differ in their appreciation and application of the main themes of AR (for example as set out in the table of methods shown on page 96 of Baskerville and Wood-Harper 1998) both share Hult and Lennung's six major characteristics of AR (Hult and Lennung 1980).

The translation of methodology into diverse cultural contexts is described in Bell (Bell 1996), and success in meeting the challenges of the incorporation of such methodologies in diverse cultures is argued there to be, in part at least[4], a function of reflective systemic practice. In undertaking the various studies contained in this chapter, and attempting to meet the need for reflective practice head on, the authors linked the learning cycle /AR concepts of:

- Participatory reflecting on the current context
- Participatory connecting with issues and opportunities
- Participatory modelling potential ways forward
- Collaborative action

(Bell 1999; Sankaran 2001; Bell and Morse 2003)

To complement the AR approach and provide it with some guarantees of inclusion and cooperation, certain principles from the application of the virtues of reflective practice and vulnerability as set out in Table 7-1 were used as themes in the research process.

The table, arising from previous research in the application of AR, is not so much a presentation of rules as the formalisation of behavioural rubrics for effective AR. The table arose from an assessment of the behaviours of Action Researchers and set out potential positive and negative responses to the vulnerability of the researcher.

---

[4] Alongside such factors as language, organisational agendas and technical capacity.

Table 7-1. Prizes of Self-Reflection in Action Research

Problem of non-self-reflective vulnerability	Prize of self-reflection with vulnerability
Unrealistic quality standards	Realistic expectation
Paranoia	Tolerance
Doubt	Humility
Self-preservation	Self-giving
Incessant self-expression	Listening
Undue self-assertion	Self-containment
Out of my depth	But I can learn
Out of my context	But I can experience
Keep it out!	But I am already part of 'it' and 'it' is part of me

The approach to be tested and applied in the four contexts contained in this chapter were adapting versions of Multiview (Wood-Harper, Antill et al. 1985; Avison and Wood-Harper 1990; Wood-Harper 1990), and SPSA Imagine (Bell and Morse 1999; Bell and Morse 2003; Planbleu 2004). In the case of Multiview, the rapid version of this described elsewhere (Bell and Wood-Harper 1998) lead to the refinement of the non-specialists practitioner guide (subsequently published in: Bell and Wood-Harper 2003). Imagine, is at the time of writing, being published by Blue Plan in the form of a bilingual Practitioners Guide - and is intended for flexible and adaptive application (Bell 2005). Multiview and Imagine strive to bridge the gap between "hard" and "soft" views on information within systems in any given context. Multiview is currently being applied in various contexts including strategic information systems (Vidgen, Avison et al. 2002) and the transport industry (McManus and Wood-Harper 2003). The Multiview and Imagine are approaches which the international researcher on the team had worked on extensively and therefore there was a need for him to see himself as an interested party and a stakeholder in the success of the mission. The approach to multi-methodology as set out in the 1998 Bell and Wood-Harper text had been developed specifically taking into account the need in diverse countries for approaches which are useful but which do not overarch the needs, priorities and value systems of local contexts (Kumar 1993; Chambers 1997). To this end the approaches are primarily focused on the use of softer and more systemic modes of understanding (Checkland 1981; Checkland and Scholes 1990; Checkland and Holwell 1998) in the early stages, rather than the more formal and technical focus of many conventional approaches regularly applied in the UK. Some of the stages of Multiview and Imagine are, in common with most problem solving and information building methods, aimed at addressing data and technical issues. However, the technical focus is set within a participative and inclusive initial analysis.

Basing our analysis on a combined approach, making use of action research concepts, linked to methods for rapid and participatory appraisal (Chambers 1992; Chambers 1997; Chambers 2002), the structure of the studies resolved themselves as:

1. an examination of the value of the application of multi-methodology in different national contexts
2. making use of participatory action research as a investigating framework
3. applying Multiview/ Imagine by means of participatory techniques – in the spirit of self-reflection and vulnerability
4. a consideration of the cultural value of Multiview/Imagine in the various contexts
5. an examination of the role of the external researchers/consultant
6. an assessment of the sustainability of the project process.

This six-step process, applied in each case, can also be seen as iterative and evolutionary, with each study linking with, providing evaluatory feedback for and feeding learning to the following study. This methodological adaptation and flexibility had been previously applied in work undertaken in the 1990s and described in Bell 1996 (Bell 1996). In this approach, adapted from the 'organised use of rational thought' in Checkland (Checkland 1985), each AR iteration can be seen as a frame by frame cycle or process of:

1. Exploring the intellectual framework of the researcher
2. Being clear on the format and structure of the methodology in use
3. Understanding the context of application and
4. Being aware of the changing strengths and weaknesses of the researcher

In a qualitative fashion, this structure operated at a meta level, overarching and acting as a reflective opportunity for rigor in the overall research process.

4.   MULTIVIEW/IMAGINE: SIMILAR AND DIFFERENT

Multiview and Imagine are multi-methodologies with significantly contrasting aspects. Whereas Multiview is an information systems analysis and design approach, Imagine is specifically intended to facilitate the participatory development of sustainability indicators. However, the approaches do have many similarities:

- Both are concerned with understanding context from the bottom up
- Both are participatory in application
- Both are concerned with producing useful information products
- Both are relevant only if they are appreciated by actors operating in the context where they are applied
- Both are concerned with improving understanding and transparency
- Both are concerned with developing information indicators as outcomes.

The common stages of Multiview and Imagine as applied in the four contexts were as follows:

Firstly variants of the Soft Systems Methodology or SSM were applied – focusing on three tools and outcomes. This was in order to gain understanding of the present situation - and not just from the perspective of technology or technologists or other 'experts', but also from the wider organisational perspective[5] – rich pictures[6] were drawn (depicting - "what is?"). These free form, cartoon type diagrams of the context were drawn by stakeholders across the context of the analysis. The rich picture exercise was followed by the development of root definitions – in this case they were to be mission statements, clearly stating:

- who the beneficiary for the analysis would be
- who will be involved in developing it
- what transformation the project is expected to achieve
- what is the main assumption contained in the transformation
- who will own the final system
- what are the major constraints operative in the context.

The rich picture presents an image of what the present situation is – from a variety of perspectives – the root definition sets out where the aspiration for the project in the future is directed ("what can be?").

Following the development of the root definition, the final stage of SSM is to develop the activity model. In this stage the stakeholders in the context develop their understanding of how they will get from the present situation to the aspired transformation set out in the root definition ("how do we get there?").

---

[5] Therefore including social, cultural and ethical issues.
[6] See figures 7-3 – 7-6 for examples.

Following the completion of the SSM, for both Multiview and Imagine, the expected outcome is clarity over the planned progression for the project. This plan can subsequently be developed in a variety of ways but in the case of Malta and Bangladesh, it was eventually progressed into a Logical Framework.

A second common aspect of Multiview and Imagine is the construction of a high level information model. In Bangladesh it was the version known as End User Information Modelling (EUIM). In this stage diverse stakeholder groups define:

- what information they need from the IS
- where it is held at present
- what the data is to provide the information
- what needs to be done to the data to create the information
- when this needs to happen.

In the Imagine projects in Malta, Lebanon and Slovenia, local members of the project teams developed models of data and information, (including entities, attributes, functions and events) to provide sustainability indicators. The main output or information modelling is to provide detailed awareness of what the key information products the project is expected to produce throughout.

Multiview goes on in a conventional IS process with four more stages: developing a socio-technical model, the human/computer interface, technical subsystems and issues of implementation. Imagine, by contrast, is more concerned with scenario making on the basis of the sustainability indicators developed, and the influencing of policy based upon the ramifications of the scenarios produced.

5.   STORIES AND TYPES OF STORY TELLING

Conventional Multiview, as originally devised, focuses its early stages on analysis on understanding: "what the organisation is trying to achieve - what it is for" (Avison and Wood-Harper 1990, page 43). By way of contrast, and as represented in the later, Bell and Wood-Harper book (Bell and Wood-Harper 2003) the Multiview approach applied in Bangladesh was directed to "help the major stakeholders in the organisation define the situation and analyse what the problem is". The movement from an approach to seek (and therefore assume the existence of) purposeful action as concentrated on in the original, 1990 version of Multiview, to one seeking to allow local actors to define their view of the problems in the context, as specified in the 2003 version, is not, we argue, merely a change of emphasis. It provides a demarcation of two different modes for applying the Multiview approach:

- The first is categorised as implicitly tending to the functional and purposive,
- the second is tending to the interpretivist - allowing stories from personal perspectives to be told and for purpose to emerge from dialogue.

This theme of interpretivist approaches is a significant aspect of Imagine as well, to some extent it has followed where Multiview has led. The forerunners to Imagine, SSA or Systemic Sustainability Analysis and SPSA or Systemic Prospective Sustainability Analysis have been said to:
"allow.. a team engaged in analysis to explore, describe and assess the level of sustainability of an agreed system by the use of indicators, in the past present and future .. By definition, SSA provides a global approach and has a dynamic characteristic because it takes into account the relations between the indicators which describe the elements of the system and their interactions."
(UNEP/MAP/BluePlan 2000)

All well and good, but the spirit of the approach means that:
"If the approach is to work it has to work for local practitioners. Without this the approach remains rarefied and the preserve of an elite. Such an approach is more likely to generate indicators for the elite and not for the population as a whole .. we saw participation as central throughout this process"
(Bell and Morse 2003, page 74)

In the application of Multiview in Bangladesh, the core team developed rich pictures of the current environment in sections and the wider NGO as whole. An example of one of the pictures is presented in Figure 7-3.
Similarly, in Malta, Lebanon and Slovenia, rich and varied diagrams were produced, setting out the wealth of the situation as was conceived by the various stakeholders (see Figures 7-4, 7-5 and 7-6).

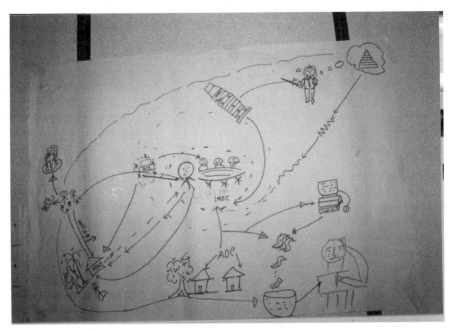

Figure 7-3. Example of a rich picture produced by NGO staff

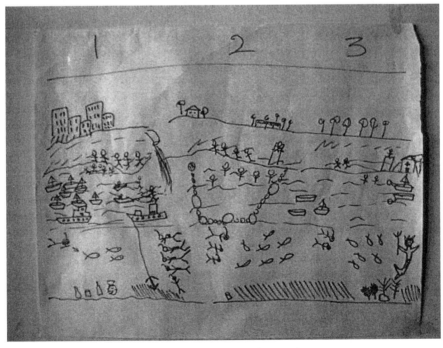

Figure 7-4. Rich Picture from Malta

Figure 7-5. Rich Picture from Lebanon

Figure 7-6. Rich Picture from Slovenia

Rich pictures, seem to be a wonderful way to engage local stakeholders and to allow them to tell the story of the project. One of the authors noted the following point in his practitioner diary in Bangladesh:

"I was really impressed with the apparent ease of all stakeholders in getting to grips with the rich picture form of presentation. Some of the pictures were really insightful and there was a great deal of honesty as to current problems and issues."

The issue of 'honesty', related to one of the known powers of the Rich Picture tool when undertaken in an action research process where issues of vulnerability are expected and respected – that participants will draw what they will not openly discuss. In all four contexts, this was pertinent to each case as it was observed in early meetings that stakeholders in the context often seemed uncomfortable at times with descriptions of accepted or reported processes and procedures. When probed further about this, team members would often volunteer the information (confidentially) that powerful stakeholders in the context were often not keen to appear to be complicit with apparent risks which could result in failures. Therefore, honesty in describing difficult and/ or failed initiatives and past failures were noteworthy explicit expressions of real problems. Further, in the Bangladesh case, the NGO in question was, at the time of the analysis, closely linked to a major political party in the country. With a general election about to occur, the NGO was experiencing a high degree of nervousness concerning its future. Political concerns and potential economic decline figured large in the minds of those engaged in the analysis. The Maltese rich picture shown here indicates three potential futures for the coastal area .. ranging from the most pessimistic to a sustainable future. The Lebanese picture makes rich use of imagery and symbol (Don Quixote tilting at windmills in the centre), as well as caricatures of rich capitalists and uncontrolled urban sprawl to make a case. The Slovenian picture shows a sustainable future, years from now, with a number of key problems and concerns overcome .. such as depopulation of the Karst area and new investment.

The rich picture exercise was adapted within the SSM element to provide stakeholders with the opportunity to express their wider concerns - and, in line with the research question for this chapter, consider deeper issues than those pertaining purely to information use and project or organisaton purpose, and to set these out in the context of the potential success or failure of the project.

In many cases, the rich pictures would show visual metaphors of corruption (money being diverted), intervention of government in NGO affairs (people with powerful sticks to beat the organisation) and internal frustrations (gestures of worry and concern) as well as the more prosaic matters of information flow and delivery.

Given the problematic and confidential nature of much of the conversation which occurred in these early stages, the authors decided that it was vital to develop room for two separate 'stories' for the analysis:

The first story was the presenting, explicit, 'published record' approach to the development of project objectives with either Multiview or Imagine - reflecting the need of those engaged in the process to develop a logical and purposeful model for the project

The second story was implicit, an outcome of a confidential talk-shop, the spoken or 'acroamatic record', where issues and concerns which could not be easily and openly discussed or publicised were dealt with[7]

To some extent, the remainder of all four projects concerned the subtle ways in which the latter story or narrative informally braided with and influenced the former. Also, it was often the second, acroamatic record, which, as observed in the enthusiasm of those taking part, provided indications of local stakeholders adopting and feeling included in the project process.

It was also evident at this stage that the first, published story could not achieve its objective - the establishment of an MIS or sustainability indicators, without the second, acroamatic story being taken into account. The acroamatic added real insight such as:

- The unwillingness of key and important actors
- The existence of other, similar or conflicting projects
- Questionable motivations
- Hidden agendas
- Alternative outcomes being sought

At any stage in the following analysis the core team were constantly aware of the potential jeopardy of their work in the light of the un-folding acroamatic story.

It is also worth noting at this point that following the rich picture exercise, the ongoing development of the projects often followed the work represented in the conventional, published story. From this point onwards the weighty issues derived from the acroamatic story often found little formal ground for open reporting - unless it were to be within another diagramming process. This observation does vary in severity, depending on which specific context is under being described, and it did not mean that important items were not discussed, rather, the outcomes of these

---

[7] The notion of an oral, insider story, not openly available to the public record has a long tradition. It is understood that Plato in his academy provided a written teaching (his Dialogues) which were supported and guided by the acroamatic teaching Szlezak, T. (1999). Reading Plato. London, Routledge.. The un-packing of the acroamatic story within the SSM aspect of Mutliview we argue, goes beyond the conventional notion of a 'soft' message in the analysis.

discussions were often not conformable with the reporting structures of the formal project structure and/or were not acceptable as issues to be openly addressed. This item is discussed in more detail in the following sections.

From this point the acroamatic story finds little or no formal 'voice' in the reporting of many projects but, it did still influence the development of the project process:

- Firstly as informal briefing at most team meetings
- Secondly as rubrics for guidance of what was /was not possible

The way in which the acroamatic story of the project and the published story braided in practice is an issue of importance for practitioners of AR - based approaches and is discussed in more detail in the latter sections of this chapter.

6.   THE 'PUBLISHED' PROJECT STORY

Although the projects described in this chapter are still in various stages of process of development, it is useful to reflect on the outcomes of the use of Multiview and Imagine to-date.

From the observed activities in all four it can be seen that, the 'soft' front end of both multi-methodologies has been adopted by local stakeholders in the various contexts. Furthermore, again, the observation of the workshops so far experienced would indicate that this adoption has been undertaken with a minimum of difficulty for those attending. The stakeholder meetings generated real enthusiasm for the approaches and there did not appear to be any problem with local people in all four locations making use of tools like the rich picture, root definition or activity model. This may in part be the outcome of the long contact that some individuals have had with a variety of project approaches adopted by major international donor agencies. In this it might be speculated that people in all four locations were culturally adapted to the general format of international projects if not the specific rigours of Multiview or Imagine. To return to the original question which guided this research:

- could these approaches yield substantial, and appropriate benefits for local people and
- could the approaches be adapted and adopted by local people or
- would they remain the specialised property of an expatriate analyst providing that analyst with a privileged understanding not available to local people?

Table 7-2 shows how the cyclic process of AR changed, case by case, Table 7-3 provides an overview of the responses to the questions set out above in all three questions, as well as some observations arising from emergent questions relating to the acroamatic stories from each project[8].

Table 7-2. Process learning from AR application

Frame	The intellectual framework for AR	The methodology in use	The area of application	The researcher – strengths and weaknesses
1	An adaptive approach to applying fixed methodology	Imagine version 1 – also called Systemic Sustainability Analysis or SSA	Malta – NW coast	Only a theoretic knowledge of the methodology
2	Seeking a 'mode 2' version of the approach – willing to change the 'fixed' features of methodology.	Multiview – mode 1, aspiring to greater flexibility in mode 2	Bangladesh	Deep knowledge of the approach plus the confidence to adapt
3	Evolving approach to all AR methodology. Willing to change in terms of the needs of the context	Imagine version 2 – called Systemic Prospective Sustainability Analysis or SPSA	Lebanon	Developing knowledge of the methodology in practice and theory. Increasing confidence to adapt
4	Settling on a new structure of Imagine. Focus on the AR components that appear to work in varied contexts	Imagine version 3. Imagine proper.	Slovenia	Confidence in the processes. Willing to change as needed.

[8] It should be noted that the table presents the author assessment of each question and codes the responses in traffic light form, where light grey indicates a broadly positive response, grey: an indeterminate response and dark grey a largely negative outcome.

Table 7-3. 'Traffic Light' Comparison of the four applications of Multi-Methodology in AR

Country / Question:	Malta	Bangladesh	Lebanon	Slovenia
Published question 1. Outcomes/ value to local community	Local stakeholders expressed high value in terms of engagement and a positive experience	Local stakeholders expressed high value in terms of engagement and a positive experience	Local stakeholders expressed high value in terms of engagement and a positive experience	Local stakeholders expressed high value in terms of engagement and a positive experience
Published question 2. Dynamic development of methodology	Some adaptation of Imagine – specifically including logframe, scenario making and comparative matrix	Some adaptation of Multiview – specifically including logframe	Some small adaptation of imagine mainly concerning the development of feasibility analysis	Significant adaptation to Imagine - specifically developing matrix use, adapting scenario making and developing meta scenario
Published question 3. Transferability of Methodology	Transferable in the short term. No evidence of long term application	Transferable in the short term. No evidence of long term application	Transferable in the short term. No evidence of long term application	Transferable in the short term. Some evidence of potential for longer term application
Acroamatic question 1 Cultural relevance of Multiview/ Imagine	No apparent contradictions between open use of methodology and local values	Some contradictions between use of methodology and local values	No apparent contradictions between open use of methodology and local values	No apparent contradictions between open use of methodology and local values
Acroamatic question 2 Braiding stories in Multiview/ Imagine	Both published and presenting stories presented	Both published and presenting stories presented	Both published and presenting stories presented	Both published and presenting stories presented
Acroamatic question 3 project sustainability for Multiview/ Imagine	Minimal sustainability for the project approach	Zero sustainability for the project approach	Minimal sustainability for the project approach	Possibly some sustainability for the project approach
Overall 'traffic light'				

The cyclic process and learning of the AR, which was first alluded to in section 3 is shown in Table 7-2.

Using both Multiview and Imagine as the 'frames' for AR, and noting the evolution of the approach frame by frame, three features of changing use in practice can be seen.

- Over the entire process the methodologies have significantly altered, evolving with need and in line with the growing confidence and facility of the researchers.
- Therefore, methodology is seen not to be fixed .. rather it changes with the need of location
- And so, it can be argued that the perspective, understanding and vulnerability of the researcher is a key variable in the evolution of the methodology and its application

Overall, and unsurprisingly, context is key.

The generalisable outcomes of the application of the approaches at the time of writing are as follows:

1. Outcomes/ value to local community. In all four cases there was an observed tendency for local stakeholders to produce a broad agreement on the nature of some of the explicitly understood, current problems as experienced by the diverse group of stakeholders. However, there are many other issues, held in the acroamatic story, which are partially understood or only assented to by certain key stakeholders and stakeholder coalitions. But, at a presenting level the response is overwhelmingly green.

2. Dynamic development of methodology?. On a matter of methodology, the Logical Framework approach to project planning appears to link in with the SSM with relatively few problems (as experienced in Malta and Bangladesh only). Only in Slovenia did there seem to be a significant adaptation to Imagine. In all four cases it seems more likely that the development of the approach was more down to innovations in the project team rather than the initiative of local groups, but the source of the innovation often arose from discussion in the various working groups.

3. It is as yet early days in the roll out of the various projects, however, it does appear that:

Transferability of methodology: The initial stages of the approaches have proved to be doable in the various contexts – and key methods, tools and techniques were adopted those local people who attended the workshops.

The outcomes in the published story appear to be acceptable as valid by most stakeholders

The preliminary stages appear to offer the potential for the development of a participative project - co-owned by local and international stakeholders

The potential for the benefits of new practice relating to the use and application of information products – as identified in the root definition and activity plan – provide concrete means to produce beneficial performance for the four locations as whole.

However, in the longer term, the Multiview and Imagine approaches did not appear to be absorbed for later application – providing a series of dark grey responses. Only in Slovenia at the time or writing, does there appear to be a commitment to the longer term adoption of Imagine.

7.   THE 'ACROAMATIC' STORY: PRACTITIONER LESSONS

The formal/ published story of the projects indicates a high degree of viability for the Multiview and Imagine approaches in the various contexts, however, from the acroamatic story, three emergent, methodological, practice challenges were observed as being critical. These have been allocated their own place in Table 7-2 and are discussed briefly here:

1. Cultural relevance of Multiview and Imagine. Multiview and Imagine are presented as a powerful, coherent means to develop information products, however, they are, by definition of origin, the product of a European mindset. They come with a tradition and with baggage which could provide obstacles to wider understanding in cultures not versed in the European experience. The adoption of an action research approach, guided by rubrics, arising from experiences in vulnerability cannot be expected to overcomes all cultural difficulties. Multiview and Imagine arose partly as eclectic mixes of tools to counter the observed failure of overly technical approaches to IS development on the one hand and information use on the other. The more recent incarnations of the methodologies have been developed to focus on soft issues. Yet, the inclusion of a participatory and human-needs centred focus cannot be assumed to be understood or welcomed by those who do not understand the raison d'etre for the methodology (see also, Puri and Sahay 2003). At various points in the extrapolation of Multiview and Imagine it proved necessary to explain not just *how* the approaches worked but *why* they worked that way and why they *needed* to work that way. This is indicative of a need in practice not to assume that the methodologies as presented made sense to those experiencing them, nor that their internal logic was self-evident or non-contestable. Rather, for participants to gain confidence in the approaches, they needed to be clearly and unambiguously (and without jargon) set out. In most of the projects described in this chapter a green/positive response resulted. Only in the Bangladesh case did local values and methodology significantly conflict. However, even in this case the conflict was not dramatic – rather it was due to some confusions over the role of the AR project and the inclusive nature of the process.

A related issue is that of social inclusion in processes of selecting tools for analysis and design. At times participants wanted to include craft skills, tools, techniques and methods from their own experience (a point also noted in: Roman and Colle 2003). These were familiar to local experts and had the added value of being developed from within the context. Conversations did include the informal application of minor tools in some cases but the project framework did not provide time or resources for extensive application. In this sense the approach did not have the formal capacity to learn from local experience and this was noted as something of a loss to the projects overall. One means to overcome this inflexibility in the Multiview and Imagine approaches are at present being tested in a UK Masters Degree course: The Open University. "The Information Systems Toolkit – T851", has subsequently been designed by one of the authors, in a specific attempt to combat problems of non-inclusion and inflexibility.

2. Facilitating braiding stories in Multiview / Imagine. In the context described in this chapter the researcher was an outsider to the context. As such, the researcher was developing personal understanding and, at the same time, initiating the methodological process. Reflective Practice (e.g. as presented in: Moon 1999) was key in facilitating the process. It was a means to learn in practice and the theoretic and practitioner literature (e.g as celebrated in: Chambers 2002) was extensively drawn upon – specifically in terms of craft skills for sensitive braiding of the published and acroamatic records of the project process.

The external researcher comes to a context with objectives and terms of reference and these need to be checked with stakeholders locally and assessed for acceptability to local people - as Chambers argues:

"Local people's knowledge and skills often qualify them as consultants" (Chambers 1997, page 218).

In the experience of the authors, the inclusion of local people in decision making and in reflective practice on decisions made is vital if there is to be any meeting of minds in any ongoing informing process – and if the acroamatic is to be effectively represented in the published story. Researchers and international consultants are sometimes experienced as an unwelcome interference by local people and can be guilty of not understanding local sensitivities. On the other hand, they can be in the privileged position of confidant to acroamatic stories and major facilitators in either assisting openness or complicit in hiding important but uncomfortable facts. The agenda of the project funder is not necessarily commensurate with the needs of those working on the ground. Reflective Practice, including welcoming informal input from local counterparts is suggested as an important craft skill for inclusion in all methodological processes.

In all four cases, both Multiview and Imagine achieved considerable success in providing opportunity and presenting results of braiding a variety of stories from the four contexts and the all four projects present as light grey.

3. Project Sustainability for Multiview and Imagine: At the time of when this paper was originally written (June 2005) the various project processes described in this chapter have undergone considerable re-alignment. Critical to the process of adjustment in all cases is the loss of personnel and resources. Despite early encouraging developments in all four contexts, the loss of personnel and resources meant that the methodology process was impaired. It appears that either a substantial re-working of the process with new people at some unspecified future date, or the adoption of a less ambitious process - and therefore project outcome - would be required. This issue of project frailty has been noted in other work, (Bell and Morse 2004; Bell and Morse 2005), the project mindset itself, and the short-termist culture which tends to accompany it is often anathema to longer term sustainability of any given methodology. Bell and Morse have referred to this short term culture as the 'Projectified World Order'.

In the authors' experience, the negative impact of the Projectified World Order is not a rare event. It appears that projects of all types progress - apparently successfully - to a point, then fail following a critical event - for example, the over-emphasis on short term targets, reduction in funding, changes in political allegiance to the project vision, the loss of a project champion (issues more widely discussed in: Bell and Mayhew 1994; Bell 1996; Bell and Morse 1997; Fortune and Hughes 1997; Fortune 1999; Bell and Morse 2003). Projects with a focus on information seem particularly prone to this type of disruption. This is an issue beyond the capacity of any methodology and has more to do with the funding priorities of donor and recipient agencies.

A related point arising from more recent contact with the project context and linked to the issues of cultural relevance already discussed above, is the emergence of levels of hostility to information concepts of transparency and accountability – what is referred to here as "Information Culture". The sustainability of any information process going forward means that powerful local stakeholders and leaders recognise that such projects do not merely mean the development and wide-scale use of technologies, it also requires information culture to be embedded (a point also flagged by Galliers, Madon et al. 1998). Information culture also comes with its own specific baggage and assumptions, but it is an underlying requirement if such projects are to be more than selective data archive. In many organisations there is a culture, fostered and encouraged, of privacy and secrecy – and a tendency to prefer the project to run to time and produce reports than result in real and significant change. Whilst not wishing to imply judgement on the reasons or necessities for these features in some organisations, if informing is attempted without openness concerning potential culture clash – issues usefully flagged in the acroamatic story - then these issues can cause the project process to fail completely in spirit if not in fact.

8. CONCLUSIONS AND TRAFFIC-LIGHT TALES

Finally, in summing up the experiences of the authors in this case, the overall message of the traffic light analysis shown in Table 7-3 needs to be told.

Perhaps, it is not surprising that a review of the final row of collated results shows that the most positive, green responses to the research carried out, both in terms of the published and the acroamatic stories are provided by the two more developed country contexts: Malta and Slovenia. Maybe, also, it is not too surprising that the least positive response to the analysis comes from the Bangladesh context – where the rigours of poverty, social exclusion and conflict are most pronounced.

A more subtle message to the readers of this book might include the observation that the AR approach is intended to provide researchers with capacity to work with and through local people and that sustainable outcomes might be expected to be a likely outcome of such work. Our response to this is stark. The sustainability of outcome is still more dependent upon the rigour and mindset of the projectified world order than the sensitivities of the project research approach – and the manner in which the projectified world order reacts with any specific project context will be key in determining the sustainability of the final project outcomes.

REFERENCES

Avison, D. E. and A. T. Wood-Harper (1990). Multiview: an exploration in information systems development. Maidenhead, McGraw-Hill.

Avison, D. E. and A. T. Wood-Harper (1997). Multiview: an exploration in information systems development. London, Alfred Waller.

Baskerville, R. and A. T. Wood-Harper (1998). "Diversity in Information Systems Action Research Methods." European Journal of Information Systems 7: 90 - 107.

Baskerville, R. and T. Wood-Harper (1996). "A Critical Perspective on Action Research as a Method for Information Systems Research." JOurnal of Information Technology 11: 235 - 246.

Baskerville, R. and T. Wood-Harper (1998). "Diversity in Information Systems Action Research Methods." European Journal of Information Systems **7**: 90-107.

Bell, S. (1996). Learning with Information Systems: learning cycles in information systems development. London, Routledge.

Bell, S. (1996). "Reflections on Learning in Information Systems Practice." The Systemist **17**(2): 54-63.

Bell, S. (1998). "Self-Reflection and Vulnerability in Action Research: Bringing forth new worlds in our learning." Systemic Practice and Action Research **11**(2): 179-192.

Bell, S. (1999). Rapid and Participatory IS Analysis and Design: A means to defy the 'Anatomy of Confusion'? Synergy Matters: Working with systems in the 21st Century. A. Castell, A. Gregory, G. Hindle, M. James and G. Ragsdell. Dordrecht, Kluwer Academic/ Plenum Publishers: 523-528.

Bell, S. (2005). A Practitioners Guide to Imagine - Systemic and Prospective Sustainability Analysis (SPSA). Sophia Antipolis, Blue Plan.

Bell, S., G. Coleman, et al. (2000). "Information Systems Project in China: Action research and soft systems methodology." Human Systems Management **19**: 181-192.

Bell, S. and P. Mayhew (1994). Lessons in the Application of Systems Analysis in Developing Countries. A paper prepared for the Second European Conference on Information Systems, Nijenrode University, Nijenrode.

Bell, S. and S. Morse (1997). Systems Thinking and Gauging Sustainable Development. Systems for Sustainability: people, organisations and environments. F. Stowall, R. Ison and R. Armson. London, Plenum Press: 407-412.

Bell, S. and S. Morse (1999). Sustainability Indicators: Measuring the immeasurable. London, Earthscan.

Bell, S. and S. Morse (2003). Learning from Experience in Sustainability. The 2003 International Sustainable Development Research Conference, University of Nottingham, UK.

Bell, S. and S. Morse (2003). Measuring Sustainability: Learning from Doing. London, Earthscan.

Bell, S. and S. Morse (2004). "Experiences with Sustainability Indicators and Stakeholder Participation: a case study relating to a 'Blue Plan' project in Malta." Sustainable Development **12**: 1-14.

Bell, S. and S. Morse (2005). "Delivering Sustainability Therapy in Sustainable Development Projects." Journal of Environmental Management **75**(1): 37 - 51.

Bell, S. and S. Morse (2005). Sustainable Development Projects: Explicit and acroamatic story telling as part of a new 'project ethnography'. Symposium on Transdisciplinary Case Study Research for Sustainable Development, Helsinki, Swiss Federal Institute for Technology.

Bell, S. and A. T. Wood-Harper (1998). Rapid Information Systems Development: systems analysis and systems design in an imperfect world: Second Edition. London, McGraw Hill.

Bell, S. and A. T. Wood-Harper (2003). How to Set Up Information Systems: a non-specialists guide to the Multiview approach. London, Earthscan.

Bell, S. and A. T. Wood-Harper (2003). How to Set Up Information Systems: A non-specialist's guide to the Multiview approach. London, Earthscan.

Bottrall, A. (1982). The Action Research Approach to Problem Solving, with illustrations from irrigation management, Overseas Development Institute.

Chambers, R. (1992). Rural Appraisal: rapid, relaxed and participatory. Brighton, Institute of Development Studies.

Chambers, R. (1997). Whose Reality Counts? Putting the first last. London, Intermediate Technology Publications.

Chambers, R. (2002). Participatory Workshops: A sourcebook of 21 sets of ideas and activities. London, Earthscan.

Checkland, P. and S. Holwell (1998). "Action Research: Its nature and validity." Systemic Practice and Action Research 11(1): 9-21.

Checkland, P. and S. Holwell (1998). Information, Systems and Information Systems: Making sense of the field. Chichester, Wiley.

Checkland, P. B. (1981). Systems thinking, Systems Practice. Chichester, Wiley.

Checkland, P. B. (1985). "From Optimisation to Learning: a development of systems thinking for the 1990s." Journal of the Operational Research Society Vol. 36(No. 9): pp. 757-767.

Checkland, P. B. and J. Scholes (1990). Soft Systems Methodology in Action. Chichester, Wiley.

Coleman, G. (1987). "Logical Framework Approach to the Monitoring and Evaluation of Agricultural and Rural Development projects." Project Appraisal Vol. 2(No. 4): 251-259.

Fortune, J. (1999). Fighting Failure. Synergy Matters: Working with systems in the 21st Century. A. Castell, A. Gregory, G. Hindle, M. James and G. Ragsdell. Dordrecht, Kluwer Academic/ Plenum Publishers: 7-12.

Fortune, J. and J. Hughes (1997). Modern Academic Myths. Systems for Sustainability: People, organizations and environments. A. Stowell, R. Ison and R. Armson. London, Plenum: 125-130.

Galliers, R., S. Madon, et al. (1998). "Information Systems and Culture: applying 'stages of growth' concepts to development administration." Information Technology for Development 8: 89 - 100.

Gamila, S. (2003). "Cross-Cultural IS Adoption in Multinational Corporations." Information Technology for Development 10(4): 249 - 263.

Gasper, D. (1997). Logical Frameworks - a critical look. Development Studies Association, University of East Anglia.

Gasper, D. (2000). "Evaluating the "Logical Framework Approach": Towards learning - orientated development evaluation." Public Administration and Development 20(1): 17-28.

Godet, M. (2000). "The Art of Scenarios and Strategic Planning: Tools and pitfalls." Technological Forecasting and Social Change 65(1).

Godet, M. (2000). "How to be rigorous with scenario planning." Foresight 2(1): 5-9.

Godet, M., R. Monti, et al. (1999). Scenarios and Strategies: a toolbox for Scenario planning, Laboratory for Investigation in Prospective and Strategy: Toolbox. 1999.

Gordon, T. (1970). Parent Effectiveness training. New York., Plume Books, New American Library Inc.

Hughes, B. and M. Cotterell (1999). Software Project Management. Maidenhead, McGraw Hill.

Hult, M. and S.-A. Lennung (1980). "Towards a Definition of Action Research: a note and bibliography." Journal of Management Studies 17(May): 241 - 250.

Johnsen, H. and R. Normann (2004). "When Research and Practice Collide: The role of action research when there is a conflict of interests with stakeholders." Systemic Practice and Action Research 17(3): 207-236.

Kumar, K. (1993). Rapid Appraisal Methods. Washington DC, World Bank Publications.

Lewin, K. (1947). "Frontiers in Group Dynamics." Human Relations **1**: 5-41.

Lousberg, M. and J. Soler (1998). "Action Research and the Evaluation of IT Projects." Active learning **8**: 36-40.

Matzdorf, F. and M. Ramage (1999). "Out of the box - into the future." Organisations and People **6**(3): 29-34.

Matzdorf, F. and M. Ramage (2000). "Planning for Many Futures." Scenarion and Strategy Planning **2**(4): 20-22.

McManus, J. and A. T. Wood-Harper (2003). Information Systems Project Management: Methods, tools and techniques. London, Financial Times Prentice Hall.

Midgley, G., J. Gu, et al. (2000). "Dealing with Human Relations in Chinese Systems Behaviour." Systemic Practice and Action Research **13**(1): 71-96.

Midgley, G. and J. Wilby (2000). "Systems Practice in China: New developments and cross cultural collaborations." Systemic Practice and Action Research **13**(1): 3-10.

Mingers, J. and J. Brocklesby (1996). "Mutlimethodology: towards a framework for critical pluralism." Systemist **18**(3): 101-131.

Molinari, M. (2000). Introducing Mini Solutions: Working towards sustainability. Reading, Ab Uno.

Moon, J. (1999). Reflection in Learning and Professional Development. London, Kogan Page Ltd.

Munro, I. and J. Mingers (2000). The Use of Multimethodology in Practice - Results of a survey of practitioners. Warwick, University of Warwick.

Paton, G. (2001). "A Systemic Action Learning Cycle as the Key Element of an Ongoing Spiral of Analyses." Systemic Practice and Action Research **14**(1): 95-112.

Planbleu (2004). http://www.planbleu.org/indexa.htm. Sophia Antipolis.

Puri, K. and S. Sahay (2003). "Participation through Communicative Action: A case study of GIS for Addressing Land/Water Development in India." Information Technology for Development **10**(3): 179 - 200.

Roman, R. and R. D. Colle (2003). "Content Creation for ICT Development Projects: Integrating normative approaches and community demand." Information Technology for Development **10**(2): 85 - 95.

Sankaran, S. (2001). "Methodology for an Organisational Action Research Thesis." Action Reserch International **Paper** 3(http:/www.scu.edu.au/schools/gcm/ar/ari/p-ssankaran01.html).

Scholz, R., D. Lang, et al. (2005). Transdisciplinary Case Studies as a Means of Sustainability Learning: Historical Framework and Theory. Symposium on Transdisciplinary Case Study Research for Sustainable Development, Helsinki, Swiss Federal Institute for Technology.

Stowell, F., D. West, et al. (1997). Action Research as a Framework for IS Research. Information Systems: an emerging discipline? J. Mingers and F. Stowell. Maidenhead, McGraw-Hill.

Szlezak, T. (1999). Reading Plato. London, Routledge.

Taylor, A. (2000). IT Projects: sink or swim. The Computer Bulletin: 24-26.

UNEP/MAP/BluePlan (2000). Systemic Sustainability Analysis within CAMP Malta: Technical specification. Sophia Antipolis, Blue Plan.

Vidgen, R., D. E. Avison, et al. (2002). Developing Web Information Systems. London, Butterworth-Heinemann.

Wadsworth, Y. (1998). "What is Participatory Action Research?" Action Reserch International **Paper 2**(http:/www.scu.edu.au/school/gcm/ar/ari/p-ywadsworth98.html).

Walsham, G. (2001). Making a World of Difference: IT in a global context. Chichester, Wiley.

Woherem, E. (1993). Information Technology in Africa: challenges and opportunities. Nairobi, ACTS Press.

Wood-Harper, A. T. (1988). Comparison of Information Systems Approaches: an action-research, Multiview perspective. Norwich, University of East Anglia.

Wood-Harper, A. T., L. Antill, et al. (1985). Information Systems Definition: a Multiview Approach. Oxford, Blackwell Scientific Publications.

Chapter 8

ACTION RESEARCH IN NEW PRODUCT DEVELOPMENT

Ola Henfridsson[1] and Rikard Lindgren[2]

[1] *Viktoria Institute & Halmstad University, Sweden;* [2] *Viktoria Institute, Sweden*

Abstract: This chapter explores the nature of action research in new product development. Characterized by pressures associated with product concept effectiveness and process performance, new product development is a challenging but rewarding setting for action research. By re-assessing a previously reported action research study in the automotive industry, we identify and analyze characteristics of managing such research in new product development. On the basis of this assessment, the chapter complements previous research on managing action research projects with specific insights applicable to settings in which new technologies are being built and tried out.

Key Words: action research, new product development, prototypes, wide-audience client

1. INTRODUCTION

The client-system infrastructure of an action research project specifies its research environment (Baskerville & Wood-Harper, 1996; Susman & Evered, 1978). In particular, it defines the researcher-practitioner relationship including dimensions such as authority level, degree of formalization, project initiation process, researcher role, risk taking, and data collection. Previous research highlights the centrality of controlling and managing the action research environment as to secure research rigor and relevance. To this end, the literature reports sets of aspects, principles, criteria, and lessons to do this (Avison, Baskerville, & Myers, 2001; Davison, Martinsons, & Kock, 2004; Lau, 1999; Mathiassen, 2002). A common denominator of this literature is its orientation towards organizational development.

Given that "IS researchers should be actively involved in studies where technologies are being built and tried out – not after the fact when they enter the market" Lyytinen and Yoo (2002a, p.387), action researchers may need to develop research alliances with those who drive technological change. Indeed, packaged software (Sawyer, 2000) and software bundled with physical products (Joglekar & Rosenthal, 2003) increasingly shape the utilization of information technology in organizations. Thus, we need to learn how to conduct action research in settings where this shaping takes place.

This chapter explores the nature of action research in such a setting: new product development (NPD). Characterized by pressures associated with product concept effectiveness and process performance (Brown & Eisenhardt, 1995), NPD is a challenging but rewarding setting for articulating the new conditions for information systems action research. By re-assessing a previously reported study in the automotive industry (Henfridsson & Lindgren, 2005; Olsson & Henfridsson, 2005), this chapter identifies and analyzes characteristics of managing action research in NPD. On the basis of this assessment, the chapter complements previous research on controlling and managing action research projects with specific insights applicable to NPD. These insights are valuable contributions to the ambition to make information systems research part of the settings in which new technologies are being built and tried out.

The remainder of the chapter is structured as follows. The following section reviews the action research literature with a specific focus on managing and controlling aspects. Section three provides a brief review of the NPD literature. Following these literature sections, section four outlines an action research study conducted in the automotive industry. On the basis of this study, we generate a set of advices to action researchers who intend to conduct action research in NPD settings. While the proposed advices conform to the extant guidelines for managing and controlling action research, they suggest ways to handle specific product development aspects that the generic guidelines virtually overlook.

2. MANAGING ACTION RESEARCH

Action research has for long been recognized as a valid research method in applied fields such as organization development and education (Baskerville and Myers 2004). In light of frequent calls for information systems researchers to make their research more relevant to practice, action research has been identified as one potential avenue. Information systems researchers have therefore tried to conceptualize the nature of information systems action research as a scientific method (McKay & Marshall, 2001). In the quest of emergent standards that help action research to become a valid research method, there have been attempts to show how various forms of action research have different models, different structures, and different sets of goals (Baskerville, 1999; Baskerville & Wood-Harper, 1998). Complementing these conceptual contributions, there are also empirical accounts that describe information systems action research projects conducted in collaboration with practitioners in organizational settings. On a general level, using different variants of action research, these articles are exemplars of researcher-practitioner collaborations for solving organizationally bounded problems (Chiasson & Dexter, 2001; Iversen, Mathiassen, & Nielsen, 2004; Lindgren, Henfridsson, & Schultze, 2004; Mårtensson & Lee, 2004; Street & Meister, 2004).

While the number of published action research articles in premier information systems journals is growing, however, information systems researchers have historically been reluctant to use this qualitative method. As asserted by Avison et al. (2001), this can be traced to the many difficulties created by the goal of combining both action and research. Stemming from the fact that the action researcher has to serve "at least two demanding masters – the client and the academic community" (Davison et al., 2004, p.71), such difficulties concern how to structure the research process and findings, to predict and control the focus of the research outcome, and to conduct systematic data collection (Mathiassen, 2002). As action research projects are highly situational (Avison et al. 2001), it is complicated to formulate general laws about how to manage such projects.

There is a number of articles suggesting general guidelines for how to organize, manage, and evaluate information systems action research projects (Avison et al., 2001; Davison et al., 2004; Lau, 1999; Mathiassen, 2002). Whereas there is no consensus on the ideal practice of conducting action research, the guidelines suggested help improve the rigor of such research by identifying a set of key management aspects. Addressing the initiation of an action research project, a first management guideline concerns *the identification and specification of a situation where problems exist*. Whereas the action researcher may discover the problems, the classic genesis of action research is that a host organization seeks assistance from a knowledgeable researcher. In such situations, problems discover the action researcher (Avison et al., 2001). An alternative approach is collaborative initiation where the action research project evolves from interactions between researchers and clients. Regardless of how action research projects are initiated, "the goal of the initiation process among both the practitioners and the researchers is the discovery of a mutual interest in solving the problem at hand" (Avison et al., 2001, p.30). The management challenge here is to formulate and organize the action research initiative as to cater for both knowledge discovery and practical problem-solving (Avison et al., 2001; Lau, 1999).

As recognized by Avison et al. (2001), the action researcher's motives are divided between research goals and organizational problem-solving goals. A second management guideline therefore concerns *the formalization of collaboration between practitioners and researchers*. Both researchers and clients may have multiple roles and responsibilities in an action research project. As action researchers typically guide the overall project process, their scope of responsibility on content issues is an important topic of negotiation (Davison et al., 2004). Because of the divergent nature of the interests involved and the emerging nature of the research focus and findings, researchers and practitioners are recommended to develop and determine control structures in the early stages of an action research project (Avison et al., 2001; Mathiassen, 2002). While action research control structures can take a variety of different forms including formal, informal, and/or evolved, such structures should include specifications of action warrants, project management structures, and processes for renegotiation and/or cancellation (Avison et al., 2001). As Mathiassen (2002, p.337) notes, formalization of collaboration in action research projects is a critical management aspect because "both researchers and practitioners will otherwise easily mismanage their projects and find it difficult to meet goals and expectations". Indeed, this management aspect may be particularly important in situations where the power domination profile comprises "clients" who are outside the immediate project team (Avison et al., 2001).

The rationale behind action research is that researchers should assist practitioners in practical problem solving and through their direct involvement in organizational change be able to expand scientific knowledge. Targeting "the dual imperative of action research" (McKay & Marshall, 2001), a third management guideline concerns *the implementation of full learning cycles of understanding, supporting, and improving practice* (Mathiassen, 2002). In the context of action research, unplanned project cancellations are likely to render negative effects on researchers and practitioners alike. This is especially true for situations where the researchers have invested considerable efforts in developing the theoretical foundation after the problem was discovered. As asserted by Avison et al. (2001), a project cancellation may also leave the host organization in an even worse condition than initially diagnosed. Apparently, a critical aspect is the sequence of steps by which action research is conducted. The cyclical nature of action research suggests that both researchers and practitioners should be involved in problem diagnosis, action planning and taking, as well as evaluation and reflection. Progressing through the different phases in a sequential fashion will help ensure that action research projects are conducted with systematic rigor (Davison et al., 2004). Indeed, as noted by Lau (1999), the length of an action research study has to be adequate too, so that appropriate problem diagnosis, action interventions, and reflective learning can take place. In this way, dedicated research efforts can target a plethora of problems and issues as the research process unfolds (Mathiassen, 2002).

One of the basic tenets of action research is that complex social systems cannot be reduced for meaningful study. Essentially, this means that the factoring of a real-life setting into variables or components will not generate valuable knowledge about the whole organization (Baskerville, 1999). Rather, as noted by Baskerville (1999, p.4), "the fundamental contention of the action researcher is that complex social processes can be studied best by introducing changes into these processes and observing the effects of these changes". Following this, however, a danger in action research is that the researcher becomes too involved in the problems of practice, thus weakening the rigor of the research effort (Baskerville & Wood-Harper, 1996; Mathiassen, 2002). Therefore, it has been found that action researchers need to apply pluralist approaches and different methods as to deal effectively with both the richness and the challenges that characterize research efforts seeking to change real world practices (Mathiassen, 2002). Targeting the need for methods to guide and focus activities in the action research situation, a fourth management guideline concerns *the systematic collection of data and suitable methods of interpretation* (Mathiassen, 2002). In order to establish systematic documentation, various types of data can be used in action research ranging from interviews, observations, document review, focus groups, surveys to experiments (Lau, 1999; Mathiassen, 2002). As asserted by Lau (1999, p.166), "it is important to describe what types of data being used, how they are being systematically collected and analyzed, and why these data sources are considered dependable".

In sum, these four guidelines provide excellent support for researcher-client collaborations with the ambition to solve organizationally bounded problems. However, for the purpose of stimulating the active involvement of information systems researchers in industry projects where new technologies are developed and tried out (cf. Lyytinen & Yoo, 2002a), it is important to recognize how such research efforts can be created and managed. This is because action research situations in firms involved in NPD are likely to pose various challenges requiring tailored research efforts. An explicit understanding of the characteristics of action research situations in NPD thus contributes to making action research more feasible and rigorous for information systems researchers.

3.   NEW PRODUCT DEVELOPMENT

The capability to develop innovative new products is critical for a firm's long-term competitive advantage (Clark & Fujimoto, 1991). However, NPD is not only a significant means by which organizations develop new customer offers. As noted in the literature, NPD is also a process that is essential for organizations' ability to adapt, diversify, and reinvent their business propositions vis-à-vis evolving market and technical conditions (Brown & Eisenhardt, 1995; Schoonhoven, Eisenhardt, & Lyman, 1990). Arguably, this is particularly true for organizations in fast-paced or competitive markets characterized by rapidly changing customer requirements and technologies (Iansiti & MacCormack, 1997).

Given its centrality to competitive advantage, NPD has attracted considerable research attention over at least three decades (Brown & Eisenhardt, 1995). On a general level, NPD is typically understood as a series of business and engineering activities that include, for example, establishing product requirements, creating a product architecture, doing detailed design, and testing (Ulrich & Eppinger, 2000). As Brown and Eisenhardt (1995) assert, the NPD literature is extensive, ranging from theoretical explorations to in-depth case studies of product development across firms and industries. However, they identify two generic themes of NPD that are reiterated regardless of research stream: *product concept effectiveness* and *process performance*. As components of an integrative model, these generic themes help synthesize factors affecting product development. Whereas product concept effectiveness concerns factors with significance for the fit between a candidate product and market needs as well as firm competencies, process performance refers to factors critical for lead-time speed and productivity of NPD. Arguing that a product that is well planned, developed, and appropriately implemented will be a success, the NPD literature suggests a set of key activities for tackling the effects that product concept and development process factors have on product development, patterns of organizing, customer involvement, and so forth.

In the context of product concept effectiveness, different NPD activities have been proposed as to increase the fit between both customer requirements and firm competencies and the new products to be developed. Denoting virtually all time and activity invested in problem/opportunity structuring (Leifer et al., 2000) and information collection/exploration (March, 1995), the fuzzy front end is typically regarded as the earliest stage of the NPD process. As recognized by Reid and de Brentani (2004), the idea that the fuzzy front end involves processes of information gathering and adoption of external sources builds on the rationale that the environment is the primary source for innovations. Reflecting the notion of absorptive capacity "the ability of a firm to recognize the value of new information, assimilate it, and apply it to commercial ends" (Cohen & Levinthal, 1990, p.128), organizations capable of developing products that outperform their competitors in the marketplace have been shown to benefit from the acquisition and use of external information (Stock, Greis, & Fischer, 2001). As absorptive capacity may lead to better acquisition and application of external information to product development, organizational processes that link corporate-level and individual-level knowledge with new information from the environment are critical. Contemporary NPD firms often seek to organize such knowledge-integrating processes so that knowledgeable organizational members operate as boundary spanners and/or gatekeepers (Reid & de Brentani, 2004). By identifying and analyzing emerging patterns in the environment, these individuals play an important role in the process of determining what new environmental information means in terms of value construction. In this vein, "gatekeepers indirectly "champion" ideas for new product innovations at the fuzzy front end" (Reid & de Brentani, 2004, p.174).

Clearly, an important determinant for successful NPD processes is that the individual, the organization, and the environment are part of a network of interactions and knowledge exchange. However, leveraging customer needs fulfillment through such boundary-spanning knowledge networking activities has proved to be a difficult, time-consuming, and critical event (Tidd, Bessant, & Pavitt, 2001). Recent NPD literature has therefore suggested that users should be directly involved in the development process as to increase the likelihood of new product success (von Hippel & Katz, 2002). As explained by Kristensson, Gustafsson and Archer (2004, p.5), the underlying logic behind user involvement is that ideas generated in the user's own environment "seem more likely to contain those unique features that companies seek but which are difficult to detect". According to Joshi and Sharma (2004), customer knowledge development denotes an organizational process in which customer engage with new product ideas, concepts, and prototypes. Because prototypes can function as catalysts for shaping and determining new product concepts, prototyping has been identified as an activity of particular importance for increased product concept effectiveness in NPD processes (Baba & Tschang, 2001).

In NPD processes, identification of users' needs and assessments of various technological possibilities are key aspects for successful product project outcomes (Iansiti & MacCormack, 1997). However, as MacCormack, Verganti, and Iansiti (2001) recognize, handling such aspects in uncertain and dynamic environments is both risky and challenging. In this type of environments, fundamental changes are likely to occur in both the customer requirements that a product must address and the technology that offers the product its ability to meet these needs (Krishnan & Bhattacharya, 2002). Indeed, in fast-cycle and high technology industries where time-to-market is critical for sustaining competitive advantage and market share, firms seek organizing principles capable of catering for efficient and rapid NPD processes (Datar, Jordan, Kekre, Rajiv, & Srinivasan, 1997). In the context of process performance, the NPD literature proposes various activities for increasing lead-time speed and productivity. The stage-gate process model is one example of a NPD activity targeting risks associated with cost and quality objectives in product innovation processes (Cooper, 1993). As Joglekar & Rosenthal (2003, p.377) express, "the stage-gate process involves an explicit top-down approval sequence for developing an innovative idea and refining it until it results in a newly launched product". In this way, the process model provides both structure and vocabulary for managing time-critical and cross-functional product-oriented development processes.

Analyzing the sequential nature of the stage-gate model, (Cooper, 1993) discusses "fuzzy" gates as mechanisms allowing for some degree of overlap of development stages in NPD processes. Introduced to leverage increased organizational flexibility, such gates promise to increase lead-time speed by tackling development uncertainty (Joglekar & Rosenthal, 2003). To further reduce development uncertainty, the NPD literature provides guidelines for applying evaluation criteria at different gates of the NPD process (Hart, Hultink, Tzokas, & Caommandeur, 2003). Moreover, integration of technical tools in NPD processes has been recognized as a means to reduce development time and goal failure (Gerwin & Barrowman, 2002). As Halman, Hofer, and van Vuuren (2003) observe, more and more technology-driven firms implement platform thinking as a basis for creation and management of platform-based product families. To support firms seeking to cope with the complexity created by attempts to offer greater product variety, the platform-based product development approach suggests sharing of product architectures, components, modules, and other assets across a family of products (Halman et al., 2003). Indeed, as noted by Gerwin and Ferris (2004), such sharing of assets is a distinguished feature of NPD projects being organized as strategic alliances where jointly developed products form complementary parts of a larger-scale system.

Given this literature review, it is fair to say that action research in organizations engaged in NPD targeting clients outside the immediate organizational setting will likely differ from traditional action research efforts. Resulting from the fact that such clients are literally dispersed, the conditions and opportunities for their direct involvement in the action research situation are affected. Ultimately, this means that the action is taken in collaboration with a product development firm capable of supporting behavioral use patterns among these distant customers. We refer to this client as the wide-audience client (cf. Tuunainen, 2003), i.e., clients who are outside the immediate reach of the AR project. Compared to traditional action research, action research in NPD settings thus comprises at least three actor groups: researchers, client organization, and wide-audience clients. In view of this backdrop, we now set out to analyze a case of information systems action research that was conducted in the setting of new telematics functionality development for the Saab 9-3 car.

4.   RESEARCH SETTING

The research setting of this chapter consists of two earlier reported action research studies that were conducted as a joint action research project called "Mobile Services for In-Car User Value" (July 2002-June 2004). The first study (Henfridsson & Lindgren, 2005) was reported with the specific purpose of contributing to a special issue on ubiquitous computing in *Information & Organization* (Yoo & Lyytinen, 2005). This study outlines socio-technical implications of multi-contextuality in ubiquitous computing by developing and evaluating an in-car ubiquitous computing support system. Throughout this chapter, we refer to this study as the "multi-contextuality study". The second study (Olsson & Henfridsson, 2005) was reported with the specific purpose of contributing to the *IFIP WG 8.2-conference* on design of ubiquitous information environments (Sørensen & Yoo, 2005). This study explores an interactional context framework for context-aware applications by developing and testing a PDA-based context-aware game for entertainment experiences linked to car traveling. Throughout this chapter, we refer to this study as the "context-aware interaction study".

We used the canonical action research method (Davison et al., 2004; Susman & Evered, 1978) for jointly managing both these sub-projects. This method is characterized by its cyclical process model, rigorous structure, collaborative research involvement, and primary goals of organizational development and scientific knowledge (Baskerville & Wood-Harper, 1998). In collaboration with practitioners at Saab Automobile (car manufacturer), Mecel (automotive systems integrator), and Vodafone (mobile network operator), we followed Susman and Evered's (1978) five traditional action research phases: diagnosing, action planning, action taking, evaluating, and specifying learning. Table 8-1 provides an overview of the "Mobile Services for In-Car User Value"-project and its two studies. In this chapter, we return to the joint action research project, including both studies mentioned above, for identifying and exploring management aspects of action research in NPD.

Table 8-1. Overview of the "Mobile Services for In-Car User Value" project

Sub-projects	The Multi-Contextuality Study (Henfridsson & Lindgren, 2005)	The Context-Aware Interaction Study (Olsson & Henfridsson, 2005)
Research methodology	While the context-aware study used canonical action research (Davison et al., 2004; Susman & Evered, 1978) in its original form, the multi-contextuality study used a variant of canonical action research called grounded action research (Baskerville & Pries-Heje, 1999).	
Research goal	Outline socio-technical implications of multi-contextuality in ubiquitous computing.	Explore an interactional context framework for context-aware applications.
Practical goal	To improve Saab Automobile's NPD capability within personal telematics.	
Prototype description	SeamlessTalk is an in-car support system that facilitates driver control of Bluetooth-equipped cell phones brought into the car.	CABdriver Space is a PDA-based context-aware game that provides entertainment experiences linked to car traveling.

Saab Automobile's NPD within personal telematics was the setting for our action research project. Personal telematics refers to the integrated use of mobile devices and embedded computing platforms for providing in-car user services. Using personal area network and location-based technologies, personal telematics solutions provide temporary and synchronized networks between vehicles and mobile devices for leveraging the convenience and safety of using phone features such as multi-party chat, mp3 music, location aware games, position enhanced directory services, personal information management, and server-based navigation (Fuchs, 2003).

As highlighted by Joglekar and Rosenthal (2003), telematics solutions are product bundles consisting of physical goods (in-car hardware such as communication devices, networks, and microprocessors) and value-adding software features. While software features can be updated frequently, telematics hardware must be introduced in conjunction with new car models. Car-integrated hardware must be specified years before production start and cater for the cars' entire lifetime. Since telecommunications hardware is outdated in a few years, the lifecycle differences between the telecommunications and automotive industries are problematic for automakers in their development of telematic offers. Indeed, this is a barrier to automakers in efforts to keep pace with aftermarket providers of telematic services. For example, aftermarket firms such as TomTom present navigation services running on car-external low-cost devices to which the lifecycle differences mentioned above are irrelevant. In order to meet the competition of aftermarket providers, automakers are therefore seeking solutions that steer away from embedded car communication and computing systems. Personal telematics is an example of such a solution. Our project was motivated by Saab Automobile's interest in the personal telematics trend. Facing what is conceived as a paradigm change (Fuchs, 2003), Saab had to determine whether they would stick to stand-alone telematic systems, or change strategy to supporting people's in-car use of consumer electronics.

In this context, it is important to note that Saab Automobile is owned by General Motors (GM). Saab's product development is therefore intertwined with initiatives at GM Europe and Corporate levels. In order to better leverage investments in NPD, GM uses a platform-based approach (Halman et al., 2003) in which cross-brand considerations are critical. In our action research project, cross-brand considerations were made on the GM Europe level including, apart from Saab, the Opel and Vauxhall brands. Throughout the project, the project had to pass a number of stage-gate decisions (Cooper, 1993). In total, there were four gates including a presentation gate (preceding the start of the project) and a closure gate. Whereas the collaboration between action researchers and Saab representatives was characterized by a mutual commitment and understanding, the gates were occasions when the fate of the project was at stake.

5. A CASE OF ACTION RESEARCH IN NEW PRODUCT DEVELOPMENT

Without prior in-house experience of mobile devices and mobile user needs, a decision to equip production cars with personal telematics support can be considered radical for an automaker. The action research project was therefore a timely and suitable alternative for Saab to investigate this venue. Through the participation of Vodafone and Mecel, it also included telecommunications and car-related wireless technology competencies that automakers seldom possess. In addition, the Viktoria Institute's experience of applied research on mobile IT was considered useful. Thus, Saab's reasoning concurred with the strategic alliance tendency in developing new products in high-technology settings (cf. Gerwin & Ferris, 2004). Following the principle of researcher-client agreement (Davison et al., 2004), control structures were set up to handle the divergent nature of interest and emergent nature of the research focus. As an example, all project organizations signed an agreement specifying their roles and responsibilities. This agreement included resource allocations and regulations for the possible commercial utilization of the research results.

While the general focus on personal telematics was formulated in the project proposal submitted to the research agency, the diagnosing phase of the project was important to identify the specific directions of the project. In this phase, the action research group developed a comprehensive range of service concepts that would be interesting to evaluate in light of the personal telematics trend. Two of these were selected as candidates for full cycles of action research. They subsequently became the sub-projects referred to as the multi-contextuality and the context-aware interaction studies in this chapter. First, the multi-contextuality study (Henfridsson & Lindgren, 2005) addressed ways to support in-car use of cell phones. In particular, we were interested in how to develop in-car support systems with the capacity to contextualize the use of general mobile services. We used this empirical work to theorize about multi-contextuality, i.e., the co-existence of different use contexts in ubiquitous computing. Second, the context-aware interaction study (Olsson & Henfridsson, 2005) explored ways to create gaming experiences in cars by using vehicle data to extend games running on PDAs. We used this empirical work to theorize about context-aware applications that go beyond mainstream applications that approximate context with location (see Schmidt, Beigl, & Gellersen, 1999).

As early as in the diagnosing phase, we discovered some essential differences between the client-system infrastructure (Susman & Evered, 1978) of this action research project and traditional, non-NPD, ones (e.g., Lindgren et al., 2004). Whereas the starting-point of the project was Saab Automobile's product development within personal telematics, we soon realized that the action taken in the project could not only be evaluated vis-à-vis the client organization's problem setting. Without relations to end users, who eventually would use the products, the "relative truth-value of the theoretical concepts underlying the action" would be poorly evaluated (Baskerville & Myers, 2004). In addition, we reasoned that including experiences originating from users' own environment was likely to generate features that cannot be detected otherwise (Kristensson et al., 2004).

Indeed, the personal telematics trend basically follows from the tremendous consumer uptake of mobile devices in recent years (Fuchs, 2003). The standardization of underlying technologies in cell phones, smart phones, PDAs, and mp3-players has created a global, mass-scale, market. It is therefore not surprising that small-volume dedicated in-car devices are difficult to market and sell for automakers. Rather than purchasing expensive add-ons to their cars, people tend to settle with their cell phone equipped with a wired hands-free solution for enabling cell phone use in cars. Given this tendency, we therefore targeted our action research to the needs of two clients – Saab Automobile and wide-audience clients. The action research group concluded that future personal telematic solutions must build on emerging in-car device use patterns. Thus, we reasoned that an investigation of particularities of everyday mobility with implications for personal telematics would be useful.

In the multi-contextuality study, we therefore decided to use a variant of canonical action research called grounded action research (Baskerville & Pries-Heje, 1999). A central feature of the grounded action research method is its use of the data analysis techniques of grounded theory (Strauss & Corbin, 1998) for theory formulation. Open, axial, and selective coding were accordingly used for complementing practical intervention with an inductive and systematic way of generating qualitative and empirically validated insights. This grounded approach was motivated by our critical need of understanding the incentives and problems associated with mobile device use in cars. To this end, the project's first encounter with wide-audience clients consisted of an interview study involving 18 IT professionals and frequent cell phone users. We collected narratives and episodes of car-related cell phone usage that would give the wide-audience client a voice in the research process to come. By identifying and analyzing emerging patterns of mobile technology use in the environment, the researchers became a type of boundary spanners performing a gatekeeping function in the action research project (cf. Reid & de Brentani, 2004). Our data analysis yielded categories and concepts that depicted typical aspects of such usage (Henfridsson & Lindgren, 2005). These study results became important inputs to the project's agenda in that they guided our prototype development and action taking. Given the hedonic character of the context-aware study, the corresponding grounding in existing use patterns was not applicable. The canonical action research method was therefore used in its original form (Susman & Evered, 1978), in which the diagnosing and action planning phases were guided primarily by a combination of a theoretical framework (Dourish, 2001a, 2001b, 2004) and Saab's product development problems. Representatives for the wide-audience client entered this study first in the evaluation phase of the project.

Reflecting the notion that prototypes can function as catalysts for shaping and determining new product concepts (Baba & Tschang, 2001), a central methodological aspect of the action research project was its design-orientation. Both studies were designed to develop and test design principles for ubiquitous computing support systems in car settings. To assess these two sets of design principles, we developed two prototypes – SeamlessTalk (Henfridsson & Lindgren, 2005: see Figure 8-1) and CABdriver (Olsson, 2004; Olsson & Henfridsson, 2005: see Figure 8-2) as fully integrated systems of the Saab 9-3 model. SeamlessTalk is an in-car support system that facilitates driver control of Bluetooth-equipped cell phones brought into the car. CABdriver Space is a PDA-based context-aware game that provides entertainment experiences linked to car traveling.

Figure 8-1. SeamlessTalk is controlled by the multi-functional control of the infotainment system

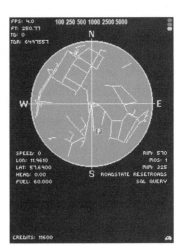

Figure 8-2. CABdriver Space screenshots

We opted for prototypes that would be tested in a real-life setting for a longer period of everyday use. This objective proved to be both costly and risky. First, the real-life ambitions meant that we had to integrate the prototypes with the existing in-car computing platform of the Saab 9-3 model. While the choice of this computing platform was important for authenticity, it also linked the fate of our action research to Saab's market strategy for the 9-3 model. Second, substantial resources were consumed on developing functionality that linked the in-car computing platform with external mobile devices using the Bluetooth protocol stack. Since this had to be reliable even outside the lab, it was imperative to reduce errors related to implementation to a minimum level. Despite Mecel's solid competence in Bluetooth technology, this prototype developmental goal was costly in terms of both time and resources.

Coinciding with the evaluation phase of the project, a termination threat emerged. Since all forms of new employments were stopped at Saab at the time, the job move of one key Saab member of the action research project threatened Saab's participation in the evaluation phase. The completion of a full learning cycle of understanding, supporting, and improving practice was at stake (cf. Mathiassen, 2002). After a few weeks' ambiguity, the car infotainment manager managed to save the project by re-allocating resources in the form of labor from another project. The termination threat halted the start of an already compressed evaluation phase. The compression of this phase was associated with its complexity. Developed for evaluating design principles, for instance, the prototypes required a rigorously administrated evaluation process.

We conducted a joint two-month evaluation of both prototypes and the design principles embedded in them. By modifying five families' private Saab 9-3 cars, we could use these families as representatives of the wide-audience client. They evaluated the SeamlessTalk and CABdriver Space prototypes in their everyday mobility for two months. Extensive coordination was required for matching their everyday car needs with available time slots at a busy Saab workshop. We also replaced the respondents' personal cell phones with SeamlessTalk-compatible 3G phones provided by Vodafone, meaning that we had to transfer contact lists to new SIM-cards and calls were re-directed from their ordinary phone numbers to new ones. In the CABdriver case, respondents were equipped with PDAs running the CABdriver client software. As most of the respondents lacked hands-on PDA experience, the action research group had to give basic PDA training, apart from a general CABdriver introduction. Given this administrative workload, we had to coordinate the SeamlessTalk and CABdriver evaluations.

In modifying the participants' cars, we intended to install flight recorders facilitating quantitative data collection and analysis of prototype use. However, in view of other costly and complex problems associated with realizing the evaluation this installation was cancelled at a late stage. Especially in the SeamlessTalk case, this was unfortunate since quantitative data could have been valuable for triangulating findings gained through qualitative methods such as interviews. Because of the integrated evaluation, up-coming stage-gates, as well as scarce project resources, we could not postpone the evaluation phase to make flight recorded data possible.

6.   DISCUSSION

The importance of controlling and managing action research projects has been recently highlighted in information systems action research literature (Avison et al., 2001; Davison et al., 2004; Lau, 1999; Mathiassen, 2002). Such management is important as to secure that the action research conducted contribute simultaneously to both rigor and relevance. Our literature review highlights four general guidelines for accomplishing this: *the identification and specification of a situation where problems exist*; *the formalization of collaboration between practitioners and researchers*; *the implementation of full learning cycles of understanding, supporting, and improving practice*; and *the systematic collection of data and suitable methods of interpretation.*

This chapter explores the nature of action research in NPD settings. Characterized by pressures associated with product concept effectiveness and process performance (Brown & Eisenhardt, 1995), NPD can be a challenging but rewarding setting for articulating the new conditions for information systems action research. The promise of action research in such development is the possibility to build alliances with those who drive technological change (cf. Lyytinen & Yoo, 2002a). As a large portion of our new technologies are developed and packaged as products, the claimed contribution of action research to relevance (Baskerville & Myers, 2004) would be stronger in the case that the methodology was applicable beyond organizational development. Thus, we believe that it is vital to understand the challenges of conducting action research in product development settings.

The action research study re-assessed in this chapter was conducted in the setting of Saab Automobile's product development within personal telematics. Throughout our canonical action research study (Davison et al., 2004; Susman & Evered, 1978), we encountered a set of problems that is atypical to previously reported information systems action research. Whereas existing guidelines for managing action research are useful in their generic form, there exist additional implications for managing action research in NPD. In what follows, we will outline these as a set of advices to researchers who intend to conduct action research in NPD. Table 8-2 outlines a summary of this discussion.

Table 8-2. Implications for managing action research in NPD

NPD themes	Case highlights	AR management guidelines	Advices to action researchers in NPD
Product concept effectiveness	- Researcher-client agreement - Two sub-projects singled out - Additional client: future end-users - Two prototypes - Researchers became wide-audience spoke-persons	- Identification and specification of a situation where problems exist - Formalization of collaboration between practitioners and researchers	- Diagnose the wide-audience problem situation - Mediate the wide-audience client role throughout the project
Process performance	- Termination threats - Costly car-prototype integration - High administrative workload in evaluation phase - Quantitative data collection cancelled at a late stage	- Full learning cycles of understanding, supporting, and improving practice - Systematic collection of data and suitable methods of interpretation	- Secure intermediate research results - Develop pluralist data collection strategies for time-dependent evaluations

Diagnose the wide-audience problem situation: The early stages of an action research project are typically geared towards identifying and specifying a situation where problems exist (cf. Avison et al., 2001). In the literature, it is typically assumed that such a situation is found within an organization. The action research team, composed by both researchers and practitioners, diagnoses the organizationally bounded situation as to identify its underlying causes (Baskerville & Wood-Harper, 1998).

Following this logic, the diagnosing phase of our project started in Saab Automobile's problem setting. In identifying their causes, however, we realized that Saab's NPD problems were intertwined with an additional client: future end users of telematic products. We refer to this client as the wide-audience client (cf. Tuunainen, 2003), i.e., clients who are outside the immediate reach of the AR project. Indeed, looking into the emerging use patterns of such clients seemed necessary to handle Saab's problem situation.

Design intensive products cannot be tightly linked to experienced use problems in real-life situations (Baba & Tschang, 2001). In the "context-aware interaction study", this difficulty was manifested in that existing use patterns did not exist. As a result, the diagnosing phase had to rely on discussions held at the action research project meetings. These discussions directed us to literature on context-aware computing and the notion of context. However, the wide-audience client was included in the evaluation phase by completing the CABdriver prototype evaluation including the five families mentioned earlier. In the "multi-contextuality study", we managed to generate design principles on the basis of incentives and problems found in existing mobile device use in cars. The wide-audience client was therefore part of both the diagnosing and evaluation phases.

An implication of the dual client of action research in NPD settings is that *the wide-audience problem situation needs to be diagnosed* (see Figure 8-3). The client organization's product development problem needs to be linked to problems related to a wide-audience client. Apparently, because NPD often is concerned with products without counterparts on the market, this can be challenging. Despite many types of action research methodologies (Baskerville & Wood-Harper, 1998), these exists little support for analyzing relations between client organizations and wide-audience clients. In particular, support for determining the type of diagnosis needed to substantiate different product concepts seems to be critical. In our action research, tools and techniques for locating relevant use experiences and settings could have helped us in diagnosing the product concept effectiveness of the two studies at an early stage.

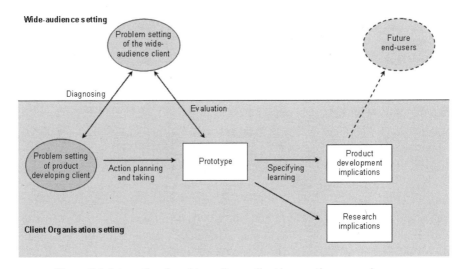

Figure 8-3. Integrating the wide-audience client in an action research process

Mediate the wide-audience client role throughout the project: The formalization of collaboration between practitioners and clients in action research projects is typically done in order to develop and determine control structures for managing the divergent nature of interests involved (Avison et al., 2001; Davison et al., 2004; Mathiassen, 2002). In our case, many of these matters were regulated by an agreement signed for specifying roles and responsibilities of the participating organizations.

However, in the context of action research in NPD, wide-audience clients cannot participate directly in formalizing and executing the researcher-client agreement. Given their centrality to a sound action research process, wide-audience clients may therefore be represented by the action researchers throughout the research process. Thus, apart from diagnosing wide-audience clients' problems, we believe that it is important that action researchers *mediate the wide-audience client role throughout an action research project* in NPD. Using existing guidelines for managing and controlling action research (e.g., Davison et al., 2004), information systems action researchers conducting projects in NPD need to negotiate terms for assessing the wide-audience client view throughout the entire research process. Essential to the field of information systems, such negotiation is important to balance the social and technical elements of NPD in seeking the phenomena that emerge when these two elements interact (cf. Lee, 2001).

A notable difference between representatives for the wide-audience client (e.g., interviewees and prototype evaluators) and client organization participants is the weaker viewpoint of the wide-audience client. In investigating wide-audience views in both the diagnosing and evaluating phases, we were urged to take on a larger responsibility in the project by acting as spokespersons for them. The wide-audience data collected in the diagnosing and evaluation phases was not only important input in directing the action research project (see Figure 8-3), but also a necessary component for making contributions to the field of information systems. Consequently, we recommend researchers who embark on action research in NPD to not only serve the client organization but also the wide-audience client. Not the least, representing the client outside the action research project team can reinforce the action researchers' power and control over the research process (cf. Avison et al., 2001).

Secure intermediate research results: Mathiassen (2002) highlights the importance of implementing full learning cycles of understanding, supporting, and improving practice. This is critical because unexpected project cancellations can have negative effects for both researchers and practitioners.

Given pressures to increase lead-time speed and productivity (Brown & Eisenhardt, 1995), NPD is a risky context for action research. Our study indicates that stage-gate processes (Cooper, 1993), time-to-market pressures (Datar et al., 1997), and platform-based development (Halman et al., 2003) made the project vulnerable throughout the entire process. As an example, the stage-gate procedure used at Saab Automobile and GM played an important role in the management of the project. One critical moment occurred in autumn 2002 when Saab was obliged by GM to do an extensive project-shakeout because of the firm's weak profitability. At the electronics division, almost all research (i.e., long-term) projects had to be put on hold. In fact, only short-term implementation projects were sanctioned. However, the project was eventually sustained by the co-funding by VINNOVA and that the car infotainment manager at Saab managed to re-classify the project as a development project.

It is imperative to manage risks by developing exit strategies as to *secure intermediate research results.* Such strategies should enable the publication of insights and results at various stages of the project. In retrospect, we would have been better positioned to do this if we had not designed the project as a single cycle but as multiple cycles of understanding, supporting, and improving practice. Multiple cycles would offer more suitable points of entry in terms of knowledge contributions. Generally, designing multiple cycles can be difficult given the linear character of stage-gated NPD processes. We therefore recommend action researchers and practitioners to negotiate a combined process that align multiple cycles of inquiry with this accepted practice of NPD.

Develop pluralist data collection strategies for time-dependent evaluations: Our literature review illustrates that systematic collection of data and suitable methods of interpretation is an important element in managing action research (see Mathiassen, 2002). The richness of research processes that seek to change real world processes make pluralist approaches to data collection valuable.

The realism needed in evaluating action taking in NPD settings is a major task as it may involve product concepts that do not previously exist. Ultimately, this makes evaluations of innovative concepts both costly and risky. In our case, the integration of the CABdriver and SeamlessTalk prototypes with the computing platform of Saab 9-3 demanded considerable coordination as to secure realistic evaluation. First, the fact that we used the private cars of five families required a firm evaluation period that was feasible for all of them. Second, given our ambition to evaluate different use situations (e.g., everyday commuting, traveling between work and customer sites, weekend trips), the timing of the evaluation period was important. Given these constraints in combination with the overall NPD pressures, we had to make trade-offs in doing this. For example, an appropriate data source such as flight recorders was cancelled at a late stage. Even more important, the data collection that we actually performed was heavily time-dependent.

Whereas evaluations in action research efforts always are situationally dependent, we believe that the seemingly single-time character of our evaluation has general implications for technology-intense action research. Rather than applying pluralist approaches that prescribe data collection over longer time periods, we recommend action researchers who embark on research in NPD to *develop pluralist data collection strategies for time-dependent evaluations.*

7. CONCLUSION

This chapter has generated a set of advices to action researchers who intend to conduct action research in NPD settings. These advices are: *diagnose the wide-audience problem situation; manage the wide-audience client role throughout the project; secure intermediate research results;* and *develop pluralist data collection strategies for time-dependent evaluations.* The proposed advices conform to extant guidelines for managing and controlling action research, but highlight ways to handle specific product development aspects that the generic guidelines virtually overlook.

Looking at the information systems literature, action research in NPD is rare. We believe that this is unfortunate since such research can play an important role in making information systems researchers part of the settings in which new technologies are developed and tried out (cf. Lyytinen & Yoo, 2002a). NPD involving IT-artifacts is dependent on the successful configuration and cultivation of business, organizational, and technological elements. In this regard, information systems researchers are well positioned for investigating product development processes through active participation.

A possible reason as to why action research has played a marginal role in product development settings is that existing action research methodologies provide limited support for conducting such research. Since product development *per se* involves products and is design-oriented, the process orientation found in most action research methodologies might be a disincentive to pursue action research in NPD settings. One example of insufficient product-orientation in extant information systems action research methodologies is their general lack of support for using artifacts as to simultaneously contributing to theory and practice (cf. Lindgren et al., 2004). More research into such methodological support is therefore important. This chapter is a modest attempt to go in this direction.

ACKNOWLEDGMENTS

VINNOVA and the participating organizations funded this work. We are also indebted to all industry participants of our action research project. Special thanks to our colleague Carl Magnus Olsson. Thanks are also due to the book editor, Ned Kock, and three anonymous reviewers for their useful comments.

REFERENCES

Avison, D., Baskerville, R., & Myers, M. (2001). Controlling action research projects. *Information Technology & People, 14*(1), 28-45.

Baba, Y., & Tschang, F. T. (2001). Product development in japanese tv game software: The case of an innovative game. *International Journal of Innovation Management, 5*(4), 487-515.

Baskerville, R. (1999). Investigating information systems with action research. *Communication of the AIS, 2*.

Baskerville, R., & Myers, M. D. (2004). Special issue on action research in information systems: Making is research relevant to practice - foreword. *MIS Quarterly, 28*(3), 329-335.

Baskerville, R., & Pries-Heje, J. (1999). Grounded action research: A method for understanding it in practice. *Accounting, Management & Information Technologies, 9*, 1-23.

Baskerville, R. L., & Wood-Harper, A. T. (1996). A critical perspective on action research as a method for information systems research. *Journal of Information Technology, 11*, 235-246.

Baskerville, R. L., & Wood-Harper, A. T. (1998). Diversity in information systems action research methods. *European Journal of Information Systems, 7*(2), 90-107.

Brown, S. L., & Eisenhardt, K. M. (1995). Product development: Past research, present findings, and future directions. *Academy of Management Review, 20*(2), 343-378.

Chiasson, M., & Dexter, A. (2001). What can we conclude when an action research process doesn't work: Implications for practice and research. *Information Technology & People, 14*(1), 91-108.

Clark, K. B., & Fujimoto, T. (1991). *Product development performance.*Boston, MA: Harvard Business School Press.

Cohen, W. M., & Levinthal, D. A. (1990). Absorptive capacity: A new perspective on learning and innovation. *Administrative Science Quarterly, 35*(1), 128-152.

Cooper, R. G. (1993). *Winning at new products: Accelerating the process from idea to launch.*Reading, MA: Addison-Wesley.

Datar, S., Jordan, C., Kekre, S., Rajiv, S., & Srinivasan, K. (1997). New product development structures and time-to-market. *Management Science, 43*(4), 452-464.

Davison, R. M., Martinsons, M. G., & Kock, N. (2004). Principles of canonical action research. *Information Systems Journal, 14*, 65-86.

Dourish, P. (2001). Seeking a foundation for context-aware computing. *Human-Computer Interaction, 16*(2-4), 229-241.

Dourish, P. (2001). *Where the action is: The foundations of embodied interaction.*Cambridge, MA: MIT Press.

Dourish, P. (2004). What we talk about when we talk about context. *Personal and Ubiquitous Computing, 8*, 19-30.

Fuchs, A. (2003). Personal telematics - a global paradigm change. *Telematics Update Magazine*(21), 14-15.

Gerwin, D., & Barrowman, N. J. (2002). An evaluation of research on integrated product development. *Management Science, 48*(7), 938-953.

Gerwin, D., & Ferris, J. S. (2004). Organizing new product development projects in strategic alliances. *Organization Science, 15*(1), 22-37.

Halman, J. I. M., Hofer, A. P., & van Vuuren, W. (2003). Platform-driven development of product families: Linking theory with practice. *Journal of Product Innovation Management, 20*, 149-162.

Hart, S., Hultink, E. J., Tzokas, N., & Caommandeur, H. R. (2003). Industrial comapnies' evaluation criteria in new product development gates. *Journal of Product Innovation Management, 20,* 22-36.

Henfridsson, O., & Lindgren, R. (2005). Multi-contextuality in ubiquitous computing: Investigating the car case through action research. *Information and Organization, 15*(2), 95-124.

Iansiti, M., & MacCormack, A. (1997). Developing products on internet time. *Harvard Business Review, 75*(5), 108-117.

Iversen, J. H., Mathiassen, L., & Nielsen, P. A. (2004). Managing risk in software process improvement: An action research approach. *MIS Quarterly, 28*(3), 395-433.

Joglekar, N. R., & Rosenthal, S. R. (2003). Coordination of design supply chains for bundling physical and software products. *Journal of Product Innovation Management, 20,* 374-390.

Joshi, A. W., & Sharma, S. (2004). Customer knowledge development: Antecedents and impact on new product performance. *Journal of Marketing, 68*(October), 47-59.

Krishnan, V., & Bhattacharya. (2002). Technology selection and commitment in new product development: The role of uncertainty and design flexibility. *Management Science, 48*(3), 313-327.

Kristensson, P., Gustafsson, A., & Archer, T. (2004). Harnessing the creative potential among users. *Journal of Product Innovation Management, 21,* 4-14.

Lau, F. (1999). Toward a framework for action research in information systems studies. *Information Technology & People, 12*(2), 148-175.

Lee, A. (2001). Editorial. *MIS Quarterly, 25*(1), iii-vii.

Leifer, R., McDermott, C. M., Colarelli O'Connor, G., Peters, L. S., Rice, M., & Veryzer, R. W. (2000). *Radical innovation: How mature companies can outsmart upstarts.*Boston, MA: Harvard Business School Press.

Lindgren, R., Henfridsson, O., & Schultze, U. (2004). Design principles for competence management systems: A synthesis of an action research study. *MIS Quarterly, 28*(3), 435-472.

Lyytinen, K., & Yoo, Y. (2002a). Research commentary: The next wave of nomadic computing. *Information Systems Research, 13*(4), 377-388.

MacCormack, A., Verganti, R., & Iansiti, M. (2001). Developing products on "internet time": The anatomy of a flexible development process. *Management Science, 47*(1), 133-150.

March, J. G. (1995). Exploration and exploitation in organizational learning. In M. D. Cohen & L. S. Sproull (Eds.), *Organizational learning* (Vol. 2, pp. 101-123). Thousand Oaks: SAGE.

Mathiassen, L. (2002). Collaborative practice research. *IT & People, 15*(4), 321-345.

McKay, J., & Marshall, P. (2001). The dual imperatives of action research. *IT & People, 14*(1), 46-59.

Mårtensson, P., & Lee, A. S. (2004). Dialogical action research at omega corporation. *MIS Quarterly, 28*(3), 507-536.

Olsson, C. M. (2004). Exploring the impact of a context-aware application for in-car use. *Proceedings of 25th ICIS,* 11-21.

Olsson, C. M., & Henfridsson, O. (2005). Designing context-aware interaction: An action research study. In C. Sorensen, Y. Yoo, K. Lyytinen & J. I. DeGross (Eds.), *Designing ubiquitous information environments: Socio-technical issues and challenges* (pp. 233-247). Cleveland, OH: Springer.

Reid, S. E., & de Brentani, U. (2004). The fuzzy frond end of new product development for discontinuous innovations: A theoretical model. *Journal of Product Innovation Management, 21,* 170-184.

Sawyer, S. (2000). Packaged software: Implications of the differences from custom approaches to software development. *European Journal of Information Systems, 9*, 47-58.

Schmidt, A., Beigl, M., & Gellersen, H.-W. (1999). There is more to context than location. *Computers & Graphics, 23*(6), 893-901.

Schoonhoven, C. B., Eisenhardt, K. M., & Lyman, K. (1990). Speeding products to market: Waiting time fo first product introduction in new firms. *Administrative Science Quarterly, 35*(1), 177-207.

Stock, G. N., Greis, N. P., & Fischer, W. A. (2001). Absorptive capacity and new product development. *Journal Of High Technology Management Research, 12*, 77-91.

Strauss, A., & Corbin, J. (1998). *Basics of qualitative research: Techniques and procedures for developing grounded theory* (2 ed.). Thousands Oaks, CA: SAGE.

Street, C. T., & Meister, D. B. (2004). Small business growth and internal transparency: The role of information systems. *MIS Quarterly, 28*(3), 473-506.

Susman, G., & Evered, R. (1978). An assessment of the scientific merits of action research. *Administrative Science Quarterly, 23*, 582-603.

Sørensen, C., & Yoo, Y. (2005). Socio-technical studies of mobility and ubiquity. In C. Sørensen, Y. Yoo, K. Lyytinen & J. I. DeGross (Eds.), *Designing ubiquitous information environments: Socio-technical issues and challenges* (pp. 1-14). New York: Springer.

Tidd, J., Bessant, J., & Pavitt, K. (2001). *Managing innovation.*New York: John Wiley.

Tuunainen, T. (2003). A new perspective on requirements elicitation methods. *Journal of Information Technology Theory and Application, 5*(3), 45-72.

Ulrich, K., & Eppinger, S. (2000). *Product design and development.*New York: McGraw-Hill.

von Hippel, E., & Katz, R. (2002). Shifting innovation to users via toolkits. *Management Science, 48*(7), 821-833.

Yoo, Y., & Lyytinen, K. (2005). Social impacts of ubiquitous computing: Exploring critical interactions between mobility, context and technology - a special issue for information and organization. *Information and Organization, 15*(2), 91-94.

Chapter 9

ACTION RESEARCH IN A VIRTUAL SETTING
Cautions from a Failed Project

Darren B. Meister and Christopher M. Gronski
The University of Western Ontario, Canada

Abstract: Virtual teams are used by leading companies around the world to address important business problems and to support critical business operations. However, the best ways of providing leadership and managing technological-based change within these teams remain challenges for the practitioner and research communities. In this project, we describe how, as part of a research team, we participated in an Action Research project within a virtual setting. While we gained insights along the way, ultimately the project failed. From this failure, we draw our personal conclusions about what happened and what Action Researchers may do in the future to avoid such problems again.

Key words: Virtual teams, action research, learning from failure

1. INTRODUCTION

Organizations have increasingly adopted virtual teams as part of their normal operations. As companies – even small ones – have extended their customer base globally, employees have become more geographically distributed. This growth has not been limited to one functional area of business. Rather, research, development, marketing and manufacturing have all increasingly used virtual teams (McDonough et al. 2001).

The term virtual team has been defined across several fields of study (Dubé and Paré 2002) and exist in various different configurations (Jackson 1999; Crampton 2001; Bell and Kozlowski 2002). In this study, we adopted a definition consistent with others (DeSanctis and Poole 1997; Jarvenpaa et al. 1998; Powell et al. 2004): a virtual team is a organizational grouping with a significant portion of its membership in different locations whose dominant communication is via telecommunications media, such as email, phone, teleconferencing, videoconference, etc.. The virtual team is assumed to be working towards a particular goal or goals that might be either the completion of a project or an on-going managerial or technical matter. While team members might meet face-to-face occasionally, the dominant form of communication within our teams of interest was telecommunications based. Hence, the teams are said to operate in a virtual setting.

Action Researchers are often located at a different physical location from their practice partners. Further, employees within these companies are not always in the same location. However, the degree to which the practitioners and Action Researchers might be separated increases significantly in a virtual team setting. Now, the researchers may never physically visit the research site, partly because the company team is distributed globally and partly because there really is no physical site to visit.

A virtual setting is a challenging environment to manage for companies. It is also an area of active on-going research interest. This combination – relevance to both practice and research – makes it an interesting setting in which to use Action Research, a research methodology that adopts the perspective that research and practice inquiry are not dialectically opposed. Rather, an Action Researcher believes that these two types of inquiry can inform one another in a constructive manner. Our research team felt that Action Research was an appropriate methodology to take into the virtual setting.

However the virtual setting poses novel challenges for an Action Researcher. As it is generally thought of, Action Research requires close interaction of the researcher and practitioners, often through intensive meetings. Commonly, this occurs in face-to-face meetings. However, when working with virtual teams, meeting face-to-face can become prohibitively expensive or it may even be impossible. Therefore, an Action Researcher is left with a choice, either to avoid virtual team settings or to develop guidelines that make Action Research work within this context.

This chapter seeks to understand if Action Research in a virtual setting is different, and what methodological steps Action Researchers can take to collaborate with virtual teams more effectively. In this paper, we will present our research design. Unfortunately, we had three related attempts before ultimately being forced to abandon the project. Within this context, we hope that our cautionary tale will help researchers better address this setting.

2.   BENEFITS OF ACTION RESEARCH IN A VIRTUAL SETTING

Why use Action Research in this setting, rather than another methodology such as case studies, surveys or ethnographies? For us, a primary reason was to engage a company with a problem that was of real interest. Rather than convincing a company that the benefits of our research would come to them in the long run or by formulating plans based on our results, we were interested in our results being their results, actionable items that were tested, evaluated and refined through dialogue. In many respects, this is a philosophical choice on the part of the researcher, a statement of how they intend to do research. We understood that perhaps we would trade off generalizability for a more nuanced understanding of the phenomenon that we wished to study. Nevertheless, Action Research is a challenging research methodology, and potentially more difficult in a virtual setting (Pauleen 2004).

First though, there are benefits in adopting Action Research when investigating a virtual setting. Not surprisingly, most are related to releasing the researcher from physical constraints. Apart from the obvious convenience of being able to conduct field research from the comfort of one's office, the possible breadth of study can be extended by allowing for full international field research without the expense of travel. On the business side, these conveniences were part of the motivation behind creating virtual teams in the first place. Business executives could participate in meetings using collaborative software, videoconferencing, or something as simple as the telephone, allowing people to "virtually" be in two places at one time.

Another benefit is that it leaves the practitioners in their *native environment*, which is quite different than assembling them for a meeting. It can be argued that the Action Researcher is less intrusive participating virtually rather than being co-located with the team in the field, possibly reducing biases such as the Hawthorne effect (Street and Meister 2004).

A third benefit of virtual research is that it presents the Action Researcher with a realistic representation of the research site, including time management challenges in the work environment. Also, the researcher needs to coordinate their schedule around virtual meetings, and manage competing time demands as opposed to the artificial situation where a time period– perhaps a half-day, day or more – is set aside and dedicated to the research project. Rather, the researcher needs to integrate research requirements into their daily routine. Also, time zone differences between the Action Researcher and other members of the virtual team could mean late night or early morning meetings, outside of one's regular day. Though sometimes time zone differences can allow work to go on "around the clock" (Haywood 1998), it can be challenging to manage these differences.

The entire experience helps the Action Researcher with contextualization, providing the researcher's audience with a proper background and context to the research setting so that the audience may understand how the situation under investigation came to be. In addition it allows the Action Researcher to critically reflect on how the social construction of the data through researcher participant interaction (Klein and Myers 1999).

There are convenience factors as well. It is quite possible that at least a portion of the Action Researcher's study can be self documenting in the virtual setting. This occurs due to the use of e-mail, chat, or other text based forms of communication. However not having to be physically present for field research is a *double edged sword*, the Action Researcher's lack of physical presence can also make research more difficult.

In order to conduct this project, we adopted a framework based on Susman and Everend (1978) as shown in Figure 9-1. For each of the stages we saw some potential difficulties that were introduced over and above those typical for Action Research. The next section outlines some issues that we anticipated.

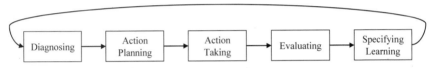

Figure 9-1. Action Research Framework (Susman and Everend 1978)

3.   CHALLENGES OF ACTION RESEARCH IN A VIRTUAL SETTING

As in many things, the benefits of using Action Research in this setting can also be cast as negatives. For example, in a typical action research project, the researcher spends time co-located with the practitioners to acclimatize themselves to the organization and the issues at hand. In a virtual setting, there is no true "site" to visit - and therefore less imposition - but visiting the team can become much more complicated. For example, twenty-four hours of site exposure can easily take twenty-four weeks to achieve, if it is all done attending weekly virtual meetings. This extended timeline may leave the organization wondering what the research team is doing "all this time".

This leads to the challenge of maintaining a presence. Like a telecommuter, their lack of physical presence requires them to justify their contribution to the organization much more rigorously than employees who are co-located (Westfall 2004). There is an old adage that says "out of sight out of mind". This could be the fate that befalls the Action Researcher. Overall, this increased the difficulty in building credibility with the practitioners.

The Action Researcher's lack of physical presence at their research site also means they are not privy to things such as casual side conversations, meeting people by chance in elevators, and the like. While this places them on an equal footing with other virtual team members, it removes an important communication channel. Various technologies such as instant messaging can be used to initiate informal side conversations but these are likely not a full substitute due to the task requirements (Daft and Lengel 1986; Dennis and Kinney 1998).

Overall, we were quite concerned about our ability in a virtual setting to get a good handle on existing strengths and weakness. However, we believed it to be very important to develop this baseline in order to provide a firm grounding for recommendations and a credible foundation for evaluation of interventions. This lead us to believe that we would need to spend what might seem to be an above-average amount of time in the initial diagnosing phase.

After diagnosis is completed though, the Action Researcher wants to introduce some interventions into the environment. This too is potentially more complicated in the virtual setting. Most managers are not going to take advice from someone who is not engaged and not really accountable for the results of their actions. It is only by achieving true membership on a team that the researcher can effectively introduce interventions. Developing team membership takes a clear role and responsibility and the development of trust. In a virtual setting this can be more difficult (Jarvenpaa and Leidner 1999)

One way to build trust is through face-to-face meetings. This is a paradox about virtual teams: they seem to function better with face-to-face contact, whereas their very nature would indicate face-to-face contact does not regularly occur. Face-to-face communication is important as it is arguably the "surest way to establish and nurture the human relationships underlying business relationships. These relationships are grounded in social bonding and symbolic expressions of commitment (Hinds and Kiesler 2002)".

Trust is important in all virtual relationships (McKnight et al. 1998; Newell and Swan 2000; Paul and McDaniel 2004), therefore it is important for the Action Researcher to build trust during their research into virtual teams. To build trust the researcher must follow through on obligations they have made to the team (Morrison and Robinson 1997; Piccoli and Ives 2003). While in all research this is important, it can be more difficult in a virtual setting.

In addition to these communication concerns, virtual teams have a harder time converging to a decision than co-located teams (McDonough et al. 2001). In some ways this difficultly provides a research opportunity to the Action Researcher, since convergence may be required for the researcher's interventions. The likelihood of convergence can be increased by agreeing to a process for decision making at the start so that method can be followed at a later date, as well as holding offline meetings between representatives with rival views (Mittleman et al. 2000).

In spite of these challenges, we felt that the benefits were greater, particularly in being able to make a unique contribution to the research literature. In the next section, we will discuss how we began to develop our Action Research project in collaboration with our practitioner partners.

4.   THE CONTEXT

Our study occurred in a large, well-known global manufacturing firm, which we will call GlobalCo. GlobalCo designs and manufactures its products on nearly every continent, serving a global clientele. Its customer service strategy mandates that it serve its customers as a single global firm, rather than as a set of coordinated nation-level companies. For example, a customer in Germany, China, or the United States deals with GlobalCo, not a local company.

This means that to coordinate regular operations and projects, GlobalCo relies extensively on virtual teams. In our preliminary discussions, one team manager stated that "almost all of my meetings – even with my local colleagues – are conducted via teleconference." We were told – and confirmed in subsequent telephone conversations – that it was typical for a mid-level or more senior manager to spend six to twelve hours per week in teleconferences for virtual team meetings.

Under these circumstances, one might expect GlobalCo's managers to be very good at working with virtual teams. However, this was not the feeling of some of its leadership. Some concerns that were raised were:

- Superhuman efforts were often required to meet deadlines
- Difficulty in virtual team members in balancing local and virtual team requirements (that is, virtual team commitments were often second to local ones)
- Hours of work were extending and intruding on home life. It was not unusual for employees to have at least one virtual team meeting sometime during the week at home.

The GlobalCo managers that we spoke to felt that there were opportunities for significant improvement that would contribute to its performance and employee satisfaction.

As one might expect, GlobalCo had internal development courses focused on virtual teams. One course was called "Virtual Team Leadership"; the other, "Virtual Team Membership". However, neither course was well-subscribed. This was attributed to a lack of awareness and a perception that the course could have better content.

4.1 The Action Research Project

Our relationship with GlobalCo started through a Research Center that had an on-going research relationship with GlobalCo. Within that relationship, our research team and GlobalCo managers began to explore how to develop a research mandate that would provide practical advice to virtual team managers and enable the research team to make a contribution to the research literature. GlobalCo, and specifically the contact managers, were in the process of implementing a new Knowledge Management platform, moving from an internally-created solution to one based on a commercial off-the-shelf package, called here CollaboraSoft. GlobalCo was interested in seeing how virtual team management practice could be improved through the implementation, and changes in underlying work processes.

GlobalCo's managers wanted the research team to specifically focus on the CollaboraSoft implementation. The research team on the other hand, despite finding CollaboraSoft to be an interesting package which was indeed becoming more prevalent in industry, was less interested in specific software functionality and more on the underlying relationship between people, processes and technology. This created a tension between understanding the problem broadly and addressing GlobalCo's "burning platform" issues, illustrating Rapoport's (1970) initiative dilemma: how to specify a research project that satisfies both a research question and a practical business need.

With time, a consensus emerged that the initiative dilemma could be solved by following five virtual teams as they implemented CollaboraSoft. The lessons learned would then be incorporated into the virtual team's leadership and membership courses. Regardless, these courses were to be updated to include advice on using CollaboraSoft. For GlobalCo, this process would enable the sharing of best practices between virtual teams and then generalization through course material delivery. For the research team, our research interests had coalesced around understanding the process by which a virtual team leader implemented technology-based change in the virtual setting. Both practitioners and researchers found this to be a useful project and signed off on a project plan, outlined in the next section.

4.2 Project Plan #1

This plan was structured according to Susman and Everend's (1978) cycle as shown in Figure 9-1. The plan was to first learn to familiarize ourselves with virtual teams at GlobalCo and diagnose opportunities for improvement. Subsequently, we would plan actions, move to have those interventions enacted, evaluate those actions and to specify the learnings before repeating the cycle. As we believed that we would need to take great care to be sure to understand the situation in which we were operating, we allocated a significant amount of time to the diagnosis stage.

The research team thought that the quickest way to understand virtual team's at GlobalCo would be to meet with several active virtual team members. In order to overcome some common issues in virtual teams, the research team thought that face-to-face meetings with several virtual team members at North America locations would assist in developing our credibility with GlobalCo. To this end, the following agreement was exchanged in the form of an email:

- Ten teams would be investigated that represent a range of performance across the organization that are currently active or have completed their work within the past six months
- The research team would require information on the team membership, contact information and a brief outline of what they did
- One or two key informants per team (approximately 15 in total) including individuals not located at the [Corporate Headquarters]
- Some informants should be physically removed from the rest of their team
- Informants could be on more than one team
- 60 minute face-to-face interviews scheduled with informants, within two months
- Team members will be surveyed (by web) following the key informant interviews

This was our pattern of communication with the GlobalCo managers. We would summarize plans reached in a teleconference and gain their confirmation in August 2003. However, a few weeks after receiving their confirmation (in October), circumstances within GlobalCo changed and they stated that they were no longer able to pay for the research team's travel expenses and that we should make different plans. We quickly secured alternative research funding to pay for the travel but GlobalCo declined our offer. Therefore we were unable to complete this stage. As a research team, we perceived that the GlobalCo managers were having difficulty securing commitment for the interviews. Security at GlobalCo is taken very seriously and we came to believe that at least part of the problem was due to perceived risks in hosting the research team at non-headquarters locations. This problem caused our first major plan adjustment where we scaled back our initial diagnosing phase.

4.3 Project Plan #2

We went back and confirmed with the GlobalCo managers to ensure they were still interested in pursuing the project in light of the new plan. They did this via e-mail. In retrospect, it might have been better if we had been able to read body language as de-escalation of their commitment had already begun. Nevertheless, we worked together to develop a new project plan. In this plan, we would gather our data by investigating five virtual teams. In effect, this was a continuation of our previous plan but we would no longer do intensive one-on-one interviews and surveys. Rather we would "observe" virtual teams in action by listening in on teleconferences and following up with virtual team leaders individually for further clarifications about practice, problems and opportunities in order to complete the initial diagnosing phase of our action research project.

The research team would follow the virtual teams for a period of time that began before the implementation of CollaboraSoft and extended to 3 months after its initial implementation, drawing on Tyre and Orlikowski (1994) to set an endpoint that likely captured the most significant period of change.

This plan was agreed to 5 months after the initial start of the project (January 2004). At this stage, we completed the university ethics review process for our new protocol. At this time we did not realize the extent to which common – and reasonable – ethics requirements become more complicated in a virtual setting.

4.3.1 Ethics Approval

A general research ethics principle is informed consent and this often means that each virtual team member must *explicitly* agree to participate. University ethics boards properly do not allow negative options in observational studies where a non-response is could be seen as *implicit* agreement, as opposed to survey research where submission of a survey can be interpreted as informed consent.

Our primary contacts started to set up phone conversations with virtual team leaders. In our conversations with the virtual team leaders, we explained what our goal was – to help identify ways in which CollaboraSoft could be used to improve virtual team management – and asked about their team. Some teams, such as those that met infrequently (less than once a month), primarily distributed information rather than facilitated active collaboration or had too few (we wanted at least 4 regular members) or too many (some teams had in excess of forty members) members, were dropped from consideration. Unfortunately due to time zones and the already jammed schedules of the virtual team leaders, we had identified, and secured the support, of only 3 virtual teams by March 2004 and in total 7 by the end of June 2004.

Rather than waiting to have all the teams lined up before starting, we started to satisfy the ethics requirements as teams were secured. After some relatively short discussions with GlobalCo's managers, it was decided that the most practical way to gain informed consent was to send an e-mail to each individual virtual team member and ask for a reply. After all, e-mail is used for almost all written communication within GlobalCo. However, herein lay a problem. GlobalCo managers receive so much e-mail that they look for ways of reducing their load; Ignoring our e-mail was probably an obvious one. In response to these slow replies or non-replies, the virtual team leaders asked their members to look for the e-mail response and to consider it positively. We were concerned that if we asked the virtual team leaders to go any further would violate individual virtual team members sense that their participation truly was voluntary.

For us, this requirement that each person affirmatively consent ended opportunities with four virtual teams before they got started; in one case, one person out of 22 did not reply, delaying the entire project. After it became obvious that someone was not going to respond, we would withdraw, a source of frustration to us and to GlobalCo's managers.

As we found that we kept losing teams to this process, we adopted with the approval of the ethics coordinator, some process changes in trying to secure the approval. The primary one was that, before sending out the invitation e-mails, a member of the research team would join a regular teleconference to explain the research project at the start of the meeting. As the failures mounted we joined additional meetings to explain the project before we requested permission. It was necessary to do this for two reasons: first, it's easy to miss a meeting and second, people often join a few minutes late. We found that speaking to the group (even if it was primarily one-way) was a useful supplement to the introductory letter that accompanied the ethics permission request as we were able to sign up more teams this way. By using this approach, we were able to ease our introduction to the research site.

4.3.2   CollaboraSoft

As mentioned earlier, the implementation of CollaboraSoft was one of the primary motivators for our GlobalCo sponsors. The software was supposed to be implemented in several teams by January 2004. However, due to some previously unrecognized limitations in the software, the implementation became significantly delayed. Concurrently, increased resistance also surfaced within GlobalCo to switching from the homegrown software as there was a perception that CollaboraSoft was not as integrated with GlobalCo's processes. The firm deadline for CollaboraSoft's "go live" came and went without a new date being set.

This caused the purpose of our project to shift – in a way that we did not recognize as very significant – towards a study of how a virtual team leader could implement technology-based tools to improve team performance, not just CollaboraSoft tools. What the research team did not fully grasp was that as we were no longer focused on the new tools some of our efforts were perceived to address old technology that was going to be phased out. The research team was focused on the process underlying the tools, while the GlobalCo managers were more focused on the tools.

We experienced another problem in relation to the tools. As virtual teams use some form of electronic communication media, the research team believed that we needed full, or at least significant, access to the tools, particularly those related to communication and meeting support. However, getting access to GlobalCo's normal IT infrastructure was very difficult for an outsider, as has also been reported by Pauleen (2004). In spite of the our sponsors' efforts, the research team was never able to get even partial access. We were restricted to exchanging email and telephone conferences. We never were able to join NetMeeting discussions for example directly in spite of signing very thorough Non-Disclosure Agreements. This limitation – one that we worked months to overcome – became a very significant limitation. For a collocated team, it is usually at least possible for someone to show you the site and to watch where you go. For a virtual team, you are flying blind.

4.3.3 Our Teams

With our new focus and with the limitations facing us on technology access, we secured permission from three teams while continuing to experience difficulties with the ethics approval process. The first team was focused on the implementation of CollaboraSoft, SoftTeam (April 2004). A second team had fourteen members from the global procurement function, ProcTeam (June 2004). Finally the third team had only two members from GlobalCo and five additional members from a GlobalCo supplier. We shall refer to this team as SupplierTeam (October 2004). It surprised us that one of the teams had more members from outside GlobalCo than from inside. After securing three teams in 10 months, we stopped trying to sign up more teams. Before discussing how we revised the plan, the next sections will document some experiences from each virtual team.

4.3.4   SoftTeam

SoftTeam was the first team that we secured full commitment. As soon as we had the last confirmation, we started to join the teleconferences (April 2004). It became obvious almost immediately that simply listening in to the teleconference was not adequate to understand the virtual team process. SoftTeam was using pilot CollaboraSoft tools and internal tools to share documents and view data and we did not have access. The SoftTeam leader supported our efforts to get access. However, in the end, all we were able to get were screenshots of agenda, work lists, etc. Unfortunately, even this quickly became an imposition for the virtual team leader and became very intermittent. It was like watching a meeting captured through still pictures rather than video.

In our first few months of observing SoftTeam, we saw many things that we expected to see. For example, the meetings were fairly structured with an agenda that the virtual team leader announced at the start of the meeting. In general, the team members updated each other on their activities and from time-to-time engaged in joint problem solving. Some non-productive activities were also observed. For example, members would sometimes arrive late for meetings or would not respond when asked a question, indicating that perhaps they had mentally left the meeting. Given the overall slowing down of the CollaboraSoft implementation, SoftTeam's sense of urgency was low and meetings were cancelled frequently.

At the end of the three months and five meetings (there should have been 12), leadership of the virtual team shifted (unexpectedly to us). The old team leader was supposed to remain on the team but he only attended a few more meetings. The new team leader was much less effective. Rather than announcing an agenda, the leader would ask if there was anything to discuss. Within a couple of meetings, attendance dropped off to the point where the first 15 minutes of the teleconference often had one person (usually but not always the virtual team leader) and the research team. The meetings then rarely lasted more than 15 additional minutes. Finally, by September the team declared that its job was over and disbanded.

This team highlighted to us the importance of a virtual team leader with strong leadership skills. The drop-off in team performance was noticeable to us when leadership changed. For the research team, this underlined the importance and value of what we were doing.

4.3.5   ProcTeam

The second team that we followed was a team of procurement managers. The dynamics of this team were noticeably different that SoftTeam.

Meetings had lively discussions that followed a well-structured agenda. In order to improve the focus at each meeting, the leader had created a pattern where one week the team held a KOAT (Keep Our Act Together, updates and frequent firefighting) meeting and the other meeting focused on longer-term issues. Fifteen to thirty minutes would be allocated to KOAT-type issues but the meeting never completely focused on short-term issues.

The team leader also built team collegiality through the use of an "inclusion" exercise. About once a month, the leader would throw out a question like "What concert would you pay not to go?" or "Where would you like to go on vacation where you've not been?" Then, each team member – no one was allowed to 'pass' – would respond. This would take 20 minutes. Even though we were impressed by the team building, we asked the leader why he used this exercise. He mentioned that the team met once every 12-18 months face-to-face and on average every two month there would be a new member. This meant that there were several people who did not know the people that they were working with closely and he found this helpful. We felt that we had found the first practice that we would try and propagate through other teams. However, we did not feel that SoftTeam would be a good place for its suggestion given the on-going attendance issues. We viewed the ProcTeam leader as highly effective and wanted to work out a way of capturing the practices that we observed.

4.3.6   SupplierTeam

The final team for which we received ethics approval was SupplierTeam. The research team initially thought that we should decline it as an option (as our intention had been to focus only on internal teams) but the team leader was really interested in participating. Effectively he convinced us that it was a good team to study. Previously, problems in making the virtual team work had created a need for a lot of face-to-face meetings and none of the team members wanted to travel as much.

We received approval very quickly and attended our first meeting. As this cross-company team used an external third-party meeting tool (WebEx) to support its meeting, we were able to experience the "real" virtual team environment. At the end of the second meeting, we were intrigued by what we were observing and were starting to look at what was working and what wasn't. In contrast to our other two teams, where we were not privy to the collaboration tools, this team provided us with a more complete picture.

Then, suddenly, the virtual team leadership shifted to a new person. The new leader failed for two meetings to send us the login information, in spite of sending reminders. We then attended one meeting (which had to be cut short due to other business issues) and then were forgotten again. Then the team went on hiatus for a couple of months as there weren't issues to discuss as one of GlobalCo's factories was being refurbished and nothing was going on. Once the team start meeting again, the leader again forgot to bring us into the loop and by the time this was worked out we had moved on to the next phase of the project.

4.4   Project Plan #3

As a reader might expect, the research team was getting quite frustrated by our lack of progress. For most of 2004, we followed one team and while it was very interesting it was not going to address either the practice or research problem adequately. We did recognize those that virtual team leaders were often very interested in the project, even if their members were less so. In conjunction with our GlobalCo sponsors, we decided to reorganize the project once again.

After discussions with GlobalCo, the following plan was agreed to:

1. The research team would continue to monitor the teams that have completed ethics approval or those undergoing it now. No new teams would be recruited.
2. With the assistance of GlobalTech's managers, 10-15 team leads would be recruited to form a research panel.
3. On a monthly basis, the research team would send these team leads a set of observations and possible suggestions for improvement to their team functioning. These would be based on the research literature and team observations. Observations would not be identified with any specific team.
4. The team leads would comment on these suggestions (would they be appropriate for their team? would they try them with their team? etc.) by email. These comments would be collated anonymously.
5. We would continue to develop these lists, collate feedback and refine the document.
6. After 4-6 months of this process (Steps 2-5), the research team would make suggestions on course content for the GlobalCo virtual team Leadership and Membership courses.

Probably for reasons of optimism more than realistic expectations, the research team and GlobalCo felt confident that this would lead to useful practice and research results. By this time, any focus on CollaboraSoft had disappeared. Indeed, a technology-focus was not even expected anymore by GlobalCo.

Before proceeding, we had to again consult the ethics committee on our new approach. The changes were approved expeditiously but it was still March 2005 before we could request the list of twenty virtual team leaders who had been identified by GlobalCo. We received these and sent out the consent forms. By May we had received a "yes" from 17 individuals and started the project. As part of this process we received a short and informal bio from 15 of the participants. The research team had sent personal bios that included information about research interests, teaching activities, hobbies and family information. We sent these in the hope that a more personal connection could be developed, similar to the inclusion exercise we observed in ProcTeam.

4.4.1 Initial Data Collection Email

Our initial data collection email asked the questions with three different purposes. For each of the questions, we began to consider interventions, based on the research literature. The purpose of the first set of questions (Table 9-1) was to capture some basic demographic information on the participants. We found that the "average" participant was on 4 teams with 15 members per team with a mix of internal and external experience, and used a wide range of tools. It was very surprising to see CollaboraSoft so high on the usage list as we had not been informed that the implementation had proceeded to that point. Therefore, we were energized to see that we might be able to bring the original aims related to CollaboraSoft back into the project.

The second set of questions (Table 9-2) related to the Diagnosing phase. Our goal was to understand whether these leaders had undergone formal training (most had not), whether there was a difference between a good team leader and a good virtual team leader (resoundingly yes) and what characteristics they felt that a good virtual team leader exhibited. While we were not surprised with any of the answers, we felt that these responses would provide a credible foundation upon which to based future interventions. For example, several respondents mentioned "cultural insensitivity" as serious problem. We planned to state that this seems to be a problem in some situations and to suggest that a document outlining culture based differences in communication and decision-making styles would be useful reading for virtual team leaders and members.

Table 9-1. Demographic Questions

Question	Response Summary	Possible Intervention
How many virtual teams are you currently leading? How many have you led at GlobalCo? In other organizations?	• 1 to 10 virtual teams • average 3.8 • mix of internal and external experience.	Sharing of experiences across leaders through our published findings would bring personal insights beyond that of which can be covered in training alone (Dubé and Paré 2002).
Please list the virtual teams are you currently a member of and how many members are on the team.	• 3 to 80 members • Averaging 15 (though skewed by the small sample and the 80 member outlier, there were numerous 20 member plus teams).	Increasing relational links between members through introducing face to face meetings, social activities, and informal communication (Powell et al. 2004) This is important as the larger teams get the greater the: complexity (Dubé and Paré 2002), the possibility for miscommunication, information overload (Hiltz et al. 1991), and potential for free-riding (Furst 1999; Crampton 2001).
What sorts of electronic medium do you use to communicate with your virtual teams?	• Various MS Office products, the Intranet, and one on one communication.	Suggest changes in medium to increase communication and therefore team effectiveness.

Table 9-2. Action Planning Questions

Question	Response Summary	Possible Intervention
Have you received formal training in virtual team leadership? If not, would it have been useful?	• Two-thirds had no formal training • Most saw formal training as useful.	Hold a virtual leadership and membership training sessions (Warkentin and Beranek 1999) including discussion to motivate positive diversity effects (Dubé and Paré 2002).
Are some individuals better suited to managing virtual teams than others? What characteristics would such an individual have?	• Yes, some are better • Cultural sensitivity and diversity, listening and communication skills, ability to deal with ambiguity, and organizational skills.	A team leader could also increase a team's effectiveness by clarify role expectations. Such clarification alleviates uncertainty and creates expectations of how members should behave (Wong and Burton 2000).
What was the most surprising challenge that you have found in leading a virtual team?	• Meeting timing, culture, language, achieving engagement of distant members, creating a sense of team.	Mitigate difficulties by suggesting changes to meeting prep, rotating meeting times (Klein and Kleinhanns 2001), and negotiating differences offline (Mittleman et al. 2000).
What are one or two things you have seen a virtual team leader do to destroy a virtual team's effectiveness?	• Poor leadership training, cultural insensitivity, disorganization, lack of preparedness, assuming consensus, excluding members.	Provide a summary list of "horror stories" to the participants without attribution. Comments seen as negative are often withheld within an organization for the sake of politeness. A third party might be able to help bring these out.

Table 9-3. Action Taking Questions

Question	Response Summary	Possible Interventions
What are the one or two key practices you use (or urge others to use) that you believe make virtual teams more effective?	• Gate keeping • frequent communication • agenda setting • informal communication.	Introduce Agendas that can explain why items are on the agenda, how they fit into overall strategy, and relevant stakeholders (Mittleman et al. 2000). Encourage leaders to help all members have a chance to express their ideas (Powell et al. 2004).
Are there important team-leadership-related things that you do outside of the actual meeting that help make the team a success? Please describe one or two of them.	• Face to face meetings • Altering travel plans • Annual "sit down" meetings • Individual meetings • Work with stakeholders • Pursuing and ensuring buy in • Organization through prep / documentation / minutes • Ensuring assignments and action items were completed.	Introduce team building exercise to build a team identity (Furst 1999) (possibly inclusion exercise as per ProcTeam) and help establish trust (Jarvenpaa et al. 1998).

The final set of questions (Table 9-3) focused on eliciting best practices from our research partners, rather than the literature. Some of the suggestions might seem trivial such as "agenda setting" but our experience with SoftTeam suggested that not all virtual team leaders did this. We viewed this as a relatively straightforward first intervention that could have some value to the participants but would not be so radical that they might be reluctant to try it.

4.5   The Project Ends

We believed that this project was finally on track. We were moving into the Action Taking stage; with the first "intervention" e-mail about to go out to the participants. While we were analyzing the first email responses to complete this draft, GlobalCo decided to end the overall research program. As we mentioned earlier, this project was part of a broader research collaboration. As unbelievable as it might seem, this was the project seeing the most progress. For example, a survey had been ready-to-go for over a year with another team and had not been distributed due to internal issues.

The research team debated trying to convince GlobalCo that we should proceed with this project as it finally seemed to be on the rails but, perhaps finally, we recognized that the interest on the practitioner side was no longer there. Therefore, we prepared a report that summarized where we were (based on the Tables 9-1 to 9-3) and withdrew.

5.   DISCUSSION

The outcome of this project was very disappointing to the research team. The research team had seen a real opportunity to make a research contribution to the processes by which best practices are adopted by virtual teams. We also believed that we would be able to bring value to GlobalCo's management. In this way, we would satisfy the twin goals of Action Research by contributing to research and practice. However, it did not happen that way. In this section, we will reflect on our reasons why we think this occurred because in spite of our result we very well might try AR in a virtual team setting again.

Initiative Dilemma: It is of no surprise that the initiative dilemma caused issues in Action Research. It is one of the most well-known concerns in an Action Research project. Nevertheless, it happened here. The project started with what we saw (and still see) as a project that was useful for both research and practice. However, the delays in implementing CollaboraSoft meant that the goals became misaligned. As researchers, our interests went beyond one technology implementation and when the project shifted to the existing technology our interests were not diminished. However, again in retrospect, the project became less interesting for GlobalCo and there was de-escalation in commitment. Therefore, over time, a misalignment developed that we did not sense.

It is also likely that, while our specific sponsors within GlobalCo were very interested this project, the rest of organization did not have the same priority. This could explain one of the reasons we had trouble getting ethics approval. Some potential participants may not have seen the value in the study and simply judged it not to be worth their time. For us this was a lesson about the effect of the fact that even relatively senior managers can have different priorities from the rest of the organization. Within the virtual setting, this was more difficult to detect.

Too Much Time Diagnosing: We were concerned that it would be difficult to develop a full understanding of the research environment. However, in retrospect, we did develop a reasonable understanding in a fairly short period of time. One characteristic of a good Action Research project – one that addresses Rapoport's Goal Dilemma – is that the practitioners really need the results of the research and are eager to see tangible signs of progress. Also, this was the first known instance of Action Research for the people we worked with. They had worked with many researchers on surveys or case studies but this was a novel method to them. Therefore, we were introducing a change into the organization but proceeded on a path that delayed benefits of value to the practitioners. We would have benefited from implementing some "quick wins" and other change management principles (Kotter 1996). In our opinion, this was the key downfall in how we designed this project.

Real System Access: We compromised in this project by proceeding without full access to the GlobalCo virtual team environment. However, getting access to a virtual team's normal IT infrastructure is often very difficult for an outsider (Pauleen 2004). We were never able to get full access. It seems that in many companies it is difficult to set up visitor accounts with permissions that allow you to read certain files within team structures but not others. This was in spite of signing very thorough Non-Disclosure Agreements. This took away one of the primary benefits that we saw in using Action Research in this setting: our ability to work within the actual setting. Together with Pauleen's experience, we believe that this is a significant caution for researchers considering this form of research in this setting.

Difficulty in Building Commitment to the Project: Before starting this project, we knew the challenges in working at a distance. However, we did not appreciate how difficult it would be to overcome them. In spite of our efforts, we never really became part of the team. While at least initially we had good goal compatibility with our GlobalCo sponsors, this did not exist with our direct work with the teams in the second phase. In the final phase, it was too early to tell whether we would have developed a good team with the researchers and the managers. Were we to do this again however, we would tend towards insisting on a face-to-face kickoff meeting to build early momentum. This would also partially address the issue of developing quick wins as some shared learning would occur.

Team Leadership: The team leadership changes in SupplierTeam and SoftTeam caused us significant challenges. However, these could have been good research opportunities for us but we effectively lost contact with the teams at these points. On our side, we should have developed contacts with more people on the team than just the leader so that the change would not have had such an effect. On the practitioner side, this brought out their version of the Role Dilemma (Rapoport 1970; Trist 1976). It is well known that an Action Researcher must balance between potentially roles as a consultant and as a researcher. What we had not articulated was the role dilemma faced by practitioners.

While the practitioners have a job to do, they need to balance their commitment to the research project. When the team leaders were re-assigned, they felt that they satisfied their commitment to the research by informing the new leader about the project but this was not sufficient to support the project. We exchanged emails with the company to reach a Research Client Agreement (Davison et al. 2004). However, we did not include elements of what to do should one of the practitioners change positions in the future. We will incorporate such contingencies in future agreements.

Evaluation: Though the project was terminated without ever reaching the Evaluation phase, in retrospect we realized that our revised research plan put us in the awkward position of being relatively unable to evaluate the effectiveness of our interventions. Specifically, we had no on site contact, and would only receive data through the team leaders we were studying. Therefore we were completely at the mercy of the leaders to both implement and report on the effectiveness of the intervention. While this is a possible problem in all Action Research projects, it could have been particularly acute in a virtual setting.

6. CONCLUSION

A fair criticism to level at the research team was that we did not know when to stop and realize that the project had become more likely to fail than succeed. While we teach our students that sunk costs should not influence forward looking decisions, this story is an example of how hard it can be to implement that advice. We persevered even when the conditions had deteriorated.

Why would we do that? It certainly was not for a lack of other things to do. Rather, we believed that there was the real opportunity to make a contribution to practice and research, the twin aims of Action Research. We still believe that the potential exists. Hopefully, we will learn from our experiences next time.

7.   ACKNOWLEDGEMENTS

The authors were only part of the research team described in this chapter. We are indebted to our colleagues who worked with us. This chapter is our personal reflections of what the lessons that we learned from our experience. Our thanks go to the Research Center that originally facilitated this contact. Also, we would like to recognize GlobalCo's managers, virtual team leaders and members who worked with us. The outcome of this project was disappointing to us as we were unable to deliver value to these hard-working individuals. Should a reader feel the need to place blame for this project it could perhaps be addressed to the authors. In our opinion, everyone associated with this project acted with honesty and integrity and we thank them for contributing to our learning.

8.   REFERENCES

Bell, B. S. and S. W. J. Kozlowski (2002). "A Typology of Virtual Teams: Implications for Effective Leadership." Group & Organization Management **27**(1): 14-49.
Crampton, C. D. (2001). "The Mutual Knowledge Problem and its Consequences for Dispersed Collaboration." Organization Science **12**(3): 346-371.
Daft, R. L. and R. H. Lengel (1986). "Organizational Information Requirements, Media Richness and Structural Design." Management Science **32**(5): 554-571.
Davison, R., M. G. Martinsons and N. Kock (2004). "Principles of Canonical Action Research." Information Systems Journal **14**(1): 65-86.
Dennis, A. R. and S. T. Kinney (1998). "Testing Media Richness Theory in the New Media: The Effects of Cues, Feedback, and Task Equivocality." Information Systems Research **9**(3): 256-274.
DeSanctis, G. and M. S. Poole (1997). "Transitions in Teamwork in New Organizational Forms." Advances in Group Processes **14**: 157-176.
Dubé, L. and G. Paré (2002). "The Multi-Faceted Nature of Virtual Teams." Cahier du GReSI **2**(11): 1-33.
Furst, S., Blackburn, R., and Rosen, B. (1999). "Virtual Team Effectiveness: a Proposed Research Agenda." Information Systems Journal **9**(4): 249-269.
Haywood, M. (1998). Managing Virtual Teams: Practical Techniques for High-Technology Project Managers. Boston, MA, Artech House.
Hiltz, S. R., K. Johnson and M. Turoff (1991). "Group Decision Support: The Effects of Designated Human Leaders and Statistical Feedback in Computerized Conferences." Journal of Management Information Systems **8**(2): 81-88.
Hinds, P. and S. Kiesler (2002). Distributed Work. Cambridge, Mass., MIT Press.
Jackson, P. J. (1999). "Organizational Change and Virtual Teams: Strategic and Operational Integration." Information Systems Journal **9**: 313-332.

Jarvenpaa, S. L., K. Knoll and D. E. Leidner (1998). "Is Anybody Out There? Antecedents of Trust in Global Virtual Teams." Journal of Management Information Systems 14(4): 29-64.

Jarvenpaa, S. L. and D. E. Leidner (1999). "Communication and Trust in Global Virtual Teams." Organization Science 10(6): 791-815.

Klein, H. K. and M. D. Myers (1999). "A Set of Principles for Conducting and Evaluating Interpretive Field Studies in Information Systems." MIS Quarterly 23(1): 67-94.

Klein, J. and A. Kleinhanns (2001). "Maximizing the Contribution of Diverse Voices in Virtual Teams." MIT Mindshare: 1-33.

Kotter, J. P. (1996). Leading Change. Cambridge, MA, Harvard Business School Press.

McDonough, E. F., K. B. Kahn and G. Barczak (2001). "An Investigation of the Use of Global, Virtual, and Colocated New Product Development Teams." The Journal of Product Innovation Management 18(2): 110-120.

McKnight, D. H., L. L. Cummings and N. L. Chervany (1998). "Initial Trust Formation in New Organizational Relationships." Academy of Management. The Academy of Management Review 23(3): 473.

Mittleman, D. D., R. O. Briggs and J. F. Nunamaker (2000). "Best Practices in Facilitating Virtual Meetings: Some Notes from Initial Experience." Group Facilitation 2(2): 5-14.

Morrison, E. W. and S. L. Robinson (1997). "When Employees Feel Betrayed: A Model of How Psychological Contract Violation Develops." Academy of Management. The Academy of Management Review 22(1): 226-256.

Newell, S. and J. Swan (2000). "Trust and Inter-Organizational Networking." Human Relations 53(10): 1287-1328.

Paul, D. L. and R. R. McDaniel (2004). "A Field Study of the Effect of Interpersonal Trust on Virtual Collaborative Relationship Performance." MIS Quarterly 28(2): 183-227.

Pauleen, D. J. (2004). "An Inductively Derived Model of Leader-Initiated Relationship Building with Virtual Team Members." Journal of Management Information Systems 20(3): 227-256.

Piccoli, G. and B. Ives (2003). "Trust and the Unintended Effects of Behavior Control in Virtual Teams." MIS Quarterly 27(3): 365-395.

Powell, A., G. Piccoli and B. Ives (2004). "Virtual Teams: A Review of Current Literature and Directions for Future Research." Database for Advances in Information Systems 35(1): 6-36.

Rapoport, R. N. (1970). "Three Dilemmas in Action Research." Human Relations 23(6): 499-513.

Street, C. T. and D. B. Meister (2004). "Small Business Growth and Internal Transparency: The Role of Information Systems." MIS Quarterly 28(3): 473-506.

Susman, G. I. and R. D. Everend (1978). "An Assessment of The Scientific Merits of Action Research." Administrative Science Quarterly 23(4): 582-603.

Trist, E. (1976). Engaging with Large-scale Systems. Experimenting with Organizational Life: The Action Research Approach. A. W. Clark. New York, Plenum Press: x, 259 p.

Tyre, M. J. and W. J. Orlikowski (1994). "Windows of opportunity: Temporal patterns of technological adaptation in organizations." Organization Science 5(1): 98-118.

Warkentin, M. and P. M. Beranek (1999). "Training to Improve Virtual Team Communication." Information Systems Journal 9(4): 271-289.

Westfall, R. D. (2004). "Does Telecommuting Really Increase Productivity?" Association for Computing Machinery. Communications of the ACM 47(8): 93-96.

Wong, S.-S. and R. M. Burton (2000). "Virtual Teams: What are their Characteristics, and Impact on Team Performance?" Computational and Mathematical Organization Theory 6(4): 339-360.

Chapter 10

HEALTHCARE
Fertile Ground for Action Research

Rajiv Kohli[1] and Ellen D. Hoadley[2]
[1] The College of William and Mary, USA; [2] Loyola College in Maryland, USA

Abstract: This chapter presents an example of action research in the healthcare industry. A synopsis of the project is provided, followed by a discussion of why action research was successful in this project and in this industry. Further discussion focuses on the overall use of action research to increase interactions between academic researchers and business practitioners. The authors propose the increased use of action research as a synergistic tool to improve the relevance of academic research while increasing rigor in the healthcare industry.

Key words: action research, healthcare, academic research, relevance, rigor

1.   INTRODUCTION

A benefit of action research (AR) is that it provides the researcher with an inside perspective on the problem, the solution, and the ongoing implementation process of a project. The benefit to the organization is that the researcher brings to bear the body of knowledge, theory, frameworks, and concepts into the less objective, highly constrained world of the business problem. AR uses these two perspectives to open the 'black box' and to study how a mechanism solves complex problems. Information systems applications in healthcare are particularly fertile grounds because dispensing quality healthcare requires a combination of technological and social skills. Information technology is mandated to increase efficiency by automating activities. Healthcare professionals, on the other hand, increase effectiveness through their diagnostic skills tempered with compassion and sensitivity. Therefore, the impact of information systems on healthcare quality is multi-faceted and, as such, the measurement variables for which are still evolving. In part due to this complexity, healthcare poses an environment in which the role of the actors is inherently susceptible to conflict. The interaction of the information systems and healthcare professionals provides a rich environment conducive to the practice of AR.

This chapter begins with a description of the AR setting, problem domain, and actions taken in a healthcare setting. We then dissect the action research project to indicate the contribution of the AR methodology and how the findings reflect its value. We also discuss healthcare research areas that provide fertile ground for action research. We use a published action research project as an example to demonstrate the opportunities in healthcare. In this action research, a physician's profiling system (PPS) was used to monitor and report clinical practices and patient outcomes with the goal of modifying physician behavior. For a comprehensive description of the PPS project and its domain, please see the published article (Kohli & Kettinger, 2004).

1.1   Criteria for Action Research Evaluation

There are concerns that AR may be limited in its impact because there is a lack of agreed upon criteria for evaluation (Baskerville, 1999b). Indeed, some researchers have also questioned whether AR can serve two masters due to possible duality of goals of the researchers and the practitioners (Kock, 1999). Baskerville (1999a) suggests four criteria for evaluating AR: (1) theory must be informed, (2) client participation in determining action should be ensured, (3) appropriate researcher involvement should be ensured, and (4) the goals of the action research should be clearly understood. In ensuring the criteria for the application of AR, the PPS project included these key components as demonstrated in Table 10-1.

The AR reported also conforms to principles of canonical action research (Davison, Martinsons, & Kock, 2004), which proposes that, in addition to Baskerville's research criteria and Susman's ARC, AR should proceed through multiple iterations to achieve the desired outcomes. The criteria of Baskerville, the principles of Davison et al., and how the PPS project conformed to these criteria and principles are synthesized in Table 10-1.

Table 10-1. Action Research Criteria in PPS Project

Baskerville Evaluation Criterion	Davison et al. Principles of Canonical AR	Characteristic of the PPS Project
(1) theory must be informed	Principle of Theory	An existing base of knowledge based in theory was applied to guide the project.
		The researchers reported theoretical findings and development based on the project outcomes.
(2) client participation in determining action should be ensured	Principle of the Researcher – Client Agreement	The project dealt with a solution to a real problem within an organization.
		The researchers and clients agreed on the roles and participation of both parties.
(3) appropriate researcher involvement should be ensured	Principle of the Researcher – Client Agreement	The researchers were actively involved in the project implementation.
	Principle of Change through Action	The researchers adapted the project directives to the organizational problem changes through two iterative action research cycles.
	Principle of the Cyclical Process Model	The researchers and clients agreed on the roles and participation of both parties.
(4) the goals of the action research should be clearly understood	Principle of Learning through Reflection	The project built upon the synergy of research experience of academic researchers and the practice skills of the organizational leadership.
		The researchers applied a prescribed evaluation and control criteria to determine the success of the project

The findings are presented in this chapter using the framework of the Action Research Cycle specified by Susman and Evered (1978): diagnosing, action planning, action taking, evaluating, specifying learning. The diagnosing is discussed in the section that describes "The Problem." We present the action planning and action taking section "Searching for a

Solution." "Learning from Failure" section describes evaluating and specifying learning steps of the AR Cycle. The researchers then completed the cycle again for a second iteration within the same project domain. The chapter concludes with a synthesis of the steps taken, the activities conducted, and the suggestions provided in Table 10-2.

1.2   Action Research Opportunities

Action Research thrives on real world situations that pose a conflict. In conflict situations the underlying issues are more complex than might first appear. Indeed, if the solutions were obvious, the conflict might not last long and therefore, other research methods may serve just as well as AR. As in most conflict situations, the actors have well-entrenched and ostensibly justified positions. Should the practitioners and researchers agree on a position and the phenomenon of interest is well defined, then survey-based research is appropriate to uncover the root issues to answer the probative question or concern at hand. On the other hand, one sign that AR may be an appropriate methodology for complex or conflict situations is when both sides appear to be justified in their positions to the researcher. One soon realizes that the variables of interest are not obvious. An AR researcher should embrace such conflict and not shy away from stepping in the middle of it, without taking sides.

2.   HEALTHCARE: THE PROBLEM DOMAIN

2.1   The Problem

Consider the environment of healthcare, especially in the United States where this project took place. With the advent of new diagnostic technologies, advanced medical treatment and newer drugs, costs have been rising faster than the rate of inflation; yet reimbursements by insurers of patient healthcare to hospitals have been getting tighter. Insurance companies find it harder to pay for expensive treatment regimes and are shifting the risk of higher costs to the hospitals by paying a fixed amount for treating patients. Thus, hospitals face increasing pressures as business entities and have worked diligently to contain those costs that are within their direct control. In addition, public and governmental awareness of the cost and quality pressures have led to increased legislation including the Medicare Prescription Drug, Improvement and Modernization Act, the Health Insurance Privacy and Portability Act (HIPPA) and a mandate by President George W. Bush to provide electronic health records to most Americans within the next ten years (Brailer, 2004).

This level of visibility and public interest has increased the desirability of solving complex and real problems by exploiting the needs of the healthcare industry and the knowledge of academics. While the operational aspects of controlling costs can be addressed through quantitative models such as those proposed by operations sciences, the need to address the challenges of getting physicians and clinical professionals to accept and adopt information technologies and act upon the information remains a challenge for hospital administrators. Uncovering the dimensions of resistance to technology use and the implications for behavioral changes to control costs in a dynamic and humanistic environment are characteristics that create an appropriate problem domain for action research.

The subject of the PPS study, St. John's Health System (SJHS) found itself in this situation. As a community hospital in the Midwest region of the United States, SJHS is a typical mid-size hospital facing the above mentioned challenges due to changes in the US healthcare industry. When as much as 80% of a hospital's costs are driven by the plans of care directed by physicians (Chilingerian & Sherman, 1990) whose primary concern is with quality of patient care, there is a clear conflict between the goals of the two actors, i.e the hospital administration that wants to control costs and physicians whose goals are to practice medicine as they see fit. Our society, physicians, and healthcare institutions value human life and would comfort patients in any way – one would like to say 'at any cost.' However, healthcare institutions are like other business entities and must conform to a fundamental law of economics. For any business entity to continue to exist, on aggregate, revenues must equal or exceed costs. The one common ground between the actors was that both admit to the inefficiencies in dispensing healthcare. However, the researchers soon discovered that such agreement was short-lived because each actor thought that the inefficiency is on the other side. Therein lies the conflict!

How can the actors, hospital and physicians, come to an agreement about the goals without affecting the quality of patient care? Who is in a better position to negotiate? What will convince one to see the other's point of view?

AR INSIGHT: Empirical research methods had uncovered cost overruns and a variance among the physicians' performance. However, understanding the reasons why such variance exists and what can be done required a deliberative approach that engaged the actors.

2.2 Searching for a Solution

The researchers hypothesized that agency theory may provide a solution for this conflict. Agency theory, also referred to as principal-agent theory, deals with the issue of motivating one party to keep the interest of another while acting on its behalf. The theory addresses the issue that the agent, the acting party, may or may not act in the best interest of the principal.

The researchers relied on prior research that indicated that if the hospital administrators (principal) provided the physicians (agents) with information about the quality and cost of care, such information would bring the physicians to the see the hospital goals as important. Previous research found that working with knowledge workers, known as *informating*, could bring the goals of the agents in alignment with those of the principal (Zuboff, 1985). As such the hospital would benefit by using their information systems to capture, process and disseminate cost and quality information among physicians resulting in a joint effort to contain costs.

The hospital administrators planned to include physician metrics of productivity and quality to enhance the current productivity tracking system which benchmarked hospital staff against norms and their peers' average performance for their activities. Theory indicated that what worked for the staff would have a good chance of modifying the behavior of the physicians as well. The hospital management expected that when the physicians were made aware of the cost of their procedures, as compared their peers within the hospital vis-à-vis the patient outcomes, they would be willing to modify their patient care plans to deliver high quality while containing costs wherever possible.

During the first iteration of the Action Research Cycle, the information system implementation was a technical success. One of the researchers assisted in the development and deployment of a system which captured more detailed patient care costs. Previously, the physicians were reluctant to accept the hospital's cost and quality information because it did not take into account the severity of illness among their patients. Some specialist physicians contended that due to their higher degree of specialization they routinely see sicker patients. They argued that costs for such patients are expected to be higher than another physician who may treat other patients in the same specialty. Furthermore, they did not trust the cost information in the computer information systems because a large percentage of it was comprised of fixed costs – something they have no control over[1]. The hospital administrators improved the methodology of cost accounting and the information systems that calculated and reported the costs. They then took the improved cost information to the physician peer group committees for review, exhorting the physicians to use the cost and quality data in the decision support system (DSS).

---

[1]   Physicians concerns and hospital administrators response are cited in (Kohli et al., 2001).

Initially, the DSS seemed to be a success. While the cardiologists used the DSS information and improved their cost performance and patient outcomes, it soon became evident that the wider physician community did not use the DSS. Even the usage among cardiologists tapered off. Now the question was how to get more physicians to adopt the use of the DSS without a hospital mandate.

AR INSIGHT: AR was particularly helpful in identifying the failure of the initial phase of the project and uncovering the reasons why it appeared to be successful at first. Contrasting AR with other approaches indicates that a survey or case study approach may have uncovered some of the reasons for failure. A cross-sectional empirical usage data would have likely concluded that the DSS was a success. The reasons for eventual failure might have eluded the researcher.

3. OUTCOMES

3.1 Learning from Failure

AR interaction with the hospital and physician actors enabled the researchers to return to a complementary theory base in the next action planning cycle. Because of the nature of physicians who perform somewhat as independent professionals, the researchers recognized the limitation of the agency theory and informating in achieving goal congruence between the hospital administrators and physicians. AR, combined with the commitment and involvement, enabled the researchers to observe that unlike the administrators, the physicians did not conform to the traditional role as agents of the hospital. Rather, the physician constituency functioned in a clan-like structure. Professional groups can behave as clans and gain legitimacy from their specialized knowledge or expertise that is greater and/or more specific than those within the organization they serve (Ruef & Scott, 1998). The literature guided the researchers to the clan characteristics and to previous findings that direct attempts at managerial control of a clan often fail. This is because the principal attempting to exercise control is not perceived as a legitimate member of clan on the basis of a lack of the technical knowledge or expertise shared by the clan (Sharma, 1997). For the hospital administrators, the question was to identify and engage a person within the physician clan who would be able to demonstrate legitimacy through professional identification and adherence to common culture.

AR INSIGHT: Note that the action researcher is now going into sociology to search for explanatory theories of legitimacy to apply to the problem. This is an indication that the complexity of healthcare field offers broad opportunities for AR. The focus is on problem solving even if it means stepping out of the traditional boundaries of information system research. Insights and learning often occur at the intersection of two or more disciplines.

The hospital appointed a boundary-spanning physician to an administrative position with the goal that the administrative physician would lead by example in using the information from the DSS and then would promulgate its acceptance among other physicians through the peer-committees. In addition, the system content and design specifications were improved so that the information concerns of the physicians were readily available at the time and place that the physicians were making their plans of care decisions for their patients.

During this iteration of the cycle at the evaluation point, the researchers and administrators realized their success. They had built on the strength of the physician clan, supporting the members themselves to shape the behavioral changes desired based on their shared values. By the end of the evaluation period, the physicians were using the DSS more widely, and the costs of physician care per patient had decreased leading to an overall cost savings to SJHS. Quality indicators had improved as well. After two years of use, the hospital administrators were pleased with the result. The technology implementation worked and provided financial payback to the hospital, and the administrators now understand that successful projects are the result of both technical and human factors.

As IT professionals, the researchers were able to work on the project over a protracted period to achieve the desired results patiently, rather than do a quick project where they remained neutral and were in and out in a matter of months. The researchers were able to put the initial phase failure into context for themselves and for the administrators. They incorporated the findings of their failed phase into the learning for the next phase – a luxury many projects are unable to afford. They were able to demonstrate the flexibility and patience required for successful action research. The learning is consistent with success criteria outlined by Baskerville (1999b).

3.2 Action Research: the Bridge over Organizational Waters

As this chapter has pointed out, the interaction between action researchers (many of whom are academics) and the practitioners in the project creates a synergy between the two worlds. The PPS project demonstrates one way that academics and practitioners can work together for mutual benefit. Yet both groups must understand the needs of each other beyond just the context of the project. This can be summed up in the age-old debate between relevance and rigor. The practitioners need outcomes that can be applied to problems in their domain, that are practical, and that can yield tangible results. The academics need issues emanating from the problem domain to which they can apply and extend their theoretical work for systematic exploration and generalizability. Through patience and mutual understanding, both groups can realize positive outcomes.

The project at SJHS was structured and examined through a research lens. From theory, the researchers proposed and predicted the likely outcomes. They controlled for criteria that they weren't interested in and evaluated success based on the criteria that they were interested in. They were able to take a long-term view of the project and see it through for a number of years. These features enhanced the rigor of the project and therefore, the generalizability of the findings.

The practitioners were able to provide a real context, real participants, and a real problem situation. When the first iteration was complete, and an action was required for the second iteration, the practitioners were able to make it happen to fit the theory. In the end, the practitioners got real solutions through the implementation of a real decision support system that included the baseline metrics and comparative modeling of physician activities and outcomes. These features enhanced the relevance of the project.

What did each party give up to participate in this project? Beyond the opportunity costs, the researchers gave up the objectivity that many academics believe is requisite for the creation of knowledge. They were engaged in the day-to-day workings of the system and the trials and tribulations of the project. The hospital's pain was their pain. On the other hand, the hospital gave up some level of speed to completion in favor of a more careful and deliberative approach to the problem. They also gave up their privacy in failure, preferring instead to learn from their shortcomings and allow others to learn as well.

3.3 Benefits for All

In this healthcare example the AR project addressed the relationship between the physicians and hospital administration. AR has also been applied in clinical settings. In a study of interprofessional collaboration in discharge planning so that patients are discharged in a timely manner, Atwal and Caldwell (2002) found that although verbal and nonverbal communication between stakeholders did not increase, it led to greater trust between them. Moreover, the study uncovered the fact that key factors in discharge delays were organizational rather than professional, a theme with which the action researchers began their study. In another healthcare application, AR was applied to understand how clinical nurses facilitate learning of junior nurses in acute care hospital setting, a simple yet critical part of dispensing healthcare (Kelly, Simpson, & Brown, 2002).

Despite its complexity, AR in healthcare can uncover special situations that can lead to building new information system theories or further enriching existing theories (Chiasson & Davidson, 2005). It is clear that in order for AR to flourish, researchers and the healthcare industry have to actively collaborate. What good does it do to continue to push ahead in the pursuit of knowledge, if no one ever gets to put the knowledge to good use? How can we expand the practicality of knowledge if, as academics, we don't pay attention to the problems that practitioners face daily? If we report a statistically significant finding but can't answer the question "Who does it help and how?", then the research outcome has limited value. Kohli (2001) proposes a proliferation of research projects between industry and academia. We propose that AR is the vehicle that can accomplish such meaningful interaction and collaboration between the industry and researchers.

It is important, therefore, for practitioners to invite their academic colleagues to work with them to solve their practice related issues. It's important for researchers to keep asking the practitioners, "What keeps you up at night?" It's important for both to keep adding to the body of knowledge, so that progress is shared among practitioners and academics alike.

The application of AR in healthcare can learn from how AR has been deployed in other areas. At the XI World Forum of the International Association of Jesuit Business Schools, a study reported on the impact on students that resulted from the collaboration between business schools and business enterprises (González Ramagli, 2005). Such collaboration resulted in a blending or colliding of the elements of three dichotomies: theory and practice, university and business, student and practitioner. The study reported increased levels of satisfaction among the participants, increased quantity and quality of social interactions about work (work issues came up more often as topics of conversation in social circumstances), improved levels of evaluation and understanding of the issues, and increased levels of personal self-confidence. In addition, students in particular reported being more satisfied with their studies when they believed that their studies or their membership in the university was transforming or changing them. This is indeed what we want action research to accomplish.

4.   CONCLUDING REMARKS

Action research does extremely well in addressing messy problems – those that do not have a clear problem definition. This lack of definition makes it challenging to find a clear solution; hence the need for establishing evaluation criteria. AR projects work remarkably well in uncovering issues sometimes with unexpected findings. In conclusion, based upon our experiences in AR, we offer some suggestions for AR researchers in Table 10-2.

Table 10-2. Steps, activities, and suggestions in an action research project. Steps and activities in Steps 2-6 follow the cyclical process suggested by Susman and Evered (1978)

Step	Activities	Suggestions
1. Identifying AR Projects	• Establish contact with organizations • Pre-diagnose whether AR will add value to the client	• Identify situations with 'messy' problems • Prefer projects where the organization is feeling the 'pain.' • Clarify how the outcome of your research findings will be published • Offer to sign a non-disclosure statement and disguise the organization and/or the data in publications
2. Diagnosing	• Establish the mutually acceptable ethical framework • Clearly articulate the problem	• Identify the areas of conflict • Seek to understand all sides • Identify informants • Establish trust with the informants • Keep meticulous notes of meetings, computer logs and emails. • Is there an IT artifact?

Step	**Activities**	**Suggestions**
3. Action Planning	• Identify alternative approaches to solving the problem • Evaluate each alternative	• Don't let your favorite theory drive the action planning • Consult colleagues within and outside your discipline for alternate theoretical perspectives • Keep facts or data separate from your observations
4. Action Taking	• Choose one of the alternatives as a course of action	• Validate your assumptions with the informants • Ensure that notice of actions taken are through customary communication channels
5. Evaluating	• Examine how the action taken addressed the problem situation	• Evaluate learning from all parties' perspective • Compare results with the criteria established at the beginning of the project • Examine how did the findings conform to those predicted by theory
6. Specifying Learning	• Document learning from the 'evaluation' step and how such learning can be applied to other AR projects	• How can be learning be shared with the organization? Who will be the beneficiaries of the findings? • Do organizational design or policies need to be adjusted as a result of the learning? • Did the theoretical grounding help or hinder AR? • Does the theory need to be adjusted?

REFERENCES

Atwal, A., & Caldwell, K. (2002). Do multidisciplinary integrated care pathways improve interprofessional collaboration? *Scandinavian Journal of Caring Sciences, 16*(4), 360-367.

Baskerville, R. (1999a). *Action Research for Information Systems.* Paper presented at the Americas Conference on Information Systems.

Baskerville, R. (1999b). Investigating Information Systems with Action Research. *Communications of AIS, 2*(19), 1-32.

Brailer, D. (2004). *Testimony Before the Subcommittee on Health of the House Committee on Ways and Means.*

Chiasson, M. W., & Davidson, E. (2005). Taking industry seriously in information systems research. *MIS Quarterly, 29*(4), 591-605.

Chilingerian, J. A., & Sherman, H. D. (1990). Managing Physician Efficiency and Effectiveness in Providing Hospital Services. *Health Services Management Research, 3*(1), 3-15.

Davison, R., Martinsons, M. G., & Kock, N. (2004). Principles of canonical action research. *Information Systems Journal, 14*(1), 65-86.

González Ramagli, A. (2005, June 5-8). *La Condición Estudiante - Trabajador: Impactos en la Evaluación del la Formación y en la Circulatión de Conocimientos Universidad - Empresa,.* Paper presented at the XI World Forum of the International Association of Jesuit Business Schools, Sao Leopoldo, Brazil.

Kelly, D., Simpson, S., & Brown, P. (2002). An action research project to evaluate the clinical practice facilitator role for junior nurses in an acute hospital setting. *Journal of Clinical Nursing, 11*(1), 90-98.

Kock, N. (1999). *IS Action Research: Can we serve two masters?* Paper presented at the Americas Conference on Information Systems.

Kohli, R. (2001). Industry-Academia Intervention: Key to IT Relevance. *Communications of AIS, 6*(15), 1-4.

Kohli, R., & Kettinger, W. J. (2004). Informating the Clan: Controlling Physicians' Costs and Outcomes. *MIS Quarterly, 28*(3), 363-394.

Kohli, R., Piontek, F., Ellington, T., VanOsdol, T., Shepard, M., & Brazel, G. (2001). Managing Customer Relationships through an E-Business Decision Support Application: A case of hospital physician collaboration. *Decision Support Systems, 32*(2), 171-187.

Ruef, M., & Scott, W. R. (1998). A multidimensional model of organizational legitimacy: Hospital survival in changing institutional environments. *Administrative Science Quarterly, 43*(4), 877-904.

Sharma, A. (1997). Professional as agent: Knowledge asymmetry in agency exchange. *Academy of Management Review, 22*(3), 758-798.

Susman, G. I., & Evered, R. D. (1978). Assessment of Scientific Merits of Action Research. *Administrative Science Quarterly, 23*(4), 582-603.

Zuboff, S. (1985). Automate Informate - the 2 Faces of Intelligent Technology. *Organizational Dynamics, 14*(2), 4-18.

Chapter 11

GENERATING DATA FOR RESEARCH ON EMERGING TECHNOLOGIES
An Action Learning Approach

Pak Yoong[1], David Pauleen[1] and Brent Gallupe[2]
[1]Victoria University of Wellington, New Zealand; [2]Queen's University, Canada

Abstract: One of the difficulties of conducting applied qualitative research on the applications of emerging technologies is finding available sources of relevant data for analysis. Because the adoption of emerging technologies is, by definition, new in many organisations, there is often a lack of experienced practitioners who have relevant background and are willing to provide useful information for the study. Therefore, it is necessary to design research approaches that can generate accessible and relevant data. This chapter begins with a description of action learning and its application to the training of e-facilitators. It will also explain the differences between action learning and action research. The chapter will then describe two case studies in which the researchers used an action learning approach to study the nature of e-facilitation for face-to-face and for distributed electronic meetings. Finally, the chapter describes some lessons learned for both practitioners and researchers.

Key words: Action learning; emerging technology; electronic meeting; virtual teams; e-facilitation.

1. INTRODUCTION

The introduction and use of emerging technologies in organisations has been found to be a complex process (Orlikowski, 1992). Collaborative technologies that supports group members in face-to-face meetings or in virtual meetings are examples of such emerging technologies. One of the difficulties in studying the introduction of collaborative technologies in organisations is the lack of experienced and knowledgeable users who are able to provide meaningful data so that researchers can better understand the actual processes of how these technologies can be successfully introduced.

One of the critical success factors in the use of IT to support face-to-face and virtual collaborative work is electronic meeting facilitation (e-facilitation). E-facilitation could be described as a set of activities carried out by the facilitator to assist a group of people to achieve its own outcomes in face-to-face and virtual environments. Research has shown that these electronic meetings can be productive (Dennis and Gallupe, 1993; Fjermestad and Hiltz, 1999; Kayworth and Leidner, 2001) but they also show that the productivity is largely due to the skill of an e-facilitator (Benbasat and Lim, 1993; Nunamaker, Briggs and Mittleman, 1996; Duarte and Tennant-Snyder, 1999). The skilled facilitator aids the group in using the technology, helps with group process and facilitates the building of relationships between members who may be separated by time and distance. Yet, because the adoption of e-facilitation is new in many organisations, there is often a lack of experienced practitioners who have relevant background and are able to provide useful information. Therefore, researchers and less-experienced practitioners continue to struggle to understand the subtleties and difficulties in the application of meeting facilitation techniques in the 'electronic' context. What is needed, then, is a way for researchers and these less-experienced practitioners to learn more about the nature of e-facilitation and the learning processes associated with becoming a facilitator of e-meetings.

The purpose of this chapter is to describe how the researchers used an *action learning* approach to produce a rigorous and flexible method for studying e-facilitation. In particular, two cases are discussed that met this need by designing research approaches that enabled the generation of easily accessible and relevant data related to e-facilitation, as well as giving practitioners the opportunity to learn such skills. In the first case, the author conducted a study that examined the question of how facilitators of conventional meetings become facilitators of face-to-face electronic meetings (Yoong, 1996) while the second explored the nature of virtual facilitation and relationship building in virtual teams (Pauleen, 2001). In both cases *action learning* was used, via an intensive training programme, as the means for data generation.

The chapter begins with a discussion on action learning. This discussion highlights the differences and similarities between action learning and action research. The second section presents each study and the application of action learning. Finally, some implications of this research approach for practice and research are outlined.

2. ACTION LEARNING

The term *action learning* was coined by Revans (1982) and is defined as "a means of development, intellectual, emotional or physical that requires its subjects, through responsible involvement in some real, complex and stressful problem, to achieve intended change to improve their observable behavior henceforth in the problem field" (p. 626-627). Action learning has now been extended and applied in information systems education (Avison, 1989; Jessup and Egbert, 1995, Yoong and Gallupe, 2001; Pauleen 2003) and organisational development (Ramirez, 1983; Gregory, 1994). In these contexts, action learning is a group learning and problem-solving process whereby group members work on real issues and problems with an emphasis on self-development and learning by doing.

Marsick and O'Neil (1999) identify three different 'schools' of thought on action learning: Scientific, Experiential and Critical Reflection. Table 11-1 provides a summary of the theoretical background to each school of thought.

Marsick and O'Neil uncovered two themes that are common to all three schools of action learning and that is, the group participants: (a) meet on equal terms and (b) are engaged in solving unstructured problems where there are no one right solution. The group of four to six participants, known as the action learning 'set', meets regularly and provides the supportive and challenging environment in which members are encouraged to learn from experience, sharing that experience with others, having other members criticise and advise, taking that advice and implementing it, and reviewing with those members the action taken and the lessons that are learned (Margerison, 1988). Many learning sets require the assistance of a 'learning coach' or 'facilitator' and the role of the coach depends on (a) whether the learning set works on one project as a team or the participants work on individual projects and (b) the level of facilitation on group process (Marsick and O'Neil, 1999).

2.1 Action learning and action research

Action learning is closely linked to action research. The relationship between action learning and action research is described by Zuber-Skerritt (1991) when she argues that action research is based on the "fundamental concepts of action learning, adult learning and holistic dialectical thinking..." (p. 88) and that action learning "...is a basic concept of action research" (p. 214). However, the use of action research is more prevalent in IS research (Lau, 1997) and typically involves the researcher's intervention in

Table 11-1. The Three 'Schools' of Action Learning (Adapted from Marsick and O'Neil, 1999; pp. 161-163)

School	Influenced by	Theoretical background
Scientific	R. W. Revans (1982)	Action learning is viewed as a model of problem solving in three stages: 1. System Alpha – design of a problem solving strategy including a situation analysis. 2. Systems Beta – the negotiation of the strategy including survey, hypothesis, experiment, audit and review. 3. System Gamma – the learning process associated with the strategy.
Experiential	D. Kolb (1984)	Based on Kolb's experiential learning cycle, proponents of this school advocate that the starting point for learning is action followed by reflection on action, preferably with the support of other group members. Any further action should focus on changing previous patterns of behaviours.
Critical Reflection	J. Mezirow (1990, 1991)	Proponents of this school see 'reflection on action' as a necessary but insufficient condition for learning. They believe that participants should also go deeper and examine the assumptions and beliefs that influence their practice. Reflection at this deeper level focuses a participant's attention on the root of the problem and transform previously held perspectives of the same problem.

an organisation's core business process in order to both improve that process and generate new and relevant knowledge from this experience (Kock, McQueen and Scott, 1997). Lau's (1997) proposed IS action research framework describes the 'classical' action research as having a focus on changing information systems related practice while the 'emergent' version has a focus of changing social and business processes with a socio-technical system or a technological innovation.

However, in the context of these e-facilitation studies, three differences between action learning and action research have been identified. First, action learning focuses on a process in which a group of people (often from different organisations or situations) coming together to help each other learn from their experience (for example, e-facilitation). Each participant may draw different learning from his or her different experiences and organisational agenda. Therefore, the learning is unique to each participant. On the other hand, action research is a process by which a team of people, often coming from the same organisation, pursues an organisational change strategy (for example, via a GSS-supported process improvement project) and the participants draw collective learning from a collective experience. Second, the researcher in an action learning project focuses on the facilitation of group members' learning, whereas, in action research, the researcher intervenes and facilitates an aspect of organisational change. Finally, while both action learning and action research require participants to collect and analyse data, in action research, the participants collect and analyse data in a more rigorous and formal manner (Davison, Martinsons and Kock, 2004).

2.2   The Appropriateness of Action Learning in the Study of Emerging Technologies

The facilitation of e-meetings with its characteristic rational and irrational components is an example of complex processes associated with introducing emerging technologies (Anson, 1990; Yoong, 1999). Understanding one's own facilitation actions, intended or unintended, is possible only with attention to situational and contextual complexities (Friedman, 1989) and with the recognition that much of what the facilitator does is active, spontaneous and flexible (Anson, 1990). There is simply little time to deliberate on their actions. If this situation is also coupled with the use of electronic meeting tools, the facilitation becomes very much more complex. How then do you design a research-focused training programme that not only deals with this complexity in the learning situation but also equips the learners to handle this complexity in 'live' situations?

To discover the personal experiences of the facilitators in these complex situations, we began to search for learning approaches which would not only explicitly acknowledge our roles as researcher, facilitator and trainer but also our intimate involvement in the study. This meant looking for a framework that would include us in the design of the study, by allowing us to take an active part in its implementation and in collecting, analyzing and interpreting the data. This is what Cunningham (1993) described as being 'engaged' in the problem as it evolves. It was proposed that *action learning* would be the appropriate and relevant approach for an e-facilitation training programme to be used in the two studies.

First, action learning focuses on tackling real 'live' organisational issues and "action learning problems are always based on real work" (Marsick and O'Neil, 1999; p. 165). Learning to facilitate in electronic environments is real and 'live' for many organisations who have or are considering introducing internet-based collaborative work spaces. Second, action learning promotes learning in collaborative groups and that group process is important to participants' learning (Marsick and O'Neil, 1999). Third, action learning is suited to turbulent environments, which are experiencing conditions of uncertainty and unpredictability (Ramirez, 1983). E-facilitation often occurs in turbulent environments where uncertainty and unpredictability are common phenomena. In these conditions, the e-facilitators, in consultation with team participants, are continually adapting the meeting agenda to accommodate to these unexpected changes (DeSanctis and Poole, 1994). In this respect, action learning is appropriate for e-facilitation training as it encourages and promotes the practice of active flexible facilitation. Finally, action learning meets the requirement that these training programmes are tailored to a group of experienced facilitators who could bring their own expertise and who, by researching their own practice, would be able to improve their own facilitation practice in the e-meeting environment.

3.   THE APPLICATION OF ACTION LEARNING

Even though there were some differences between how action learning was applied in the two studies, the approach to be described in this section is a generalized version of action learning based on our collective experiences.

3.1   The Action Learning Programmes

As described in an earlier section, we did not have ready access to research participants who had relevant e-facilitation experiences to provide the research data for our studies. So we had to design training programmes for data generation purposes. We also had to offer research participants, who were busy professionals, something in exchange for their time and effort, and the training programmes provided an environment in which they could receive knowledge and a safe place to improve their e-facilitation skills.

Two factors have influenced the adoption of action learning for both studies, which commenced in 1991 and 1998 respectively. The first factor was a desire to ground the studies on the practical experiences of professional practitioners. We believe in making research relevant and have a strong commitment to engage in research projects that have practical implications for business organisations.

The second factor was a desire to be engaged with the participants during the research process. We were interested in improving our own level of e-facilitation skills. By being engaged in a 'co-learner' role with the research participants, we were able to share new skills and knowledge as they were generated during the project.

When designing the action learning programmes, we were guided by the following set of principles:

Facilitators are encouraged to learn in groups and to use the learning groups to:
- work and gather data on real issues and problems associated with e-facilitation,
- reflect and improve on their facilitation by the appropriate incorporation of the e-meeting tools,
- interlink their action and reflection,
- share their action and reflection with others, and
- create and sustain a supportive and challenging community of critically informed facilitators. (Adapted from Revans, 1982; Margerison, 1988)

Action learning has an iterative cyclical nature often involving the same learning group. The learning group continues in successive cycles until an appropriate level of self-development and learning is achieved. In our studies, each iterative cycle involved a new learning group. This is a modification of the action learning approach and was made to improve data collection. It should be pointed out that each action learning training programme was evaluated at the end of each cycle and changes were made to the training programme before the next cycle. As for the participants, although their involvement with their action learning set ended at the end of each cycle they were invited to get in touch with us if they wanted to discuss new experiences or insights. In fact, in the first training programme, some of the fifteen participants formed a community of practice and continued to learn and share new e-facilitation knowledge and skills for many years after their training (Yoong, 1998).

3.2 An Outline of the Two Case Studies

Case study 1: Face-to-face Electronic Meetings Facilitation

This first study investigated the question: *How do facilitators of conventional meetings make the transition to facilitating face-to-face electronic meetings?* The study aimed to develop a model representing the learning processes and experiences of conventional meeting facilitators who were undergoing training in the facilitation of computer supported problem-solving meetings (Yoong, 1998). Three action learning programmes were conducted and five facilitators took part in each programme. Each training programme consisted of three modules as shown in Table 11-2.

Table 11-2. The Components of a Electronic Meetings Facilitation Training Programme

Module Number	Title of Module	Brief Description of the Module
1	The Tools of an Electronic Meetings	This module provides the necessary hands-on skills and knowledge of the e-meeting product (GroupSystems V or VisionQuest).
2	Planning and Managing an Electronic Meeting	This module focuses on (a) how to plan and design an agenda for an electronic meeting, (b) how to balance human and computer interactions, and (c) the role of the facilitators in electronic meetings.
3	Putting It All Together	This practical module provides opportunities for trainees to plan and facilitate 'live' electronic meetings.

The facilitators studied Modules 1 and 2 during the two full-day and two half-day sessions. The practical component, 'Putting It All Together', took place soon after the training. During this module the facilitators were expected to demonstrate the skills and knowledge acquired from the preceding training programme. They did this by planning, managing and facilitating a 'live' electronic meeting which lasted about three hours.

Examples of action learning activities

In this section, we will describe the use of three action learning activities during a typical group training session:

Learning the GSS tools: During each training session, the trainees were encouraged to learn the GSS tools. The learning of each GSS tool was structured as described by Bostrom et al. (1991) - "Model it, let them experience it, discuss and process it, let them experience it again. Build in structured 'playtimes' - individual time for them to play with the technology" (p. 33). This approach was often followed by a group discussion on how and when to use the tools during an electronic meeting. Boud's (1993) notion that learners actively construct their own experience has been found to be a useful principle. The trainees found that they had to construct their learning of GSS tools differently according to a meeting's context. For example, facilitating a meeting where conflict resolution is a high priority requires a different approach to the use of GSS tools than in a meeting where the participants conduct planning scenarios. Each trainee was encouraged to think about how these shared learnings can be incorporated into their individual facilitation style.

Mini-meetings: As well as learning the different GSS tools, the trainees were given the opportunity to integrate them into an electronic meeting. Each trainee demonstrated the use of the tools during 15 minute structured mini-meetings with their peers as participants in the meeting, and in each of the meetings the topic was a current interest of the facilitator-in-practice. Immediately after the session, self- and peer feedback comments on each trainee's performance was given. It should be noted that these mini-meeting sessions were also used to increase the trainees' repertoire of facilitation skills and knowledge. The opportunity to observe each other's experience during the practice sessions served as another source of learning.

The 'Live' Electronic Meeting: The practical module - 'Putting It All Together' - took place after the training. Trainees demonstrated the skills and knowledge acquired from the preceding training programme by planning, managing and facilitating a 'live' electronic meeting which lasted about three hours. The participants in each meeting were told that, even though the meeting facilitator was undergoing training, they should use the meeting to deliberate on 'live' issues that were important to them. In other words, they were not in a 'mock' meeting. All the meetings were videotaped and the recordings used for giving feedback to the trainees and as research data for this study.

Case study 2: Virtual Teams Facilitation

The second study investigated the question: *How do facilitators of virtual teams build relationships with their virtual team members?* A pilot programme involving one facilitator and two action learning programmes, involving three facilitators each, were conducted in this study. Each training programme was ten weeks long. The content of the programme covered virtual team issues and processes of concern to a facilitator (Table 11-3). During the training programmes, each participant planned for, evaluated the use of, or actually initiated and facilitated a virtual team within their own organisational context. The three facilitators and the trainer/researcher in each program met every two weeks for two hours.

Table 11-3. Outline of Virtual Team Action Learning Program

Virtual Team Action - Learning Program
Session One Virtual Team Implementation and Project Planning **Session Two** Developing Virtual Team Purpose, Communication Strategies and Protocols and Technology **Session Three** Developing Team Identity, Building Relationships and Intercultural Communication Issues **Session Four** Preparing for and Facilitating Virtual Meetings **Session Five** Concluding a Virtual Team and Other Training Issues. Virtual Teams in the Organisation

Examples of action learning activities

In this section, we will describe the use of action learning activities during a typical group training session.

An Action Learning Virtual Practice Team (first training program): Because these participants were busy professionals working on diverse projects, it was unlikely that they would be carrying out the implementation and facilitation of their virtual teams in lock step, and would therefore not always have the same issues to discuss in the training sessions. Therefore, it was proposed that they consider themselves to be a virtual team and work together outside of the training sessions experimenting with electronic communication channels and discussing virtual team issues raised in the training sessions. This gave them another avenue to gain practical and relevant experience. To this end, the facilitators were given the team name, *VT Pioneers*, before training Session 1, and during each training session were asked them to do small tasks as shown in Table 11-4. Their experiences with these tasks were discussed in the subsequent training sessions.

Table 11-4. Session 1 Simulation Task for Virtual Pioneers (Cycle One Participants)

Session 1
Virtual training – contact *VT Pioneers* using 2 – 3 different media; note and evaluate your experiences

Virtual Team Simulation Redux (second training program): based on the feedback from the first training program participants, a second virtual team simulation was developed. Before the participants met face to face in the training program, an email was sent to them with the simulation exercise in Table 11-5. This exercise generated an enormous amount of virtual activity. No name was agreed upon, but the participants had all managed to introduce themselves online prior to the first face to face meeting. We tried to keep the stimulation going with another task to be completed online between program sessions. This task was not completed either, and it became clear that interpersonal and team issues, including non-participation by two members, were already coming to the fore and impairing the team's performance. In the end, the simulation was discontinued, but it had generated significant discussion and learning, as evidenced by theis comment from one of the participant, "One of the big things that struck me about what was happening here in that this simulation actually mirrored a number of experiences I have had in virtual teams".

Table 11-5. Virtual Team Simulation Exercise – Part 1

Virtual Team Action Training Program
Cycle Two Session One

Simulation Exercise # 1

Your CEO, an inventive, 'follow her intuition sort of character', and founder of *Mission Possible Software Solutions* would like to do an impromptu experiment on the initiation of a virtual team. So she randomly contacts a few of the company's employees from different offices and functions and asks them to form a virtual team to look into an as yet unidentified organisational issue.

The first task of this team is to choose a team name and logo. She offers no other input.

You have been chosen to be a member of this team. The other team members are:

    1. RR   RR@poll.nz

    2. RA   ARA@AX.co.nz

    3. CC   CC@inno.net.nz

    4. JD   JD@trader.co.nz

    5. SS   SLS@IS.org.nz

Deadline: Team name and logo to be presented in Session One 25 January 2000

(For the purpose of this simulation, your role in this company is similar to your current role in your current company, ie manager = manager, analyst = analyst))

Online Synchronous Tutorial: Another activity involved organizing an online tutorial using Netmeeting. In this online session, we explored the issues in facilitating online desktop videoconferencing. The session highlighted many of the difficulties of facilitating online synchronous meetings, but was considered a valuable learning experience, with at least one participant saying he learned a lot in the session.

3.3   Collecting and Analyzing Data from the Programme

This section begins with a discussion of some field work issues associated with both studies.

Field Work Issues

The field work in both studies was divided into three blocks of activity. For the first study, we had three training programmes whilst the second study involved a pilot project and the two training programmes. Dividing the studies into blocks of activity proved to be a useful approach. The extended period between each block of fieldwork provided time for transcription and analysis of the interview data. Equally importantly, these in-between periods were used for reflection, interpretation and strategy building. These reflective periods, which are built into the action learning cycle (Yoong, 1996), significantly influenced the way the next period of fieldwork was conducted. The following two examples from the second study are illustrative: the difficulties the researcher encountered in the pilot project working with a single individual, encouraged him to think strategically about his data collection methods and consequently to devise a training programme for several participants so as to ensure adequate data collection; the interim results from the first training programme helped him to determine the selection of the second programme participants based on the principle of theoretical sampling (Glaser and Strauss, 1967). Facilitators in the second training programme were selected because of their differences to those from the first training programme, both in their experience with virtual teams and in the global nature of their virtual teams and team projects. As a result, the researcher was able to compare and contrast the emerging theory with the data as prescribed by the constant comparative method.

Data Collection and Analysis

Several methods of data collection have been used in both studies primarily based on semi-structured interviews and discussions between the researcher and the facilitators and informal facilitator reports, the researcher's journal, participants' notes, and organisational documentation. Video-recordings of the 'live' electronic meetings were also collected in the first study while copies of electronic conversations (i.e. e-mail) were used in the second study.

Semi-structured interviews were conducted with the facilitators after each of the following training events: briefing meeting, the training sessions and the 'live' electronic meeting (used only for the first study). The list of questions in the interview guide was flexible and "not a tightly structured set of questions to be asked verbatim as written ... it is a list of things to be sure to ask about when talking to the person being interviewed" (Lofland and Lofland, 1995; p. 85). This flexible and guided conversation then flowed on from the initial leading questions.

We were also participants in the programme and took on two major roles: the first as trainer and coach and the second, as observer. We identified ourselves as both a member of the training group and as an observer of the training sessions. That is to say that we both gathered information and participated in the training activities.

However, as participant observers, we were able to learn at first hand how the facilitators' actions corresponded with what was described as important in subsequent interviews when the "interview questions that develop through participant observation (were) connected to known behavior, and their answers ... therefore ... better interpreted" (Glesne and Peshkin, 1992; p. 39). These contextual cues were found to be especially useful during the analysis and interpretation stages. Therefore, there was an explicit connection between the observations that we gathered and the facilitators' accounts of their experience. We also gathered data on what we had heard and seen during the training sessions.

As is common in qualitative research, a large volume of data was collected in both studies (Gopal and Prasad, 2000), and we began to analyse the data by listening to and transcribing each recorded interview and discussion. Transcripts were returned to the participants for member checking and validation.

Our first step in the analysis of the data was to code all the transcripts as well as relevant documents such as facilitators' journals. We used open coding techniques, a process of labelling the events and ideas represented in the data (Baskerville and Pries-Heje, 1999). We coded most our data using NVIVO, a computer software program developed especially to be used with qualitative research methods (Richards and Richards, 1994). We perused the transcript and assigned one or more conceptual codes to each line, sentence or paragraph, most often in terms of properties and dimensions (ibid.). As grounded theory researchers, we also tried to approach the data without any particular preconceived notion or framework (Trauth and Jessup, 2000) and simply assign a descriptive label.

At the end of the first action learning cycles, we began looking for connections between conceptual codes through the use of several strategies. As suggested by Baskerville and Pries-Heje (1999) we used grounded theory notation such as memos and diagrams. We created a set of emergent models based on the codes and categories that were taking shape, as well as our intuition guided by increasing levels of theoretical sensitivity. We also wrote narrative, chronological case studies of each of the participants. This gave us another lens through which to view the data and to draw cross linkages between the experiences of each of the participants. These cases also gave us a valuable way to engage in 'member checking' with the participants when they read through them and verified their experiences as we had written them up.

We repeated the data collection and analysis processes for the remaining training programmes, comparing emerging categories with those from the previous cycles. The notion of 'theoretical sensitivity' is particularly useful at these stages. It is "the attribute of having insight, the ability to give meaning to data, the capacity to understand, and capability to separate the pertinent from that which isn't" (Strauss and Corbin, 1990; p. 42-43). This sensitivity can be achieved by a variety of approaches including extensive literature search in related fields of study and a series of reflections on personal and professional experience. Any further data collection and analysis become more selective and are guided by the emerging theory and a process known as 'theoretical saturation'. This means that the entire process continues until no additional data, coding, or sorting contribute to the extension of the theory.

4.   RESEARCH RESULTS

Case study 1: GSS[1] Facilitation
The major outcome of the first study is the *Grounded Theory of Reflective GSS Facilitation* (from now on referred to as *Reflective GSS Facilitation*). *Reflective GSS Facilitation* describes the processes and issues associated with how facilitators of conventional meetings – the trainees who took part in this study – become facilitators of electronic meetings. The processes and issues were documented from the time the facilitators entered the program until the time they had facilitated their first electronic meeting, a period defined as the transitional period. The research findings from this study, which occurred in one setting, are inductively derived from what took place during it.

---

[1]   GSS is the acronym for Group Support Systems

Reflective GSS Facilitation is a unifying framework for the two inter-related theoretical components: *The Stages of GSS Facilitation Development* and *Reflective Practice*. Figure 11-1 shows the inter-relationship between the two theoretical components.

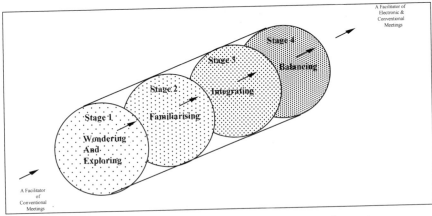

Figure 11-1. The Stage Theory of GSS Facilitation Development

The first of these two theoretical components, *The Stages of GSS Facilitation Development*, describes the four stages that the trainees go through in the transition from being facilitators of conventional meetings to being facilitators of electronic meetings. The four stages are: *Wondering and Exploring, Familiarising, Integrating*, and *Balancing*.

The second theoretical component, Reflective Practice, describes the trainees' ways of thinking about how to facilitate electronic meetings and the context in which these thoughts take place. Reflective Practice itself consists of two components: Active Reflection and Contextual Factors.

Case study 2: Virtual Facilitation

The major outcome of the second study is a *Grounded Theory of Virtual Facilitation* that investigated the issues facing virtual team facilitators as they implemented and led virtual teams see members (Pauleen, 2003-04). A specific outcome of the study was a model of how virtual team facilitators build relationships with their virtual team members. This model (Figure 11-2) includes a unifying framework of three inter-related theoretical steps: *Assessing Conditions, Targeting Level of Relationship*, and *Creating Strategies*. This study was the first to identify the steps a virtual team leader undertakes when building relationships with virtual team.

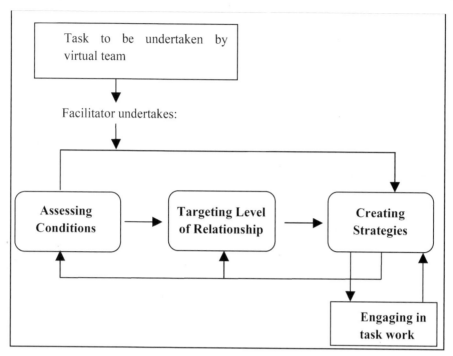

Figure 11-2. The Three Steps in Facilitating Virtual Relationships (in organisational context)

5.   DISCUSSION AND IMPLICATIONS

Based on the evidence from these two cases, we believe that the action learning approach is a useful method for supporting practitioner learning, and for providing data to the researcher so that useful theory can be developed. We found that using the action learning approach made the introduction of the technology "real" to the practitioners. We found this to be important because it motivated the practitioners to heighten their awareness and reflections about what they were doing, and hence provide the researchers with rich and relevant data. Action learning may not be appropriate in all cases of introducing new technologies into organisations, but in these two cases it was found to be useful for both practitioners and researchers.

We believe there are a number of implications of the action learning approach described in this chapter. First, learning to facilitate electronic meetings is a complex and difficult experience. The action learning approach provides the facilitator with the means to combine both experience and reflection as the learning is taking place.

Second, the action learning approach enables the researcher to better understand what the learner is experiencing, and therefore better able to adapt his/her approaches to make the learning more efficient and effective. The action learning approach goes beyond some interpretative techniques in that it enables the subject to express their own thoughts about what is being learned and how the learning is occurring rather than being interpreted by the researcher. This "direct" link to the data is an important benefit for the researcher from the action learning approach.

Third, the action learning approach has potential beyond research into e-facilitation. Information Systems researchers in general, might consider this approach when studying learning in complex situations involving emerging technologies. For example, we believe that this form of practice-focused research will become more pervasive as organisations learn to manage emerging technologies.

Finally, implementing action learning approaches to generate data in the use of emergent technologies is not without potential pitfalls or difficulties. Organisations and individuals value their time and require persuasive reasons to participate in any kind of research agenda. Action learning requires a significant time and energy commitment. Marquardt (1999) identifies a number of other pitfalls including: (a) inappropriate problem, (b) lack of organisational support, (c) lack of commitment to learning, and (d) poor group facilitation. However, the action learning approach as a research tool also possesses distinct advantages that organisations and individuals can readily grasp: chief of these is the opportunity to engage in hands-on learning and use of new technologies with peers in a safe, guided environment. Organisational and peer learning are the hallmarks of successful organisations in the current knowledge age and action learning research has a key role to play.

6.   CONCLUSIONS

In conclusion, we believe that action learning is a powerful approach in the training of organisational users of emergent technologies as well as an effective method for researchers to collect relevant data based on the users' experience. The approach offers the potential to develop emergent theories of new information technology applications that are based on actual practice.

It is hoped that this chapter, which describes the action learning approach in two cases, will promote identification of and discussion about the many complex issues associated with the introduction of new technology in the workplace.

REFERENCES

Anson, R. (1990). Effects of Computer Support and Facilitator Support on Group Processes and Outcomes: An Experimental Assessment. Unpublished doctoral dissertation, Indiana University.

Avison, D. (1989). Action Learning for Information Systems Teaching. International Journal of Information Management. 9, 41-50.

Baskerville, R., & Pries-Heje, J. (1999). Grounded action research: a method for understanding IT in practice. Accounting Management and Information Technologies. 9, 1-23.

Benbasat, I. & Lim, L. (1993). The Effects of Groups, Task, Context, and Technology Variables on the Usefulness of Group Support Systems: A Meta-Analysis of Experimental Studies. Small Group Research. 24(4), 430-462.

Bostrom, R., Clawson, V., and Anson, R. (1991). Training People to Facilitate Electronic Environments. Working Paper, Department of Management, University of Georgia, Athens, GA 30602.

Boud, D. (1993). Experience as a Base for Learning. Higher Education Research and Development. 12(1), 33-44.

Cunningham, J. (1993). Action Research and Organizational Development. Westport, Connecticut: Praeger.

Davison, R.M., Martinsons, M.G. and Kock, N. (2004). Principles of Canonical Action Research, Information Systems Journal. 14(1), 65-86.

Dennis, A.R. and Gallupe, R.B. (1993). GSS Past, Present, and Future. Jessup, L. and Valacich, eds. Group Support Systems: New Perspectives. New York: Macmillan:, 59-77.

DeSanctis, G. and Poole, S. (1994). Capturing the Complexity in Advanced Technology Use: Adaptive Structuration Theory. Organization Science. 5(2), 121-147.

Duarte, N., and Tennant-Snyder, N. (1999). Mastering Virtual Teams: Strategies, Tools, and Techniques that Succeed. San Francisco: Jossey-Bass.

Fjermestad, J., and Hiltz, S.R. (1999). An assessment of group support systems experiment research: methodology and results. Journal of Management Information Systems. 15(3), 7-15.

Friedman, P. (1989). Upstream Facilitation: A Proactive Approach to Managing Problem-Solving Groups. Management Communications Quarterly. 3(1), 33-51.

Glaser, B., & Strauss, A.L. (1967). The Discovery of Grounded Theory: Strategies for Qualitative Research. New York: Aldine De Gruyter.

Glesne, C. and Peshkin, A. (1992). Becoming Qualitative Researchers: An Introduction. White Plains, N.Y: Longman.

Gopal, A., & Prasad, P. (2000). Understanding GDSS in symbolic context: shifting the focus from technology to interaction. MIS Quarterly. **24**(3), 509-545.

Gregory, M. (1994). Accrediting Work-Based Learning: Action Learning - A Model For Empowerment. Journal of Management Development. **13**(4), 41-52.

Kayworth, T.R. and Leidner, D.E. (2001). Leadership effectiveness in global virtual teams. Journal of Management Information Systems. **18**(3), 7-40.

Jessup, L. and Egbert, J. (1995). Active Learning in Business Education With, Through, and About Technology. Journal of Information Systems Education. **7**(3), 108-112.

Kock, N., McQueen, R. and Scott, J. (1997). Can Action Research be Made More Rigorous in a Positivist Sense? The Contribution of an Iterative Approach. Journal of Systems and Information Technology. **1**(1), 1-24.

Lau, F. (1997). A Review on the Use of Action Research in Information Systems Studies. Lee, A.S., Liebenau, J. and J.I. DeGross, J. I. eds. Information Systems and Qualitative Research. London: Chapman and Hall, 31-68.

Lofland, J. & Lofland, L. (1995). Analyzing Social Settings; A Guide to Qualitative Observation and Analysis. Belmont, California: Wadsworth Pub.

Margerison, C. (1988). Action learning and excellence in management development." Journal of Management Development. **7**(5): 43-55.

Marquardt, M. (1999). Action Learning in Action. Palo Alto, California: Davis-Black Publishing.

Marsick, V. and O'Neil, J. (1999). The Many Faces of Action Learning. Management Learning. **30**(2), 159-176.

Nunamaker, J.F. Jr., Briggs, R.O. and Mittleman, D.D. (1996). Lessons from a Decade of Group Support Systems Research. The Proceedings of the 29th Annual Hawaii International Conference on System Sciences, 418-427.

Orlikowski, W. (1992). The Duality of Technology: Rethinking the Concept of Technology in Organization. Organization Science. **3**(3), 398-427.

Pauleen, D. (2001). A Grounded Theory of Virtual Facilitation: Building Relationships with Virtual Team Members. Unpublished doctoral thesis. Wellington, New Zealand: Victoria University of Wellington.

Pauleen, D. (2003). Leadership in a Global Virtual Team: An Action Learning Approach. Leadership and Organizational Development Journal. **24**(3), 153-162.

Pauleen, D. (2003-4). An Inductively Derived Model of Leader-Initiated Relationship Building with Virtual Team Members. Journal of Management Information Systems 4, (3), 227-256.

Ramirez, R. (1983). Action Learning: A Strategic Approach for Organizations Facing Turbulent Conditions. Human Relations, **36**(8), 725-742.

Revans, R. (1982). The Origins and Growth of Action Learning. Bromley: Chartwell-Bratt.

Strauss, A. L., and Corbin, J (1990). Basics of Qualitative Research: Grounded Theory Procedures and Techniques. Newbury Park: Sage Publications.

Trauth, E. M., and Jessup, L.M. (2000). Understanding computer-mediated discussions: positivist and interpretative analysis of group support system use. MIS Quarterly. **24**(1), 43-79.

Yoong, P., and Gallupe, B. (2001). Action learning and groupware technologies: a case study in GSS facilitation research. Information Technology and People. **14**(1), 78-90.

Yoong, P. (1998). Training Facilitators for Face-to-Face Electronic Meetings: An Experiential Learning Approach. Journal of Informing Science. **1**(2), 31-36.

Yoong, P. (1996). A Grounded Theory of Reflective Facilitation: Making The Transition From Traditional To GSS Facilitation. Unpublished doctoral thesis. Wellington, New Zealand: Victoria University of Wellington.

Yoong, P. (1999). Making Sense of GSS Facilitation: A Reflective Practice Perspective. Journal of Information Technology and People. **12**(1), 86-112.

Zuber-Skerritt, O. (1991). Professional Development in Higher Education: A Theoretical Framework for Action Research. Brisbane: Griffith University.

Chapter 12

A TEST OF THE COMMUNICATION FLOW OPTIMIZATION MODEL THROUGH AN ACTION RESEARCH STUDY AT A DEFENSE CONTRACTOR

Ned Kock
Texas A&M International University, USA

Abstract: Operational-level approaches to process redesign have traditionally focused on "workflows", or the chronological flows of activities in processes. It is argued in this chapter that while this makes some sense in materials-transformation processes, whose final product usually is a tangible manufactured item (e.g., a car engine), this orientation is fundamentally inconsistent with the communication-intensive nature of the vast majority of processes found in organizations today. This chapter shows, through an action research study, that a focus on communication flow representations and methods is likely to lead to better process redesign outcomes than a focus on representations and methods in connection with "workflows". It does so by developing a set of research questions based on the communication flow optimization model, and answering those questions in the context provided by three process redesign projects facilitated by the researcher at a defense contractor in the US.

Key words: qualitative research; action research; data triangulation; process redesign; organizational communication; electronic communication

1. INTRODUCTION

Recently, organizational development approaches centered on business process redesign (or, simply, "process redesign") have become popular, particularly due to the emergence of business process re-engineering in the late 1980s and early 1990s (Hammer, 1996; Hunt, 1996). In spite of this recent popularity, an argument can be made that process redesign is a much older approach than re-engineering; one that has probably influenced management thinking since management's emergence as a separate field of study and practice. According to this view, process redesign can be seen as dating back to the early 1900s, when Frederick Taylor (1911) published *The Principles of Scientific Management*. The scientific management movement strongly influenced organizational development ideas and approaches throughout the Second Industrial Revolution (1850-1950). During this period, process redesign was primarily concerned with productivity (i.e., efficiency) improvement in manufacturing plants, and was centered on the optimization of "times and motions" in situations of high work specialization and division of labor.

Taylor was faced with the challenge of increasing productivity in manufacturing plants employing a workforce that was largely uneducated and unskilled. His solution involved an emphasis on the use of standard work methods and strict division of labor. In Taylor's time, manufacturing was the main wealth creator; unlike today, when service is the main contributor to the gross national product of most developed and developing countries. Accordingly, Taylor's approach involved breaking processes down into simple activities that usually involved sequences of physical motions, which were then designed to be carried out in the minimum amount of time and with the minimum amount of effort by specialized manual workers.

The value of Taylor's approach in rationalizing production is indisputable and its impact on the development of mass-production techniques has been widely recognized. Yet, it provoked resentment and opposition from labor representatives when carried to extremes, which seems to have happened often (Clutterbuck and Crainer, 1990). This might have been at least partially motivated by Taylor's depiction of workers in general as mindless executors of activities designed by management, to whom (i.e., the workers, as opposed to management) he sometimes referred as being as "stupid" and destined to back-breaking manual work as an "ox" (Taylor, 1911).

Even though it often raised factory workers' salaries, by tying individual financial compensation to increased productivity, Taylor's scientific management led to what many believe to have been as a dehumanization of the workplace, which set the stage for more "humane" schools of management to emerge and flourish. The work of Elton Mayo in the early and mid-1900s (Mayo, 1945) and that of others such as McGregor, Maslow, and Herzberg represented the emergence of the "humanist" school of management (Clutterbuck and Crainer 1990; Herzberg et al., 1959; Maslow, 1954), which tried to shift the focus of organizational development from "processes" to "people". While these management thinkers, who were very successful during the mid 1900s, can be seen as having proposed ideas that minimized the importance of processes as competitiveness drivers in organizations, process redesign was far from "dead".

The work of the "humanists" set the stage for the emergence of what many saw as a more "humane" process redesign school of thought, generally known as total quality management (Walton, 1991), which have not only succeeded scientific management as a process-based method for organizational development, but also represented a shift in focus from productivity to quality in the improvement of processes (Deming, 1986). While heavily based on statistical methods in its inception, this approach soon acquired a broader orientation (Deming, 1986; Ishikawa, 1986; Juran, 1989). Total quality management began in Japan after the World War II, largely due to the work of William Deming and Joseph Juran, and is widely credited as having propelled Japan to economic superpower status (Bergner, 1991; Chapman, 1991; Deming, 1986; Juran, 1989; Walton, 1989). In the 1980s, total quality management became widely practiced in the US and other Western capitalist countries (Deming, 1986; Juran, 1989; Walton, 1989; 1991). Similarly to scientific management, its primary focus was the improvement of manufacturing operations.

Business process re-engineering (Davenport, 1993; Hammer and Champy, 1993) replaced total quality management as the predominant school of thought in connection with process redesign in the early 1990s. Michael Hammer (together with James Champy) and Thomas Davenport independently developed business process re-engineering as, respectively, a better alternative (Hammer and Champy's version) and a complement (Davenport's version) to total quality management. Their work was based on the premise that the incremental gains in productivity obtained through the implementation of total quality management methods were insufficient for organizations to cope with the accelerated rate of change of the 1990s, brought about by new information technologies (Davenport, 1993; 1993a; Davenport and Short, 1990; Hammer, 1990; Hammer and Champy, 1993). Differently from scientific management and total quality management, business process re-engineering was presented as a method for the improvement of service as well as manufacturing operations.

In spite of being initially touted as a "new" idea, it became apparent that business process re-engineering had built on ideas and methods that were similar to those proposed by Taylor's scientific management (Earl, 1994; Waring, 1991). This is particularly true of "operational" versions of business process re-engineering (Hammer and Stanton, 1995; Hunt, 1996), which, unlike more strategic ones (Caron et al., 1994; Clemons et al., 1995), look into the inner workings of individual processes in order to improve them. In fact, throughout the history of process redesign, operational-level approaches to process redesign consistently maintained a focus on "workflows", or chronological flows of activities in processes (Kock and McQueen, 1996). It is argued in this chapter that while this orientation makes some sense in materials-transformation processes, whose final product usually is a tangible manufactured item (e.g., a car engine), this orientation is fundamentally inconsistent with the communication-intensive nature of the vast majority of processes found in organizations today, where Kock and McQueen (1996) argue much more information (an intangible item) is handled than materials (or tangible items).

This chapter attempts to show that a focus on communication flow representations and methods is likely to lead to better process redesign outcomes than a focus on "workflows". It does so by developing and answering a set of research questions based on the communication flow optimization model proposed by Kock (1999) and Kock and Murphy (2001) through an exploratory action research study of three process redesign projects conducted at a defense contractor in the US. The communication flow optimization model provides a theoretical basis for the claim that the focus of process redesign should be on how communication interactions take place in a process, and provides guidelines on how process redesign can be accomplished in a way that is consistent with this focus.

2.   RESEARCH BACKGROUND

Much research on process redesign has been conducted in the 1990s, addressing important questions raised by re-engineering. Success factors and preconditions for effective process redesign have been identified (Bashein and Markus, 1994; Clemons et al., 1995), new methods and techniques for managing change in connection with process redesign have been proposed (Kettinger and Grover, 1995; Stoddard and Jarvenpaa, 1995), potentially damaging "myths" have been identified (Davenport and Stoddard, 1994), the role of information technology in process redesign efforts has been clarified (Venkatraman, 1994), new insights on the implementation of new process designs has been gained (Grover et al., 1995), and new methods and information technology tools to support process redesign have been proposed (Kock, 1999; Nissen, 1998).

One area that has received relatively little attention, however, is that of process representation frameworks and their impact on process redesign (Katzenstein and Lerch, 2000). This is an important area of research, because it addresses the way process redesign practitioners "look at" processes, or the representational "lenses" through which they "see" a process, which arguably are likely to have a strong influence on how processes are redesigned (Hammer and Champy, 1993; Katzenstein and Lerch, 2000). For example, a focus on the flow of activities in a process (or "workflow") is likely to lead to changes in how *activities* flow in the process, whereas a focus on the flow of information in a process is likely to lead to changes in how *information* flows in the process (Davenport, 1993; Kock, 1999).

An analysis of process redesign practices throughout the 100-year period from the development of scientific management to the emergence of business process re-engineering suggests an interesting, perhaps cyclic, pattern. Even though business processes changed significantly since Frederick Taylor's times, the process redesign practices employed then seem very similar to those of the 1990s and beyond in terms of the focus of process redesign, which has consistently been the sequence of activities, or "workflow", of a process (Kock, 1999; Kock and McQueen, 1996; Waring, 1991).

The scientific management method (Taylor, 1911) consisted in breaking down a business process into component activities, for which a pictorial as well as a quantitative model was generated. The pictorial model depicted the flow of execution of the activities and the associated motions, whereas the quantitative model included information about physical distances associated with motions and the times needed to perform each of the activities. Taylor showed that managers could empirically devise optimal (or quasi-optimal) business process configurations that could then be standardized through financial incentives to workers (Taylor, 1885; 1911).

Many have argued that business process re-engineering is a "modernized" version of scientific management (Earl, 1994; Kock and McQueen, 1996; Rigby, 1993; Waring, 1991). Re-engineering's popularity reached its peak by the mid 1990s and slumped since due to a number of reported failures. James Champy, one of re-engineering's pioneers, argued that 70% of all re-engineering projects failed to achieve their goals (Champy, 1995). In spite of this, re-engineering created renewed interest in process redesign, making it (i.e., process redesign) one the most widely practiced modern forms of organizational development (Biggs, 2000; Davenport, 2000; Hammer, 2000). However, unlike during the "heyday" of scientific management, when business process improvement meant "materials flow" improvement, today most of what flows in business processes is information. As pointed out by Peter Drucker, already in the early 1990s: "In 1880, about nine out of 10 workers made and moved things; today, that is down to one out of five. The other four out of five are knowledge people or service workers" (Drucker, 1993, p. 50). A study by Kock and McQueen (1996) shows that, even in manufacturing organizations, approximately 80% of what flows in business processes is data (carrying information), while the other 20% is made up of materials (in service organizations, these proportions are usually very close to 100% and 0%, respectively). These figures seem to confirm the once thought to be visionary claims that "we are living in an information society" (Toffler,

1991) and that organizations have become "information organizations" (Drucker, 1989). The high proportion of information flow is also consistent with the widespread use of information technologies in organizations, and its increasing importance in the improvement of business processes.

In spite of the above, most process redesign practices today mirror Taylor's approaches of the early 1900s in one key respect – they appear to be tailored to the optimization of the flow of materials, which involves sequences of interrelated physical actions, and not the flow of information (Katzenstein and Lerch, 2000; Kock, 1999), which involves communication. This conclusion is reached based on the observation that most of today's process redesign practices focus on the analysis of business processes as sets of interrelated activities, and pay relatively little attention to the analysis of the communication flow in business processes (Archer and Bowker, 1995; Harrington et al., 1998; Kock and McQueen, 1996). Systems analysis and design methods (Davis, 1983; Dennis and Wixom, 2000), on the other hand, do address communication in processes, but they have traditionally been relegated to process *automation*, and had seldom been applied to process *redesign* (Harrington, 1991; Harrington et al., 1998; Kock and McQueen, 1996). More recently, object-oriented analysis and design methods have contributed a more communication-oriented view of processes, particularly those in connection with the unified modeling language (Booch et al., 1998; Rumbaugh et al., 1998), but they have also been faulted by what some see as an excessive activity orientation – see e.g., Chuang and Yadav (2000), who use this argument to explain the relative lack of success of object-oriented analysis and design methods in comparison with object-oriented programming methods.

A focus on the flow of activities makes particularly good sense in manufacturing processes, e.g., assembly-line processes, because those processes usually involve sequential steps that add complexity and value to tangible items. Since manufacturing processes embody "action" in the physical sense, they can generally be easily represented as chronological sets of activities that bring tangible items together, such as car parts or chemical components, to produce other complex and value-added tangible items, such as a car engine or a complex chemical product. That is, it is natural to think of manufacturing processes as sequences of activities. However, this is not the case with non-manufacturing processes in general, where the output of the process is usually a service (which is usually consumed while it is produced) or an information product (e.g., a report or a computer program). It has been argued that in non-manufacturing processes in general, activity flow-based modeling attempts usually lead to overly complex and somewhat misleading representations, which are not useful for process redesign (Kock, 1999; Kock and McQueen, 1996).

Perhaps due to the fact that until recently manufacturing processes played a key role in wealth creation, the most widely adopted normative approaches for process redesign embody general guidelines that place no special emphasis on the redesign of communication activities, thus arguably disregarding the information-intensive nature of business processes (Kock and McQueen, 1996). This is also true for the US Department of Defense and its contractors (arguably the single largest group of employers in the US), where the IDEF0 approach for process redesign (Ang and Gay, 1993), an activity flow-based approach, has been chosen as the official process redesign approach and is by far the most widely used (Dean et al, 1995; Kock and Murphy, 2001). One widely used activity flow-oriented approach proposed by Harrington (1991, p. 108), goes as far as stating that: "As a rule [information flow diagrams] are of more interest to computer programmers and automated systems analysts than to managers and employees charting business activities" (see also Harrington et al., 1998). While this opinion is obviously at odds with the notion that information processing is the main goal of business processes (Galbraith, 1977), it is in line with re-engineering's original claims (Hammer and Champy, 1993) and most of the current process redesign practice.

The communication flow optimization model (Kock, 1999; Kock and McQueen, 1996; Kock and Murphy, 2001; Kock, 2002; Kock et al., 1997) is an attempt to address the problems above from a theoretical perspective. The theoretical model forms the basis from which the research questions that guide this study were derived, and is discussed in the section below.

3. THE COMMUNICATION FLOW OPTIMIZATION MODEL

The communication flow optimization model (Kock, 1999; Kock and McQueen, 1996; Kock and Murphy, 2001; Kock, 2002; Kock et al., 1997) was developed based on grounded-theory research (Glaser and Strauss, 1967; Strauss and Corbin, 1990; 1998). Given space limitations, the model is only briefly summarized here – see particularly Kock (1999) and Kock and Murphy (2001) for more details. It emerged from real-world process redesign projects conducted over a period of 6 years. Evidence from those projects suggested that the flow of information could generally be seen as analogous to the flow of materials in processes, and that the former (i.e., the flow of information) could be subsumed by what is referred to as the "communication flow", or the web of communication interactions of a process. One of the key findings of those projects was that the communication flow structure of processes was a particularly strong determinant of most of the quality and productivity problems associated with processes, more so than either the activity flow or the material flow structure of the processes. Nevertheless, the evidence also suggested that, unlike in traditional systems analysis and design projects (Davis, 1983; Dennis and Wixom, 2000), rarely process redesign groups favored communication flow representations of processes over activity flow representations early on in their projects, because the former were seen as more difficult to generate, or "less natural" than the latter. The theoretical model proposes that communication flow representations of processes are perceived as more difficult to be generated than activity flow representations because the latter are better aligned with the way humans are cognitively programmed to envision "action" in the physical sense. That is, processes, which essentially represent "action", are more naturally seen as sequences of interconnected activities than communication interactions.

According to the model, optimal communication configurations can be obtained by redesigning the flow of communication in processes through the application of communication flow-oriented process redesign guidelines. It is hypothesized that the level of optimization of the communication configuration of a process will account for a substantial amount of the variation in quality and productivity achieved through the redesign. Process productivity is measured through the ratio of output capacity (e.g., the number N of complete insurance policies executed per month by an insurance underwriting process) versus costs (e.g., the direct and indirect costs associated with executing N insurance policies). Process quality is measured as the customer satisfaction in connection with the outputs of the process, where a customer can be internal (e.g., an insurance agent) or external to an organization (e.g., an insured corporation or individual).

While acknowledging differences between manufacturing and non-manufacturing processes, the communication flow optimization model argues that a focus on the flow of communication within a process will, on average and when applied to a number of processes, lead to better process redesign results than a focus on other elements, including activities and/or materials. The model does not dismiss the usefulness of process redesign techniques based on operations research, linear programming, and other traditional assembly-line and factory design techniques (Buzacott, 1996; Childe et al., 1994; Maull et al., 1995; Misterek et al., 1992), whose focus on "times and motions" often leads to quantum-leap productivity gains. Nor does the theoretical model dismiss the usefulness of methods that address coordination issues among processes. By expanding their scope beyond the individual process, such coordination improvement methods often require the consideration of process dimensions other than the communication flow dimension, including various socio-technical dimensions (Checkland and Scholes, 1990; Katzenstein and Lerch, 2000; Teng et al., 1998). Rather, the communication flow optimization model argues that at the individual process level, where usually redesign is done by looking at how elements (e.g., activities, materials, data etc.) flow within the process (Hunt, 1996; Ould, 1995), a focus on communication interactions is likely to yield results that are, on average, better than if other elements were targeted. The key reason for this is, according to the theoretical model, the higher frequency in organizations today of communication-intensive processes, whose quality and productivity are more strongly determined by their "flow of communication" than non communication-intensive processes.

Even though its scope is relatively limited, the communication flow optimization model provides useful guidance for efforts that take a more operational approach to process redesign – rather than a more strategic one, where the focus may be on broad management strategies and not necessarily on how individual processes are executed (Champy, 1995; Hammer, 1996). The model addresses an important gap, since a large number of process redesign efforts are conducted at the operational and individual process levels, or at least start at those levels.

4. RESEARCH QUESTIONS

The research questions that guided this action research study were derived from the communication flow optimization model. The questions are answered within the context provided by three process redesign groups conducted at a US defense contractor. The researcher provided methodological facilitation to the groups. To avoid facilitation-induced bias, as well as foster a multiple-perspective view of the targeted processes, the process redesign groups were encouraged by the researcher to generate both communication flow as well as activity flow representations.

Given the emphasis of contemporary process redesign practices on activity flows (Katzenstein and Lerch, 2000; Kock, 1999), the study addressed two key predictions of the communication flow optimization model: (a) that process redesign groups would favor activity flow representations of processes over communication flow representations early on in their projects, because the latter would be seen as more difficult to generate, or "less natural" than the former; and (b) a focus on communication flow would, on average, lead to better process redesign results than a focus on the flow of activities. Four research questions were formulated and answered based on the action research study. Below is question **Q1**.

Q1: *Will process redesign group members perceive communication flow representations of business processes as more difficult to generate than activity flow representations?*

Question **Q1** follows from the communication flow optimization model's argument that processes, which essentially represent "action", are more naturally seen as sequences of interconnected activities than communication interactions. It is important to answer this question empirically to assess the communication flow optimization model's claim (Kock and Murphy, 2001) that process redesign groups rarely think of processes in terms of communication interactions at the outset of their process redesign efforts, rather thinking of processes in terms of chronological sequences of interrelated activities, or activity flows. This claim is central to the model because it provides an explanation for the apparently generalized preference for activity flow-based process redesign approaches today (Katzenstein and Lerch, 2000; Kock, 1999). The model also predicts a "change of mind" after the beginning of a process redesign project, reflected as a preference for communication flow representations, particularly as the project moves from process analysis to process redesign. The key reason for this is the heavy role that information technologies are likely to play on process redesign implementations, and the consequent need to address the flow of communication in the processes targeted for redesign (Kock, 1999). This leads us to research questions **Q2** and **Q3**.

Q2: *Will process redesign groups employ communication flow representations of business processes more extensively than activity flow representations when making redesign decisions?*

Q3: *Will process redesign groups employ communication flow representations of business processes more extensively than activity flow representations when making decisions about information technology solutions to implement the redesigned business processes?*

Questions **Q2** and **Q3** follow from the model's claim that, at the process level of analysis, a focus on the flow of communication is likely to yield results that are better than if other elements were targeted, including activity flows. Those two questions provide the basis on which to investigate whether process redesign groups will, when given the choice between communication flow and activity flow representations during the project, behave: (a) according to predictions based on the model; and (b) rationally (Galbraith, 1977) by choosing the one type of representation that is likely to yield the best results. However, if this choice is made, one key consideration will still remain, formalized through research question **Q4**.

Q4: *Will process redesign groups that employ communication flow representations of business processes more extensively than activity flow representations, when making redesign decisions and when making* *decisions about information technology solutions to implement the redesigned business processes, generate more successful redesigns than groups that do not?*

Research question **Q4** makes explicit a reasonable assumption in connection with questions **Q2** and **Q3**, which is that the choice of focusing on communication flow representations rather than on activity flow representations will only be meaningful if it leads to increased process redesign success. For the purposes of this study, process redesign groups were considered as either successful or unsuccessful, according to criteria proposed in the process improvement literature (Burke and Peppard, 1995; Davenport, 1993; Hammer and Champy, 1993). Following those criteria, process redesign groups were categorized as successful if the process changes recommended by them were implemented fully or partially and led to "positive" observable results (e.g., improvements in customer satisfaction, cost reductions, production capacity increases etc.).

Process redesign groups may decide to use communication flow representations of processes more extensively than activity flow representations when making redesign decisions and when making decisions about information technology solutions to implement the redesigned business processes. However, if those preferences lead to no improvements in the outcomes produced by the process redesign groups (and, consequently, in their likelihood of success) then there is no reason to believe that those preferences are warranted. Research question **Q4**, which is the most difficult to answer in practice because it entails an assessment of the actual business impact of process redesign groups, can be seen as a "reality checkpoint" in the broader operational theoretical framework represented by the four research questions.

5. RESEARCH METHOD

5.1 Action research

Peters and Robinson (1984), as well as Elden and Chisholm (1993) provide general, discipline-independent reviews of action research. Lau (1997) presents a review of action research within the field of information systems research, where research on process redesign has flourished since the mid 1990s. There is a body of literature on the use of action research in organizational studies in general, as well as in the more specific context of information systems research (Avison et al., 1999; Baskerville, 1997; Baskerville, 1999; Baskerville and Wood-Harper, 1996; 1998; Myers, 1997; Olesen and Myers, 1999). This literature is not reviewed here. Rather, a concise definition of action research is borrowed from Rapoport, (1970, p.

499): "Action research aims to contribute both to the practical concerns of people in an immediate problematic situation and to the goals of social science by joint collaboration within a mutually acceptable ethical framework."

The roots of organizational action research are in studies of social and work life issues (Fox, 1990; Lewin, 1946; Trist et al., 1970). Organizational action research is often uniquely identified by its dual goal of both improving the organization (or organizations) participating in the research study, and at the same time generating knowledge (Elden and Chisholm, 1993; Lau, 1997). Although typically applying very little, if any, control on the organization being studied, the action researcher is expected to apply positive intervention on the organization (Jonsonn, 1991), which is often realized by the researcher providing some form of service to the organization and its members. One of the key reasons for the emergence and relative success of action research has been the recognition that the behavior of an organization, group, or individual, can be more deeply understood if the researcher collaborates with the subject or subjects being studied. In the case of an organization, this can be achieved when the researcher facilitates improvement-oriented change in the organization, which was the case in the study described in this chapter. The collaboration between researcher and subjects that characterizes action research is believed to foster free information exchange and a general commitment from the researcher as well as the subjects toward both research quality and organizational development (Fox, 1990).

Action research was employed in the investigation described in this chapter for one key reason, which his that it places the researcher in the "middle of the action", allowing for close examination of real-world business situations in their full complexity, and thus is a particularly useful research approach for the study of relatively "new" business topics and research questions such as those addressed by this research study.

5.2   The role played by the researcher

The researcher provided process redesign training and facilitation to the members of three process redesign groups involving employees and management from one major defense contractor based in the US. The facilitation was solely methodological (e.g., no specific process redesign suggestions were offered), and also "methodologically neutral" so as not to bias the perceptions of the subjects about the redesign approaches used. The process redesign groups conducted their work independently from each other.

5.3 The process redesign groups

A process redesign group is typically small in size (usually less than 15 members) and has a short lifetime (from a few days to typically no more than a few months) during which its members define, analyze, and search for alternatives to improve one or a few organizational processes (Choi, 1995; Choi and Liker, 1995; Hammer and Stanton, 1995). Each of the process redesign groups studied lasted approximately 3 months, had a "core" membership of 3 to 5 members (assigned nearly full-time to the process redesign projects), and had a "peripheral" membership of 5 to 10 members (which involved external advisors, consultants, and administrative support personnel assigned on a part-time basis to the process redesign projects). All of the groups were cross-departmental (i.e., they involved members from more than one department) and targeted cross-departmental processes (i.e., processes that involved more than one department in their execution). The term "departments" is used here to refer to organizational units that aggregate employees with expertise in related organizational functions, e.g., marketing department, computer support department, and quality control department.

The literature suggests that, generally speaking, successful process redesign groups usually conduct their activities along three main conceptual stages, namely *definition*, *analysis*, and *redesign* (Davenport, 1993; Davenport and Short, 1990; Dennis et al., 1999; Hammer and Champy, 1993; Hammer and Stanton, 1997; Harrington, 1991; Harrington et al., 1998; Kock, 2001). In the definition stage, the process redesign group selects a process for redesign. In the analysis stage, the group studies the process in detail. Finally, in the redesign stage, the group proposes process design modifications. These stages are followed by the implementation of the modifications. The process redesign groups studied followed this general structure.

In the analysis stage, each process redesign group developed both communication flow and activity flow representations of their target processes. Communication flow representations were adaptations of data flow diagrams (Davis, 1983; Dennis and Wixom, 2000), and were generated following the modified format proposed by Kock (1999). Activity flow representations followed the general format proposed by Harrington et al. (1998) for functional timeline flowcharts. While both types of representations contained different types of information, they generally embodied the same "amount" of information (i.e., neither was substantially more "information-rich" than the other). See appendices A and B for examples of these representations.

In the redesign stage, each process redesign group independently proposed several major process changes, without interference from the researcher. A list of generic process redesign guidelines, compiled from a large body of literature on process redesign by Kock (1999), was provided to the groups to guide their work. To avoid biasing group member decisions, the guidelines were chosen so that: (a) three of the guidelines were more meaningful in the context of communication flow than activity flow representations, (b) three of the guidelines were more meaningful in the context of activity flow than communication flow representations, and (c) two of the guidelines could be applied in both contexts. See Appendix C for detailed descriptions of these guidelines.

Communication flow and activity flow representations of the new processes, with major changes incorporated into them, were then generated. Following this, each process redesign group developed a "generic" information technology "solution" (i.e., a product-independent computer-based infrastructure and system specification) to implement the new process. These generic information technology solutions were illustrated through rich pictorial representations with icons representing computers, databases and organizational functions. Process redesign group members generally saw these pictorial representations as important aids in explaining the new processes to peers and managers.

The above stages were followed by the implementation of the recommended process changes, which lasted from three to six months. Process performance reviews were conducted approximately nine months after the implementation of those changes. The reviews were based primarily on unstructured interviews and aimed at assessing the bottom-line business impact of the process redesign projects.

5.4   Data collection and analysis

Three main types of research data were collected and compiled in connection with the process redesign groups: focus group discussion notes (Creswell, 1998; Sommer and Sommer, 1991), participant observation notes (Creswell, 1994; 1998), and unstructured interview notes (Patton, 1980; 1987). *Focus group discussions* were conducted twice with process redesign group members, once midway through and once at the end of the work of each process redesign group. *Participant observation notes* were generated based on direct observation of process redesign group members as well as other employees who were not directly involved in process redesign groups yet observed or were affected by the work of the groups. *Unstructured interviews* were conducted with all process redesign group members, as well as with other employees who were not directly involved in process redesign groups yet interacted with group members or were directly affected by the work of the groups. Over sixty unstructured interviews were conducted in total.

In contrast to experimental studies, control groups are not normally employed in action research. Thus action researchers often have to rely on "comparison" data (Maxwell, 1996) so that they can draw conclusions based on the data collected through their investigations. This study relied on previously published comparison data related to the success rates of early process redesign projects, and was obtained from a large multinational survey of success rates of process redesign attempts based on total quality management principles (Choi and Behling, 1997), and a large survey of American and European companies of process redesign attempts employing business process re-engineering principles (Champy, 1995). As previously mentioned, for the purposes of this study, process redesign groups were seen as either successful or unsuccessful, according to criteria proposed in the process redesign literature (Burke and Peppard, 1995; Davenport, 1993; Hammer and Champy, 1993) – process redesign groups were categorized as successful if the process changes recommended by them were implemented fully or partially and led to positive observable results.

In order to increase the robustness of the data analysis, the three sources of research data – focus group discussion notes, participant observation notes, and unstructured interview notes – were extensively triangulated (Jick, 1979; Maxwell, 1996; Yin, 1994). The data set was thoroughly examined for evidence in connection with each of the research questions, and all the evidence obtained was carefully compared and checked for inconsistencies. Additionally, the study employed Scriven's (1974) "modus operandi" approach, whereby the researcher searches for clues as to whether or not expectations clearly match the evidence at hand (see Maxwell, 1996). The application of the "modus operandi" approach entailed asking what would be expected from an event, in terms of evidence arising from the data analysis, if the researcher's predictions (based on the theoretical model) were wrong.

5.5   Ethical considerations

Permission to use the research data for analysis was sought and obtained from the management of the organization, as well as from each individual contributor. The anonymity of the organization and of all individual contributors was protected. Given that the organization studied was a defense contractor, all information deemed as classified or sensitive was disguised.

6.   RESULTS

Below we discuss evidence in connection with each of the research questions that guided our study of the three process redesign groups, referred to below as G1, G2 and G3. Because the research was conducted at a defense contractor that viewed much of the information about its internal operations as classified, no further details about the individual groups and the processes they targeted can be provided here. Rather, the evidence presented and discussed in this section relates specifically to the research questions.

Different pieces of evidence presented here are given codes that are later used to summarize them in a table. The codes are built on acronyms that indicate the source of each piece of evidence – unstructured interview notes (UIN), participant observation notes (PON), and focus group discussion notes (GDN).

6.1   Research question Q1

Q1: *Will process redesign group members perceive communication flow representations of business processes as more difficult to generate than activity flow representations?*

Had group members perceived activity flow representations as more difficult to generate than communication flow representations, which would suggest a negative answer to **Q1** and contradict the communication flow optimization model, one would expect most of those who discussed the relative difficulty of each process representation approach to say so in unstructured interviews and focus group discussions – i.e., that they perceived activity flow representations as more difficult to generate. If that were the case, one would also expect most groups to generate communication flow representations *before* they did activity flow representations, because it seems natural that they would generate first the easiest type of process representation, and then the most difficult. Neither of these expectations matched what actually happened.

The analysis of the unstructured interview notes (UIN) suggested that most (more than two thirds) of the group members who were interviewed perceived communication flow representations as more difficult to be generated than activity flow representations (UIN.E01), which suggests a positive answer to **Q1**. The quote below is representative of the comments provided in interviews regarding this perception pattern.

"The flowcharts are easier to create because they are basically what we do ... the other diagrams, the [communication flow diagrams], are not as easy to work out; they show the forms, documents, faxes, emails that we send back and forth, but not really what we do ... When we think about the things

that we do, we think in terms of steps, or activities, not documents going back and forth."

The magnitude, or strength, of the perception above is unclear, but a content analysis (Creswell, 1998; Sommer and Sommer, 1991) of interviews points at a slight difference in difficulty (suggested by the absence of superlatives and other modifiers – e.g., "very", "drastic", "a lot" etc. – that would indicate a stronger perception trend).

The perception above is consistent with the analysis of participant observation notes (PON), which indicated that all groups generated activity flow representations of their targeted processes *before* they generated communication flow representations (PON.E01), and then generated communication flow representations based on those initial activity flow representations, which also suggests a positive answer to question **Q1**. That is, if we assume that a group would generate the easiest (or most "natural") type of representation first, this suggests that groups (i.e., the majority of their members) saw activity flow representations as easier to produce than communication flow representations.

A third pattern of evidence in support of a positive answer to question **Q1** comes from focus group discussions notes (GDN), which suggested that most (all but one individual) of the focus group discussion participants perceived communication flow representations as more difficult to be generated than activity flow representations (GDN.E01). The one individual who disagreed was neutral in his view; that is, he did not think that either representation was more difficult to produce than the other.

6.2 Research question Q2

Q2: *Will process redesign groups employ communication flow representations of business processes more extensively than activity flow representations when making redesign decisions?*

Research question **Q2** does not relate to perceptions, but actual behavior, and assumes that the behavior of the group members indicates an underlying difference in usefulness between process representations (which, given the answer to **Q1,** could be the opposite of the perceived ease of use of the representations). Thus, the key type of evidence to answer the question comes from our participation observation of the process redesign groups (discussed below). Nevertheless, it is interesting to note that most group members perceived communication flow representations to be more useful than activity flow representations when used as a basis for process redesign decisions. The quote below illustrates this perception.

"[Communication flow diagrams] are really where you see that useless and inadequate tasks are being executed. Why does a piece of information go from A to B, and then from B to C, when it could go straight from A to C? When you see in a [communication flow] diagram the same piece of information going back and forth, without being turned into something else, you immediately know that something is wrong. Activity flow diagrams tell you nothing about that kind of problem."

Participant observation notes (PON) provided relatively strong evidence in connection with **Q2**. In one of the groups (G1), seven out of eight process redesign decisions were made entirely based on communication flow representations (PON.E02). In another group (G2), five out of eight process redesign decisions were entirely based on communication flow representations of its target process (PON.E03). In the remaining group (G3), three out of four decisions were made in the same way (PON.E04). That is, in all process redesign groups, communication flow representations were used significantly more extensively than activity flow representations as a basis for making process redesign decisions, which provides support for a positive answer to question **Q2**.

6.3   Research question Q3

Q3: *Will process redesign groups employ communication flow representations of business processes more extensively than activity flow representations when making decisions about information technology solutions to implement the redesigned business processes?*

As with **Q2**, research question **Q3** does not relate perceptions, but actual behavior. Therefore, similarly to what was done in connection with **Q2,** the key type of evidence to answer the question comes from our participation observation of the process redesign groups (discussed below). Nonetheless, perceptions by group members also allow for a tentative positive answer to the research question, as they suggested that most group members perceived communication flow representations to be more useful than activity flow representations when used as a basis for making decisions about information technology solutions to implement the redesigned business processes. This is illustrated by the quote below, which is representative of statements made by group members in unstructured interviews.

"When one looks at a generic IT solution to automate a redesigned process, it looks almost like the [communication] flow representation of the process, because both show essentially the same thing – the flow of information in the business process – one with technology [details] and the other without. The activity diagrams are almost useless at that point, unless

you want to make a presentation for management or something like that ... even so, the [communication flow] diagrams are probably better, because they show more or less how databases will be set up and which people will need to access data in them."
Participant observation notes (PON) also suggested the existence of relatively strong evidence in connection with the use of communication flow representations when making decisions about information technology solutions to implement the redesigned business processes. In all of the three groups the "generic" information technology "solution" and rich pictorial representation were developed entirely based on communication flow representations (PON.E05), which provides support for a positive answer to question **Q3**.

6.4   Research question Q4

Q4: *Will process redesign groups that employ communication flow representations of business processes more extensively than activity flow representations, when making redesign decisions and when making decisions about information technology solutions to implement the redesigned business processes, generate more successful redesigns than groups that do not?*
This is a difficult question to answer based on this study, because the sample of process redesign projects studied was small, and thus no statistical analysis could be performed on evidence pertaining to question **Q4**. Nevertheless, two assumptions seemed appropriate and useful in analyzing the evidence with the goal of answering this research question. The first assumption was that the three process redesign groups studied should be seen as a homogeneous group when answering this question, since they all employed communication flow representations more extensively than activity flow representations when making redesign and information technology solution decisions. The second assumption was that, to provide a negative answer to **Q2**, one would expect: (a) that most group members would provide hints in focus group discussions and/or unstructured interviews that they perceived their groups as not very successful (here more in-depth probing was critical, because most people are less than willing to admit failure in connection with tasks they performed); and (b) that an inspection of the outcomes of the actual implementation of the redesigned processes would suggest a rate of success lower than that reported in the general literature on process redesign (arguably the latter, based on our

previous discussion, is largely based on activity-flow oriented process redesign projects). As it will be shown below, the evidence supported neither of these two expectations.

Focus group discussion notes (GDN) suggested that all groups members perceived their groups as likely to be very successful according to the adopted criteria for success – that recommended process changes that were implemented fully or partially and led to "positive" observable results (GDN.E02), which provides support for a positive answer to question **Q4**. No evidence from unstructured interviews contradicted this general perception.

Moreover, unstructured interview notes (UIN) suggested, based on interviews with managers (who had not been "core" group members) after the new process implementations, that all of the three groups recommended process changes that were successful according to those same criteria (UIN.E02). If the success rate here were equal or lower than the success rates of process redesign projects reported in the literature, which have been consistently found to be 34 percent or less (Choi and Behling, 1997; Champy, 1995), we would expect no more than one group out of three to be successful. So, this evidence cannot be seen as contracting the positive answer to question **Q4** provided above based on focus group discussions and unstructured interviews.

Table 12-1 summarizes the main pieces of evidence discussed above in connection with the research questions. Table 12-1(a) shows individual patterns of evidence. As above, the evidence is grouped based on its source and indicated by specific acronyms that point to the source of each piece of evidence – unstructured interview notes (UIN), participant observation notes (PON), and focus group discussion notes (GDN). Table 12-1(b) provides a description of each evidence pattern shown in Table 12-1(a).

Table 12-1. Key pieces of evidence in connection with the research questions

(a) Individual patterns of evidence in connection with the research questions

	Unstructured interview notes	Participant observation notes	Focus group discussion notes
Q1	UIN.E01	PON.E01	GDN.E01
Q2		PON.E02, PON.E03, PON.E04	
Q3		PON.E05	
Q4	UIN.E02		GDN.E02

(b) Descriptions of the individual patterns of evidence

Evidence	Description
UIN.E01	Most of the group members (more than two thirds) interviewed perceived communication flow representations as more difficult to be generated than activity flow representations.
UIN.E02	All groups recommended process changes that were implemented fully or partially and led to "positive" observable results, according to interviews with managers (who had not been "core" group members) after the implementations.
PON.E01	All groups generated activity flow representations of their targeted process before they generated communication flow representations.
PON.E02	Most (seven out of eight) process redesign decisions made by group G1 were entirely based on communication flow representations of its target process.
PON.E03	Most (five out of eight) process redesign decisions made by group G2 were entirely based on communication flow representations of its target process.
PON.E04	Most (three out of four) process redesign decisions made by group G3 were entirely based on communication flow representations of its target process.
PON.E05	All groups developed a "generic" information technology "solution" and rich pictorial representation entirely based on communication flow representations of its target process.
GDN.E01	Most (all but one individual) of the focus group discussion participants perceived communication flow representations as more difficult to be generated than activity flow representations.
GDN.E02	All group members perceived their groups as very successful according to the adopted criteria for success – that recommended process changes that were implemented fully or partially and led to "positive" observable results.

The patterns of evidence summarized above provide general support for positive answers to all of the research questions. Since the questions were developed based on the communication flow optimization model and positive answers are aligned with predictions based on the model, it can be concluded that the patterns of evidence also provide general support for the model. Consistently with the model's predictions, process redesign group members seemed to perceive communication flow representations of processes as more difficult to be generated than activity flow representations. Given their behavior, it is plausible to conclude that this was related to activity flow representations being better aligned with the way humans are cognitively programmed to envision "action" in the physical sense.

Also, consistently with the communication flow optimization model's predictions, process redesign group members "shifted" their behavior away from their initial perceptions (which were more favorable toward activity flow representations), employing communication flow representations of business processes more extensively than activity flow representations when making decisions in connection with process redesign itself and information technology solutions to implement the redesigned processes. This shift apparently had no negative impact on group success – in fact, the evidence suggests a positive impact, though based on a small sample. Moreover, it is fair to assume that process redesign group members made a rational and relatively well-informed choice, particularly given that they were involved in "real" process redesign projects, with all the personal risks associated with not doing a good job. Thus, it is reasonable to conclude that a focus on communication flow structures in processes is indeed advisable, and likely to lead to "better" results than a focus on the flow of activities.

7.   CONCLUSION

This chapter reviewed the literature on process redesign and identified a problematic focus on "workflows" (or chronological sequences of activities), particularly in operational-level process redesign approaches. Building on the communication flow optimization model, it is shown that a focus on communication flows is more advisable than a focus on "workflows". This is an important contribution, because it signals the need for a re-orientation of process redesign practices to meet the demands posed by the communication-intensive nature of contemporary business processes. Given the current predominance of "workflow"-based process redesign approaches (Harrington et al., 1998; Katzenstein and Lerch, 2000), this re-orientation may have a deep impact on the future practical success of operational-level process redesign approaches. The recent emergence of "virtual organizations", "virtual teams", and "e-business", and the consequent explosion in organizational communication demands (Burn and Barnett, 1999; Fingar et al., 2001; Sucham and Hayzak, 2001), is likely to make this re-orientation even more urgent in the near future.

Still, much more research is needed to further test and refine the communication flow optimization model. Notably, it is not clear from this research study whether a limited use of activity flow representations may be beneficial early on in process redesign projects whose focus is on communication flow representations and techniques. This issue is addressed below in our discussion of implications for future research, which is followed by a discussion of implications for practice and limitations of the research study.

One key area of future research in connection with the communication flow optimization model relates to the refinement of the model by incorporating predictions regarding the combination of communication flow-based representations and techniques with other types of representations and techniques, including activity-based ones. This follows from one of communication flow optimization's own theoretical propositions, supported by this research, which states that activity flow representations are easier to generate than communication flow representations. It may be advantageous to generate simplified activity flow representations, as an initial step in the analysis of a business process, before communication flow representations are generated. Since the process redesign groups investigated did that, it is not clear what would have happened had they not followed that path. This suggests that even though a focus on activity flows may be undesirable, as argued by the communication flow optimization model, a limited use of activity flow representations may be beneficial. This issue should be addressed in future research.

This study also provides the basis on which other methods and techniques can be developed and investigated in areas that are related to but go beyond the scope of business process redesign. Information systems design is one such area. For example, the recent success of object-oriented programming has led to the emergence of object-oriented analysis. However, the scope of use of object-oriented analysis pales when compared with that of its object-oriented programming "cousin". Chuang and Yadav (2000) argue that this is due to object-oriented analysis' excessive activity orientation, which they addressed by developing and validating, with positive conceptual results, a new methodology for object-oriented analysis. This new methodology built on early communication flow optimization model principles proposed by Kock and McQueen (1996), and suggests the potential of the model to serve as a basis for the refinement of that methodology and development of other methodologies.

A key implication of this research for managers involved in operational-level process redesign projects is that they should carefully consider the focus of their projects, especially when the goal is to redesign individual processes with an "eye" on quality and productivity improvements. If that focus is on activities and their flow, which may be advocated by proponents of popular activity flow-based methods such as Hammer's (1996) and Harrington et al.'s (1998), they should consider shifting that focus toward communication and its flow in business processes.

At a minimum, managers should strive to strike a balance in process redesign projects between activity flow and communication flow methods and techniques. This is particularly important in broad projects that target primarily service processes, where the flow of materials is minimal, such as the recent organization-wide initiatives by the US Department of Defense to improve acquisition practices (Graves, 2001). In projects of such magnitude, even single-digit success rate increases can lead to savings in the range of millions of dollars.

Like any research study, this study presents some limitations that need to be acknowledged so the reader can qualify its findings. One of the main limitations of this study is the small sample of process redesign projects investigated. While the research approach used, action research, makes it impractical to study samples of much larger size than that targeted by this study, it provides an exploratory basis on which further confirmatory research based on larger samples may be conducted. If this limitation is properly addressed, additional insights into the predictive power of the communication flow optimization model can be obtained. Given the "intensive" nature of action research, this would probably require the use of other research approaches such as case and survey research to be accomplished in an "economical" way.

Another way in which the above limitation could be addressed without resorting to other research approaches would be to conduct similar action research studies in the future; trying to ensure that the level of similarity with this study is high enough so that the research data obtained through those studies could be combined with the data collected in this study. This could be done iteratively until the combined sample size obtained is large enough to allow for unequivocal conclusions in connection with the validity of the communication flow optimization model's predictions, particularly regarding process redesign group success.

8. ACKNOWLEDGEMENTS

This chapter is a revised version of an article by the author published in 2003 in the journal *IEEE Transactions on Professional Communication*. The research study described in this chapter has been funded in part by grants from the US Department of Defense's External Acquisition Research Program, and Temple University's Office of the Vice Provost for Research. The author would like to thank the individuals and organizations that participated in the action research study for their time and support. He would also like to thank: Kim S. Campbell, for several suggestions in connection with previous versions of this chapter; the management and employees of the defense contractor that participated in this study for their time and support; Fred Murphy for his advice and ideas in connection with the main topic of this paper and its theoretical foundations; as well as Mark Nissen and Ira Lewis, for their work in connection with the External Acquisition Research Program of the US Department of Defense, without which this research project would not be have been possible.

9. REFERENCES

Ang, C.L. & Gay, R.K.L. (1993). IDEF0 modeling for project risk assessment. *Computers in Industry*, 22(1), 31-46.

Archer, R. & Bowker, P. (1995). BPR consulting: An evaluation of the methods employed. *Business Process Re-Engineering & Management*, 1(2), 28-46.

Argyris, C. & Schon, D.A. (1991). Participatory action research and action science compared. W.F. Whyte, ed. *Participatory Action Research*. Newbury Park, CA: Sage, 85-96.

Avison, D., Lau, F., Myers, M.D. & Nielsen, P. (1999). Action research. *Communications of the ACM*, 42(1), 94-97.

Bashein, B.J. & Markus, M.L. (1994). Preconditions for BPR success. *Information Systems Management*, 11(2), 7-13.

Baskerville, R. (1997). Distinguishing action research from participative case studies. *Journal of Systems and Information Technology*, 1(1), 25-45.

Baskerville, R. (1999). Investigating information systems with action research. *Communications of the AIS*, 2(19), 1-25.

Baskerville, R. & Wood-Harper, T. (1996). A critical perspective on action research as a method for information systems research. *Journal of Information Technology*, 11(3), 235-246.

Baskerville, R. & Wood-Harper, T. (1998). Diversity in information systems action research methods. *European Journal of Information Systems*, 7(2), 90-107.

Bergner, J.T. (1991). *The New Superpowers: Germany, Japan, the US, and the New World Order*. New York, NY: St. Martin's Press.

Biggs, M. (2000). Enabling a successful e-business strategy requires a detailed business process map. *InfoWorld*, 22(10), 64.

Booch, G., Jacobson, I. & Rumbaugh, J. (1998). *The Unified Modeling Language User Guide*. New York, NY: Addison-Wesley.

Burke, G. & Peppard, J. (Eds) (1995). *Examining Business Process Re-engineering*. London, UK: Kogan Page.

Burn, J. & Barnett, M. (1999). Communicating for advantage in the virtual organization. *IEEE Transactions on Professional Communication*, 42(4), 215-222.

Buzacott, J.A. (1996). Commonalities in reengineered business processes: Models and issues. *Management Science*, 42(5), 768-782.

Caron, J.R., Jarvenpaa, S.L. & Stoddard, D.B. (1994). Business reengineering at CIGNA Corporation: Experiences and lessons learned from the first five years. *MIS Quarterly*, 18(3), 233-250.

Champy, J. (1995). *Reengineering Management*. New York, NY: Harper Business.

Chapman, W. (1991). *Inventing Japan: The Making of a Postwar Civilization*. New York, NY: Prentice Hall.

Checkland, P. & Scholes, J. (1990). *Soft Systems Methodology in Action*. New York, NY: John Wiley & Sons.

Childe, S.J., Maull, R.S. & Benett, J. (1994). Frameworks for understanding business process re-engineering. *International Journal of Operations & Productions Management*, 14(12), 22-34.

Choi, T.Y. (1995). Conceptualizing continuous improvement: Implications for organizational change. *Omega*, 23(6), 607-624.

Choi, T.Y. & Behling, O.C. (1997). Top managers and TQM success: One more look after all these years. *The Academy of Management Executive*, 11(1), 37-47.

Choi, T.Y. & Liker, J.K. (1995). Bringing Japanese continuous improvement approaches to U.S. manufacturing: The roles of process orientation and communications. *Decision Sciences*, 26(5), 589-620.

Chuang, T. & Yadav, S.B. (2000). A decision-driven approach to object-oriented analysis. *Database for Advances in Information Systems*, 31(2), 13-34.

Clemons, E.K., Thatcher, M.E., & Row, M.C. (1995). Identifying sources of reengineering failures: A study of the behavioral factors contributing to reengineering risks. *Journal of Management Information Systems*, 12(2), 9-36.

Clutterbuck, D., & Crainer, S. (1990). *Makers of Management*. London, England: MacMillan.

Creswell, J.W. (1994). *Research Design: Qualitative and Quantitative Approaches*. Thousand Oaks, CA: Sage.

Creswell, J.W. (1998). *Qualitative Inquiry and Research Design: Choosing Among Five Traditions*. Thousand Oaks, CA: Sage.

Davenport, T.H. (1993). *Process Innovation*. Boston, MA: Harvard Business School Press.

Davenport, T.H. (1993a). Need radical innovation and continuous improvement? Integrate process re-engineering and total quality management. *Planning Review*, 21(3), 6-12.

Davenport, T.H. (2000). *Mission Critical: Realizing the Promise of Enterprise Systems*. Boston, MA: Harvard Business School Press.

Davenport, T.H. & Short, J.E. (1990). The new industrial engineering: Information technology and business process redesign. *Sloan Management Review*, 31(4), 11-27.

Davenport, T.H. & Stoddard, D.B. (1994). Reengineering: Business change of mythic proportions? *MIS Quarterly*, 18(2), 121-127.

Davis, W.S. (1983). *System Analysis and Design: A Structured Approach*. Reading, MA: Addison-Wesley.

Dean, D.L., Lee, J.D., Orwig, R.E., & Vogel, D.R. (1995). Technological support for group process modeling. *Journal of Management Information Systems*, 11(3), 42-63.

Deming, W.E. (1986). *Out of The Crisis*. Cambridge, MA: Center for Advanced Engineering Study, Massachusetts Institute of Technology.

Dennis, A. & Wixom, B.H. (2000). *Systems Analysis and Design: An Applied Approach*. New York, NY: John Wiley & Sons.

Dennis A.R., Hayes G.S., & Daniels, R.M., Jr. (1999). Business process modeling with group support systems. *Journal of Management Information Systems*, 15(4), 115-142.

Drucker, P.F. (1989). *The New Realities*. New York, NY: Harper & Row.

Drucker, P.F. (1993). Professional's productivity. *Accross the Board*, 30(9), 50.

Earl, M.J. (1994). The new and the old of business process redesign. *Journal of Strategic Information Systems*, 3(1), 5-22.

Elden, M. & Chisholm, R.F. (1993). Emerging varieties of action research. *Human Relations*, 46(2), 121-141.

Fingar, P., Aronica, R. & Maizlish, B. (2001). *The Death of "e" and the Birth of the Real New Economy*. Tampa, FL: Meghan-Kiffer Press.

Fox, W.M. (1990). An interview with Eric Trist, father of the sociotechnical systems approach. *The Journal of Applied Behavioural Science*, 26(2), 259-279.

Galbraith, J. (1977). *Organizational Design*. Reading, MA: Addison-Wesley.

Galliers, R.D. (1991). Choosing appropriate information system research approaches: A revised taxonomy. H. Nissen, H.K. Klein, & R. Hirschheim, eds. *Information Systems Research: Contemporary Approaches and Emergent Traditions*. New York, NY: North-Holland, pp. 327-345.

Galliers, R.D. (1992). Choosing information systems research approaches. R. Galliers, ed. *Information Systems Research: Issues, Methods and Practical Guidelines*. Boston, MA: Blackwell Scientific Publications, 144-162.

Glaser, B.G. & Strauss, A.L. (1967). *The Discovery of Grounded Theory: Strategies for Qualitative Research*. Chicago, IL: Aldine Publishing.

Graves, R.H. (2001). Seeking defense efficiency. *Acquisition Review Quarterly*, 8(3), 47-60.

Grover, V., Jeong, S.R., Kettinger, W.J., & Teng, J.T.C. (1995). The implementation of business process reengineering. *Journal of Management Information Systems*, 12(1), 109-144.

Hammer, M. (1990). Reengineering work: Don't automate, obliterate. *Harvard Business Review*, 68(4), 104-114.

Hammer, M. (1996). *Beyond Reengineering*. New York, NY: HarperCollins.

Hammer, M. (2000). Reengineering redux. *CIO Magazine*, 13(10), 143-156.

Hammer, M. & Champy, J. (1993). *Reengineering the Corporation*. New York, NY: Harper Business.

Hammer, M. & Stanton, S.A. (1995). *The Reengineering Revolution*. New York, NY: HarperCollins.

Hammer, M. & Stanton, S.A. (1997). The reengineering revolution. *Government Executive*, 27(9), 2-8.

Harrington, J.H. (1991). *Business Process Improvement*. New York, NY: McGraw-Hill.

Harrington, J.H., Esseling, E.K.C. & Van Nimwegen, H. (1998). *Business Process Improvement Workbook: Documentation, Analysis, Design, and Management of Business Process Improvement*. New York, NY: McGraw-Hill.

Herzberg, F., Mausner, B., & Snyderman, B. (1959). *The Motivation to Work*. New York, NY: Wiley.

Hunt, V.D. (1996). *Process Mapping: How to Reengineer your Business Processes*. New York, NY: John Wiley & Sons.

Ishikawa, K. (1986). *Guide to Quality Control*. Tokyo, Japan: Asian Productivity Organisation.

Jick, T.D. (1979). Mixing qualitative and quantitative methods: Triangulation in action. *Administrative Science Quarterly*, 24(4), 602-611.

Jonsonn, S. (1991). Action research. H. Nissen, H.K. Klein, & R. Hirschheim, eds. *Information Systems Research: Contemporary Approaches and Emergent Traditions*. New York, NY: North-Holland, 371-396.

Juran, J. (1989). *Juran on Leadership for Quality*. New York, NY: The Free Press.

Katzenstein, G. & Lerch, F.J. (2000). Beneath the surface of organizational processes: A social representation framework for business process redesign. *ACM Transactions on Information Systems*, 18(4), 383-422.

Kettinger, W.J. & Grover, V. (1995). Toward a theory of business change management. *Journal of Management Information Systems*, 12(1), 9-30.

Kock, N. (1995). *Process Reengineering, PROI: A Practical Methodology*. Sao Paulo, Brazil: Editora Vozes (in Portuguese).

Kock, N. (1999). *Process Improvement and Organizational Learning: The Role of Collaboration Technologies*. Hershey, PA: Idea Group Publishing.

Kock, N. (2001). Compensatory adaptation to a lean medium: An action research investigation of electronic communication in process improvement groups. *IEEE Transactions on Professional Communication*, 44(4), 267-285.

Kock, N. (2002). Managing with web-based IT in mind. *Communications of the ACM*, 45(5), 102-106.

Kock, N. (2005). *Business Process Improvement through E-Collaboration: Knowledge Sharing through the Use of Virtual Groups*. Hershey, PA: Idea Group Publishing.

Kock, N. & McQueen, R.J. (1996). Product flow, breadth and complexity of business processes: An empirical study of fifteen business processes in three organizations. *Business Process Re-engineering & Management*, 2(2), 8-22.

Kock, N. & Murphy, F. (2001). *Redesigning Acquisition Processes: A New Methodology Based on the Flow of Knowledge and Information*. Fort Belvoir, VA: Defense Acquisition University Press.

Kock, N., McQueen, R.J. & Corner, J.L. (1997). The nature of data, information and knowledge exchanges in business processes: Implications for process improvement and organizational learning. *The Learning Organization*, 4(2), 70-80.

Lacity, M.C. & Janson, M.A. (1994). Understanding qualitative data: A framework of text analysis methods. *Journal of Management Information Systems*, 11(2), 137-155.

Lau, F. (1997). A review on the use of action research in information systems studies. A.S. Lee, J. Liebenau, & J.I. DeGross, eds. *Information Systems and Qualitative Research*. London, England: Chapman & Hall, 31-68.

Ledford, G.E. & Mohrman, S.A. (1993). Self-design for high involvement: A large-scale organizational change. *Human Relations*, 46(2), 143-173.

Ledford, G.E. & Mohrman, S.A. (1993b). Looking backward and forward at action research. *Human Relations*, 46(11), 1349-1359.

Lewin, K. (1946). Action research and minority problems. G.W. Lewin, ed. *Resolving Social Conflicts*. New York, NY: Harper & Row, 201-216.

Maslow, A.H. (1954). *Motivation and Personality*. New York, NY: Harper and Row.

Maull, R.S., Weaver, A.M., Childe, S.J., Smart, P.A. & Bennett, J. (1995). Current issues in business process re-engineering. *International Journal of Operations and Production Management*, 15(11), 37-52.

Maxwell, J.A. (1996). *Qualitative Research Design: An Interactive Approach*. London, England: Sage.

Mayo, E. (1945). *The Social Problems of an Industrial Civilization*. New York, NY: Macmillan.

Misterek, S.D., Dooley, K.J. & Anderson, J.C. (1992). Productivity as a performance measure. *International Journal of Operations & Production Management*, 12(1), 29-45.

Mumford, E. (2001). Advice for an action researcher. *Information Technology & People*, 14(1), 12-27.

Myers, M.D. (1997). Qualitative research in information systems. *MIS Quarterly*, 21(2), 241-242.

Nissen, M.E. (1998). Redesigning reengineering through measurement-driven inference. *MIS Quarterly*, 22(4), 509-534.

Olesen, K., & Myers, M.D. (1999). Trying to improve communication and collaboration with information technology: An action research project which failed. *Information Technology & People*, 12(4), 317-332.

Orlikowski, W.J. & Baroudi, J.J. (1991). Studying information technology in organizations: Research approaches and assumptions. *Information Systems Research*, 2(1), 1-28.

Ould, M.A. (1995). *Business Processes: Modelling and Analysis for Re-engineering and Improvement*. Chichester, England: John Wiley & Sons.

Patton, M.Q. (1980). *Qualitative Evaluation Methods*. Beverly Hills, CA: Sage.

Patton, M.Q. (1987). *How to Use Qualitative Methods in Evaluation*. Newbury Park, CA: Sage.

Peters, M. & Robinson, V. (1984). The origins and status of action research. *The Journal of Applied Behavioral Science,* 20(2), 113-124.

Popper, K.R. (1992). *Logic of Scientific Discovery*. New York, NY: Routledge.

Rapoport, R.N. (1970). Three dilemmas in action research. *Human Relations*, 23(6), 499-513.

Reason, P. (1993). Sitting between appreciation and disappointment: A critique of the special edition of Human Relations on action research. *Human Relations*, 46(10), 1253-1270.

Rigby, D. (1993). The secret history of process reengineering. *Planning Review*, 21(2), 24-27.

Rumbaugh, J., Jacobson, I. & Booch, G. (1998). *The Unified Modeling Language Reference Manual*. New York, NY: Addison-Wesley.

Scriven, M. (1974). Maximizing the power of causal investigations: The modus operandi method. W.J. Popham, ed. *Evaluation in Education: Current Applications*. Berkeley, CA: McCutchan, 66-84.

Siegel, S. & Castellan, N.J. (1998). *Nonparametric Statistics for the Behavioral Sciences.* Boston, MA: McGraw-Hill.

Sommer, B. & Sommer, R. (1991). *A Practical Guide to Behavioral Research.* New York, NY: Oxford University Press.

Stoddard, D.B. & Jarvenpaa, S.L. (1995). Business process redesign: Tactics for managing radical change. *Journal of Management Information Systems,* 12(1), 81-107.

Strauss, A.L. & Corbin, J.M. (1990). *Basics of Qualitative Research: Grounded Theory Procedures and Techniques.* Newbury Park, CA: Sage.

Strauss, A.L & Corbin, J.M. (1998). *Basics of Qualitative Research: Techniques and Procedures for Developing Grounded Theory.* Thousand Oaks, CA: Sage.

Sucham, J. & Hayzak, G. (2001). The communication characteristics of virtual teams: A case study. *IEEE Transactions on Professional Communication,* 44(3), 174-186.

Taylor, F.W. (1885). *A Piece Rate System.* New York, NY: McGraw-Hill.

Taylor, F.W. (1911). *The Principles of Scientific Management.* New York, NY: Norton & Company.

Teng, J.T.C., Seung, R.J. & Grover, V. (1998). Profiling successful reengineering projects. *Communications of the ACM,* 41(6), 96–102.

Toffler, A. (1991). *Powershift.* New York, NY: Bantam Books.

Trist, E.L., Higgin, G.W., Pollock, A.E. & Murray, H.A. (1970). Sociotechnical systems. P.B. Smith, ed. *Group Processes.* Middlesex, UK: Penguin Books, 41-54.

Truex, D.P., III (2001). Three issues concerning relevance in IS research: Epistemology, audience, and method. *Communications of the AIS,* 6(24), 1-11.

Venkatraman, N. (1994). IT-enabled business transformation: From automation to business scope redefinition. *Sloan Management Review,* 35(2), 73-87.

Walton, M. (1989). *The Deming Management Method.* London, England: Mercury.

Walton, M. (1991). *Deming Management at Work.* London, England: Mercury.

Waring, S.P. (1991). *Taylorism Transformed.* Chapel Hill, NC: The University of North Carolina Press.

Yin, R.K. (1994). *Case Study Research.* Newbury Park, CA: Sage.

10. APPENDIX A: ACTIVITY FLOW REPRESENTATION USED

The partial functional timeline flowchart (Harrington, 1991; Harrington et al., 1998) below, generated by one of the groups, illustrates the activity flow representations used by the process redesign groups. Activity names (not shown below) were listed next to the flowchart.

Activity	Processing Time (Days)
1	1
2	1
3.1	1
3.2	5
3.3	1
3.4	5
3.5	7.5
3.6	3
4	1
5	0.5
6	3
7	5
7.1	3
7.2	3
8	1
9	2.5
10	3
11	1
12	1
13	1
14	3
14.1	1
14.2	1
14.3	2
14.3.1	2
14.3.3	1
14.4	1
15	1
	62.5

11. APPENDIX B: COMMUNICATION FLOW REPRESENTATION USED

The partial communication flow diagram (Kock, 1999; Kock and Murphy, 2001) below, generated by one of the groups, illustrates the communication flow representations used by the process redesign groups.

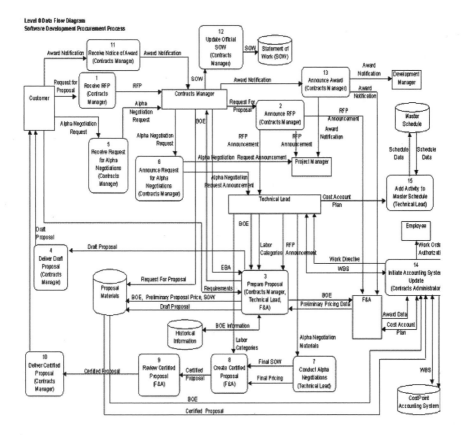

12.   APPENDIX C: PROCESS REDESIGN GUIDELINES USED

The process redesign groups used the following guidelines, which have been compiled from a large body of literature on process redesign, and are discussed in more detail by Kock (1999; 2005). In the list below, each guideline is followed by a brief description of why it may lead to process improvement, using generally the same language and rationale as those presented to the participants.

To avoid bias, the set of guidelines was balanced in terms of its communication and activity flow orientation. Guidelines 1–3 are more meaningful in the context of communication flow than activity flow representations. Guidelines 4–5 can be applied in both contexts. Guidelines 6–8 are more meaningful in the context of activity flow than communication flow representations.

1. *Foster asynchronous communication.* When people exchange information they can do it synchronously, i.e., interacting at the same time, or asynchronously, i.e., interacting at different times. One example of synchronous communication is a telephone conversation. If the conversation takes place via e-mail, it then becomes an example of asynchronous communication. It has been observed, especially in formal business interaction, that, almost always, asynchronous communication is more efficient. For example, synchronous communication often leads to wasted time (e.g., waiting for the other person to be found) and communication tends to be less objective. Asynchronous communication can be implemented with simple artifacts such as in-and out-boxes, fax trays, and billboards. These artifacts work as dynamic information repositories.

2. *Eliminate duplication of information.* Static repositories, as opposed to dynamic repositories, hold information in a more permanent basis. A student file maintained by a primary school, for example, is a static repository of information. Conversely, the data entry form used to temporary stored information about a student that will be entered into the student file is not a static repository. Duplication of information in different static repositories often creates inconsistency problems, which may have a negative impact on productivity and quality. Kock (1995; 2005) describes a situation where a large auto maker's purchasing division tried to keep two supplier databases updated; one manually and the other through a computer system. Two databases were being kept because the computer database had presented some problems and therefore was deemed unreliable. This, in turn, was causing a large number of inconsistencies between the two databases. Each database stored data about over four hundred parts suppliers.

3. *Reduce information flow.* Excessive information flow is often caused by an over-commitment to efficiency to the detriment of effectiveness. Information is perceived as an important component of processes, which drives people to an unhealthy information hunger. This causes information overload and the creation

of unnecessary information processing functions within the organization. Information overload leads to stress and, often, the creation of information filtering roles. These roles are normally those of aides or middle managers, who are responsible for filtering in the important bit from the information coming from the bottom of, and from outside, the organization. Conversely, excessive information flowing top-down forces middle managers to become messengers, to the damage of more important roles. Information flow can be reduced by selecting the information that is important in processes and eliminating the rest, and by effectively using group support and database management systems.

4. *Reduce control.* Control activities do not normally add value to customers. They are often designed to prevent problems from happening as a result of human mistakes. In several cases, however, control itself fosters neglect, with a negative impact on productivity. For example, a worker may not be careful enough when performing a process activity because he knows that there will be some kind of control to catch his mistakes. Additionally, some types of control, such as those aimed at preventing fraud, may prove to be more costly than no control at all. Some car insurance companies, for example, have found out that the cost of accident inspections, for a large group of customers, was much more expensive than the average cost of frauds that that group committed.

5. *Reduce the number of contact points.* Contact points can be defined as points where there is interaction between two or more people, both within the process and outside. This involves contacts between functions, and between functions and customers. Contact points generate delays and inconsistencies and, when in excess, lead to customer perplexity and dissatisfaction. In self-service restaurants and warehouses, for example, the points of contact were successfully reduced to a minimum. Additionally, it is much easier to monitor customer perceptions in situations where there are a small number of contact points. This makes it easier to improve process quality.

6. *Execute activities concurrently.* Activities are often executed in sequence, even when they could be done concurrently. This has a negative impact primarily on productivity, and is easier to spot on process flowcharts than in data flow diagrams. In a car assembly process, for example, the doors and other body parts can be assembled concurrently with some engine parts. This has been noted by several automakers, which, by redesigning their processes accordingly, significantly speeded up the assembly of certain car models.

7. *Group interrelated activities.* Closely interrelated activities should be grouped in time and space. Activities that use the same resources, i.e. artifacts or functions, may be carried out at the same location and, in some cases, at the same time. Kock (1999; 2005) illustrates this point using the case of a telephone company that repaired external and internal house telephone connections. This company had two teams, one team for internal and another for external repairs. An internal repair occurs, by definition, within the boundaries of a commercial building or residence; external repairs involve problems outside these boundaries. Whenever the telephone company received a customer complaint, it used to send first its internal team. Should this team find no internal connection problem, the external team would then be dispatched check the problem. It took a process

improvement group to show the company that it was wasting thousands of dollars a year, and upsetting customers due to repair delays, by not combining the two teams into a single repair team. This was because, when complaints were categorized and counted, it was found out that most of the problems were external.

8. *Break complex processes into simpler ones.* Complex processes with dozens (hundreds in some cases) of activities and decision points should be "broken" into simpler ones. It is often much simpler to train workers to execute several simple processes, than one complex process. It is also easier to avoid mistakes in this way, as simple processes are easy to understand and coordinate. In support of this point, Kock (1999; 2005) discusses the case of an international events organizer, which was structured around two main processes: organization of national and international events. After a detailed analysis of these two processes, which embodied over a hundred activities each, it was found that they both could be split into three simpler sub-processes: organization of exhibitions, conferences, and exhibitors participation. This simplification improved the learning curve for the processes, as well as reducing the occurrence of mistakes. It did not, however, lead to an increase in the number of employees needed. The reason is because, with simpler processes, one person could perform functions in various processes at the same time.

Part III. Current Debate on IS Action Research

Chapter 13

EDUCING THEORY FROM PRACTICE

Richard Baskerville
Georgia State University, USA

Abstract: This chapter explores the discovery of new or enhanced theory within the action research process. Action research is an empirical research method with two purposes: (1) to solve an immediate practical problem, and (2) to develop new scientific knowledge. Action research projects sometimes succeed at the first, but fail at the second. The highly practical nature of action research sometimes leads to results that have little to contribute in terms of new scholarly knowledge. Although a difficult practical problem may have been resolved, academic publications will often reject reports of the results because the theoretical value is trivial. Action research that encounters difficulties in the attempts to employ existing theory in resolving an immediate practical problem is a more promising venue for developing new or enhanced theory. The most valuable venues for action research lie in the intractable problems of practice, problems that existing knowledge cannot seem to fix.

Key words: Action Research, Epistemology, Information Systems, Research Method

1. ACTION RESEARCH

Action research provides a method that both solves an immediate practical problem while developing social scientific knowledge. It is usually based on collaboration between researchers and research subjects, and is often a cyclical process that builds learning about change into a given social system (Hult & Lennung, 1980).

The discipline of information systems (IS) is appropriate for the use of action research because it is a highly applied field, almost vocational in nature (Avison, Lau, Myers, & Nielsen, 1999; Banville & Landry, 1989). Action research methods are highly clinical and place IS researchers in a "helping-role" within the organizations being studied. (cf. Schein, 1987, p.11). Action research is not only used by academic researchers, but is also widely used for its practical value. Action research has been characterized as the "touchstone of most good organizational development practice" and as remaining "the primary methodology for the practice of organizational development" (Van Eynde & Bledsoe, 1990, p. 27). Because action research merges research and practice, it produces highly relevant research findings. Relevance, together with rigor, become the two most important measures of the significance of IS research (Keen, 1991).

The label "action research" can be legitimately applied to a wide range of research methods (Baskerville & Wood-Harper, 1998). The essence of action research is still a simple two-stage process. First, the diagnostic stage involves a collaborative analysis of the social situation by the researcher and the subjects of the research. Theories are formulated concerning the nature of the research domain. Second, the therapeutic stage involves collaborative change experiments. In this stage changes are introduced and the effects are studied (Blum, 1955). The two stages are iterated until the problem is solved.

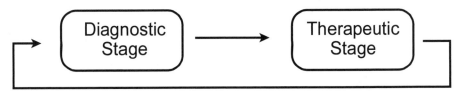

Figure 13-1. Action research as a simple two-stage process

The simple two-stage model is rarely found in practice. To help guide the research process, most action researchers expanded the structure that guides the research. The most common example is the five phase, cyclical process (Susman & Evered, 1978) that is couched within the establishment of a client system infrastructure or research environment. The iterated phases are

1. diagnosing,
2. action planning,
3. action taking,
4. evaluating, and
5. specifying learning.

The client system infrastructure constitutes the research environment by agreement between the researchers and the host organization. This agreement specifies the authority by which the researchers and host practitioners may specify actions.

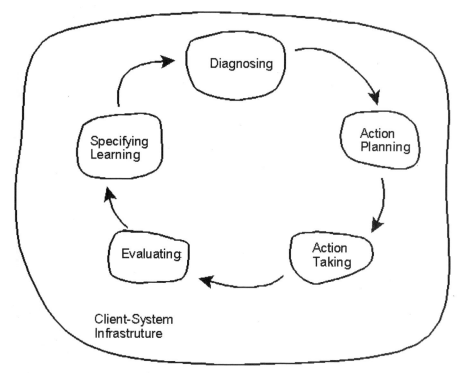

Figure 13-2. Five-stage model of action research (Susman & Evered, 1978)

Diagnosing involves identifying the primary problems that are the root causes driving the need for change. This diagnosis usually operates with several theoretical assumptions (i.e., a working hypothesis) about the nature of the problem.

Action planning requires researchers and practitioners to collaborate in determining actions that should relieve or improve the practical problem. The theoretical framework developed in the diagnosis stage guides action planning.

Action taking implements the plan, again involving collaboration between the researchers and practitioners for the purposes of developing the action.

Evaluating includes a determination of whether the theoretically expected effects of the action developed, and whether these relieved the problem. If successful, the evaluation must determine the degree to which the action drove the success. If unsuccessful, researchers and practitioners must collaboratively develop a revised theoretical framework for the next iteration of the action research cycle.

Specifying learning is usually an ongoing process that formalizes the knowledge gained in the action research, whether the results were successful or unsuccessful.

The action research cycle continues as the project iteratively progresses toward a solution of the practical problem. Such a solution validates the final form of the theory used to drive the actions taken in developing the solution. In this way the action research project develops two outcomes: (1) resolution for the practical problem, and (2) a new or extended theory about the social state of nature in which the problem developed.

Action research authorities distinguish between "participatory action research" and forms that are less participatory. The originators of action research viewed the methodology as a form of field experiment, in which the researchers were technical experts and clinicians brought into the organization to help solve a difficult practical problem. An alternative form, participatory action research, shares much more responsibility with client participants (Whyte, Greenwood, & Lazes, 1991). In other words, practical, client participants earn "co-researcher status" in the action research project (Elden & Chisholm, 1993).

2.   EXEMPLAR: INFORMATING THE CLAN

To illustrate how researchers educe theory from practice and practical problem settings, we will consider an action research project conducted by Rajiv Kohli and William Kettinger (2004). This case centered on a community hospital that was encountering severe financial problems because the hospital administrators could not control the treatment costs of their patients. Their efforts to influence the physicians in recommending lower-cost treatments and avoiding unnecessary high-cost treatments were proving fruitless. This was an intractable problem shared by many hospitals in many different forms. Existing theories of management were failing to resolve such problems. In this case the action researcher was forced to develop new theories by extending and conflating existing theories. This activity resolved the problem.

Initially, the hospital felt that a new information system would enable the hospital to track physician performance. The hospital management believed that they could use this information to improve the cost-effectiveness of physicians. It was based on the theoretical assumption that you cannot manage what you cannot measure. Hospital management believed that the proposed new system would not only improve the cost-effectiveness by monitoring physician performance, but would also improve the quality of patient outcomes.

Initially, the action researchers drew on Zuboff's (1988) informated induced transparency (as modified agency theory). Under this theory hospital management was considered the principal, and physicians were regarded as agents of the hospital. The theory stated that by illuminating agent behavior with information, management would ultimately be able to reconfigure the work. In more practical terms, the system would bring the physicians costs and outcomes into the light, and this illumination alone would lead to more cost-effective decisions by the physicians. The theory holds that the physicians would make better decisions simply because they were aware that their decisions were visible to management. Stated differently the activities of the agents were made visible to the principal by the information system.

Based on this theory, the action research team planned and built new capabilities in the hospital's clinical decision-support system to track the activities of physicians and patients. The system capabilities were carefully deployed. However, the outcome was failure. The physicians failed to use the new clinical decision-support system. This highlighted the intractable nature of this practical problem. In evaluating the learning, the action researchers realized that the physicians did not see the hospital managers as legitimate medical leaders. In their eyes, only trained physicians were capable of evaluating the decisions of other physicians. The information provided as feedback to the physicians was not regarded as legitimate. As a result there was no change in behavior, and the problem setting endured.

In reforming the diagnosis, the researchers recognized that the physicians were operating using a form of control by clan (Ouchi, 1980). According to this theory, the physicians and the managers possessed asymmetric technical knowledge. This asymmetric knowledge legitimated the professional entities as clans. The physicians only respected control by other physicians. Control within the clan is peer based, and hospital management, being external to the clan, is not permitted to set norms.

As a result of this diagnosis, the researchers adopted a new theory that conflated Zuboff's informated induced transparency with Ouchi's clan control. In this situation the induced transparency was to be developed among the clan members. It is important to note how this theory was educed, or drawn out of the problem setting. The revised problem setting was the interaction of the old theory (informating) and the problem situation. The solution was not quite deduced or induced, but simply apparent to observers with the right background and enough courage to act on their observations.

Based on this extended theory the researchers planned and built new capabilities into the clinical decision-support system. They created a physician profile system that permitted the physicians to compare their own results with their peers. This illuminated for each physician his or her performance in relation to other physicians in the same hospital. The outcome was satisfying. The physicians used the clinical decision-support system to maintain the best patient service, along with maintaining their own status among their peers for both economy and care.

The theoretical discovery concerns the legitimacy of informating differently in different kinds of situations. The informating process will work even when it is not used between principals and agents. It will work in different kinds of organizational arrangements, such as clans. The revised theory was successfully applied in resolving an intractable practical problem. The new theory is validated in action.

3.   SERVING TWO MASTERS

Regardless of the exact form of the action research methodology in use, nearly every action research project serves two masters: these masters are (1) the practical goals of the clients driving them to participate in the project, and (2) the research goals of the scientific community driving the researchers to participate in the project (Kock & Lau, 2001). The clients are usually driven to participate in the action research project by their immediate problem situation. The researchers are often driven by the need to develop new and interesting social theory. The originators of action research recognized that these two goals could be synergistic when the organization harvested their problem solution from the project, and the researchers harvested new scientific theory. But in many cases the diversity of roles and goals in the project gives rise to conflicts and dilemmas.

Rapoport (1970) specified the three dilemmas of action research as ethical, goal and integrity. Warmington (1980) delineated the ethical dilemmas as goal, value, and role. An examination of these reveals that each dilemma can be further polarized when action research and consulting are mixed within the same project.

Goal dilemmas. Two goal sets sometimes compete for both project direction and resources. One set of goals represents the practical problems at-hand, including client-system (the organization) and client-component (the individuals) goals. Warmington noted that organizational goals are inextricably commingled with personal ones. The second goal set consists of the research goals (the institution or the project) and the researcher goals. It follows that this last goal set may become equally commingled with institutional and individual goals.

Role dilemmas. Warmington believed that action researchers should not present themselves as experts with definitive techniques or packaged methods, ready to make externally referenced recommendations to the client. The researcher's position can be difficult and ambiguous, and they should enact a role as a fellow student, a collaborator and an investigator of equal status with the client participants. Trist (1976) refers to both professional and scientific responsibilities that must be accepted by the researchers. Researchers accept a commitment to the advancement of scientific knowledge, and in order to be collaborative, both client and researcher must explicitly accept this fundamental commitment. In settings where the role dilemma is severe, the client system and the researcher may become victims of each other, because of the difficulty with which clients can assess the competence of the researcher, and the dependence of the researcher on the tasks set by the client (Clark, 1976).

Value dilemmas. The dual goal sets in action research may also evoke distinctions between the cultures of the clients and the researchers. Culturally determined expectations, such as contrasting values of the academic and management cultures, can lead to conflict. Sometimes the imbalance of priorities in value conflicts is between the immediate, patent needs of the client system and the anticipated, but potent needs of the scientific community (Seashore, 1976). For example, consider the contrast between the need for critical reflection or decisive action. The former is valued in the academic community, the latter an admired quality in the management profession. The researcher faces certain credibility doubts among professional managers if critical reflection is mistaken as indecision, thus leading to pressure for incomplete initial data collection and theorization.

The potential conflict between practical and research goals may sometimes center on the role of theory in the project. An exciting and groundbreaking new theory provides the kind of widespread and general impact for which many researchers are most strongly rewarded. For practitioners with an immediate problem, the widespread and general impact is of little concern. As a result, it is often the sole responsibility of the researchers to be mindful of the potential for theory development and to ensure that this part of the action research process is carefully enacted and satisfactorily complete.

4.   THEORY AND THEORY DISCOVERY

The role of action research as a social scientific method is anchored in pragmatic philosophy (Baskerville & Myers, 2004). This branch of philosophy arose in the company of the nineteenth century genesis of the social sciences as an expedient search for knowledge through the results of using knowledge. The value of any concept is engendered by the achievement of some desirable condition through the use of the concept. If an idea works as a means to an end, then it achieves certain face validity. Pragmatists habitually bypass unnecessarily complex abstraction in thought in favor of ideas that work in practice. While this is liberating for some, it is negligent to others (Menand, 1997). Perhaps nowhere is this tension more evident in action research than in the discovery and application of theory.

Theory is, after all, a potentially complex abstraction. It is not a term with a concise, scientific meaning. It has such general meaning that dictionaries of philosophy may avoid the entry altogether (e.g. Bullock & Stallybrass, 1977; Flew, 1979.). Webster's defines the term as "a belief, policy, or procedure proposed or followed as the basis of action." The *Oxford English Dictionary* (*Oxford English Dictionary*, 1989) defines the term as "A conception or mental scheme of something to be done, or of the method of doing it; a systematic statement of rules or principles to be followed." It more expansively adds, "A scheme or system of ideas or statements held as an explanation or account of a group of facts or phenomena; a hypothesis that has been confirmed or established by observation or experiment, and is propounded or accepted as accounting for the known facts; a statement of what are held to be the general laws, principles, or causes of something known or observed."

Theories may be formulated to explain why things are the way they are, and why things behave the way they do (Harré, 1972). In the natural sciences, theories (or "theoretical laws") are distinguished from experimental laws by such a lessened degree of observability that the components are tantamount to assumptions (Nagel, 1961). These assumptions may connect together a set of experimental laws into a logical collection (Kuhn, 1977). In the social sciences, however, there are no experimental laws available for logical connection into a cogent theory. The body of social theory includes explanations and models that vary widely in scope and grounding, but will typically be a system (perhaps a system of hypotheses) that explains phenomena, or some sort of guiding framework for action.

It is beyond the scope of this paper to ruminate further the meaning of "theory." However, given our context of action research, it is notable that theory, and most of its forms, provides a basis for action. Action research seeks to validate theory through actions in a social setting that are driven by the theory.

5.   THEORY IN PRACTICE

Kurt Lewin, regarded as the father of action research, said, "There is nothing so practical as a good theory." (Hunt, 1987, p. 4) The role of theory in providing a framework for action highlights the importance of theory to action. Theory driven action, or phrased differently, theory driven practice should operate smoothly as long as the theory is valid for the setting. The discovery of tension between theory and practice implies that the particular theory is inappropriate for the particular practical setting. Such a discovery usually means that the practices are going poorly.

Action researchers are used to regarding theory as a basis for actions taken to solve a practical problem. However, theory is also closely related to the practical problem itself. This relationship unfolds in the following way. Typically long before the action researcher is engaged in the client's organization or setting, a reasonably competent practitioner has taken actions in that setting that are planned to solve or avoid organizational problems. These actions either failed to solve the problem or inadequately solved the problem. As a consequence, the problem remained an annoyance (or possibly something more severe) for the organization. It is important to recognize that the practitioner was probably operating on the basis of a set of assumptions that we might regard as constituting that practitioner's theory. The action failed to achieve its goal and provided an indication that the theory was not valid for the setting.

Action researchers, as a consequence, frequently enter an organization that has been applying known theories with surprisingly poor results. To a certain extent, the researcher is encountering a failed theory. A primary mission of the action researcher is to help the organization evaluate its setting and help the organization determine if the theories it has been using are appropriate for that setting.

Because the setting is based on a failed theory, the researcher is driven toward one of three possible conclusions. First, the organization has misapprehended the problem setting and they used the wrong theory. In this case, it is important to engage practitioners from within the organization in order to reevaluate the problem setting and reevaluate the theory, or the type of theory, being drawn upon for resolving the problem. In the simplest case, recognizing that the problem setting is fundamentally different from the assumptions previously made, and choosing a more appropriate theory may enable the organization to directly solve this problem. Second, the organization may have been correct in its apprehension of the problem setting and correct in its choice of an appropriate theory, but the theory may simply be unworkable. Again, choosing a more appropriate theory may help solve the problem. However, it may be the case that there is no other theory appropriate for this problem setting. Third, the organization may have misapprehended the problem setting, but there is in fact no appropriate theory available to solve such a setting.

Any of these conclusions will lead to action, but the basis of that action on theory will vary. In some cases the researchers and the clients will select a new theory as the basis for further action. If this theory solves the problem, such that no further action is necessary, then the clients will be happy, and the researchers rather less so. The researchers' discovery is limited to replicating the use of a known theory in solving a known problem setting. This discovery is neither exciting nor very publishable.

Induction thinking is of value in such settings. It involves recognition and enumerating a number of separate facts or particulars in the problem setting, and this helps generalize the setting to compare with similar settings where other theories may have worked.

Deductive thinking is also most valuable where known theories exist. It involves the process of drawing a conclusion from a principle already known or assumed. This mode of thought is appropriate for applying a existing theory to the problem setting. It is not a wholly simple operation, since the action researcher must know the theory, and be able to recognize the appropriateness of the setting.

However, in other cases the researchers and the clients will select a new theory as the basis for further action, but discover that this theory does not solve the problem (or does not completely solve the problem). Based on this result, one of two possible actions may be appropriate. One is to select yet another theory and continue with the action research cycles. Another is to modify the most recently used theory and continue with the action research cycles using a modified theory. In this latter case, the theory may be said to evolve through practice. In this way, existing theory is extended to cover new problem settings. Once the problem setting is solved, the clients will be happy, and the researchers will be happy. The discovery of extensions to theory is exciting and publishable.

In still other cases the researchers and the clients may be unable to find any new theory as the basis for further action. Given the complexity of the social setting in many different kinds of organizations, this outcome is not as uncommon as we might imagine. In this setting, the researchers and the clients must be creative in discovering a new theoretical basis for taking action in the problem setting. The discovery of new theory, especially when empirically validated, is always very exciting and very publishable.

6.   EDUCTION

The process of discovering new theory involves creativity, invention, and problem solving skills. Discovery takes place at the frontiers of social scientific knowledge. Encountering a problem setting where existing theory fails to resolve the practical problem is a strong indication that the researcher is standing on these frontiers.

These problem settings may arise because of entirely new social settings. The problem may arise within a new kind of organization, a new generation of workers, a new technology, or a new industry. A new problem setting may pose a challenge for existing theory such that the theory fails to solve the problem and the boundaries of the theory's application become established.

These problem settings may not necessarily be new settings. It is always possible that the problem is an old one, an intractable problem for which none of the existing theories had really ever provided satisfactory resolutions. Intractable problems can be the most exciting of challenges. Intractable problems have effectively defeated practitioners and researchers who have encountered the problems in the past. To a degree an encounter with an intractable problem is more exciting than an encounter with a completely new problem.

While inductive and deductive reasoning are helpful in the discovery of new theory and practice, a different mode of thinking may also be useful. Eductive thinking involves drawing forth, eliciting, or developing ideas from a state of latent, rudimentary, or potential existence. Educing is the act of extracting principles from data (*OED*, 1989). In an action research setting, induction is a mode of thinking that draws theory from action. In this case the action is also practice, so the researcher educes theory from practice.

A certain degree of courage is necessary to confront an unknown problem setting. The researchers have to be very independent and confident in their capabilities. Since eductive theory is highly creative, it is difficult to set forth any repeatable process. However, in Root-Bernstein's (1989) treatise on the history of scientific discovery, he offered a number of principles gleaned from a study of major scientific breakthroughs. These include,

- All talents and skills are useful. In many cases the discovery chooses the discoverer rather than the other way around.
- Action creates results, discovery requires exploration. Try many things. Truth comes out of error more rapidly than out of confusion.
- Discoveries can be serendipitous, and arise in eccentricity. Do things that make your heart leap. Explore places where there is no light.
- Choose important problems, these lead to important discoveries. Do not confuse importance with difficulty. Formulating the problem is more essential than its solution.
- Recognize anomalies. Watch for contradictions between theory and data; and between observations and orthodoxy.
- Speculate. Turn it on its head.
- Seek simplicity, it arises from understanding complications.

While this list may seem like a series of platitudes, closer thinking reveals that major scientific discoveries arise from creative and courageous thinking. The individual researcher will possess a unique background that enables this person to see things differently from others. Such major discoveries come from individuals who realize that only they can see what they see, and have the courage to act upon it.

7.   CONCLUSION

While the literature on discovery explores deductive and inductive logic, eduction is almost overlooked entirely. Perhaps this is because eductive logic is illusory. If one thinks of the problem setting as a text, then the source of eduction might best be thought of as being between the lines or in the margins. More than just recognizing a pattern, eduction is the discovery of meaning as intentional actions engage with settings. It is a form of reasoning that builds from ideas in motion: the interaction of thought and action.

What are the tips and traps of theory eduction? Both center on action. Actions in research should certainly be carefully considered, planned, and executed. However, neither learning nor theory building will accelerate until action is underway. Interventions in the problem setting should not be unnecessarily delayed. The reasoning underlying the action should be well understood. Discoveries are most likely to follow actions that, while based on clear reasoning, fail to achieve the desired outcomes. The question, "Why didn't that work?" lays open a path to discovery of new theories. Where the actions are aimed at solving an intractable problem, the potential for discovery of important new theories is greatly increased.

Action research provides a method that is intended to solve an immediate practical problem while simultaneously developing new social science. The form of this new social science is usually extended or novel theory. Action research involves an internal conflict between the goals of the clients and the goals of the researchers. This may lead to a number of dilemmas for the researchers, some of which revolve around the need for theory. The importance of theory in action research is not entirely concordant with the basic pragmatic philosophy that underlies the action research methodology. Action research deemphasizes theorizing in favor of action. The theory arises from the learning that follows the action. As a result, theory emerges as the action research study evolves. It is up to the researcher to discover the theory as it appears in the action, not quite deductively, not quite inductively, but rather eductively.

8. REFERENCES

Avison, D. E., Lau, F., Myers, M. D., & Nielsen, P. A. (1999). Action research. *Communications of The ACM, 42*(1), 94-95.

Banville, C., & Landry, M. (1989). Can the field of MIS be disciplined? *Communications of the ACM, 32*(1), 48-61.

Baskerville, R., & Myers, M. (2004). Special issue on action research in information systems: Making IS research relevant to practice--foreword. *MIS Quarterly, 28*(3), 329-335.

Baskerville, R., & Wood-Harper, A. T. (1998). Diversity in Information Systems Action Research Methods. *European Journal of Information Systems, 7*(2), 90-107.

Blum, F. (1955). Action research--A scientific approach? *Philosophy of Science, 22*(1), 1-7.

Bullock, A., & Stallybrass, O. (Eds.). (1977). *The Fontana Dictionary of Modern Thought*. London: Fontana.

Clark, A. (1976). The client-practitioner relationship. In A. Clark (Ed.), *Experimenting with Organizational Life: The Action Research Approach* (pp. 119-133). New York: Plenum.

Elden, M., & Chisholm, R. F. (1993). Emerging Varieties of Action Research: Introduction to the Special Issue. *Human Relations, 46*(2), 121-142.

Flew, A. (1979.). *A Dictionary of Philosophy*. London: Pan.

Harré, R. (1972). *The Philosophies of Science, An Introductory Survey*. London: Oxford University Press.

Hult, M., & Lennung, S. (1980). Towards A Definition of Action Research: A Note and Bibliography. *Journal of Management Studies, 17*, 241-250.

Hunt, D. E. (1987). *Beginning with ourselves: In practice, theory and human affairs*. Cambridge, Mass: Brookline Books.

Keen, P. (1991). Relevance and Rigor in Information Systems Research: Improving Quality, Confidence Cohesion and Impact. In H.-E. Nissen, H. Klein & R. Hirschheim (Eds.), *Information Systems Research: Contemporary Approaches & Emergent Traditions* (pp. 27-49). Amsterdam: North-Holland.

Kock, N., & Lau, F. (2001). Information systems action research: serving two demanding masters *Information Technology & People, 14*(1), 6-12.

Kohli, R., & Kettinger, W. J. (2004). Informating the clan: Controlling Physicians' costs and outcomes. *MIS Quarterly, 28*(3), 363-394.

Kuhn, T. (1977). *The Essential Tension: Selected Studies in Scientific Tradition and Change*. Chicago: University of Chicago Press.

Menand, L. (Ed.). (1997). *Pragmatism: A Reader*. New York: Vintage.

Nagel, E. (1961). *The Structure of Science: Problems in Scientific Explanation*. London: Routledge and Kegan Paul.

Ouchi, W. (1980). Markets Bureaucracies and Clans. *Administrative Science Quarterly 25*, 129-141.

Oxford English Dictionary. (2nd ed.)(1989). 2nd ed.). Oxford: Oxford University Press.

Rapoport, R. (1970). Three Dilemmas of Action Research. *Human Relations, 23*(6), 499-513.

Root-Bernstein, R. S. (1989). *Discovering: Inventing and Solving Problems at the Frontiers of Scientific Knowledge*. Cambridge, Mass.: Harvard University Press.

Schein, E. (1987). *The Clinical Perspective in Fieldwork*. Newbury Park, Calf: Sage.

Seashore, S. (1976). The design of action research. In A. Clarke (Ed.), *Experimenting with organizational life: The action research approach* (pp. 103-117). New York: Plenum.

Susman, G., & Evered, R. (1978). An Assessment of The Scientific Merits of Action Research. *Administrative Science Quarterly, 23*(4), 582-603.

Trist, E. (1976). Engaging with Large-scale Systems. In A. Clark (Ed.), *Experimenting with Organizational Life: The Action Research Approach* (pp. 43-75). New York: Plenum.

Van Eynde, D., & Bledsoe, J. (1990). The changing practice of organization development. *Leadership & Organization Development Journal, 11*(2), 25-30.

Warmington, A. (1980). Action Research: Its Method and Its Implications. *Journal of Applied Systems Analysis, 7*(4), 23-39.

Whyte, W. F., Greenwood, D. J., & Lazes, P. (1991). Participatory Action Research: Through Practice to Science in Social Research. In W. F. Whyte (Ed.), *Participatory Action Research* (pp. 19-55). Newbury Park: Sage.

Zuboff, S. (1988). In the Age of the Smart Machine: The Future of Work and Power: Basic Books.

Chapter 14

A CRITICAL ASSESSMENT OF INFORMATION SYSTEMS ACTION RESEARCH

Ravi Narayanaswamy and Varun Grover
Clemson University, USA

Abstract: The debate between rigor and relevance in information systems research has motivated methodological pluralism in the information systems field. In the recent years IS researchers have applied various methodologies; one such method that is gaining prominence is action research. As qualitative method that emphasis collaboration between researchers and practitioners' action research has been applied to study IS in various organizational settings. In this chapter we address the issues associated with action research. In doing this we develop a set of criteria to assess the quality of information systems action research. We then provide recommendations to improve both the incidence and the quality of action research in the field.

Key words: Action research, Information systems, Information system researchers, Information systems field

1. INTRODUCTION

Over the past few decades the information systems (IS) field has experienced criticisms of its research methods and philosophy. Many of these criticisms narrow down to the question of the relevancy of IS research to practice (Benbasat and Zmud, 1999; Davenport and Markus, 1999; Hirschheim and Klein, 2003; Holland, 2003). While IS researchers have predominantly followed positivist methods (Orlikowski and Baroudi, 1991) these criticisms have provided impetus for greater methodological pluralism in IS research. Some researchers assert that qualitative approaches are appropriate for an applied field like IS (Baskerville and Myers, 2004; Susman and Evered, 1978). However in their study Orlikowski and Baroudi (1991) found that interpretive studies represented only 3.2 percent of the total IS research. For the past few years IS scholars and premier journals have been promoting use of qualitative approaches in IS research (Hirschheim and Klein, 2003; Vessey, et al., 2002); one such method that is gaining prominence is action research.

Action research combines theory and practice through change and reflection to address an immediate problematic situation within a mutually acceptable ethical framework. (Rapoport, 1970). The research process is collaborative and iterative, that is, it requires both the researcher and practitioner to act jointly on a particular cycle of activities - problem diagnosis, action intervention, and reflective learning (Baskerville and Wood-Harper, 1996). Unlike other interpretive methods where researchers only observe and interpret a phenomenon, action research encourages researchers to influence change through intervention and reflective learning. Due to its collaborative nature some scholars feel action research to be an ideal research method for a "vocational" field like IS (Baskerville and Wood-Harper, 1996). However only 0.6 percent of IS research has applied action research as their research method (Orlikowski and Baroudi 1991). Exploring the reasons behind this limited application reveals that action research has been pushed to the periphery of legitimate scientific methodologies because of its post-positivist foundations which brings the discussion of research findings under dispute (Baskerville and Wood-Harper, 1998; Baskerville and Wood-Harper, 1996). Further there is little consensus on which criteria IS action research should be judged (Baskerville, 1999; Lau, 1999). Consequently, prominent action researchers claim that lack of unified framework to conduct and review action research (Lau, 1997; 1999), diverse views held by researchers regarding action research process (Baskerville, 1999), the challenge of serving both world of science and world of practice (Kock and Lau, 2001) has inhibited scholars from applying action research in mainstream IS research.

To address these issues we develop a comprehensive framework for assessing action research by reviewing and integrating the key strengths of extant action research frameworks. We believe that developing such a framework would help researchers' gain better understanding of action research process. For reviewers it would serve as a tool to evaluate published research and as a guide for conducting future action research. To test the applicability of the proposed framework, we use it to assess the quality of IS action research studies published in premium North American and European IS journals. Finally, through this process we offer recommendations to improve both the incidence and quality of action research in the field.

2.   ACTION RESEARCH IN IS

Action research has been linked to systems theory since its inception. Some of the early work such as Client-system structure by (Susman and Evered, 1978), ETHICS by Mumford (Mumford and Weir, 1979), Mutiview by Wood-Harper (1985) and Checkland's (1981) soft systems methodology has made seminal connections between action research and the IS community. All these efforts coupled with specialized conferences (for example, IFIP 8.2) and invitations extended by premium journals (for example, MIS Quarterly's special invitation for action research studies in year 2004) have fostered application of action research in IS field (Baskerville and Wood-Harper, 1998; Baskerville and Wood-Harper, 1996; Lau, 1999). However, the breadth and intensity of action research in mainstream IS research has been limited. For instance, only one action research article was found among 155 major research publications between 1983 and 1988 (Orlikowski and Baroudi, 1991). In another instance, only 29 action research studies were found in IS research spanning 25 years (1971-1995) (Avison, et al., 1999). Most of the action researchers contend that lack of integrated framework for evaluating action research studies, different meanings held by researchers and lack of precise guidelines addressing deeper complexity of the research process has hindered application of action research (Lau, 1997; Lau, 1999; Baskerville, 1999; Baskerville and Wood-Harper, 1996; Lau, 1997; Lau, 1999). At this juncture we believe that offering a comprehensive set of evaluative criteria would facilitate benchmarking and improvement in the quantity and quality of IS action research studies

3.   EXISTING CRITERIA OF ACTION RESEARCH

Over the years researchers have held diverse views about the term action research. They have used it to refer streams such as action science, participatory research and a general class of methods in social inquiry (Baskerville, 1999; Lau, 1997; Lau, 1999). These divergent views have made action research literature rather imprecise in its basic terminology (Baskerville and Wood-Harper, 1996). Consequently there exists different assessment criteria described in the social science and IS literature. We identified five[1] key set of criteria that have been widely adopted by most action research studies:

---

[1]   The five set of criteria were selected by scanning through the bibliography of published action research studies. In addition we chose only those criteria which offered general guidelines and not addressing a particular type of action research for example, canonical

1. Hult and Lennung (1980) build on the definition offered by Rapport (1970). They define action research as – a simultaneous process which assists in practical problem-solving, expands scientific knowledge and enhances the competence of the respective actors; it is a collaborative process which involves both researcher and practitioner and is performed in an immediate problem situation using data feedback in a cyclical process aimed at an increased understanding of the totality of a given situation primarily applicable for the understanding of change processes in social systems undertaken within a mutually acceptable ethical framework. Put differently, they claim that an action research study must depict –

    a. Existence of real problem situation
    b. Nature of collaboration between the researcher and the practitioner
    c. Application of theoretical assumptions to analyze the problem
    d. The cyclical nature of the research. The cyclical process is further divided into five stages - Diagnosing, Action planning, Action taking, Evaluating, Specifying (see Susman and Evered, 1978 for more details)
    e. The manner in which the participants' competency was enhanced.

We use these five characteristics as the key corner stones for developing the integrated framework. Further to ensure completeness we include the key aspects offered by extant action research assessment frameworks.

2. Chisholm and Elden (1993) in the process of differentiating emergent form of action form classical ones identified five criterions:

    a. Level of analysis
    b. Degree of formalization of the research process
    c. Goal and purpose of the research effort
    d. Role of the researcher and participants
    e. Extent of openness in the research process.

3. Jonsson (1991) builds upon the definition offered by Argyris, et al. (1985) and advocates use of interpretive or critical perspectives as a philosophical base for conducting action research. The criteria suggested are:

    a. Exemplifying the link between the research objective and the perspective employed
    b. Utilizing a ethical framework, that is the level of discretion the researcher has to discuss some of the research issues

---

action research etc. However, we ensured that the proposed framework includes all the criteria important for promoting rigor of the research process. The model offered by Susman and Evered (1978) is not explicitly mentioned because the five stages are often embedded in most of the identified framework.

   c. Clarity in access and exit points
   d. Employing multiple sources to collect and interpret data
   e. Reflective learning

4. Checkland (1981; 1991) proposed FMA (framework, methodology and area of application) structure where the primary objective to promote rigor of action research. The highlights of the FMA structure are:

   a. Including an intellectual framework (theoretical assumptions) to guide the effort,
   b. Clarifying methodological details
   c. Stating the role of the researcher
   d. Elucidating the cyclical process, that is, the process of problem diagnosis, the nature of the intervention, the extent of reflection and learning intended, and whether there is new knowledge to be gained.

5. Lau (1997; 1999) built upon the above listed set of criteria to develop a unified framework with four dimensions:

   a. Conceptual foundation – includes the research aim, theoretical assumptions, perspective/tradition, and stream of action research used.
   b. Study design - describes the methodological details of a study similar to those described by Chisholm and Elden (1993) and Checkland (1981;1991)
   c. Research process - refers to the sequence of steps by which action research is conducted.
   d. Role expectations - explicates the capacity and expectations of the researcher and participants taking part in the study.

In addition to these five studies we also include concerns put forth by other research highlighting the centrality of controlling (Avison, et al., 2001) and managing the action research environment (Baskerville 1999) to secure research rigor and relevance. A properly designed control structure allows action researchers to balance between action and research. (Avison, et al., 2001). In the literature three aspects of control[2] have been identified: the procedures for initiating an action research project, those for determining authority within the project, and the degree of formalization (Avison, et al., 2001). We believe these aspects are critical for promoting rigor in the research. For example, the goal of initiation process is to develop mutual interest between the researcher and practitioner in enhancing the problem situation. Articulating these in the research report will not only help the audience understand the commitment level of the researcher, but help the researcher avoid conflicts in the research process. Similarly process of

---

[2] Details of the three control aspects can be found in Avison, et al., 2001.

determining the authority aids the researcher to determine the level of involvement required to ensure project success. Third degree of formalization helps the researcher avoid scope creep. In addition to these three aspects we include role of researcher, role of participants and ethical issues under control structure. Further elucidating details of the research process and the criteria by which to judge the research can enhance the quality of action research (Baskerville and Myers, 2004; Baskerville, 1999). The framework presented here includes all the criteria aforementioned with an objective to define an integrated perspective for conducting and assessing action research[3]. There are six dimensions in the framework:

(1) Study design – refers to the context of the study, the nature of the problem addressed in the research. This serves as a basis for transferability of results and clarifies the need for action research i.e., to relieve from immediate problem situation (Hult and Lennung, 1980). In addition it also includes the description of the perspective[4] and stream[5] being employed which facilitates understanding of the logic behind the research processes.

(2) Control issues – describes the procedures for initiating an action research project, those for determining action warrants within the project, and the degree of formalization. In addition it also addresses the ethical issues, role of researcher and role of participant. Explicating these issues helps the audience evaluate the authenticity of the research effort (Avison et.al. 2001; Checkland 1991). Further it aids the project success by avoiding scope creep, and team conflict.

(3) Structure – illustrates the use of theories to guide the research effort, data collection procedure, and duration of the project. Exemplifying these issues fosters rigor in the action research process. For instance Checkland (1991) asserts that using theoretical assumptions prior to interventions validates the study as a research and promotes rigor.

---

[3] Since each action research, to some extent at least, is unique and it is difficult to propose general laws for each action research type. Thus in this study we develop a comprehensive and parsimonious which we believe can serve as baseline for further development/other types of actions research.

[4] Action research may be interpretive, critical or even positivistic depending on the perspective of the researcher (Jonsson, 1991, Baskerville and Wood-Harper, 1998).

[5] There are several streams of action research - participator action research (PA) involves practitioners as both subjects and co-researchers; action learning (AL) advocates group participation, programmed instructions, spontaneous questioning, real actions, and experiential learning in different social and organizational contexts; action science (AS) emphasizes on understanding participants' behaviors as theories-in-use versus their beliefs as espoused theories, and the use of single and double-loop learning for self-improvement (Argyris, C., and Schon, D.A. "Participatory action research and action science compared," *American Behavioral Scientist* (32:5), 1989, pp. 612-623.)

(4) Methodology – refers to the actions undertaken by the researcher to enhance the problem situation. It includes planning, implementing and reflective learning stages of action research. Illustration of these issues can serve as a powerful evidence for audience/researchers to evaluate the practical effectiveness of an underlying theory.

(5) Application – describes the efforts made by the researcher to improve the competency level of participants in dealing with their practical problem through the change process instigated. Further it also captures whether the level of competency has indeed improved. Articulating these issues demonstrate the researcher's proficiency in applying the theoretical framework to enhance the problem situation (Baskerville, 1999; Lau, 1999; Susman and Evered, 1978)

(6) Specifying learning – refers to articulation and presentation style of the new knowledge created through action research. It is important for the researchers to ensure that lessons learned are credible, transferable, dependable and confirmable to be considered a contribution to new knowledge (Hult and Lennung, 1978; Jonsson, 1991; Lau 1999).

Different assessment criteria are used to capture these six dimensions. To reduce subjectivity we use objective questions to evaluate a published action research and provide clear rationale for each criterion. Finally we assert that quality of action research is reflected in the depth to which these criterions are described and not the number of criterion being addressed (Baskerville and Wood-Harper, 1998). Table 14-1 summarizes the criteria, their description, rationale and the evaluation question used for evaluating IS action research.

Table 14-1. Criteria for Assessing Information Systems Action Research

Criteria	Description	Rationale	Evaluation
Study design			
Site description	The sites/company's) chosen/participated	Illuminates context of the study and serves as a basis for transferability of results.	Does it give enough information to understand the total social situation?
Problem description	Nature of the problem	Clarifies the need for action research i.e., to relieve from immediate problem situation (Hult and Lennung, 1980).	Is the practical problem well identified?
Perspective/tradition	Approach adopted (interpretive, critical, positivist)	Facilitates understanding of the research process.	Is the approach defined?
Stream	Kind of action research adopted (PA, AL, AS)	Helps understand the logic behind research activities.	Is the research stream defined?

Table 14-1. Criteria for Assessing Information Systems Action Research (*Continued*)

Criteria	Description	Rationale	Evaluation
Control Issues			
Initiation	Who initiated the project?	Helps determine the level of commitment of both the researcher and the practitioner. In addition fosters understanding of the research process and the outcome (Avison, et al., 2001).	Is the nature of research clearly stated such that presence of mutual interest between the parties can be determined?
Degree of formalization	Information on researcher-client agreement (formal, informal or emerging).	Assists differentiate the research from consulting (Avison, et al., 2001). It also helps in avoiding project scope creep and team conflict.	Is the project process pre-defined or emergent?
Nature of action warrants	The authority under which action may be taken.	Clarifies role and involvement of the researcher and participants. Also, helps elucidate ethical issues (Avison, et al., 2001).	Who exercises authority over planning, designing and implementing actions?
Role of researcher	Researcher's involvement and contribution in enhancing the problem situation	Clarifies whether the researcher was an observer outside the action or a participant in the action (Checkland, 1981). Helps differentiate research from consulting.	Were the roles and responsibilities of the researcher specified explicitly?
Role of Participants	Participant profile and their contribution in enhancing the problem situation	Helps evaluate and understand the degree of collaboration in the process. Further it also enables audience to understand the motivation of the client organization to improve the problem situation (Mathiassen, 2002).	Were the roles and responsibilities of the client organization/participants specified explicitly?
Ethical issues	People's who will be affected by the change effort and their acceptance of actions	Emphasize the importance of participation by those primarily affected by the planned change (Hult and Lennung, 1980).	Did the researcher seek clients' approval before implementing the planned actions?
Structure			
Theoretical assumption's	Theories used to guide the interventions.	Theory or set of theories used to guide the research. Using theoretical assumptions prior to interventions validates the study as a research. Further it is important so that the findings can make more sense to the audience (Checkland, 1991).	Were the theories used as a premise to guide interventions?
Domain of investigation	Research question /objectives	Helps understand the scope of the project (Baskerville, 1999).	Is the research question or objective well defined?
Data collection and Analysis	Data sources used, methods used to analyze data	Serves as a basis for assessing the validity of research findings (Baskerville, 1999)	Are the data reliable and plausible?
Duration	Timing of actions taken	Helps understand the progress of the project.	Were the activities planned according to the schedule?

Table 14-1. Criteria for Assessing Information Systems Action Research (*Continued*)

Criteria	Description	Rationale	Evaluation
Methodology			
Action interventions	Planned change to improve the problem situation	Helps understand the efforts made by the researcher to improve the problem situation (Hult and Lennung, 1980).	Is the planned change clearly declared?
Reflective learning	Adjustments made to interventions based on the outcomes of the previous iteration.	Represents the continuous learning process (Hult and Lennung, 1980; Susman and Evered, 1978)	Did the researcher reflect on the outcomes of the intervention?
Iteration	The cyclical process – series of actions taken to relieve the immediate problem situation.	Serves as a powerful evidence to evaluate the practical effectiveness of an underlying theory (Baskerville, 1999).	Did the project follow the cyclical process model or justify any deviation from it?
Application			
Action implementation	Actions taken at each phase/cycle	Facilitates understanding of the efforts made by the researcher to improve the problem situation (Baskerville, 1999; Lau, 1999; Susman and Evered, 1978)	Were the planned actions realized by the participants?
Evaluation of actions	Consequences of actions implemented.	Helps understand the successful/unsuccessful changes. Further it guides the researcher to make necessary adjustments to the theoretical framework for the next iteration cycle (Lau, 1999; Susman and Evered, 1978)	Were the actions implemented evaluated consistently?
Competency enhancements	Efforts made to foster understanding of the participants about the practical and theoretical applicability of the actions	Helps understand the degree of collaboration and depicts impartiality in the role of researcher (Baskerville, 1999; Lau, 1999).	Did researcher make efforts to improve the proficiency of the participants?
Access	Details on level of access to resources.	Helps understand the degree of collaboration and participation of the organization (Lau, 1999).	Is level of access to resources taken into consideration while planning/implementing action?
Point of Exit	Details on when researcher exited from the project.	Indicates the commitment of the researcher.	Did the researcher clearly articulate the point of exit?
Specifying Learning			
Presentation	Clear and adequate information about the findings at each phase and the overall project.	Helps determine whether the action/project was a success or a failure and explore reasons behind them. Further, assists the client considers the results for further action in this situation.	Did the researcher clearly articulate the conclusion of the project (project objectives being met or not, follow-up projects, etc)?

Table 14-1. Criteria for Assessing Information Systems Action Research (*Continued*)

Criteria	Description	Rationale	Evaluation
Generalization	General applicability of the findings. Implications for research and practitioner community	Allows practitioners to use the results in different settings, or for scientists to build further studies on the knowledge (Baskerville and Wood-Harper, 1998).	Were the results considered in terms of implications for the research and practitioner community?

4. ASSESSING IS ACTION RESEARCH

The proposed framework is used to assess the existing IS action research studies published in premium Europe and North American IS journals. Journals were selected using the world journal ranking[6] published by Lowry et al (2004). *MIS Quarterly, Information System Research*, and *Journal of Management Information System* were selected to represent North American IS outlets. For European journals *European Journal of Information Systems, Information System Journal* and *Information technology and People* were selected. Articles were retrieved from *EBCOhost* and *ProQuest* databases using keywords action research, action learning, participatory research and action science. A total of 15 studies from North American journals and 17 studies from European journals were considered for assessment[7]. The assessment was two fold, first we determined whether a particular criterion was explicitly addressed in the article in which case √ - was assigned. Second we examined whether there was sufficient description[8] provided about the criterion such that is facilitates better under standing among the audience, in this case √ √ was assigned. If the article failed to address a criterion then - - was assigned. To illustrate this let us consider an example of project duration, if an article simply mentioned that the total length of the project was 6 months then √ - was assigned. If the article provided a break

---

[6] Top three journals in each region were selected. We recognize that these journals may not provide a complete coverage of action, but believe that sample adequately represents the population. Further we believe that assessing all extant action research studies using the proposed framework can be a worthwhile effort in future.

[7] The titles, abstract and the key words of all the articles were collected and were scanned for the following words – action research, participatory action research, action science, canonical action research, dialectical action research, etc. The number of articles included in our assessment though not exhaustive we believe they adequately represent IS action research.

[8] We do acknowledge the space availability and journal publication policies may restrict the length of discussion. Hence during our evaluation we analyzed the intensity of discussion rather than number of lines written.

Table 14-2. Assessing IS action research in North American journals

	(Kaiser and Bostrom, 1982)	(Levine and Rossmoore, 1993)[9]	(Levine and Rossmoore, 1994)	(Baskerville and Stage, 1996)	(Briggs, et al., 1998)
Site description	√ -	√ √	√ √	√ √	√ √
Problem description	√ √	√ √	√ √	√ √	√ √
Perspective/tradition	√ √	√ √	√ √	√ √	√ √
Stream	- -	√ √	√ √	- -	√ √
Initiation	- -	- -	- -	√ -	√ -
Degree of formalization	√ -	- -	- -	√ √	- -
Nature of action warrants	- -	- -	- -	- -	- -
Role of researcher	√ √	√ √	√ √	√ √	√ √
Role of Participants	√ -	√ √	√ √	√ √	√ √
Ethical issues	√ √	- -	- -	- -	√ √
Theoretical assumption's)	√ √	√ √	√ √	√ √	√ √
Domain of investigation	√ √	√ √	√ √	√ √	√ √
Data collection and Analysis	√ √	√ √	√ √	√ √	√ √
Duration	√ √	- -	√ √	- -	√ √
Action interventions	√ √	- -	√ √	√ √	√ √
Reflective learning	- -	- -	√ √	√ √	√ √
Iteration	- -	- -	√ √	√ √	√ √
Action implementation	√ -	- -	√ √	√ √	√ √
Evaluation of actions	- -	- -	√ √	√ √	√ √
Competency enhancements	√ -	√ -	√ √	√ √	√ √
Access	- -	√ -	- -	√ √	√ √
Point of Exit	- -	√ -	- -	√ √	√ √
Presentation	√ √	√ √	√ √	√ √	√ √
Generalization	√ √	√ -	√ -	√ √	√ √

Note: √ √ the first √ is assigned if the criterion is explicitly addressed in the article; the second √ is assigned if there is sufficient information describing whether the criterion has been successfully achieved or not.

down of time lines for each activity then √ √ was assigned and if there was no mention about the duration then - - was assigned. At this point we would like to reiterate that the objective of our assessment is to assess the quality of IS action research and not single out good (or bad) studies. Assessment of selected studies is illustrated in Table 14-2 and Table 14-3.

[9]   Part of a larger study

Table 14-2. Assessing IS action research in North American journals (*Continued*)

	(Straub and Welke, 1998)	(Vreede, 1997)	(Pauleen, 2003)[10]	(Braa, et al., 2004)	(Hengst and Vreede, 2004)
Site description	√ √	√ √	- -	√ √	√ √
Problem description	√ √	√ √	√ √	√ √	√ √
Perspective/tradition	√ √	√ √	√ √	√ √	√ √
Stream	√ -	√ √	√ √	√ √	√ √
Initiation	√ -	- -	- -	√ √	√ √
Degree of formalization	√ -	- -	- -	√ √	√ √
Nature of action warrants	√ √	- -	√ √	√ √	√ √
Role of researcher	√ √	√ √	√ √	√ √	√ √
Role of Participants	√ √	√ √	√ √	√ √	√ √
Ethical issues	√ √	- -	- -	√ √	√ √
Theoretical assumption's)	√ √	√ √	√ √	√ √	√ √
Domain of investigation	√ √	√ √	√ √	√ √	√ √
Data collection and Analysis	√ √	√ √	√ √	√ √	√ √
Duration	√ √	√ √	- -	√ √	√ √
Action interventions	√ √	√ √	- -	√ √	√ √
Reflective learning	√ √	√ √	- -	√ √	√ √
Iteration	√ √	√ √	- -	√ √	√ √
Action implementation	√ √	√ √	- -	√ √	√ √
Evaluation of actions	√ √	√ √	- -	√ √	√ √
Competency enhancements	√ √	√ √	- -	√ √	√ √
Access	√ √	- -	- -	√ √	√ √
Point of Exit	√ -	√ -	- -	√ √	√ √
Presentation	√ √	√ √	√ √	√ √	√ √
Generalization	√ √	√ √	√ -	√ √	√ √

Note: √ √ the first √ is assigned if the criterion is explicitly addressed in the article; the second √ is assigned if there is sufficient information describing whether the criterion has been successfully achieved or not.

[10] Exploratory study

Table 14-2. Assessing IS action research in North American journals (*Continued*)

	(Iversen, et al., 2004)	(Kohli and Kettinger, 2004)	(Lindgren, et al., 2004)	(Mårtensson and Lee, 2004)[11]	(Street and Meister, 2004)
Site description	√√	√√	√√	√√	√√
Problem description	√√	√√	√√	√√	√√
Perspective/tradition	√√	√√	√√	√√	√√
Stream	√√	√√	√√	√√	√√
Initiation	√√	√√	√√	√√	√√
Degree of formalization	√√	√√	√√	√√	√√
Nature of action warrants	√√	√√	√√	√√	√√
Role of researcher	√√	√√	√√	√√	√√
Role of Participants	√√	√√	√√	√√	√√
Ethical issues	√√	√√	√√	√√	√√
Theoretical assumption's)	√√	√√	√√	√√	√√
Domain of investigation	√√	√√	√√	√√	√√
Data collection and Analysis	√√	√√	√√	√√	√√
Duration	√√	√√	√√	√√	√√
Action interventions	√√	√√	√√	√√	√√
Reflective learning	√√	√√	√√	√√	√√
Iteration	√√	√√	√√	√√	√√
Action implementation	√√	√√	√√	√√	√√
Evaluation of actions	√√	√√	√√	√√	√√
Competency enhancements	√√	√√	√√	√√	√√
Access	√√	√√	√√	√√	√√
Point of Exit	√√	√√	√√	√√	√√
Presentation	√√	√√	√√	√√	√√
Generalization	√√	√√	√√	√√	√√

Note: √ √ the first √ is assigned if the criterion is explicitly addressed in the article; the second √ is assigned if there is sufficient information describing whether the criterion has been successfully achieved or not.

[11] Explores a new form of action research called Dialogical action research - collaborative research process where the researcher does not speak or teach the scientific theory but considers the practitioner to be an expert of the problem situation. The dialogue itself serves as the interface between world of science and world of practice.

Table 14-3. Assessing IS action research in European Journals

	(Songkhla, 1997)	(Vidgen, 1997)	(Kock and McQueen, 1998)	(Gregor and Jones, 1999)	(Olesen and Myers, 1999)	(Davison and Vogel, 2000)
Site description	√ √	√ √	√ √	√ √	√ √	√ -
Problem description	√ √	√ √	√ √	√ √	√ √	√ -
Perspective/tradition	√ √	√ √	√ √	√ √	√ √	- -
Stream	- -	√ √	√ -	- -	√ √	- -
Initiation	√ -	√ -	√ √	√ √	√ √	√ √
Degree of formalization	√ -	√ √	- -	√ -	√ √	√ √
Nature of action warrants	√ √	√ √	- -	- -	√ √	√ √
Role of researcher	√ -	√ √	√ √	√ √	√ √	√ √
Role of Participants	√ -	√ √	√ -	√ √	√ √	√ -
Ethical issues	- -	√ -	- -	- -	- -	√ -
Theoretical assumption's)	√ √	√ √	√ √	√ √	√ √	√ √
Domain of investigation	√ √	√ √	√ √	√ √	√ √	√ √
Data collection and Analysis	√ √	√ √	√ √	√ √	√ √	√ √
Duration	- -	√ √	√ √	√ √	√ √	√ √
Action interventions	√ -	√ √	√ √	√ √	√ √	√ √
Reflective learning	√ -	√ √	√ √	- -	√ √	√ √
Iteration	√ -	√ √	√ √	√ √	√ √	√ √
Action implementation	√ √	√ √	√ √	- -	√ √	√ -
Evaluation of actions	√ √	√ √	√ √	- -	√ √	√ -
Competency enhancements	√ √	√ √	√ √	√ √	√ √	√ -
Access	√ -	√ √	√ -	√ √	√ √	√ -
Point of Exit	- -	√ √	√ -	√ -	√ √	√ -
Presentation	√ -	√ √	√ √	√ √	√ √	√ √
Generalization	√ √	√ √	√ √	- -	√ -	- -

Note: √ √ the first √ is assigned if the criterion is explicitly addressed in the article; the second √ is assigned if there is sufficient information describing whether the criterion has been successfully achieved or not.

Table 14-3. Assessing IS action research in European Journals (*Continued*)

	(Simon, 2000)	(Salmela, et al., 2000)	(Chiasson and Albert, 2001)	(Davison, 2001)	(Kock, 2001)	(Davison and Martinsons, 2002)
Site description	√√	√√	√√	√√	√√	√√
Problem description	√√	√√	√√	√√	√√	√√
Perspective/tradition	√√	√√	√√	√√	√√	√√
Stream	√√	√√	√√	√√	√-	√√
Initiation	√√	√-	√-	√√	√-	√√
Degree of formalization	√√	√-	--	√√	√√	√√
Nature of action warrants	√√	√√	--	√√	√√	√√
Role of researcher	√√	√√	√-	√√	√-	√√
Role of Participants	√√	√-	√-	√√	√-	√√
Ethical issues	√√	√√	--	√√	--	--
Theoretical assumption's)	√√	√√	√√	√√	√-	√√
Domain of investigation	√√	√√	√√	√√	√√	√√
Data collection and Analysis	√√	√√	√√	√√	√√	√√
Duration	√√	√√	--	√√	√√	√√
Action interventions	√√	√√	√√	√√	√√	√-
Reflective learning	√√	√√	√√	√√	√-	√-
Iteration	√√	√√	--	√√	√√	√-
Action implementation	√√	√√	--	√√	√√	√-
Evaluation of actions	√√	√√	√√	√√	√√	√-
Competency enhancements	√√	√√	√√	√√	√√	√-
Access	√√	√√	--	√√	√√	√-
Point of Exit	√√	√√	√-	√√	√-	√-
Presentation	√√	√√	√-	√√	√√	√-
Generalization	√-	√√	√-	√-	√√	√-

Note: √ √ the first √ is assigned if the criterion is explicitly addressed in the article; the second √ is assigned if there is sufficient information describing whether the criterion has been successfully achieved or not.

Table 14-3. Assessing IS action research in European Journals (*Continued*)

	(Rose, 2002)	((Vidgen, 2002)[12]	(Grant and Ngwenyama, 2003)	(Lindgren, et al., 2003)	(Champion, et al., 2005)[13]
Site description	√ √	√ √	√ √	√ √	√ √
Problem description	√ √	√ √	√ √	√ √	√ √
Perspective/tradition	√ √	√ √	√ √	√ √	√ √
Stream	√ √	√ √	√ -	√ √	√ √
Initiation	√ √	√ √	√ √	√ -	√ -
Degree of formalization	√ √	√ √	- -	- -	- -
Nature of action warrants	√ √	√ √	√ √	- -	√ √
Role of researcher	√ √	√ √	√ √	√ -	√ -
Role of Participants	√ √	- -	√ √	√ -	√ -
Ethical issues	√ -	- -	√ √	- -	- -
Theoretical assumption's)	√ √	√ √	√ √	√ √	√ √
Domain of investigation	√ √	√ √	√ √	√ √	√ √
Data collection and Analysis	√ √	√ √	√ √	√ √	√ √
Duration	√ √	√ √	√ √	√ √	- -
Action interventions	√ √	√ √	√ √	√ -	√ √
Reflective learning	√ √.	√ √	√ √	√ -	√ √
Iteration	√ √	√ -	√ √	√ -	√ √
Action implementation	√ √	√ √	√ √	√ -	√ √
Evaluation of actions	√ √	√ √	√ √	√ -	√ √
Competency enhancements	√ √	√ -	√ √	√ √	√ √
Access	√ √	√ -	√ √	√ -	√ -
Point of Exit	√ √	√ -	√ √	- -	√ √
Presentation	√ √	√ √	√ √	√ √	√ √
Generalization	√ √	√ -	√ √	√ √	- -

Note: √ √ the first √ is assigned if the criterion is explicitly addressed in the article; the second √ is assigned if there is sufficient information describing whether the criterion has been successfully achieved or not.

[12] Ongoing research
[13] Research in progress

5. FINDINGS AND RECOMMENDATIONS

Overall trend implies that the number of IS action research studies has increased in the recent years. Moreover, recently published articles seem to incorporate most of the elements mentioned in the framework (see Table 14-4). For instance, the research aims and underlying theoretical assumptions are well defined in almost in all articles. Further authors seem to have gained better understanding of the research processes and offer their own set of evaluation criteria to appraise their research (see Bra et al. 2004; Iverson et al. 2004).

On the other hand, very few articles seem to be explicit in describing ethical issues. Further very few articles illustrate the process of how authority over the research process was achieved. In sum, rigor in IS action research though not complete, it seem to increasing. Below, we discuss our findings and recommendations for each of the six dimensions listed in the framework.

5.1 Study Design

The study designs for most of the articles are explicit, appropriate and adequate in most respects. However, recent articles offer more explicit definition or description of the term and stream of action research than the ones published earlier. For example, Braa et al (2004) explicitly declare use of participatory action research to design, implement and sustain health information systems. Further there is a clear link between the stream and the sequence of activities presented. On other hand in Kock and McQueen (1998) the stream (participatory action research) is implicit.

Recommendation: While stream can be implicitly inferred from the data collection and later stages. Precise articulation in the beginning of the study would help readers understand the logic behind the research activities. For instance, one may adopt the action research stream that focuses on changing practice, the action science stream for conflict resolution, the participatory action research stream for participant collaboration, or the action learning stream through experiential learning (Lau, 1997; Baskerville and Wood-Harper, 1998). Explicating these may help researcher maintain consistency between the design and reporting of the study.

Table 14-4. Summary of findings

Criteria	Cumulative		
	√ √	√ -	- -
Study design			
Site description	90 %	6 %	4 %
Problem description	97 %	3 %	None
Perspective/tradition	97 %	None	3 %
Stream	72 %	13 %	15 %
Control issues			
Initiation	53 %	30 %	17 %
Degree of formalization	53 %	16 %	31 %
Nature of action warrants	68 %	14 %	28 %
Role of researcher	85 %	15 %	None
Role of Participants	70 %	27 %	3 %
Ethical issues	46 %	8 %	46 %
Framework			
Theoretical assumption's)	97 %	3 %	None
Domain of investigation	100 %	None	None
Data collection and Analysis	100 %	None	None
Duration	81 %	None	19 %
Methodology			
Action interventions	84 %	9 %	7 %
Reflective learning	76 %	12 %	12 %
Iteration	76 %	12 %	12 %
Application			
Action implementation	76 %	12 %	12 %
Evaluation of actions	78 %	9 %	13 %
Competency enhancements	81 %	16 %	3 %
Access	60 %	24 %	16 %
Point of Exit	54 %	30 %	16 %
Specifying learning			
Presentation	91 %	9 %	None
Generalization	64 %	27 %	9 %

Note: *(Applies for Table 14-4 and 14-5)*
1. √ √ the first √ is assigned if the criterion is explicitly addressed in the article; the second √ is assigned if there is sufficient information describing whether the criterion has been successfully achieved or not.
2. Values are rounded; Total number of studies = 32; Studies from North American journals = 15; Studies from European journals = 17

Table 14-5. Summary of findings (categorized region wise)

Criteria	North American			European		
	√ √	√ -	- -	√ √	√ -	- -
Study design						
Site description	86 %	7 %	7 %	94 %	6 %	None
Problem description	100 %	None	None	94 %	6 %	None
Perspective/tradition	100 %	None	None	94 %	None	6 %
Stream	80 %	7 %	13 %	65 %	18 %	17 %
Control issues						
Initiation	47 %	20 %	33 %	59 %	41 %	None
Degree of formalization	53 %	14 %	33 %	53 %	18 %	29 %
Nature of action warrants	60 %	7 %	33 %	76 %	22 %	24 %
Role of researcher	100 %	None	None	70 %	30 %	None
Role of Participants	93 %	7 %	None	47 %	47 %	6 %
Ethical issues	67 %	None	33 %	24 %	17 %	59 %
Framework						
Theoretical assumption's)	100 %	None	None	94 %	6 %	None
Domain of investigation	100 %	None	None	100 %	None	None
Data collection and Analysis	100 %	None	None	100 %	None	None
Duration	80 %	None	20 %	82 %	None	18 %
Methodology						
Action interventions	86 %	None	14 %	82 %	18 %	None
Reflective learning	80 %	None	20 %	71 %	24 %	5 %
Iteration	80 %	None	20 %	71 %	24 %	5 %
Application						
Action implementation	80 %	7 %	13 %	71 %	18 %	11 %
Evaluation of actions	80 %	None	20 %	76 %	18 %	6 %
Competency enhancements	80 %	13 %	7 %	82 %	18 %	None
Access	67 %	6 %	27 %	53 %	41 %	6 %
Point of Exit	60 %	20 %	20 %	47 %	41 %	12 %
Specifying learning						
Presentation	100 %	None	None	82 %	18 %	None
Generalization	80 %	20 %	None	47 %	35 %	18 %

5.2 Control issues

Most of the articles are explicit and appropriate in defining the roles of the researchers and participants, only few refer to ethical issues, initiation, and degree of formalization (see Table 14-4). Some studies are explicit in addressing the control issues while in others it can be implicitly inferred from later stages. For example, Simon (2000) clearly describes the invitation received by the organizations and provides details on personnel/process involved in determining the nature of action warrants. In another study Street and Meister (2004) openly demonstrate the negotiation process held with the agency officer in determining the project goals, clarifying authority issues and developing a mutually ethical framework. In some studies control issues are implicit because of the nature of research. For example, the study by Straub and Welke (1998) began as a non-intervention case study, opportunity for intervention arose only after the engagement had begun, and hence details on nature of action of warrants, degree of formalization can be inferred from later stages of intervention. These observations imply that description of control issues largely depend on the research context.

Recommendation: Given that control issues are complex in real setting, elucidating them in the beginning of the study would help the audience assess the validity of the study. Clear illustration of how control structures evolved in terms of shifts occurred during the project, informal or formal mechanisms used aids understanding of the seriousness and complexity of the problem being addressed (Avison, et al., 2001). From a research process perspective shaping control structures in early stages of the project will avoid scope creep and reduce possibility of losing control during the project (Avison, et al., 2001). Further adequate framing of control issues will assist the researcher to develop a mutually acceptable ethical framework (as seen in Street and Meister (2004) study), currently this appears naïve in many reports. Given that coercive situations are common in information systems work it becomes more imperative for IS action researchers to address ethical issues (Lau, 1999). Finally, elucidating control issues will help audience to differentiate action research from consulting, which is often cited as a dilemma in action research (Rapoport, 1970).

Framework

Our analysis shows a steady increase in the proportion of articles applying theoretical framework to guide the research (see Table 14-4). Some studies use a combination of methods ranging from ethnography, soft systems methodology, to evaluation research. The description of data collection process appears to vary in quality within and across journals. A common theme observed across most articles is that authors do not explain complexity involved in the data collection process. For example, in Salmela et al. (2000) the authors mention a fourteen page report was developed from the interviews but do not offer details[14] on the interview process and the route adapted to develop planned changes from the collected data. Nevertheless some studies stand as good examples in describing the process.

---

[14] We do recognize that space limitations might preclude complete description of the process.

For example in Martensson and Lee (2004), the authors clearly illustrate the measures taken to maintain the quality of data and explain different sources (interviews, internal documents, archival reports, etc) and techniques (hand-written notes, use of tape-recorder, one-one sessions, etc) used to collect data.

Recommendation: In action research the data collection process serves as a premise for planning actions and cycle of activities. Further given the criticisms faced by action researchers (post-positivist approach, action research being similar to consulting, etc) it is imperative that researchers present a rigorous documentary records of the process; this can serve as basis for audience to judge the validity and quality of undertaken actions and its consequences.

Methodology

Most of the articles use theories for guiding the interventions. Further they provide sufficient details on the specific interventions undertaken and cycle of activities (see Table 14-4). For example, Lindgren et al. (2004) use Susman and Evered (1978) model to develop an iterative process to test the design principles. The series of activities and interventions undertaken are demarcated in two action research cycles and explicitly presented. However some studies describe the iteration process as a sequence of activities without clear link between each step. It appears that the researcher is so involved in the immediate practical effects of the research they neglect the scientific discipline. For example, Kaiser and Bostrom (1982) mention using integrative problem solving perspective to enhance system success but fail to provide details on interventions and cycle of activities undertaken.

Recommendation: Some action researchers (for example see, Baskerville and Wood-Harper, 1996; Rapoport, 1970) assert that a rigorous action research must adhere resolutely to the constructs of cyclical theoretical infrastructure and clearly depict the cycle of activity to promote validity of the pronounced theory. Thus, articulating the sequence involved or the link between theory and intervention would promote validity of the theory under test. In addition since rigorous action research cannot disguise negative effects of some action, as these action failures are important as action successes (Baskerville and Wood-Harper, 1996) demonstrating the steps through which intervention were planned, implemented and evaluated would endorse authenticity of the research effort/process. Finally reflective learning is an important characteristic of action research hence illustrating how it was achieved is a worthwhile effort.

Application

The components of application - implementation, evaluation of actions, and competency enhancements are explicit in most articles (see Table 14-4). However, the nature of involvement of the practitioner in the evaluation process is not well explained. This can misguide the audience in interpreting the impartiality of the researcher. For instance, Davison and Vogul (2000) describe involvement of Chief Information Officer and team members in the planning the interventions but do not offer details on how the interventions were evaluated. There is variation in the way researchers elucidate their level of access to resources which poses difficulty in assessing the participants'/researchers commitment to enhance the problem situation. Finally the point of exit is often not explicit, it is important to illustrate whether the objectives were achieved or not, and was the project completed within proposed time. For example, Davison and Vogul (2000) recommend significant information technology related improvements and organizational culture change, but details on whether this was achieved is absent.

Recommendation: Since even seasoned researchers sometime have problems on delineating action research from consulting (Jonsson, 1991), clear description of criterions under application dimension would help one appreciate the researcher's loyalty and commitment to the project. An important part of action research is to improve the competency level of participants in dealing with their practical problem through the actions instigated. Hence, the questions whether there is any effort to improve the competency of the participants, and whether their level of competency has indeed improved, becomes imperative for promoting authenticity of the research effort. The increased competency may refer to increase in participants' performance, or heightened awareness of the problem through reflections on how to cope with it effectively. Delineating these issues as a part of research process would help researcher adjust his/her actions accordingly in order to achieve the project goals.

Specifying Learning

Since action research is situational and context bound, generalization and presentation plays a vital role in promoting validity of the research. Number of articles with explicit discussion of generalization and contribution to the creation of new knowledge in IS has increased (see Table 14-4). Apparently, some authors state their tacit experience as generalized new knowledge while few others portray generalization as a draw back. For example, Levine and Rossmoore (1995) contend that political considerations must be part of any organizational IT diagnosis; and summarize their findings but do not present ways to extend them to different contexts.

Recommendation: Generalization makes theories relevant and allows expansion of knowledge. The quality of action research is often reflected in the manner in which it is presented (Baskerville 1999). Appropriate presentation of the findings is necessary in order to facilitate extended use of research by both scientific community and practitioners. For a vocational field like IS, it is generalizability of the findings that interests majority of the scientists (Baskerville and Wood-Harper, 1996).

6.   IMPLICATIONS

The increase in number of IS action research studies indicates growing acceptance of action research within the IS community. Given that relevance in action research is obvious; efforts have to be made to promote rigor in the process. Failing to do so will reduce incidence of action research as it did in social psychology and social science research (Sanford, 1976).

The framework developed here provides opportunities for action researchers to gain scientific rigor by following some/all of the criteria listed (refer table 14-1). Further the researcher must understand and apply the key characteristics of action research such as enhancing a immediate problem situation, using iterative process of planning, taking, and evaluating organizational actions. The interventions act as interface between world of science and world of practice, hence it is vital that researchers adhere to scientific knowledge while planning the interventions. Collaboration is a key aspect of action research, researchers should motivate subjects to participate in the research process and also attempt advance subject's knowledge through learning cycles. Planning the duration and utilizing a rich data collection process will avoid project scope creep. Conventional wisdom says that a good theory will stand the test of time and apply across different contexts; hence it is necessary to ensure that the research findings apply across diverse scenarios. Consequently it is important to report the findings in a manner that allows expansion of knowledge within the scientific and practitioner community.

IS action researcher serves two different *masters*, namely the research client and the research community as a whole. The needs of these two masters are usually entirely different, and sometimes conflict with each other. Fulfilling them is rarely easy, and certainly the main challenge that all IS action researchers have to face (Kock and Lau, 2001). The IS action research framework proposed in this paper provides a general set of guidelines for both researchers and readers to recognize and engage in good IS action research studies. In particular, for those engaging in conducting IS action research, this framework provides an extensive set of criteria and questions that should be taken into account when designing, conducting and publishing a study. For readers and reviewers of IS action research studies reported in the literature, this framework can serve as a comprehensive checklist with its repertoire of criteria and questions to critically assess the quality of a given study. Finally, we feel that no approach is without problems, the difficulty with action research is matter of degree and not absolute. We hope that this work can serve as a catalyst to guide and improve future action research in IS.

7. CONCLUSION

Action research offers unique opportunity to bridge theory and practice. The pragmatism provided by action research directly promotes the calls for increasing relevance in IS. With information technology becoming a key enabler of business processes that lead into new forms and practices, the use of action research as a scientific approach seems appropriate for understanding of such "agile" phenomena. Thus we suggest IS scholars to focus on answering important research questions rather than debating on the validity of positivistic and interpretive approaches. By applying intensive methodologies such as action research, the IS field will enhance its pragmatic utility. We hope that the guidelines presented here serve as a vehicle for vehicle for this.

REFERENCE

Argyris, C., Putnam, R., and Smith, D.M. *Action Science: Concepts, Methods, and Skills for Research and Intervention,*, Jossey-Bass Publishers, San Francisco, CA, 1985.

Argyris, C., and Schon, D.A. "Participatory action research and action science compared," *American Behavioral Scientist* (32:5), 1989, pp. 612-623.

Avison, D., Baskerville, R.L., and Myers, M.D. "Controlling action research projects," *Information Technology & People* (14:1), 2001, pp. 28-45.

Avison, D., Lau, F., Myers, M.D., and Nielsen, P.A. "Action research," *Communications of the ACM* (42:1), 1999, pp. 94-97.

Baskerville, R., and Myers, M.D. "Special Issue on Action Research in Information Systems: Making IS Research Relevant to Practice — Foreword," *MIS Quarterly* (28:3), 2004,

Baskerville, R., and Wood-Harper, A.T. "Diversity in information systems action research methods.," *European Journal of Information Systems* (7:2), 1998, pp. 90-107.

Baskerville, R.L. "Investigating information systems with action research," *Communications of the Association for Information Systems* (2:19), 1999, pp. 2-32.

Baskerville, R.L., and Stage, J. "Controlling Prototype Development Through Risk Analysis," *MIS Quarterly*), 1996, pp. 481-504.

Baskerville, R.L., and Wood-Harper, A.T. "A critical perspective on action research as a method for information systems research.," *Journal of Information Technology* (11:3), 1996, pp. 235-246.

Benbasat, I., and Zmud, R.W. "Empirical Research in Information Systems: The Practice of Relevance," *MIS Quarterly* (23:1), 1999, pp. 3-16.

Braa, J., Monteiro, E., and Sahay, S. "Networks of Action: Sustainable Health Information Systems Across Developing Countries," *MIS Quarterly* (28:3), 2004,

Briggs, R.O., Adkins, M., Mittleman, D., and Kruse, J. "A technology transition model derived from field investigation of GSS use aboard the U.S.S. CORONADO," *Journal of Management Information Systems* (15:3), 1998, pp. 151.

Champion, D., Stowell, F., and O'Callaghan, A. "Client-Led Information System Creation (CLIC): navigating the gap," *Information Systems Journal* (15), 2005, pp. 213-231.

Checkland, P. *Systems Thinking, Sytems Practice*, John Wiley & Sons, Chichester, 1981.

Checkland, P. "From framework through experience to learning: the essential nature of action research," In *Information Systems Research: Contemporary Approaches and Emergent Traditions*, P. A. Nielsen and e. al. (eds.), Elsevier, Amsterdam, 1991,

Chiasson, M., and Albert, S.D. "System development conflict during the use of an information systems prototyping method of action research: Implications for practice and research," *Information Technology & People* (14:1), 2001, pp. 91-108.

Chisholm, R.F., and Elden, M. "Features of emerging action research," *Human Relations* (46:2), 1993, pp. 275-298.

Davenport, T.H., and Markus, M.L. "Rigor vs. Relevance revisited: Response to Benbasat and Zmud," *MIS Quarterly* (23:1), 1999, pp. 19-23.

Davison, R. "GSS and action research in the Hong Kong police," *Information Technology & People* (14:1), 2001, pp. 60-77.

Davison, R., and Martinsons, M.G. "Empowerment or enslavement? A case of process based organisational change in Hong-Kong," *Information Technology & People* (15:1), 2002, pp. 42-59.

Davison, R., and Vogel, D. "Group support systems in Hong Kong: An action research project," *Information Systems Journal* (10), 2000, pp. 3-20.

Grant, D., and Ngwenyama, O. "A report on the use of action research to evaluate a manufacturing information systems development methodology in a company.," *Information Systems Journal* (13:1), 2003, pp. 21-36.

Gregor, S., and Jones, K. "Beef producers online: diffusion theory applied," *Information Technology & People* (12:1), 1999, pp. 71-85.

Hengst, M.D., and Vreede, G.-J.D. "Collaborative Business Engineering:A Decade of Lessons from the Field," *Journal of Management Information Systems* (20:4), 2004, pp. 85-113.

Hirschheim, R., and Klein, H. "Crisis in the IS Field? A Critical Reflection on the State of the Discipline," *Journal of the Association for Information Systems* (4:5), 2003, pp. 237-293.

Holland, C.P. "Information Systems Research and Practice: IT Artifact or a Multidisciplinary Subject," *Communications of the AIS* (12), 2003, pp. 599-606.

Hult, M., and Lennung, S. "Towards A Definition of Action Research: A Note and Bibliography,," *Journal of Management Studies* (17), 1980, pp. 241-250.

Iversen, J.H., Mathiassen, L., and Nielsen, P.A. "Managing Risk in Software Process Improvement: An Action Research Approach," *MIS Quarterly* (28:3), 2004,

Jonsson, S. "Action research," In *Information Systems Research: Contemporary approaches and emergent tradition*, H. E. Nissen, H. K. Klien and R. Hirschheim (eds.), North-Holland, Amsterdam, 1991, pp. 371-396.

Kaiser, K.M., and Bostrom, R.P. "Personality Characteristics of MIS Project Teams: An Empirical Study and Action-Research Design," *MIS Quarterly* (6: 4), 1982, pp. 43-60.

Kock, N. "Asynchronous and distributed process improvement: the role of collaborative technologies," *Information Systems Journal* (11), 2001, pp. 87-110.

Kock, N., and Lau, F. "Information systems action research: serving two demanding masters," *Information Technology & People* (14:1), 2001,

Kock, N., and McQueen, R.J. "Groupware support as a moderator of interdepartmental knowledge communication in process improvement groups: an action research study," *Information Systems Journal* (8), 1998, pp. 183-198.

Kohli, R., and Kettinger, W.J. "Informating the Clan: Controlling Physicians' Costs and Outcomes," *MIS Quarterly* (28:3), 2004,

Lau, F. "A Review On The Use of Action Research in Information Systems Studies," In *Information Systems and Qualitative Research*, A. Lee, J. Liebenau and J. DeGross (eds.), Chapman & Hall, London, 1997, pp. 31-68.

Lau, F. "Toward a framework for action research in information systems studies," *Information Technology & People* (12:2), 1999, pp. 148.

Levine, H.G., and Rossmoore, D. "Diagnosing the human threats to information technology implementation: A missing factor in systems analysis illustrated in a case study," *Journal of Management Information Systems* (10:2), 1993, pp. 55.

Levine, H.G., and Rossmoore, D. "Politics and the function of power in the case study of IT implementation," *Journal of Management Information Systems* (11:3), 1994, pp. 115-133.

Lindgren, R., Henfridsson, O., and Schultze, U. "Design Principles for Competence Management Systems: A Synthesis of an Action Research Study," *MIS Quarterly* (28:3), 2004,

Lindgren, R., Stenmark, D., and Ljungberg, J. "Rethinking competence systems for knowledge-based organizations," *European Journal of Information Systems* (12:1), 2003, pp. 18.

Mårtensson, P., and Lee, A.S. "Dialogical Action Research at Omega Corporation," (28:3), 2004,

Mathiassen, L. "Collaborative practice research," *Information Technology & People* (15:4), 2002, pp. 321-345.

Mumford, E., and Weir, M. *Computer Systems Work Design: The ETHICS method*, Associated Business Press, London, 1979.

Olesen, K., and Myers, M.D. "Trying to improve communication and collaboration with information technology An action research project which failed," *Information Technology & People* (12:4), 1999, pp. 317-332.

Orlikowski, W., and Baroudi, J. "Studying information technology in organisations: research approaches and assumptions," (2:1), 1991, pp. 1-28.

Pauleen, J.D. "AniInductively derived model of leader-initiated relationship building with virtual team members," *Journal of Management Information Systems* (20:3), 2003, pp. 227-256.

Rapoport, R. "Three Dilemmas of Action Research," *Human Relations* (23:6), 1970, pp. 499-513.

Rose, J. "Interaction, transformation and information systems development - an extended application of soft systems methodology," *Information Technology & People* (15:3), 2002, pp. 242-268.

Salmela, H., Lederer, A.L., and Reponen, T. "Information systems planning in a turbulent environment," *European Journal of Information Systems* (9:1), 2000, pp. 3.

Sanford, N. "Whatever happened to action research?," In *Experimenting with social life:The social life approach*, A. Clark (ed.) Plenum, New York, 1976,

Simon, S.J. "The reorganization of the information systems of the US Naval Construction Forces: An action research project," *European Journal of Information Systems* (9:3), 2000, pp. 148.

Songkhla, A.N. "A soft system approach in introducing information technology A case study of an international broadcasting programme in Japan," *Information Technology & People* (10:4), 1997, pp. 275-286.

Straub, D.W., and Welke, R.J. "Coping with Systems Risk: Security Planning Models for Management Decision Making," *MIS Quarterly* (22:4), 1998, pp. 441-469.

Street, C.T., and Meister, D.B. "Small Business Growth and Internal Transparency: The Role of Information Systems," *MIS Quarterly* (28:3), 2004,

Susman, G., and Evered, R. "An Assessment of The Scientific Merits of Action Research," *Administrative Science Quarterly* (23:4), 1978, pp. 582-603.

Vessey, I., Ramesh, V., and Glass, L.R. "Research in Information Systems: An Empirical Study of Diversity in the Discipline and Its Journals," *Journal of Management Information Systems* (19:2), 2002, pp. 129-175.

Vidgen, R. "Stakeholders, soft systems and technology: seperation and mediation in the analysis of information systems requirements," *Information Systems Journal* (7), 1997, pp. 21-46.

Vidgen, R. "Constructing a web information system development methodology," *Information Systems Journal* (12), 2002, pp. 247-261.

Vreede, G.-J.d. "Collaborative business engineering with animated electonic meetings," *Journal of Management Information Systems* (14:3), 1997.

Chapter 15

IS ACTION RESEARCH AND ITS CRITERIA

Peter Axel Nielsen
Aalborg University, Denmark

Abstract: There is little agreement on which criteria should be used in the design and evaluation of IS action research. Much action research is not at all explicit about the applied criteria. This chapter seeks to remedy this by eliciting from twenty odd years of action research six criteria. The epistemology of action research has traces back to pragmatism and with this as background the six criteria are presented and illustrated through a piece of recent action research. The contributions of the chapter are the six criteria, how to model these in their context of research activities and research contributions, and how to understand these criteria in a pragmatist view.

Key words: action research criteria, pragmatism, experience, problem solving, research design, research evaluation.

1.   INTRODUCTION

In the mid-1980'ies when I came to Lancaster University, UK, to study for my Ph.D. I was struck by the clarity with which Checkland and his colleagues explained their use of action research. Their particular use of action research had already then led to many advances in their research on problem-solving methodology in what is commonly known as Soft Systems Methodology (Checkland, 1981). I came from a Scandinavian background where action research was legitimate, but never well understood as a means for researching information systems. In retrospect, I think it is fair to state that it was more luck and good intentions that had led us to a reasonable research process. When I came to Lancaster, I was for the first time confronted with a clear intellectual account of action research. I was pleased to find that we had implicitly practiced action research – at least in part –, but it was also painfully apparent that we had much to learn. The Lancaster account of action research influenced our research practice immensely and we have since been seeking to explain with clarity what we have done and why our findings amounted to research contributions. Much has happened with action research in the last twenty years and its use has diffused to larger parts of information systems research.

In this chapter I present how we now explain the criteria by which we design and evaluate action research. We have for many years used action research to study and improve the professional practice of information systems development. A few pieces of our action research are: the study of the use of methods in practice (Nielsen, 1990), a summary of the research on reflective systems development (Mathiassen, 1998), improvement of development practices (Iversen et al., 1999), the organization of action research and collaborative practice research (Mathiassen, 2002), an organizational view on software process improvement (Mathiassen et al., 2002). We first used the now six criteria explicitly in (Iversen et al., 2004). The purpose I will pursue in this chapter is to discuss pragmatism as the underlying research epistemology as well as how research activities, contributions, and criteria come together in designing and evaluating action research.

2.   ACTION RESEARCH EPISTEMOLOGY

Most accounts of action research focus on its methodology, i.e., what to do and why. Action research methodology has often been traced back to Lewin (US) and to Tavistock (UK) where the discussions have concerned its therapeutic intentions. The epistemology underlying action researches has so far received little attention. Jönsson attribute his criterion of truth to the pragmatists James and Mead (Jönsson, 1991, p. 392). Baskerville & Myers in their foreword to the special issue on action research in *MIS Quarterly* suggest that pragmatism is its underlying philosophy (Baskerville & Myers, 2004). In this chapter I shall follow the same traces of action research epistemology.

The emergence of pragmatism as a philosophical discourse was for the most part due to William James though he attributed its principles to Charles S. Pierce more than a hundred years ago. An excellent historical account of pragmatism can be found in *The Metaphysical Club* (Menand, 2001). James summarises Pierce's pragmatism with the idea of clearness:

> "To attain perfect clearness in our thoughts of an object, then, we need only consider what conceivable effects of a practical kind the objects may involve. ... The ultimate test for us of what a truth means is indeed the conduct it dictates or inspires." James, 1907, cited here from (Menand, 1997).

Thus, what we take to be a true theory is a theory that has some consequence in action. If it does not have a consequence, it is not a clear theory and thus not relevant to consider. To pragmatists, it does not make sense to think of a theory as a mirror of reality; a theory (or knowledge as the later pragmatists prefer to call it) is an instrument or organ of successful action (Dewey, 1908-09, cited here from (Menand, 1997)).

John Dewey who was influenced by James developed pragmatism much further in his integrated theory of knowledge as holistic, of politics as democratic, and of education as progressive. A core idea not only to his theory of learning-by-doing, but in all his work is that knowing and doing are inseparable aspects of the same process.

To Dewey, "the function of knowledge is to make one experience freely available in other experience" (Dewey, 1916). While experience is central in his thinking it is not so that all experience will lead to knowledge or will be educative:

"Experience and education cannot be directly equated to each other. For some experiences are mis-educative. Any experience is mis-educative that has the effect of arresting or distorting the growth of further experience." (Dewey, 1938, p. 25)

Dewey is not concerned with action research, but his concept of experience is very relevant to understand better the action aspects of this particular kind of research. It is from the action we are trying to elicit the research findings. Dewey would say that, irrespective of whether we are looking at education or problem solving, experience is foundational. Therefore everything rest on experience:

"Everything depends on the *quality* of the experience which is had. The quality of any experience has two aspects. There is an immediate aspect of agreeableness or disagreeableness, and there is its influence upon later experiences." (Dewey, 1938, p. 27)

Based on this Dewey developed two criteria for experience (Dewey, 1938, p. 35-44):

1. The *principle of continuity of experience* whether that is due to habit or explicit value-making discriminates desirable and successful actions from those that are failed action, not desirable outcomes or perhaps just less desirable consequences. Growing experience is a special case of the principle of continuity. This may also be referred to as progress – progress according to a set of values.

2. The *principle of interaction* puts equal concern on the immediate experience and the influence on lasting experience. Taken together they form what Dewey calls a situation.

Donald Schön does not refer much to Dewey (at least not directly), but it is evident that his theory of problem solving rests on a similar pragmatic view of knowledge as "knowing and doing are inseparable" (Schön, 1983, p. 165). Schön seeks to explain in various ways and for several professional disciplines how knowing and doing come together in knowledge-in-action and in reflection-in-action. Reflection-in-action is particularly directed at explaining professional practitioners' thinking in action. In reflection-in-action:

1. Situations are seen as unique though the professionals bring past experience to bear through *seeing-as* experimentation based on a repertoire of examples, images, understandings, and actions (Schön, 1983, p. 138). Dewey would undoubtedly refer to this repertoire as experience and possibly even as continuity of experience as the repertoire becomes tested over time.
2. Inquiry is seen as problem setting where means and ends are mutually dependent and therefore are set in the same process. The framing and re-framing of the situation happens gradually when the practitioner listens to the situation's back-talk (Schön, 1983, p. 132). This is in other terms the principle of interaction.
3. Progress in problem setting is measured in terms of whether it leads to successful actions (Schön, 1983, p. 133-134): Can the problem be solved? Has the situation become coherent? Have we kept inquiry moving? This is equal to the principle of pragmatism and it is a practical way to exercise the principle of continuity.

Schön's theory of reflection-in-action is relevant to mention within a pragmatist view of action research because it reflects a concern for action and for research where the two are inseparable. Schön's theory influences the relationship between research and professional practice and between researchers and professional practitioners. Schön does not distinguish between these.

The criteria for action research should from a pragmatist viewpoint be congruent with Dewey's two principles (continuity of experience and interaction) and follow Schön's three principles of reflection-in-action. In our action research we have long been influenced by Schön's theory. His theory is particularly relevant to us as our focus has always been that our research should be useful to practitioners of information systems development. The traces back to Dewey and pragmatism has daunted on us only gradually within the last years. In the following I will try to relate our view on action research criteria to Schön's theory and pragmatism to provide a better foundation for the criteria and how we use these.

3. ACTION RESEARCH CRITERIA

Action researchers seek relevance in their results by committing themselves to a particular problem situation. This unfortunately leads to a number of limitations and pitfalls (Baskerville & Wood-Harper, 1996): (1) lack of impartiality of the researcher; (2) lack of discipline; (3) mistaken for consulting; and (4) context-dependency leading to difficulty of generalizing findings.

Criteria for action research are intended to reduce the inherent limitations and pit-falls, but have in general not been common until recently. Many have been influenced by Checkland's criterion of usefulness for his research on Soft Systems Methodology (Checkland, 1981), and that criterion I will return to later. Probably the first introduce explicit criteria into IS action research was Checkland in 1990 at the IFIP WG 8.2 conference in Copenhagen where he introduced the criterion of declaring a framework (Checkland, 1991). In the following I will present some of the existing criteria and discuss these briefly from a pragmatist viewpoint. I will then continue by presenting our six criteria and also discuss these from a pragmatist viewpoint.

3.1 Existing Criteria

Lau summarizes the criteria already in the literature in the late 1990'ies on action research (Lau, 1999) based on a few selected sources (Checkland, 1991; Hult & Lennung, 1980; Jönsson, 1991). He applies these criteria on the action research papers he has found in the mainstream literature by 1999. Lau's criteria are directed at reviewing journal articles. An example of a criterion is whether the reported action research led to appropriate and adequate changes in the situation in which the action research intervened into? When planning action research and when in the midst of action you cannot know whether the resulting changes are appropriate and adequate. Our argument has always been that it is part of the action research to figure this out and it depends among other things on the actors in the situation. The principle of interaction implies that it is in the situation that appropriateness of changes can be assessed. Based on Schön I will also argue that the appropriateness of changes must be seen as problem-setting and it cannot really be determined prior to engaging into action. While Lau's criteria are all argue to be relevant for reviewing journal papers I shall maintain that action research criteria should be applicable throughout the endeavor, from designing, over engaging in action, to making sense of the findings and evaluating.

Recently, a set of principles for canonical action research was established and for each of the five principles there are a number of detailed criteria (31 in total) (Davison et al., 2004). These criteria are all very detailed and each criterion can in principle be answered with 'yes' or 'no'. An example of a criterion is: "Was the focus of the research project specified clearly and explicitly?" It is also our experience that it is reasonable to ask this question, but in addition we have often been in research projects where the focus has changed – and with good reasons. Our research projects have often been longitudinal and our main concern has always been to design action research and hence also to redesign it when we had good reasons. That is, based on the principle of interaction and Schön it becomes apparent (as with Lau's criteria) that these criteria are directed at evaluating action research, but suffer from a static view on the intrinsic relationship between action and research. I am not rejecting these criteria, but our experience with action research has led us in a different direction where attention is directed at creating and maintaining cohesion between our action and our thinking about research and its potential contribution. That is Dewey's principle of interaction enacted.

Checkland made a very important point when he claimed that it is insufficient for action research to claim that some coherent action was useful. It is only proper action research if a framework is declared in advance and the framework allows for the formulation of lessons that can be learned from the action (Checkland, 1991). Following Checkland we also apply these two criteria, which I shall return to in the next section. Checkland's two criteria have later been supplemented with the criterion of recoverability (Checkland & Holwell, 1998a). They argue that the action research process should be recoverable "by anyone interested in subjecting the research to critical scrutiny" (Checkland & Holwell, 1998a, p. 18). For research that is sound principle. For action research it is a much better principle that reproducibility which for obvious reasons does not make sense in action research. Recoverability addresses the heart of the principle of continuity. As research is a social activity the consumers of research should be able to see on which ground the action researcher claims a successful outcome, i.e., for research the principle of continuity should be exercised in public.

3.2 Six Criteria

In our use of action research criteria we have strived at setting-up the criteria in order to be relevant when designing an action research effort, while in the midst of the effort, and when evaluating past action research. The six criteria that we developed for (Iversen et al., 2004) are:

- **Roles:** Clarify the roles of researchers and practitioners.
- **Documentation:** Explain the data collection approach and how data quality is maintained.
- **Control:** Explain the control measures.
- **Usefulness:** Establish the usefulness of the findings in the problem situation.
- **Frameworks:** Relate the actions taken as well as the findings to frameworks to support the study.
- **Transferability:** Explicate conditions for transfer of findings to other situations.

We have come use these criteria only gradually. We have for many years used these criteria more implicitly and mostly directed our full attention to explicating the usefulness and the frameworks. We believe that with these six criteria we are able to explain our action research better as research.

3.2.1 Roles

Clarifying roles can help establish our impartiality as researchers and explicate the discipline in collaborating with practitioners (Baskerville & Wood-Harper, 1996). Action researchers cannot be disinterested observers (Checkland, 1981, p. 152; Susman & Evered, 1978, p. 589). There are several roles in action research, e.g., client, sponsor, champion, practitioner, and researcher, that overlap and sometimes interchange in ways that cannot be fully anticipated (Clark, 1972). An action researcher "acts and simultaneously observes himself acting" (Mansell, 1991, p. 30). A reflective practitioner is, conversely, a researcher into his own practice (Clark, 1972, p. 72-73). Action research requires in this way "a partnership of practitioner-researchers and researcher-practitioners" (Schön, 1983, p. 323).

From a pragmatist viewpoint the roles should be clarified because of the principle of continuity. What is to be taken as successful outcomes is very likely to depend on who have been involved in which activities and which values they may bring to bear on these activities. Hence to be able to act, research and report on what in the situation was taken to be successful actions and reflection-in-action the roles needs to be clear. Because of the principle of interaction it also becomes important to be clear about how the researchers interact with practitioners. In general, it becomes interesting how researchers and practitioners get feed-back from the situation and how they come to listen to the situation's back-talk (in Schön's sense).

3.2.2   Documentation

Explaining the data collection approach in detail is a key discipline that distinguishes research from consulting (Baskerville & Wood-Harper, 1996). Action research is such a empirical research and "there are two kinds of processes to record in social action research, the learning process of the host [practitioners], and the discovery and interpretation process of the guest [researchers]" (Jönsson, 1991, p. 391). Our experience is that proper data collection is often easier than done and we have had to look at other empirical approaches for relevant techniques.

Longitudinal research on organizational change (Pettigrew, 1990) offers a useful approach to documentation of action research. Pettigrew's approach is based on the assumptions that: (1) change processes should be studied in the context of change at another level of analysis, (2) the importance of revealing temporal interconnectedness, and (3) the need to explore context and action where context is a product of action and action is a product of context (Pettigrew, 1990, p. 269-270). These assumptions have implications for what we should collect data about. Pettigrew's data collection techniques are: in-depth interviews, documentary and archive data, and observational and ethnographical material. To this list we have added diary writing (Jepsen et al., 1989), i.e., the action researchers reflect in writing on events, ideas and actions as they evolve over time. Diary writing is appropriate since it offers data collection when the researchers are involved in the activities and they play an active role, which is a core characteristic of action research. These techniques address how we may collect data. Indicators of the quality of data are: (1) the extent to which the data cover Pettigrew's three assumptions, and (2) the extent to which the techniques have been systematically applied.

Where (Checkland & Holwell, 1998b) refers to recoverability as a criterion we prefer documentation in stead as it a prerequisite for later establishing recoverability. We have struggled with documentation for several years. For any particular action research effort we never take it lightly how we should document and without careful consideration it is easy to collect too much data, too little data or simply irrelevant data.

From a pragmatist viewpoint it is crucial to understand that in action research we need to see the principles of continuity and interaction not only against the background of the situation into which we intervene. We should also see it against the background of the action researchers' situation as part of a larger research community. I will refer both these backgrounds as one, namely the research situation. In action research it means that the research situation can easily have two kinds of back-talk from the situation, i.e., from action and from research, but in general there is no reason to believe that there will be just these two kinds and that they will be that simple to explain. Primarily for the purpose of research we need to collect data and the data need to reflect the whole of the research situation and its back-talk. Without data the reporting will be less believable for other researchers.

3.2.3 Control

Action research is a social activity. It is emergent in nature and control issues are therefore relevant to consider in order to make sense of the research process and its outcomes. Avison et al. propose three control structures that we should be aware of and report on: control over initiation, determination of authority, and degree of formalization (Avison et al., 2001, p. 38). Initiation may be by: (1) the researchers (if they have theories or approaches to be tried in practice), (2) the practitioners (if they are facing difficult problem situations), or (3) it may evolve from existing collaboration. Authority may largely be determined by: (1) the client organization and the existing structure, (2) migration of power between stakeholders as part of the action research process, or (3) the researchers being identical to the practitioners. The degree of formalization may be characterized by: (1) formal contracts between researchers, practitioners, and the client organization, (2) informal agreement and commitment between the partakers, (3) or by the formality evolving over time as part of the action research process.

Through our experience with action research we have recently come to realize that the control of the research situation must be addressed. The social aspects of creating continuity and interaction in the research situation also deal with power and how power is exercised. What is taken to be successful outcomes in the principle of continuity is value-based and there may well be conflicting value sets. The conflicting values do not only have to be between practitioners' interests and researchers' interests. If there are conflicting values and interests it is our experience that it is often between practitioners. There are several ways to report of this. One is to use the control framework in (Avison et al., 2001). Another will be to analyze stakeholder interests or find other ways to map out various interests and how these may influence continuity of experience, interaction with the research situation, and specifically the problem-setting in the practitioners' situation.

3.2.4 Usefulness

Usefulness is perhaps the most important criterion, and it is also the criterion most commonly reported on in action research. Establishing usefulness of findings in the problem situation supports the impartiality of action research and creates a baseline upon which the results might be transferred to other similar situations (Baskerville & Wood-Harper, 1996). Experienced usefulness is the pragmatic basis for evaluating action research. Checkland states that the "criterion by which the research was judged internally was its practical success as measured by the readiness of actors to acknowledge that learning had occurred, either explicitly or through implementation of changes" (Checkland, 1981, p. 253). Baburoglu and Ravn (1992) argue similarly that action research generates action knowledge, i.e., knowledge that actors are ready to act on or actually act on.

From a pragmatist viewpoint the criterion of usefulness deals with both the principle of continuity and the principle of interaction. If, as I the quote from Checkland, the practitioners willing claim that learning has occurred and progress has been made in their situation then from their perspective there is continuity of their experience. I shall call this first-order continuity. Second-order continuity happens when the researchers are willing to claim that it is progress in the research situation. This second-order continuity depends on the first order continuity to be stated, but there is not a 1-1 relationship.

Some of the least interesting action research I have participated in happened in a software company where the activities took the practitioners through significant learning, and though the framework we applied proved useful in the situation we did not learn anything new. The problems this company's practitioners experienced were common problems in managing large software projects and we tried successfully to reduce the effects of these problems by means of an analytical framework for assessing specific management issues. Unfortunately for us this did not amount to a research contribution as no new understanding came up. Hence, there was no second-order continuity of experience. It could be argued that we did actually have continuity of experience because the framework was confirmed, but it was just to little progress to report to the research community.

3.2.5   Frameworks

Relating results to an existing framework or to an existing body of knowledge supports the impartiality of our research, it is a key discipline in all research that distinguishes it from consulting, and it provides a basis for discussing transferability of results (Baskerville & Wood-Harper, 1996). Checkland and Holwell argue that "it is clear that the recognition that the changes have occurred and lessons have been learnt will be much helped if we have declared in advance the intellectual framework within which 'lessons' are defined" (Checkland & Holwell, 1998b, p. 24). They therefore argue that the framework on which we base the research intervention should be explicated. Explicating the framework, its background and the reseachers' background will assist the interested reader in recovering the course of action more convincingly (Checkland & Holwell, 1998a, p. 18). In this way we can turn the focus away from the experience *per se* to how the obtained experience and results draw upon and relate to existing bodies of knowledge.

This criterion addresses directly the principle of continuity. It is never straight forward what the quality of our experience is: what experience conforms to the immediate agreeableness or disagreeableness of the present situation and what experience should readily influence later experience in another situation. In action research this is even more difficult largely because of the difference between first-order and second-order continuity. In research we need to relate any experience that we claim can be transferred to other situations to what the research community at any given time agrees to be sound experience or sometimes even sound knowledge. In second-order continuity, frameworks are central to communicating experience between researchers. Frameworks are thus central in the research situation and whether a framework becomes believable and agreeable to the research community is a matter of back-talk. It is not easy, not to say impossible, to listen to this back-talk from the research situation if we are not communicating by means of frameworks. It should be noted here that I use the term 'framework' to cover also published research knowledge and theories; but I prefer to call it framework though in (Iversen et al., 2004) we call it 'theory'. I prefer 'framework for 'theory' as 'theory' often gets confused with the positivist notion of a predictive theory which makes less sense for action research.

3.2.6 Transferability

Explicating conditions for transferability of research findings addresses the situation-dependency of action research and reveals the limitations that apply to generalizing the findings (Baskerville & Wood-Harper, 1996). By relating results to existing bodies of knowledge we explicate the research contribution and increase the transferability to similar situations. In addition, we need to explicate the general characteristics of the findings and the conditions for transferring them to other situations.

While many refer to this criterion as generalisability we have come to prefer to call it transferability. This preference we based on the idea that results from action research tend to be concrete and not abstract. For the purpose of continuity of experience the experience does not have to be general and abstract in order to be transferred to another situation where it is applicable. According to the pragmatists continuity of experience depends not on the generality of the experience. It depends on the *quality* of the experience (Dewey, 1938, p. 27).

3.3   The Six Criteria in Context

The six criteria exist in the context of the research situation. This is similar to the dual processes of action research found in (McKay & Marshall, 2001), but the focus here is on the criteria, see figure 15-1.

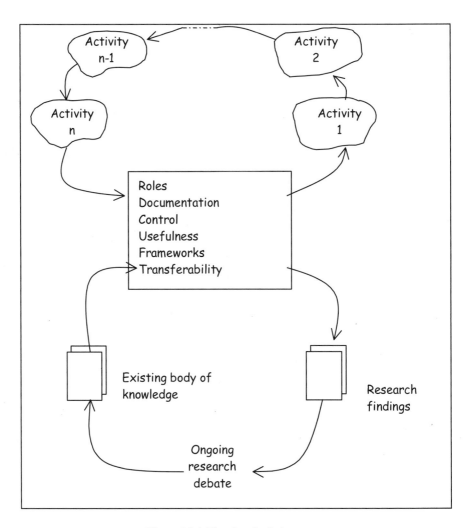

Figure 15-1. The six criteria in context

The criteria constrain the activities by adding requirements to their planning and later to the evaluation thus enforcing the research aspects of action research. The activities should be performed through the designed roles, documenting the activities, exercising the agreed control measures and utilizing the frameworks. As activities are performed the situation may well change and the activities may then lead to a revised set of roles, documentation, control, and frameworks. The activities also eventually lead to assessments of usefulness and transferability of findings.

The activities should be understood as a set of necessary activities where the arrows depict the logical dependencies between the activities. This is in accordance with the idea of a conceptual model of a human activity system as used in Soft Systems Methodology (Checkland, 1981). The overall outcome of the activities are the research findings.

The criteria are in place not only to regulate the activities, but also to constrain what can be taken as research findings. Research findings in turn are feed into the ongoing research debate in the research community. From the ongoing debate stems the existing body of knowledge from which the frameworks may be formulated and relative to which contribution and transferability may then be explained.

The relatedness of the criteria underlines that they should be seen as a coherent whole. In our thinking about these six criteria we have come to see these as relevant for both the design of action research efforts as well as for their evaluation.

3.4 Example of Design and Evaluation Using the Six Criteria

We have used the six criteria explicitly in (Iversen et al., 2004) and it may serve as an illustration of the six criteria. Figure 15-2 summarizes the research design.

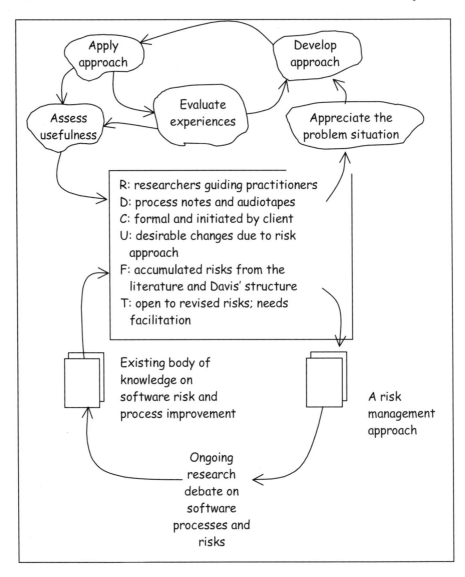

Figure 15-2. Research design with the six criteria

The action research is reported in detail in (Iversen et al., 2004) where in particular the criteria, the research process and the framework are explained. Figure 15-2 has been drawn in retrospect, but the elements of the conceptual model were explicit at the time where we did the research.

For brevity the details are referred to the original paper, but a brief explanation is in place. The research was done in the IT department of a large bank. In this IT department we worked together with a group of practitioners that were responsible for improving software development processes. As a part of that effort we worked for a period of five months on creating and improving an approach to the used eventually by the practitioners in managing risks related to software process improvement. We created the risk management approach through first studying the relevant research literature on software risk approaches and the reported risks with software process improvement. That was combined with the practitioners experience with the risks of improvement in their IT department. Based on this we built a new risk management approach addressing directly the risks of software process improvement. The structure of the approach we got from (Davis, 1982). The new approach was applied, evaluated, and modified through four consecutive iterations each dealing with an improvement effort, e.g., the project responsible for implementing a new quality assurance processes.

The criteria were applied in the following way. From the beginning the researchers were guiding the practitioners in risk management and in particular in the activity 'Apply approach' (Roles). Data about the activities 'Apply approach' and 'Evaluate experiences' that we performed together with the practitioners were recorded in the researchers' process notes and on audiotape (Documentation). There was a formal contract between the IT department and its practitioners on the one hand and the researchers on the other hand (Control). The practitioners took the initiative to work on a risk management approach for software process improvement (Control). Through the activity 'Assess usefulness' we tracked the actual changes in the IT department that could be traced back to the applied risk approach (Usefulness). The research literature on risk management and software process improvement was studied in detail and based on the activity 'Appreciate the problem situation' the core ideas in the framework were selected and the approach was developed in the activity 'Develop approach'. The framework came to be the accumulated risks and resolutions from the literature as well as a structure of the risk approach from Davis' approach for risk strategy determination (Frameworks). The limitation on transferability came late in the process as part of the assessment of the usefulness. We evaluated based on our use of the approach that though it was useful it also would need to be facilitated by a practitioner competent in this approach and with good knowledge of likely risks (Transferability). We also assessed that the risk approach would not be difficult to transfer to similar situations because the specific risks in the approach could gradually be revised when experience in another situation would call for it (Transferability).

Several issues related to the six criteria are noticeable. First, the criteria changed during the course of action – not radically, but sufficient to notice. This is important to pay attention to during the action. If changes are merely implicit our experience tells us that we can easily encounter difficulty at a later stage. For example, if our framework has changed, but we have not been aware whether that should also lead to a change of the documentation we might end up not being able to document our finding in a recoverable way. Similarly, if we are not performing the planned activities the roles may change, control measures are not appropriate, and documentation is not adequate for later asserting the usefulness of the findings.

Second, four of the six criteria influenced the activities directly. Roles, documentation, control, and frameworks have immediate consequence for the activities. Usefulness and transferability are different, as they do not in the same way influence activities. These two criteria, on the other hand, address directly the quality of the experience and hence how we exercise the principle of continuity.

Third, three of the six criteria are related to the research outcome. Usefulness, frameworks, and transferability direct affect the research outcome.

Fourth, the six specific criteria make sense only in their context of activities and research contributions. The meaningfulness of the six specific criteria has to be asserted in the light of which activities lead to which contributions. The six criteria seen in context form a whole where relatedness and internal consistency is important.

Fifth, the six criteria are not generic; they are specific to the action research effort, i.e., to the research situation. The framework is specific to the problem situation. The criterion of usefulness is specific to the framework addressing what a risk approach is and the developed approach being applied in a software organization. Similar arguments can be used for the other criteria.

Sixth, it is not difficult to envisage that there could be more than one such explanation of wholes. Soft Systems Methodology and all of its soft systems thinking (Checkland, 1981) could then be applied to make sense of several action research wholes – referred to as systems or holons (Checkland & Scholes, 1990).

4.   DISCUSSION

To look for consistency between the six criteria seen in their context deserves a more detailed discussion. Consistency has two sides: in designing action research it means we will be striving at creating specific criteria, planning activities and contributions that have a high degree of consistency; in evaluating action research it means we will scrutinize their consistency in retrospect. By consistency of the whole we mean:

1. The six criteria are internally consistent. A few examples are: (i) the roles have to match who has the initiative according to the control measures; (ii) the documentation has to be built to elicit the traces of usefulness to appear during the activities; (iii) the selected frameworks have implications for which data should be collected during documentation.
2. The six criteria are consistent with the activities. For example, there has to be a convincing way in which the activities can be documented and the roles exercised through the activities.
3. The six criteria are consistent with the research contributions. For example, the research contributions concern the frameworks directly.
4. There are too many possible consistencies to enumerate, but the point here is not to establish a rigorous mechanism for assessing all aspects of consistency. The point is rather that we should be able to defend the choices of criteria we have made.
5. Consistency is important to pursue because it leads to a coherent explanation of the action research effort.

As already mentioned the criteria are specific to the action research effort. More precisely, the specific criteria are unique to each unique action research effort (as used in figure 15-2). The six types of criteria on the other hand have emerged through twenty odd years of practicing action research and those we find gradually more useful across our action research.

We have only shown a single example above, but to illustrate the point further we may take the action research reported in (Lindgren et al., 2004) and show how an overview of the research design can easily be presented. Briefly, what Lindgren et al. have done is that they have experimented with competence management systems in two significantly different action research cycles, the first cycle was based on existing and traditional systems, and the second cycle was based on prototypes built on new design principles. They make a contribution to both the knowledge on competence management and design principles for competence management systems. They have evaluated their research using the criteria from (Davison et al., 2004), but let us look at their research in the light of the six criteria, see table 15-1.

Table 15-1. The six criteria compared for two action research studies

	(Iversen et al., 2004)	(Lindgren et al., 2004)
Roles	Researchers guiding practitioners	Researchers interviewing, designing and monitoring prototype experiments
Documentation	Process notes and audiotapes	Interview data and prototyping results
Control	Formal and initiated by client	Formal and initiated through partner contract
Usefulness	Desirable changes due to risk approach	Use of prototypes based on design principles influenced by F were feasible
Frameworks	Accumulated risk items from the literature and Davis' structure for the process	Skill-based view of competence management and a competence typology
Transferability	Open to revised risks; needs facilitation	Design principles seen as hypotheses to be tested further

The point here is not to evaluate Lindgren et al.'s research as that has already been done in their paper. This is a merely an illustration that the criteria for the two studies are very different and there is little sense in trying to reconcile these differences. Our study's research contribution was an approach to risk management. Lindgren et al.'s research contribution was a set of design principles for a special branch of information systems called competence management systems. These two research contributions are worlds apart and their design and evaluation criteria will remain apart as well.

Based on Schön's arguments for problem solving as reflection-in-action we can elaborate on this. Since all problem solving situations unique so are also action research efforts. Action research problems are set with ends (criteria) and means (activities) being mutually dependent. As in problem solving progress is measured in terms of whether the research led to successful action in the client organization (Usefulness).

How then can we ever hope that action research can live up to the accumulative research ideal? Because of experience, the pragmatist will say. The principle of continuity of experience says that lasting experience influences and has consequence for later experience. When Checkland claimed that Soft Systems Methodology was a result of several hundred applications (Checkland, 1981), he was judging based on continuity of experience. The explication of criteria as they have been presented in this chapter supports the evaluation of desirable outcomes. The principle of interaction says that there should be equal concern for the immediate experience faced in the unique situation (and alleviating the perceived problems) as for the influence on lasting experience (as that is filtered through scholarly documented knowledge). This chapter's idea of explicating unique criteria supports the evaluation of action as well as research. That is action research; neither action nor research is primary.

5. CONCLUSION

In this chapter I have first traced the epistemology of action research back to pragmatism. A clear theory in pragmatism is a theory that has consequence in action or for action. Whether these consequences are desirable can only be judged through the continuity of experience and through the interaction between immediate experience and lasting experience. Problem solving according to Schön is based on similar ideas with a focus on situations' uniqueness, seeing-as a way to bridge experience, inquiry as problem setting, and progress measured by successful actions being taken.

Through twenty odd years of action research we have come to rely on six criteria for designing and evaluating action research. The six criteria thus identified are: roles, documentation, control, usefulness, frameworks, and transferability. The six criteria were used in (Iversen et al., 2004) and I have used this to illustrate the criteria in the context of activities and contributions. Based on that I tend to conclude that the six criteria made it possible to reason about the design of the research effort and whether the criteria, the activities and the expected research outcome were consistent and formed a coherent explanation.

I have then discussed the implications of using the six criteria. The criteria cannot be general; they must remain specific though the six types of criteria seem to be useful for many different action research efforts.

In the spirit of pragmatism, the six criteria are temporary; i.e., they are currently the best explanation we have.

6. ACKNOWLEDGEMENT

The chapter builds on experience (in the pragmatists' sense) that I have shared with several action researchers and practitioners. In particular it builds on many discussions with Jakob Iversen and Lars Mathiassen through the piece of action research where we first used the six criteria (Iversen et al., 2004).

7.   REFERENCES

Avison, D. E., Baskerville, R., & Myers, M. D. (2001). Controlling action research projects. *Information Technology & People, 14*(1), 28-45.

Baburoglu, O. N., & Ravn, I. (1992). Normative Action Research. *Organization Studies, 13*(1), 19-34.

Baskerville, R., & Myers, M. (2004). Special Issue on Action Research in Information Systems: Making IS Research Relevant to Practice - Foreword. *MIS Quarterly, 28*(3), 329-335.

Baskerville, R., & Wood-Harper, A. T. (1996). A Critical Perspective on Action Research as a Method for Information Systems Research. *Journal of Information Technology, 11*, 235-246.

Checkland, P. (1981). *Systems Thinking, Systems Practice.* Chichester: Wiley.

Checkland, P. (1991). From framework through experience to learning: the essential nature of action research. In H.-E. Nissen, H. K. Klein & R. A. Hirschheim (Eds.), *Information Systems Research: Contemporary Approaches and Emergent Traditions* (pp. 397-403). Amsterdam: North-Holland.

Checkland, P., & Holwell, S. (1998a). Action Research: Its Nature and Validity. *Systemic Practice and Action Research, 11*(1), 9-21.

Checkland, P., & Holwell, S. (1998b). *Information, Systems and Information Systems - making sense of the field.* Chichester: Wiley.

Checkland, P., & Scholes, J. (1990). *Soft Systems Methodology in Action.* Chichester: Wiley.

Clark, P. A. (1972). *Action Research and Organizational Change.* London: Harper and Row.

Davis, G. B. (1982). Strategies for information requirements determination. *IBM Systems Journal, 21.*

Davison, R. M., Martinsons, M. G., & Kock, N. F., Jr. (2004). Principles of canonical action research. *Information Systems Journal, 14*, 65-86.

Dewey, J. (1916). *Democracy and Education.* New York: Macmillan.

Dewey, J. (1938). *Experience and Education.* New York: Touchstone by Simon & Schuster.

Hult, M., & Lennung, S.-A. (1980). Towards a Definition of Action Research: A Note and Bibliography. *Journal of Management Studies*(May), 241-250.

Iversen, J., Nielsen, P. A., & Nørbjerg, J. (1999). Situated Assessment of Problems in Software Development. *The DATABASE for Advances in Information Systems, 30*(2), 66-81.

Iversen, J. H., Mathiassen, L., & Nielsen, P. A. (2004). Managing Risk in Software Process Improvement: An Action Research Approach. *MIS Quarterly, 28*(3), 395-433.

Jepsen, L. O., Mathiassen, L., & Nielsen, P. A. (1989). Back to Thinking Mode: Diaries for the Management of Information Systems Development Projects. *Behaviour and Information Technology, 8*(3), 207-217.

Jönsson, S. (1991). Action Research. In H.-E. Nissen, H. K. Klein & R. A. Hirschheim (Eds.), *Information Systems Research: Contemporary Approaches and Emergent Traditions.* Amsterdam: North-Holland.

Lau, F. (1999). Toward a framework for action research in information systems studies. *Information Technology and People, 12*(2), 148-176.

Lindgren, R., Henfridsson, O., & Schultze, U. (2004). Design Principles for Competence Management Systems: A Synthesis of an Action Research Study. *MIS Quarterly, 28*(3), 435-472.

Mansell, G. (1991). Action research in information systems development. *Journal of Information Systems*, 29-40.

Mathiassen, L. (1998). Reflective Systems Development. *Scandinavian Journal of Information Systems, 10*(1&2), 67-117.

Mathiassen, L. (2002). Collaborative Practice Research. *Information Technology & People, 15*(4), 321-345.

Mathiassen, L., Pries-Heje, J., & Ngwenyama, O. (Eds.). (2002). *Improving Software Organizations: From Principles to Practice*. Reading, MA: Addison-Wesley.

McKay, J., & Marshall, P. (2001). The dual imperatives of action research. *Information Technology & People, 14*(1), 46-59.

Menand, L. (2001). *The Metaphysical Club: A Story of Ideas in America* New York: Farrar, Straus & Giroux.

Menand, L. (Ed.). (1997). *Pragmatism: A Reader*. New York: Vintage Books.

Nielsen, P. A. (1990). *Learning and Using Methodologies in Information Systems Analysis and Design*. Unpublished PhD, Lancaster University, Lancaster, UK.

Pettigrew, A. M. (1990). Longitudinal Field Research on Change Theory and Practice. *Organization Science, 1*(3), 267-292.

Schön, D. A. (1983). *The Reflective Practitioner: How Professionals Think in Action*. New York: Basic Books.

Susman, G. I., & Evered, R. D. (1978). An Assessment of the Scientific Merits of Action Research. *Administrative Science Quarterly, 23*, 582-603.

Chapter 16

ACTION RESEARCH AND CONSULTING:
Hellish Partnership or Heavenly Marriage?

Robert M. Davison and Maris G. Martinsons
City University of Hong Kong, Hong Kong

Abstract: A number of criticisms have been levelled at Action Research over the years. Among these has been the observation that the practice of Action Research is insufficiently distinct from Consulting. Indeed, some academics appear to see consulting as little short of making a deal with the Devil. In contrast, we believe that there is the potential for a heavenly marriage between Action Research and Consulting: not only do they have much to learn from each other but they also can usefully complement each other. This chapter focuses on how the practice of Consulting would benefit from the adoption of specific Action Research principles. We briefly review the background literatures of both Action Research and Consulting, particularly Management Consulting. We also consider a previously-developed set of principles and associated criteria that help to ensure the rigor and relevance of Canonical Action Research. The discussion section highlights how the principles and criteria for Action Research can usefully contribute to high quality consulting practice. We conclude with a call for more dialogue and hands-on interaction between practitioners of Action Research and Consulting.

Key words: Action Research, Consulting, Synthesis, Relevance, Rigour

1.   INTRODUCTION

Action Research (AR), as a methodology, has been the subject of considerable criticism over the years. Some critics have asserted that AR tends to produce either "research with little action or action with little research" (Dickens and Watkins, 1999, p.131). Others have suggested that AR has placed an undue focus on methodological rigour, at the expense of organizational relevance, and vice versa (cf. Cohen and Manion, 1980).

In response to these types of criticisms, we have developed, in an earlier article (Davison et al., 2004), a detailed set of structured principles and associated criteria that can be used to ensure both the rigour and the relevance of action research. Our principles and assessment criteria were designed specifically for Canonical Action Research (CAR), one of the twelve or so recognised forms of the AR method. Nevertheless, the five principles we have articulated represent a general framework that can be applied to most forms of AR, helping authors and reviewers to assure the quality of an AR project.

In response to criticisms that AR and consulting are almost synonymous, some scholars have attempted to identify the differences between these two areas (cf. Baskerville and Wood-Harper, 1988). They commonly assert that, among other differences, consultants work exclusively for a client, whereas action researchers work for both a client and the broader research community, to which they must report their findings. Subsequently, the related and vexed question of 'serving two masters' has been discussed in the AR literature (cf. Kock and Lau, 2001; Kock et al., 1999; McKay and Marshall, 2001).

For some scholars, 'consulting' remains a dirty word, an activity to be shunned as they pursue the truth and contribute to the advancement of 'scientific' knowledge. Academic researchers who cooperate with business consultants may be seen as making a deal with the Devil. In contrast, we see that there may be considerable potential for consulting (C) and AR to leverage each other's strengths, each learning from each other. However, at present the two disciplines, and in particular their proponents, seem to be so far apart as to stifle any attempt to harness any complementary effects. In this chapter, we explore the benefits that may be realized if consultants in general, and information systems (IS) consultants in particular, were to use AR as one of their many process methodologies. Benefits can also accrue to action researchers, who can usefully glean insights and research opportunities through consulting assignments.

In the following sections, we first briefly review the relevant background to AR, with a particular focus on CAR. We aim to show that AR has the potential to enhance both the rigour and the relevance of research that focuses on organizations, management and information systems. We also summarize the five principles that we have developed previously (Davison et al., 2004) to ensure relevant and rigorous AR. We then provide a similar background section on consulting (C), which highlights some of its long-standing deficiencies. We aim to show that many of the key deficiencies are related to ideas that have been addressed in the AR literature. Following this background and literature section, we consider how the principles and guidelines that were developed in Davison et al. (2004) lend themselves to application in the consulting domain. This section is primarily discursive: we do not lay out new principles and guidelines here, but rather assess the likely interaction effects between AR and C. This leads to an overall assessment of whether AR+C is a hellish partnership, a marriage made in heaven, or something else altogether. Finally, we conclude the chapter with insights drawn from our analysis and suggestions for future application of the AR+C concept.

2. ACTION RESEARCH

2.1 Essentials

Historical accounts of the evolution of AR are both numerous and varied in their quality. We will not repeat the history here, but refer interested readers to Baskerville and Wood-Harper (1998), Baskerville (1999) and Davison et al. (2004). Around a dozen or so forms of AR have now been identified and classified, each characterised by different models, structures and goals, viz.: CAR, Dialogical Action Research, Information Systems Prototyping, Soft Systems, Action Science, Participant Observation, Action Learning, Multiview, ETHICS, Clinical Field Work, Process Consultation, Reflective Systems Development and Collaborative Practice.

"CAR is unique among all the forms of AR in that it is iterative, rigorous and collaborative, involving a focus on both organizational development and the generation of knowledge" (Davison et al., 2004; cf. Baskerville and Wood-Harper, 1998). As an iterative method, one or more 'cycles' of activities are expected to occur, each cycle leading the action researcher closer to a complete solution of the identified problem. This cyclical approach is a major contributing factor to the rigour of the method. It also means that as the action researcher and members of the organizational client team proceed, so they develop a better understanding of the nature of the organizational problem. This places them in a progressively better position to devise and implement solutions that are relevant and appropriate, and thus beneficial to the client. In this way, rigour and relevance are mutually supportive: it is difficult to envision how AR could be rigorous without also being relevant.

As a collaborative method, it is expected that the action researcher will collaborate actively and openly with the organizational client team. This means that the action researcher must not dominate the process or minimise the extent to which the client can be involved. CAR mandates the interweaving of theory and practice "through change and reflection in an immediate problematic situation within a mutually acceptable ethical framework" (Avison et al. 1999, p.94), with the two-fold objective of both ameliorating organizational practice and contributing to research knowledge (cf. Eden and Huxham, 1996).

Given the fact that AR occurs in an environment 'populated' by both organizational clients and emergent organizational circumstances, not to mention the vagaries of organizational culture and the prevailing status quo, the action researcher is seldom able to exact complete control over interventions (cf. Davison and Vogel, 2000; Mumford, 2001). This means that it is impractical (quite apart from being undesirable) to pre-specify a 'plan of action' that will be followed dogmatically throughout the research process. Instead, the interventions that the action researcher deploys must therefore be adapted to "the infinite variety of circumstances, rather than simply following pre-determined techniques and styles of inquiry" (Davison et al., 2004).

2.2   Five Principles

We have previously proposed and elaborated a set of five principles designed to ensure both the rigour and the relevance of CAR (Davison et al., 2004). The five principles focus on: a researcher-client agreement; a cyclical process model; theory; change through action; and learning through reflection. For each of the five principles, we have also developed explicit assessment criteria. Those undertaking AR as well as those reviewing the reports of completed AR projects can apply these criteria to assure quality in planning, execution, and documentation. We do not discuss all 31 criteria in detail here (this appears in Davison et al., 2004), but instead list those criteria related to each principle in Tables 16-1–16-5 below. Following this discussion of the principles, we consider their existing and potential applicability in consulting practice.

The Researcher-Client Infrastructure (RCI) provides the structural foundation for an AR project. It includes protocols that determine some of the basic 'rules of engagement' for the researcher, as well as the roles, responsibilities and expectations for behaviour on both sides. In order for the RCI to work effectively, it is essential that the client organization and its key officers understand what CAR is and how it works, as well as what the benefits and drawbacks are for the organization. The RCI should be designed so as to engender trust among the various internal and external stakeholders. It should also promote a 'spirit of shared inquiry': the action researcher should not take a dominant role nor should the clients expect to stand by and watch. All should be involved.

After the establishment of an initial RCI, the action researcher should start work on the project. Typically, CAR projects follow a cyclical design, starting with diagnosis, then action planning, intervention, evaluation and finally reflection. The completion of one step leads sequentially to the next, thus helping to ensure that a CAR project is conducted with systematic rigor. As a cycle, there is the suggestion of a linear, unidirectional flow. However, in our experience some iteration between stages may well occur. This should not be discouraged, given our earlier statements about the emergent nature of the CAR process. For example, if an action plan seems unworkable, there may be a return to a diagnostic phase before proceeding to intervention.

Table 16-1. Criteria for the Principle of the Researcher-Client Infrastructure

1a	Did the researcher and the client agree that AR was the appropriate approach to use in the organizational situation?
1b	Did both the client and the researcher make explicit commitments to the project before it began?
1c	Were the scope and boundaries of the project specified explicitly before it began?
1d	Were the roles and responsibilities of the researcher and client organization members specified explicitly before the project began?
1e	Were the project objectives and evaluation measures specified explicitly before the project began?
1f	Were the data collection methods specified explicitly before the project began?

Table 16-2. Criteria for the Principle of the Cyclical Process Model

2a	Was there adherence to the cyclical process model or a clear justification for a deviation from it?
2b	Did the project begin with a diagnosis of the organizational situation that resulted in the identification of the factor(s) causing the problem?
2c	Was an explicit action plan formulated based upon the results of the diagnosis?
2d	Were the planned actions implemented and evaluated?
2e	Was there explicit reflection on the results of the planned actions and on the value of the theoretically based model?
2f	Was this reflection followed by an explicit decision on whether or not to proceed through an additional process cycle?
2g	Was the exit of the researcher and the conclusion of the project due to either the project objectives being met or some other clearly articulated justification?

The third principle involves the application of relevant theory. Philosophically, this is important since a basic premise of CAR is that action and theory can and should be interwoven so as to create a solution that is of value to both researchers and clients. Some scholars (e.g. McKay and Marshall, 2001) go so far as to assert that AR without theory is not research at all, insisting that a clearly articulated theoretical framework be imposed on the phenomenon of interest. Not all agree, however, with this position, suggesting that it may be counter-productive to apply theory too early (cf. Bunning, 1995; McTaggart, 1991). Cunningham (1993, p.61) is representative in this respect, cautioning: "it is highly unlikely that the researcher can know definitely and in advance the exact theory that will be used or developed". Indeed, theorising too early may also lead to complications if the data collected does not support that theory.

In similar vein, Heller (1993) observed that "there are still very many social issues for which no paradigmatic model and no appropriate evidence exists. In those circumstances, a research phase, wherever possible with the people who experience the problems, has to precede action". This research phase may well be operationalized as a theory-free episode of action learning.

Some scholars suggest that AR can incorporate a grounded theory approach so as to fulfil the requirement that action research includes theory (e.g. Baskerville and Pries-Heje, 1999). This is a rather risky choice, however, since if a grounded theory does not emerge from the data, then explicit theorising will become necessary. This may be problematic at such a late stage in an AR project, with significant progress already made towards a solution to the organizational problem situation.

Table 16-3. Criteria for the Principle of Theory

3a	Were the project activities (diagnosis, planning, action taking, evaluation) guided by a theory or set of theories?
3b	Was the domain of investigation, and the specific problem setting, relevant and significant to the interests of the researcher's community of peers as well as the client?
3c	Was a theoretically based model developed to explain the observed problem(s) and its cause(s)?
3d	Was the intervention based upon and consistent with this theoretically based model?
3e	Were the changes in the organizational situation that resulted from the action taking subsequently evaluated against a plausible explanatory theory?

The fundamental basis for CAR is the taking of actions in order to address an organizational problem situation and its associated unsatisfactory conditions (cf. Curle, 1949; Eden and Huxham, 1996; Hult and Lennung, 1980). The principle of change through action, indeed the indivisibility of change and action, reflects this essential quality of CAR.

Table 16-4. Criteria for the Principle of Change through Action

4a	Did the researcher have an explicit motivation to effect change and improve the organizational situation?
4b	Did the client expect that the project would improve the organizational situation?
4c	Were the problem and its cause(s) clearly understood and specified as a result of the diagnosis?
4d	Were the planned actions designed to address the specified problem?
4e	Was the status of the organizational situation measured both before and after the intervention?
4f	Did the client approve the planned actions before they were implemented?
4g	Were the timing and nature of the actions taken clearly and comprehensively documented?

The last of the five principles - the explicit specification of learning - is by no means the least, and indeed is not the easiest to accomplish either. Indeed, Lau (1997) asserts that it is the most critical of the five activities, given the two-fold nature of the action researcher's responsibilities: to the research community as well as to organizational clients.

Table 16-5. Criteria for the Principle of Specifying Learning

5a	Was the change in the organizational situation evaluated by the researcher and communicated to the client?
5b	Did both the researcher and the client reflect upon the results of the project?
5c	Were the results considered in terms of their implications for further action in this organizational situation?
5d	Were the results considered in terms of their implications for action to be taken in related research domains?
5e	Were the results considered in terms of their implications to the research community (general knowledge, informing/re-informing theory)?
5f	Were the results considered in terms of their implications for the applicability of CAR?

3.   CONSULTING

3.1   Development and Deficiencies

The consulting industry has grown rapidly in recent years, with the demand for consulting services shooting up during the 1990s. In 2000, over 140,000 consultants sold over US$70 billion of advice (Careers in Consulting, 2001). Simultaneously, management consulting became the career of choice for graduates of top MBA schools (Hasek, 1997). The overall growth of consulting has been paralleled by rising numbers of less than successful consulting engagements (Monteleone, 2000; Shapiro et al., 1993). These include engagements that failed to meet client expectations or failed to result in meaningful organizational change (Gable, 1997). Inappropriate advice provided by consultants was a major factor contributing to these failures, but so too was the inability of clients to act upon the advice offered.

These various failures tend to validate the criticisms of consulting practice, and management consulting in particular, that have been expressed by outside observers as well as industry insiders (cf. Wright and Kitay, 2002). The internal critics include Michael Porter's Monitor Group and top managers from the major consulting firms such as McKinsey & Company and Deloitte & Touche Consulting. The Monitor Group has for many years included in its promotional materials a claim that (presumably in contrast to its own performance) its competitors not only make excessive promises but also fail to achieve key objectives.

The aforementioned general criticisms of the consulting industry have been mirrored by specific comments that have been made over the years by some of the industry's most prominent leaders. Those speaking out include McKinsey & Company's former Managing Partner Rajit Gupta and Deloitte & Touche's CEO William Parrett. Gupta was forced to acknowledge that his own firm was doing a poor job of managing its knowledge at the same time as it was providing high-priced advice on the topic to its clients. Meanwhile, Parrett publicly stated that business consultants, presumably including those who work for his firm, were commonly failing their clients by giving inadequate consideration to implementation issues. Industry analysts and business journalists have also reported many cases where consultants have provided advice that seems to completely ignore the implementation context (Caulkin, 1997; O'Shea and Madigan, 1997). Unsurprisingly, many potential clients have become sceptical of management consultants as a breed (Easley & Harding, 1999; Monteleone, 2000).

In order to consider whether AR can improve consulting practice, there is a need to understand the underlying causes of these engagement failures. The recent literature (Kumar et al., 2000; McLachlin, 1999) suggests that these various failures, criticisms and scepticism can be largely attributed to three specific deficiencies of consulting: 1) informal and unsystematic process methodologies; 2) inadequate involvement of client organization members; and 3) difficulties implementing consultants' recommendations.

3.2 IS Consulting and AR Principles

Although this literature is based primarily on studies of *management* consulting, it is also relevant to IS consulting. Indeed, with more than half of all capital budgets now involving computing in one form or another, the distinction between management consulting and IS consulting has been blurred. Consulting engagements today commonly address the management of people as well as the management of information and technology.

As the Internet was commercialized in the 1990s, many small IS consulting firms sprang up to join larger and more established counterparts. Their common aim was to capitalize on the growing interest in information technology. These firms, as well as individual entrepreneurs, rode the rising wave of Internet-related business development before the dot-com bubble burst. With rapidly growing demand for IS consulting in the 1990s, the industry as a whole and many of its participants enjoyed an unprecedented period of prosperity. The attractiveness of IS consulting and its low entry barriers rapidly resulted in a relatively immature and highly fragmented industry. At the height of the dot-com bubble, many people with inadequate qualifications and limited experience were providing IS consulting services to often naïve clients.

The relative immaturity of the IS consulting industry was (and to a large extent still is) reflected in its common practices. The industry developed quickly as thousands of managers simultaneously became concerned that their traditional businesses would be swept aside by emerging on-line rivals. In most cases, these managers had limited knowledge of IS and IT. As a result, they failed to seek answers to many of the questions that are critical to selecting the most appropriate consultant and successfully completing the appropriate project.

Instead, many businesses and their managers acted hastily to hire consultants who could help them to develop new e-business capabilities or IT applications. This contracting was typically done without adequately specifying the scope and boundaries for the project, clearly establishing its objectives, or identifying measures that would be used to evaluate its success. Many clients also left critical IS project decisions to the discretion of the consultant rather than being actively involved in the project. Corporate managers who blindly placed their faith in the advice of external experts were clearly doing a disservice to their companies. More relevant to our thesis, these shortcomings clearly violated our first principle of AR, which focuses on the need for an infrastructure to define the rules of the engagement.

Given a degree of discretion by their clients, many IS consultants proceeded to design and implement a standardized e-business solution, failing to apply the kind of context-specific planning advocated by Martinsons (1993) and others. A 'cookie-cutter' solution gives the consultant a high profit margin and, in most cases, satisfies some of the client's basic needs. However, it violates our second principle of AR in failing to diagnose the specifics of the organizational situation. As a result, they typically neglected to identify all of the factor(s) that were causing the performance deficiencies or threatening the future competitiveness of the business. The lack of a diagnosis also meant that the problem and its cause(s) were not clearly understood and specified, thus violating another of our AR principles – the Principle of Change through Action. As a result of these violations, the e-business solution faced significant resistance during its implementation and was far from optimal in contributing to the improvement of organizational performance.

A subsequent failure to reflect on what was done and what could have been done differently represents a further violation of our principles. The seriousness of problems was often increased by failing to follow a systematic process (which is specifically identified as a key criterion for our Principle of a Cyclical Process Model) and/or neglecting to evaluate the change that resulted from the intervention (which is suggested by our Principle of Specifying Learning). The client was unable to modify the initial solution, and in many cases was left with the choice of using a poorly-performing IT application or hiring yet another consultant to provide another (hopefully better) solution. Systematic evaluation and reflection on the consequences of the implementation, ideally based upon a theoretically-based model as suggested by our third principle of AR, would provide invaluable guidance for initially implementing an IT application or improving an existing application.

A performance management tool such a balanced scorecard adapted for IS (Martinsons et al., 1999) may be used to compare the situation before and after the consulting engagement, and thus evaluate the success of the project. Meanwhile, general adherence to a systematic process, such as the cyclical process model highlighted by our second principle of AR, would not only help to ensure a successful outcome for the current consulting project, but also provide the consultant with valuable knowledge that could be leveraged in subsequent engagements. Table 16-6 summarizes the major failings of IS consulting in the past and relates them to specific violations of our AR principles.

Table 16-6. Major Failings of IS Consulting

Major Failing	Violated Principle(s) of AR
Inadequate preparation by the client prior to engaging a consultant	Researcher-Client Infrastructure
Inadequate involvement of the client during the consulting engagement	Researcher-Client Infrastructure
Insufficient definition of the project in terms of scope and boundaries	Researcher-Client Infrastructure
Insufficient specification of project objectives and evaluation measures	Researcher-Client Infrastructure
Inadequate diagnosis of the organizational situation to identify the factors causing the problem	Cyclical Process Model
Lack of theory/model that links the planned actions to specific aspects of performance and/or factors causing the problem	Theory
Unclear or underspecified understanding of the problem and its cause(s)	Change through Action
Failure to evaluate the change that occurred and the implications for further action	Cyclical Process Model and Specifying Learning
Failure to reflect on the consequences of the engagement and the implications for further action	Cyclical Process Model, Theory and Specifying Learning

3.3   IS Consulting Today

There is little doubt that the IS consulting industry has made significant efforts to address its major failings. An industry shakeout as the dot-com bubble burst has reduced the number of active participants. This consolidation has reduced the size of the industry but increased the strength of the remaining rivals and its overall maturity. There is little doubt that IS consulting practices now adhere more closely to our five principles of AR than they did in the late 1990s.

In addition to formalising and systematising their methodologies, IS consultants have tried both to involve their clients more directly in the consulting process, and to build long-term relationships with those clients. Meanwhile, the clients themselves have sought to become more knowledgeable about IS so that they can ask the right questions and critically evaluate the proposed work and actual performance of the consultants that they hire. In this way, both the consultants and their clients have taken significant steps that enable them to promote meaningful discussion during the consulting process and to facilitate the implementation of specific recommendations. For example, our anecdotal evidence from several leading IS consulting firms indicates that members of the client firm's management are now commonly much more active participants in the consulting project than they were five or ten years ago.

Nevertheless, the activities of the IS consulting profession and their clients could still be more coherently planned and consistently implemented. Furthermore, it does not appear that consultants have recognized the full potential that action research offers to their field. We believe that action research, and particularly the principles and criteria that we have developed to help assure rigor and relevance, has the potential to address these deficiencies in a holistic and comprehensive manner.

Notwithstanding the violations of the principles that we have proposed, it is also fair to ask a more general question: why has AR not been adopted more widely by IS consultants? We suggest three major explanations for the limited adoption of AR in consulting: Action Research-oriented engagements are likely to take considerably longer, with the implication that they will be less profitable; training consultants on the principles and operational aspects of AR can be very time-consuming and may be seen as downtime that does not accrue revenue; resistance to change is likely to be strong, especially in consulting firms that are successful with their current portfolio of process tools. In consequence, deciding that the front-end investment in AR is a worthwhile one is by no means simple. Those who are motivated by short-term goals are unlikely to make the investment in AR for the benefit of themselves and their clients.

4.   DISCUSSION

In considering how AR may usefully be applied to IS consulting practice, it is appropriate to note that IS research in general has been the subject of sustained criticism for its lack of relevance to organizational life. Robey and Markus (1998) for instance note the lack of practical advice emanating from IS research, while Senn (1998) identifies the perceived impossibility of undertaking research that is both rigorous and relevant as being both unfortunate and naïve. Good (IS) research should be both rigorous and relevant – but of course this is much easier said than done.

Benbasat and Zmud (1999, p.5) assert that relevant research should "focus on concerns of practice [and] provide real value to IS professionals" while Zmud (1996, p.xxxviii) characterises "strong relevance" as an attribute of research that "not only surfaces findings relevant to practice but also reveals both how the findings would be implemented in practice and the validity-in-practice of those findings. Thus, essentially any research effort claiming strong relevancy would by definition possess an action research component". These various opinions on the state of IS research, its relevance to organizational practice, and the potential impact that an AR-oriented approach may exert on the relevance of research outcomes are certainly helpful. Extending these ideas further to incorporate consulting is not a huge step. However, it may constitute a leap of faith for those who believe that consultants have lost their intellectual souls as a result of making a Faustian deal with the capitalist Devil.

Nevertheless, consulting has much to gain from adopting some of the principles of AR. In very general terms, one of the major problems facing AR is access to 'relevant' organizational problems that are suitable for analysis and intervention-based solutions. This, however, is the 'bread and butter' of consulting. Meanwhile, as noted above, one of the major criticisms of current consulting practice is the failure to apply process methodologies in a systematic and rigorous fashion. However, AR is designed to be precisely such a methodology. The principles and criteria that we have developed for AR specifically aim to ensure both a systematic and rigorous approach.

There are, nonetheless, some significant differences between the practice of AR and C that should not be neglected. Quite apart from issues of remuneration (action researchers are often academics who may not charge for their services), the most significant difference is that of reporting. Consultants have a primary responsibility to report their findings to the client. Clients often pay substantial amounts of money for the consulting advice and expect to have exclusive rights over that advice. Confidentiality clauses make it impossible to share that advice with other, potentially competing organizations, let alone publish it in academic or practitioner journals.

Action researchers, on the other hand, have an ethical obligation not only to solve a client's organizational problems, but also to report back on their findings to the research and practitioner community. As noted earlier, this is a major dilemma for AR: it must serve and satisfy two demanding masters. Traditionally, action researchers have managed to mitigate client concerns about revelations of confidential material by disguising the identity of organizations and indeed also by insisting that clients both play a significant role in the course of the action research and engage in writing up and reviewing any papers that emerge from the project. This involvement is often specified in a Researcher-Client Agreement. More generally, a Researcher-Client Infrastructure serves as the overall framework to set and help ensure specific standards of performance.

In principle, it is not difficult to imagine that similar guarantees could be written into what may be termed a Consultant-Client Agreement, even though such a procedure deviates from that usually practiced by consultants. Given that the AR method remains relatively unknown and poorly understood within the consulting profession, it is appropriate to envisage joint teams with both consultants and academic researchers involved. This would enable consultants and academic researchers to learn from each other and to demonstrate their methodologies in action.

In the spirit of this paper, we propose not only that AR and C be integrated on specific projects, but also that action researchers and consultants strive to learn from each other informally on a continual basis. Such an approach will not only facilitate the smoother operation of the AR process, but also facilitate the generation of papers that disseminate information back to the research and practitioner communities.

Recognising the disadvantages associated with AR from the consultant's perspective (primarily extended project time, reduced profitability, and the potential for resistance to change), we would like to recommend that a subset of our criteria be applied to consulting (see Table 16-7). These six criteria do not capture every aspect of CAR, but adhering even to these six would be likely to improve IS consulting practice significantly.

Table 16-7. AR Criteria to Improve Consulting Practice

Relevant Criteria	**Consequence for Consulting**
1c Explicit specification of the project's scope and boundaries	Enables a shared understanding of what will be included in the project
1e Explicit specification of the project's objectives and evaluation measures	Enables both the client and the consultant to determine whether the project has been completed successfully
2b Diagnose the organizational situation in order to identify the specific factor(s) causing the problem	Helps to ensure that the consulting project addresses the causes of the problem
3c/d Planning and implementation based upon a theoretical model that explains the observed problem(s) and its cause(s)	Enables the project to draw upon relevant insights from both the scholarly literature and previous experience

Table 16-7. AR Criteria to Improve Consulting Practice (*Continued*)

Relevant Criteria	Consequence for Consulting
4e Measure the status of the organizational situation before and after the intervention	Helps to determine how the intervention affected key performance indicators
5b/c Reflect upon the results of the project and consider their implications for further action in this organizational situation	Provide guidance for future actions in line with concept of continuous improvement

Our original motivation for writing this chapter was to consider the potential for action research and consulting to learn from and benefit each other. We believe that the evidence presented is strongly suggestive of a positive relationship between the two. Consultants have much to learn from action researchers and could usefully apply the principles and criteria that we developed previously (Davison et al., 2004) to their consulting practice. Indeed, we advise that consultants include AR in their toolbox of process methodologies. However, neither can AR be applied blindly and rigidly, nor should it be assumed that AR comes at no cost.

Much contemporary AR is emergent in character, i.e. it evolves as a project moves forwards. As such, it may be used to complement the more formal and rigid methods that are traditionally used to plan and manage IS projects. This would be analogous to the strategic innovation paradigm that has been used to create a synergy between formal planning and action-based learning at the strategic level of the organization (Martinsons, 1993). Indeed, consulting firms need to make a strategic investment in AR, and to persuade their clients of the appropriateness of this investment, if they are to reap the full benefits that AR has to offer.

The fundamental nature of AR means that it has to be applied sensitively and flexibly. A particular AR project should be designed to fit the prevailing circumstances of an organizational problem situation, a situation that will itself change over time. Consultants would be well advised to work with experienced action researchers as they explore how they can beneficially apply the principles of action research. Through this joint approach to deployment of the method, action researchers will benefit as well, with access to organizational problems and consulting expertise and experience.

5. CONCLUSION

In this chapter, we have explored some of the possible ways that consulting practice could benefit by adopting the principles of action research. In so doing, we have deliberately attempted to cast aside the common and long held belief that action research should remain distinctly separate from consulting. We do not believe that action researchers who work as, or co-operate with, consultants are making a deal with the Devil. Instead, we believe that both action research and consulting have much to offer each other. This is particularly the case with respect to the principles for canonical action research that were developed in Davison et al. (2004). The five principles and their associated criteria can be used to increase the rigour and reliability of consulting practice, for the benefit of consultants and clients alike.

We believe that action researchers need to overcome their current bias against consulting, while consultants need to overcome a similar bias against academic research. We envision that despite the obstacles that we have identified (time and effort required, resistance to change), some consultants will add AR to their toolkit. We have shown how consulting professionals can help ensure the quality of their work by adopting our principles of CAR in whole or in part. We strongly suggest that the adoption of these principles be done in collaboration with action researchers, who have considerable experience in successful deployment of the AR method. Otherwise, there is a danger that AR methods and our principles may be misapplied.

Whether AR+C will be a marriage made in heaven or a hellish partnership will depend on the circumstances prevailing in a particular problem situation, together with the action researchers and consultants themselves. While the focus of this chapter has been on the benefits of AR to consulting, we also believe that the consulting profession and individual consultants could potentially make some significant contributions to AR. As with most partnerships, a consulting engagement offers the potential for both marital bliss and acrimonious divorce. A more realistic scenario may well involve temporary relationships between consultants and action researchers that last for the duration of a specific project or as long as both parties find the association to be productive and mutually beneficial.

ACKNOWLEDGEMENT

This chapter incorporates and extends material previously published in Davison et al. (2004). We would like to thank the book editor and two anonymous referees for their helpful comments on an earlier version of this chapter.

6. REFERENCES

Avison, D.E., Lau, F., Myers, M. & Nielsen, P.A. (1999). Action Research. *Communications of the ACM,* **42**(1), 94-97.

Baskerville, R. (1999). Investigating information systems with action research. *Communications of the AIS,* **2** (19), 1-32.

Baskerville, R. & Pries-Heje, J. (1999). Grounded action research: A method for understanding IT in practice. *Accounting, Management and Information Technology,* **9**(1), 1-23.

Baskerville, R. & Wood-Harper, A.T. (1998). Diversity in information systems action research methods. *European Journal of Information Systems,* **7**(2), 90-107.

Benbasat, I. & Zmud, R. (1999). Empirical research in information systems: The practice of relevance. *Management Information Systems Quarterly,* **23**(1), 3-16.

Bunning, C. (1995). *Placing Action Learning and Action Research in Context.* International Management Centre: Brisbane.

Careers in Consulting (2001). Facts and trends in Consulting, available online at http://www.careers-in-business.com/consulting/mc.htm

Caulkin, S. (1997). The great consulting cop-out, Management Today, **58**(3), 32-36.

Cohen, L. & Manion, L. (1980). *Research Methods in Education,* 2nd Ed. Croom Helm: Dover, NH.

Cunningham, J.B. (1993). *Action Research and Organizational Development.* Praeger Publishers: Westport, CT.

Curle, A. (1949). A theoretical approach to action research. *Human Relations.* **2**, 269-280.

Davison, R.M. & Vogel, D.R. (2000). Group support systems in Hong Kong: An action research project. *Information Systems Journal,* **10**(1), 3-20.

Davison, R.M., Martinsons, M.G. and Kock, N.F. (2004). Principles of Canonical Action Research, *Information Systems Journal,* **14**(1), 65-86.

Dickens, L. & Watkins, K. (1999). Action research: rethinking Lewin. *Management Learning,* **30**(2), 127-140.

Easley, C.F.. and Harding, C.F. (1999). Client versus consultant, *Journal of Management Consulting,* **10**(4), 3-8.

Eden, C. & Huxham, C. (1996). Action research for management research. *British Journal of Management,* **7**(1), 75-86.

Gable, G.G. (1997). A multidimensional model of client success when engaging external consultants, *Management Science,* **42**(8), 1175-1198.

Hasek, G. (1997). The era of experts, *Industry Week,* 246(10), 60-67.

Heller, F. (1993). Another look at action research. *Human Relations,* **46**(10), 1235-1242.

Hult, M. & Lennung, S.-Å. (1980). Towards a definition of action research: A note and bibliography. *Journal of Management Studies,* **17**(2), 241-250.

Klein, H.K. & Myers, M.D. (1999). A set of principles for conducting and evaluating interpretive field studies in information systems. *Management Information Systems Quarterly,* **23**(1), 67-94.

Kock, N. & Lau, F. (2001). Introduction to the special issue: Information systems action research serving two demanding masters. *Information Technology & People,* **14**(1), 6-11.

Kock, N., Avison, D., Baskerville, R., Myers, M. & Wood-Harper, T. (1999). IS action research: can we serve two masters? *Proceedings of the 20th International Conference on Information Systems.* De, P. and DeGross, J. (eds.), 582-585. The Association for Computing Machinery, New York, NY.

Kumar, V., Simon, A., and Kimberley, N. (2000). Strategic capabilities which lead to management consulting success, *Management Decision,* **38**(1-2), 24-35.

Lau, F. (1997). A review on the use of action research in information systems studies. In: *Information Systems and Qualitative Research*, Lee, A.S., Liebenau, J. & DeGross, J.I. (eds.), 31-68. Chapman and Hall, London.

Martinsons, M.G., Davison, R.M. and Tse, D. (1999). The balanced scorecard: A foundation for the strategic management of information systems, *Decision Support Systems*, **25**(1), 71-88.

Martinsons, M.G. (1993). Strategic innovation, *Management Decision*, **31**(8), 4-11.

McKay, J. & Marshall, P. (2001). The dual imperatives of action research. *Information Technology & People*, **14**(1), 46-59.

McLachlin, R.D. (1999). Factors for consulting engagement success, *Management Decision*, **37**(5), 394-402.

McTaggart, R. (1991). Principles for participatory action research. *Adult Education Quarterly*, **41**(3), 168-187.

Monteleone, F. (2000). Anyone need a consultant?, *Computerworld*, **34**(5), 52.

Mumford, E. (2001). Advice for an action researcher, *Information Technology & People*, **14**(1), 12-27.

O'Shea, J. and Madigan, C. (1997). Dangerous company: The consulting powerhouses and the businesses they save and ruin, Times Books, New York, NY.

Robey, D. & Markus, M.L. (1998). Beyond rigor and relevance: Producing consumable research about information systems. *Information Resources Management Journal*, **11**(1), 7-15.

Senn, J. (1998). The challenge of relating IS research to practice. *Information Resources Management Journal*, **11**(1), 23-28.

Shapiro, E.C., Eccles, R.G. and Soske, T.L. (1993). Consulting: Has the solution become part of the problem, *Sloan Management Review*, **34**(4), 89-95.

Wright C. and Kitay J. (2002). But does it work? Perceptions of the impact of management consulting', *Strategic Change*, **11**(5), 271-278.

Zmud, R. (1996). Editor's comments: on rigor and relevancy. *Management Information Systems Quarterly*, **20**(3), xxxvii-xxxviii.

Chapter 17

A PLEA FOR ACTION RESEARCH IN ACCOUNTING INFORMATION SYSTEMS

C. Richard Baker
Adelphi University, USA

Abstract: In recent years there has been a growing appreciation of the use of action research in information systems (see Baskerville and others in this volume). A comparable use of action research has not been seen in Accounting Information Systems (AIS). Because AIS is an important sub-area of the accounting discipline, this chapter makes a plea for an increased use of action research in AIS.

Key words: action research; accounting; accounting information systems; managerial accounting.

1. SITUATING ACTION RESEARCH WITHIN THE ACCOUNTING DISCIPLINE

As Figure 17-1 indicates, the accounting discipline can be divided into several sub-disciplines, including financial, managerial, auditing, tax and AIS. Accounting academics and accounting practitioners typically concentrate in one of the sub-disciplines, often to the exclusion of the others. Each sub-discipline has certain academic journals which provide a focus for the research within the sub-discipline, and the research topics and methodologies often differ substantially among the sub-disciplines. For example, research in financial accounting is typically based on methodologies derived from financial economics and involves extensive use of econometric methods, while research in managerial accounting and auditing tends to be more behavioral in nature, involving methods derived from psychology and sociology. Thus, it might be expected that managerial accounting would be more receptive to action research than would financial accounting.

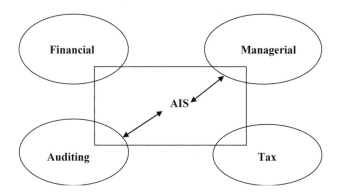

Figure 17-1. The sub-disciplines of accounting

Because accounting systems are ubiquitous and necessary for the functioning of an organization, AIS interacts with all of the sub-disciplines of accounting. In a general sense, however, AIS has closer links with managerial accounting and auditing than with financial accounting and tax. This is because the information requirements of financial accounting and tax accounting systems are usually established by outside entities (i.e. FASB and IRS), while the information requirements of managerial accounting and auditing tend to be based on the needs of organizational participants, or those who review and evaluate the AIS (i.e. auditors). Hence, the most likely space to encounter an increased use of action research in AIS would be at the intersection of AIS and managerial accounting or AIS and auditing. Since there has been little use of action research in accounting in a general sense, the following sections discuss some examples of research involving the sub-disciplines of accounting and AIS where qualitative and interpretative methods have been used that appear to approximate the principles of action research.

2.   ACTION RESEARCH IN MANAGERIAL ACCOUNTING

Kaplan (1998) provides one example of research located at the boundary between managerial accounting and AIS and relating to action research. Kaplan's work is intriguing because it provides a retrospective analysis of the consulting, teaching and case writing that Kaplan and his colleagues Robin Cooper and David Norton performed over a twenty-five year period with major American corporations. Kaplan's *Innovation Action Research* focuses on the introduction and implementation of Activity Based Costing (ABC) and the Balanced Scorecard into American business. Whether

Innovation Action Research ought to be considered under the general rubric of action research may be open to question. However, Kaplan's work has received the approval of Chris Argyris (Argyris & Schön, 1978, 1991) as a form of action research, and because of Kaplan's stature within the academic accounting community, it is important to review this type of action research.

Kaplan indicates that Innovation Action Research involves the following steps:

- Observe and document innovative practices
- Teach and speak about the innovations
- Write journal articles and books
- Implement the concept in new organizations.

These steps are similar to the action research steps in information systems as described by Baskerville (1999 and this volume); clearly there is some overlap between the approaches. In Kaplan's approach, *observing and documenting* is similar to Baskerville's first step of *diagnosis*. *Teaching and speaking* and *writing of journal articles* might comprise parts of an *action plan*, and *implementing the concept in new organizations* can also be viewed as part of an action plan. What is not apparent in Kaplan's approach is the *evaluating* and *iterative* aspects. Nevertheless, Kaplan (1998) does address this issue by indicating that implementing innovations in organizations is important for the following reasons:

- Validating new knowledge
- Providing new learning opportunities
- Learning about effective implementation processes
- Engaging in a second loop around the innovation action research cycle.

Therefore, it can be seen that Kaplan's Innovation Action Research is similar to Baskerville's approach to information systems action research. The difference between the two approaches lies primarily in Kaplan's suggestion that evaluation can be done by persons external to the action research project. In Kaplan's case, the evaluation of ABC and the Balanced Scorecard was conducted by various researchers over a period of years using a variety different research methods. Kaplan has been confident about the success of his interventions because the innovations were evaluated by other researchers and deemed to be successful in practice. This provides an interesting view of validation, in that most action research projects are not subject to validation by parties outside of the specific organization or social setting in which the action research project takes place.

Apart from Kaplan, there are few other examples of action research at the boundary of managerial accounting and AIS. One example would be Johansson & Baldvinsdottir (2003), who studied performance-evaluation processes in two small companies in Sweden—a firm of consultants, and a manufacturing company. At the consulting firm, the research approach was a longitudinal case study. The empirical material was collected over a period of four years and consisted of interviews, video recordings, and field observations. In contrast, the research at the manufacturing company was described as an action research study where one of the authors remained with the company for over a year, observing and participating in real-life situations. The authors used an interpretive scheme derived from Institutional Economics whereby institutions are seen as embodying the social linkage between individuals and are created and re-created by the habits of thought and actions of individuals. Unlike previous studies in which performance evaluation has been viewed as a tool for improving organizational performance, the authors did not find such a clear relationship. By focusing instead on the AIS role in the action–reaction chain between evaluator and evaluated, it became apparent that performance evaluation is largely dependent on trust. While this study is described by the authors as an action research study, it does not appear to follow the principles of action research in an explicit manner. Rather, it is more like a participant observation study. The differences between an in-depth longitudinal case study, a participant observation study, and an action research study may not always be clear. However, in a general sense, action research requires a problem focus and a change orientation. It is not obvious in this instance whether a change orientation was present. Nevertheless, what can be learned from this study is that there are similarities between action research and participant observation. Because participant observation is a well established methodology in several of the social sciences, including sociology, anthropology and management (Diesing, 1991; Baker, 1977), a researcher contemplating a study using action research might want to draw on the similarities between action research and participant observation in order to enhance the validity of their methodology.

Finally, in another study with some similarities to action research, Ezzamel et al. (2003) focused on a problem in a factory setting. Their paper is representative of a growing segment of "critical accounting research" which seeks to change not just the social setting in which the research takes place, but the larger society (see Neu et al., 2001). Ezzamel et al.'s paper focused on the role of the AIS in tense management–labor relationships during a reorganization of manufacturing processes. Their methodology involved a longitudinal case study of a manufacturing plant in a large multinational company. It included participant observation and extensive interviewing. The focus of the study was on the ways in which pressures to enhance productivity and improve profits led to several attempts by senior management to introduce changes in production methods, management style, and the AIS. Shop floor workers interpreted these initiatives as being intended to reduce head counts, which caused them to resist the initiatives over a period of 13 years. During this period, the rhetoric of corporate governance was confronted by the workers' expression of their own interests. While Ezzamel et al. did not set out to specifically solve a problem or change a social setting; they did set out to modify the larger social setting by demonstrating the existence of class conflict in labor relations in a manufacturing setting. They sought to create a critical understanding of labor processes such that the words 'new' and 'better' in referring to AIS were revealed as code words for ways to reduce labor costs. What can be learned from this study is that the definition of a "problem" in a particular social setting which needs to be changed through AR may be contested.

3. ACTION RESEARCH IN AIS

As mentioned before, there has been little or no action research in AIS or accounting generally. Therefore, this section reviews some AIS studies which seem to have some similarities with action research. For example, Van der Veeken & Wouters (2002) describe the results of a case study that investigated the implementation of an accounting information system by operations managers in a road building company in the Netherlands. In this study there was considerable preplanning (diagnosing) before the execution of project activities, but task uncertainty during the implementation phase required corrective action (evaluating). In the AIS design phase, information about prices and expected costs was needed for the design and preplanning purposes, but during the project implementation phase, higher-level managers focused primarily on information about low performing projects, while lower-level managers focused on information about specific work locations and the prices of various inputs. Learning over time occurred through experimentation with different action plans and building up a repertoire of solutions that worked (or did not work). The study indicated that when there is high task uncertainty, AIS may not function to aid managerial decision making, because managers may use 'action-centered' skills instead. 'Action-centered' skills focus on negotiation of contracts and may not utilize information produced by systems designed for cost analysis and cost management. The study also suggests that direct observation of processes is more informative than the formal representation that occurs in AIS design.

Another example of an AIS research study that appeared to follow the principles of action research is Hunton & Gibson (1999). In their study, Hunton & Gibson conducted a longitudinal field experiment that was designed to examine the impact of group discussion when soliciting user requirements for AIS. The results of the study indicate that group discussion among users of the system enhances the quality of data input. Hunton & Gibson suggest that this type of research could be used in the design of AIS. With traditional systems reliability evaluations, "accountants tend to ignore development processes, wait until the system is implemented, search for errors, and then suggest corrective measures" (Hunton & Gibson, p. 616). Under an alternative approach there would be an attempt to build quality into the AIS upfront. In order to do this, accountants need to be engaged during the systems development process. The principles of action research would then be used during the design and assurance function.

4.   OTHER TYPES OF ACTION RESEARCH IN ACCOUNTING SETTINGS

Apart from these few examples of action research in the accounting literature as described above, studies involving action research in accounting settings have also appeared in information systems journals. Usually these studies do not focus directly on AIS. Kohli & Kettinger (2004) provide one example of an action research project which appeared recently in *MIS Quarterly*. Their study focused on the implementation of a physicians' profiling system (PPS) which was used to monitor the costs of delivering of medical services. The problem was that physicians ignored the information system designed by non-physician managers. The authors suggest that this was because the principal (i.e. management) in a principal/agent setting did not possess sufficient legitimacy to require the agent's (i.e. the physicians) use of information to control costs. Using the principles of action research, the authors shifted their theoretical perspective to the concept of "informating the clan." Informating refers to the idea that information systems can play a central role in making behaviors more transparent between parties (Zuboff, 1988). The clan refers to the concept of clan based controls, in which control by professional peers is more important than control by hierarchical management. This study provides an understanding of how to control the behavior of autonomous professionals. The findings suggest that a clan can be controlled (i.e. informated) if management can improve the perceived legitimacy of the information, and facilitate an environment where clan-based discussion, using the information provided by the principal, is incorporated into the control process.

5.   A DEBATE ABOUT INCREASED USE OF ACTION RESEARCH IN AIS

A commentary by McSweeney (2000) on Baker's (2000) call for increased use of action research in AIS revealed some additional challenges for the use of action research in AIS. McSweeney advanced several reasons why there should not be an increased use of action research in AIS. These reasons focused on questions of power and participation, causality, theory, and validity. Some counter-arguments to McSweeney are expressed as follows. Regarding power and participation, McSweeney argued that in corporate settings participation in action research is problematic because of organizational conflict. He appears to view organizations through a lens of conflict where it is always assumed that employees will never willingly participate in activities that improve the efficiency and effectiveness of an organization. This assumption is questionable, and it is probably less valid in AIS settings than in traditional factory settings. It is also less valid in certain geographic regions (e.g. North America and Asia) than in others (e.g. Europe). The increased use of action research in MIS provides evidence regarding the ability of action researchers to secure participation from organizational actors, albeit not necessarily from lower level employees of an organization.

With regard to causality, McSweeney made an incorrect assumption about action research with respect to an assumed linkage between action taking and intended outcomes. Contrary to his assumption, the action researcher does not necessarily know in advance what the outcome of a particular action plan will be. Instead, it is through an iterative process of evaluating outcomes from action plans, and the learning that is achieved, that successful outcomes may ultimately be reached.

McSweeney also criticized action research for its emphasis on action instead of theory. He maintained that action research that is uninformed by theory is not really research. This criticism is not pertinent for several reasons. First, as Baskerville (1999) points out, the "key assumptions of the action researcher are that social settings cannot be reduced for study and that action brings understanding" (p. 3). Therefore, there is a theory underlying action research (i.e. action brings understanding), but it may not be the type of theory that McSweeney would acknowledge as being such. Second, as McSweeney himself points out, scientific discoveries are often made through careful observation without a statement of theory in advance. Third, theories in social science are often like fashions; yesterday's theories are considered outmoded by the proponents of more recent theories. Ultimately, the importance of theory for action research lies in its potential to "educe" new theory through solutions to difficult problems (see Baskerville, this volume).

Finally, McSweeney criticized action research on grounds of validity, arguing that because action research has features which resemble consultancy, it lacks validity. While it may be true that action research focuses on solutions to particular problems, and that this focus may mean that there is little that is generalizable about the research, evaluating action research on this basis is beside the point. Instead, the validity of action research, for the researcher and the organizational participant, is based on the successful resolution of the problem.

6.   SUGGESTIONS FOR FUTURE ACTION RESEARCH IN AIS

Several suggestions for future research using action research in AIS can be made. These suggestions are grouped into three categories: design and implementation of AIS; action research in public sector AIS; "critical" action interventions. The first category of action research in AIS involves the design and implementation of a specific AIS. This category of action research is similar to the studies done by Hunton & Gibson (1999) and Kohli & Kettiner (2004) in which a problem existed with regard to the design or implementation of an AIS and the researcher sought to solve the problem. Neither of these studies explicitly stated that they were following the principles of action research, but the studies could have been changed slightly to emphasize a change focus that is a necessary component of action research.

The second category of suggestions for future action research in AIS, relates to the public sector, including governments, hospitals, schools and other similar organizations. These organizations often need help with problems related to AIS implementation. Action research could help to solve the problems faced by these organizations and also provide a research venue for researchers interested in action research. For some examples of accounting research in the public sector with similarities to action research, please see Broadbent (1995), Broadbent & Laughlin (1997) and Broadbent et al. (1994).

Finally, while not necessarily of interest to all accounting researchers, some researchers might be interested in "critical" action interventions as suggested by Neu et al. (2001). This type of research has been rarely been seen in accounting or AIS research. It involves an explicit assumption of a political position and an attempt to conduct the research so as to contribute to change in a particular social setting where a problem is perceived to exist. This type of research has similarities with the types of action research seen previously in the field of education (see for example Carr and Kemmis, 1986; Grundy, 1982).

7. CONCLUSION

While there has been little action research in AIS, it is encouraging to note that in the mission statement of the recently established *Canadian Accounting Perspectives* journal, Richardson (2004) indicates that the journal intends to provide space for "applied research" in accounting, including action research. In recommending action research, Richardson comments that it "may provide the best approach to bridging the schism between academe and practice" (p. 129). Thus, we may be seeing the emergence of a greater appreciation of action research in the accounting discipline. The goal of this chapter has been to argue that action research ought to be more widely used in AIS research and accounting research generally. Action research includes a variety of qualitative and interpretive techniques that have as their objective the simultaneous pursuit of useful knowledge and the creation of plans for social change. Action research has features which resemble consulting and some which resemble field research. Action research is generally cyclical, participative, qualitative, reflective and responsive. While mainstream accounting research often follows a defined set of methodological principles in the name of rigor and scientific knowledge, such research often has little impact on real world organizations. Action research seeks not only the attainment of useful knowledge, but effective change in organizations and social settings. Therefore, it ought to be more widely used in AIS research.

REFERENCES

Argyris, C. & Schön, D. (1978). *Organizational Learning: A Theory of Action Perspective.* Reading, MA: Addison-Wesley.

Argyris, C. & Schön, D. (1991). Participatory action research and action science compared. Whyte, W. (ed.) *Participatory Action Research.* Newbury Park, NJ: Sage, 85-96.

Baker, C.R. (1977). An observation study of a large public accounting firm. *Human Relations,* **30**(11), 1005-1024.

Baker, C.R. (2000). Towards the increased use of action research in accounting information systems. *Accounting Forum,* **24**(4), 1-13.

Baskerville, R. (1999). Investigating information systems with action research. *Communications of the Association for Information Systems,* **12**(19)(October), 1-24.

Broadbent, J. (1995). The values of accounting and education: Some implications of the creation of visibilities and invisibilities. *Advances in Public Interest Accounting* **6**, 69-98.

Broadbent, J. and Laughlin R. (1997). Evaluation the 'New Public Management' reforms in the UK: A constitutional possibility? *Public Administration* **75**(3), 487-507.

Broadbent, J., Laughlin, R., and Willing-Atherton, H. (1994). Financial control and schools: Accounting in public and private Spheres. *British Accounting Review* **26**, 255-279.

Carr, W. and Kemmis, S. (1986). *Becoming Critical: Education Knowledge and Action Research.* London: Falmer Press.

Diesing, P. (1991). *How Does Social Science Work?: Reflections on Practice*. Pittsburgh, Pa.: University of Pittsburgh Press.

Ezzamel, M., Willmott, H. & Worthington, F. (2003). Accounting and management–labour relations: the politics of production in the 'factory with a problem'. *Accounting, Organizations and Society*, **29**(3/4), 269-302.

Grundy, S. (1982). Three modes of action research. Kemmis, S. & McTaggert, R. (eds.) *The Action Research Reader* (3rd edition). Geelong: Deakin University Press.

Hunton, J. & Gibson, D. (1999). Soliciting user-input during the development of an accounting information system: investigating the efficacy of group discussion. *Accounting, Organizations and Society*, **24**(October), 597-619.

Johansson, I. & Baldvinsdottir, G. (2003). Accounting for trust: some empirical evidence. *Management Accounting Research*, **14**(3)(September), 219-234.

Kaplan, R. (1998). Innovation action research: Creating new management theory and practice. *Journal of Management Accounting Research*, 10, 89-113.

Kohli, R. & Kettinger, W.J. (2004). Informating the clan: Controlling physicians' cost and outcomes. *MIS Quarterly*, **28**(3), 363-394.

McSweeney, B. (2000). 'Action research': mission impossible? Commnetary on 'Towards the increased use of action reach in accounting information systems' by C. Richard Baker. *Accounting Forum*, **24**(4), 379-390.

Neu, D., Cooper, D.J., and Everett, J. (2001). Critical accounting interventions. *Critical Perspectives on Accounting* **12**(6), 735-762.

Richardson, A.J. (2004). Applied research in accounting: A commentary. *Canadian Accounting Perspectives*, **3**(2), 149-169.

Van der Veeken, H. & Wouters M. (2002). Using accounting information systems by operations managers in a project company. *Management Accounting Research*, **13**(3)(September), 345-370

Zuboff, S. (1988). *In the Age of the Smart Machine: The Future of Work and Power*. New York: Basic Books.

Chapter 18

INSIDER AS ACTION RESEARCHER

John Teofil Nosek
Temple University, USA

Abstract: Usually, the action researcher is someone who is external to the organization, provides expertise in an organizational intervention, and systematically evaluates the intervention to gain knowledge from the action. The responsibility for the research role by researcher and practitioner within action research can vary along a continuum from where the researcher takes full responsibility for research-oriented tasks to where the researcher coaches the practitioner in fulfilling research-oriented tasks. This chapter explores the end of the continuum where the inside practitioner is provided with the theory and research structure to fulfill more of the research-oriented tasks. The ill-structured problem domain of business planning is used to illustrate. Executives, who are students within an Executive MBA Program and are also participants in organizational interventions, fulfill the role of insider-as-researcher. Results indicate that insider action researchers can provide sensitive data to which outsider action researchers may not have access and are capable of systematically evaluating organizational interventions.

Key words: action research; sensemaking; qualitative research; ill-structured problems; decision theory; business planning; strategy

1.   INTRODUCTION

Usually, the action researcher is someone who is external to the organization, provides expertise in an organizational intervention, and systematically evaluates the intervention to gain knowledge from the action (Baskerville and Myers, 2004). While it can be valuable to study an organizational intervention from the perspective of an external observer (Baskerville and Myers, 2004), being an outsider also has limitations (Levin et al, 2002). An outsider may not have access to participants, and most importantly, organizational participants may not sufficiently trust someone who is perceived to be an outsider to share important, but sensitive, data

(Levin et al, 2002). This may be especially true if the intervention does not enjoy full acceptance within the organization and is not perceived as successful by some participants (Iversen and Mathiassen, 2003).

Advocates of action research stress the importance of client-researcher relationships (Iversen et al, 2004); some even advocate the mutual responsibility of theorizing (Iversen et al, 2004). This chapter focuses on exploring the issue of providing insiders with the knowledge and capabilities to fill more of the research role in action research projects. This chapter should not be considered a complete action research project. The insiders were not trained as action researchers. The insiders were provided some minimal exposure to theory to help them elicit information that may not be easily forthcoming to outside researchers. At the same time, the chapter does provide additional evidence that, even under these limited circumstances, insiders can take on more of the research role and provide access to information not easily available to outsiders.

We first review some basic principles of action research as a qualitative research method. We then discuss the class of ill-structured problems where it may be difficult for outsiders to gain trust of insiders and quickly gain sufficient organizational knowledge to properly diagnose the situation. We then provide examples of the insider-as-researcher relevant to the diagnosing and reflective learning stages of action research (Baskerville and Myers, 2004; Kock, 2003).

2.   ACTION RESEARCH – A QUALITATIVE RESEARCH METHOD

Myers (1999) provides a comprehensive overview of qualitative research, which includes action research; others provide comprehensive reviews that focus on action research (Baskerville and Wood-Harper, 1998; Kock and Lau, 2001; Davison et al., 2004). While qualitative research broadly deals with understanding and explaining social phenomena (Myers, 1999); action research deals specifically with a planned intervention stage (Davison et al., 2004). However, the kinds of effort to understand the situation before an event (whether a planned or unplanned intervention) and understand the situation after an event are common to qualitative methods in general (Myers, 1999; Davison et al., 2004).

In the canonical action research project, the planned theoretical-based intervention is known a priori (Davison et al., 2004). In this case, it is the application of the classical experimental design of measuring before, applying the treatment (in this case intervention), measuring after, but applied to social units and not individual subjects. However, there are many situations where the issues are not well understood (Heller, 1993) and the researcher can not know the exact theory-based intervention to apply. Some researchers advocate iterative design (Baskerville and Wood-Harper, 1998; Mathiassen, 2002). In iterative-oriented action research projects, much of the reflective learning stage overlaps the diagnosing stage for the next planned intervention (Baskerville and Wood-Harper, 1998; Mathiassen, 2002).

Roles of researcher and practitioner within action research varies along a continuum from where the outside researcher takes full responsibility for the research-oriented tasks to where the external researcher coaches the inside practitioner in fulfilling research-oriented tasks. The roles can overlap and can interchange in unanticipated ways (Clark, 1972). Lindgren et al (2004) emphasize the important role of practitioners in the diagnosing and evaluating stages of action research where they jointly hold responsibility with researchers. Clearly, researchers can not do the job without practitioners, however, how would the outcomes of these stages change if the practitioner performed more of the role of researcher? Would the insider-as-researcher ask different, more organizationally-relevant questions? Is it more important in some situations than others for insiders to be girded with research skills? For example, what if organizational knowledge is paramount to success, the researcher's gap of organizational knowledge is great, and there is limited time for action? What if the researchers do not have the appropriate security clearance to access information? The next section explores the class of ill-structured problems to illustrate a class of problems where insider-as-researcher may provide valuable and unexpected insights.

3.   ILL-STRUCTURED PROBLEM DOMAINS

In ill-structured problem domains such as business planning and new product design, participants, who are increasingly distributed, face the existence of multiple and conflicting interpretations about an organizational situation. They are not certain about what questions to ask, and if questions are posed, no clear answer is forthcoming (Daft and Lengel, 1986). They grope through a recursive, discontinuous process of many difficult steps subjected to interference, feedback loops, and dead ends that more closely resembles fermentation than an assembly line (Mintzberg et al., 1976). Managers' experience-based intuitive understanding may depend on insufficient or no-longer-relevant experience (Dreyfus and Dreyfus, 1986), and problem solving requires all those involved to exchange and argue their many viewpoints, ideas, values, and concerns (Rittel, in Conklin, 1987).

3.1   Business planning example

Figure 18-1 presents a modified model of Organizational Interpretation Modes, while Table 18-1 provides the scanning characteristics by category of these interpretation modes. As the assumptions about the environment change from analyzable to unanalyzable, the source of data moves from internal, impersonal to external, personal and the data acquisition techniques move from regular, routine, reports, many obtained from organizational information systems, to irregular reports from external contacts and feedback from the environment (Daft and Weick, 1984; Dreyfus and Dreyfus, 1986). "The decision maker is faced with a "corporate primordial soup" of customer, industry and technology news; assessments of the news; competitor moves; agent's call reports; alliances; rumors; deals coming and done; problems and solutions; suggestions and scenarios" (Lee and Brookes, 1993).

3.2   New product design

New product development increasingly demands that designers, end users, manufacturers/product developers, and marketers are actively involved throughout design, development, and deployment. Multi-departmental/disciplinary design increases complexity as team members compare disparate frames of reference, educate partners about one's own terminology, explain conclusions that are not obvious to anyone outside one's own specialty, etc., in other words, "...a good deal of the work lies in formulating the background for decision making, not just in the final selection of one or more alternatives (Whitaker et al, 1995, p. 7)."

Design rationale includes the process model, the debate, and the justifications leading to a particular design. Observational studies validate the criticality of design rationale in steering and justifying the course of design. To a great extent "...the explanation for a final product lies in the historicality of its design process and not necessarily in deterministic decision making on predictable technical and functional issues" (Whitaker et al., 1995, p. 31).

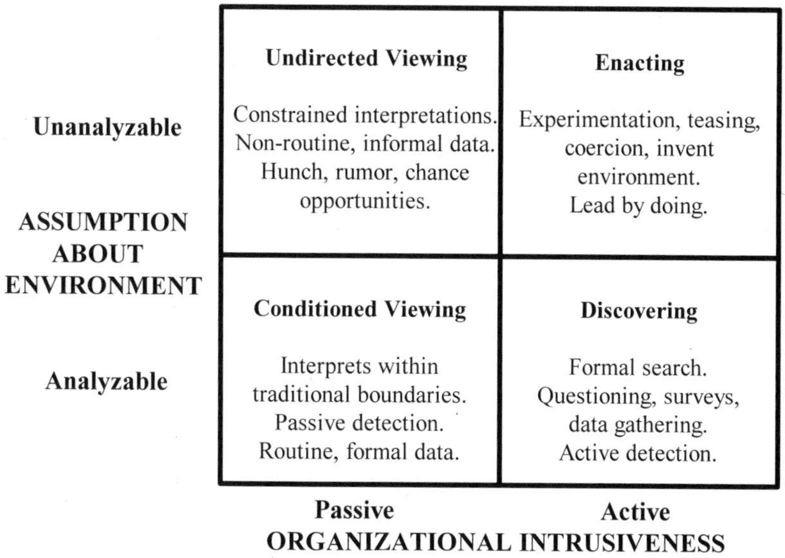

	Undirected Viewing	Enacting
Unanalyzable **ASSUMPTION ABOUT ENVIRONMENT**	Constrained interpretations. Non-routine, informal data. Hunch, rumor, chance opportunities.	Experimentation, teasing, coercion, invent environment. Lead by doing.
	Conditioned Viewing	**Discovering**
Analyzable	Interprets within traditional boundaries. Passive detection. Routine, formal data.	Formal search. Questioning, surveys, data gathering. Active detection.
	Passive	**Active**

ORGANIZATIONAL INTRUSIVENESS

Figure 18-1. Model of organizational interpretation modes (adapted from Daft and Weick, 1984)

Table 18-1. Scanning characteristics by category (adapted from Daft and Weick, 1984)

Category	Organization Mode	Data Source	Data Acquisition
Enacting	unanalyzable, active	external, personal	no department, irregular reports and feedback from environment, selective information
Undirected Viewing	unanalyzable, passive	external, personal	no scanning department, irregular contacts and reports, casual information
Discovering	analyzable, active	internal, impersonal	separate departments, special studies and reports, extensive information
Conditional Viewing	analyzable, passive	internal, impersonal	no department, although regular record keeping and information systems, routine information

4.   THEORETICAL-BASIS FOR DIAGNOSING, INTERVENING, AND REFLECTING

As noted earlier, in iterative-oriented action research projects, much of the reflective learning stage overlaps the diagnosing stage for the next planned intervention and the examples to be presented are meant to illustrate the value of insider-as-researcher, especially in the diagnosing and reflective learning stages of action research, rather than report on complete action research projects.

In this example, action researchers are to use the same theory-based technique for diagnosing, intervening, and reflecting. In diagnosing, insiders use the theory-based technique to understand the current decision-process in use or recently used. Using the same theory-based technique, insiders can modify and hopefully improve their direction setting process. Finally, in reflective learning, insiders use the technique, to evaluate success and diagnose for follow-on action research cycles. Insiders were instructed in Nutt's model of choice and direction setting (1993). In the next sections we summarize the theory-based instruction insiders received and review the technique they were to use. This is followed by three examples where insiders used the technique to understand and diagnose the situation.

4.1   Decision making background

Figure 18-2 provides an overview of three models of decision making by Simon (1960), Daft and Weick (1984), and Osborn-Parnes in Parnes et al. (1977). Simon (1960) characterized the basic decision-making process as consisting of three major steps: intelligence, design and choice. During intelligence activities groups try to identify and define a problem by sharing information and searching the environment. During design activities groups generate and refine alternate solutions. Finally, choice involves the selection and implementation of one of the proposed alternatives.

While terms to differentiate the phases of decision making may be different, decision making activities can be grouped into two general phases: activities that occur during sensemaking and activities that occur during action-making. Traditional decision making has focused on courses of action during the action-making phase represented by the shaded region of Figure 18-2. During sensemaking we are concerned with understanding the situation (Weick and Meader, 1993). Good questions to ask include: "what is going on here?" and "should I even be asking this question now?" During sensemaking, we first want to find variables in the problem situation and create an understanding of the important relationships between them

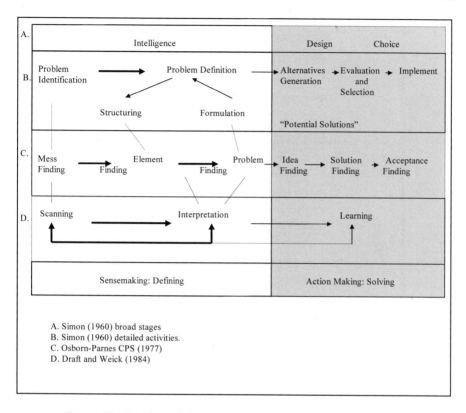

Figure 18-2. Problem solving (adapted from Massey and Clapper, 1995)

(Massey and Clapper, 1995). Activities occurring during this phase are represented by the non-shaded region of Figure 18-2, however, as noted below, sensemaking can continue through stages normally distinguished as action-making.

4.2 Choice and direction setting within the decision-making process

Figure 18-3 draws from Nutt (1993) and the work reported in this study. While historically researchers show choice as the culmination of the decision process, Figure 18-3 shows that decision-makers and stakeholders evaluate and make choices, sometimes tacitly, throughout the formulation process for organizational decisions. Nutt (1993) defines formulation as "a process that begins when signals [See top part of Figure 18-3], such as performance indicators, are recognized by key people and ends when one or more options have been targeted for development."

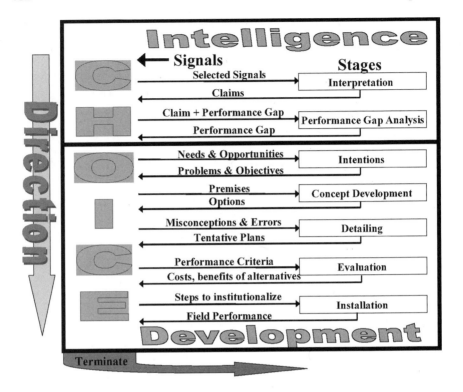

Figure 18-3. Choice and direction setting within the decision-making process

The stages, noted in Figure 18-3, are related activities that can be grouped together and identify the types of information that should be collected. These stages can be done by staff or performed by the decision-makers themselves. Not all stages are necessarily performed and they are not necessarily performed in sequential order.

The Choice Phase of the decision-making process overlaps with the Intelligence and Development Phases in decision making. Initially, stakeholders receive signals from the environment and select some for interpretation [See top of Figure 18-3]. Of the available signals, the first choice occurs, when a subset of signals are chosen to interpret. As noted earlier, many times this choice is tacitly performed, i.e., the decision makers are neither aware of the set of available signals nor of the selection of available signals. Once selected, The Interpretation Stage is initiated which generates a number of claims for the decision makers to evaluate and choose. Assessing the importance of each claim, the decision-maker chooses a claim and identifies the performance gap criteria used to analyze any performance gap that may exist. From this performance gap, the decision-maker identifies needs or opportunities suggested by the selected claim which initiates the Intentions Stage, the first step within the Development Phase.

The Development Phase "identifies the staging of information gathering activity carried out to fashion and implement the decision" (Nutt, 1993). Within the Intentions Stage problems and objectives are identified that clarify the needs or opportunities. The decision-maker states premises, which are used during Concept Development, to identify options that will deal with problems or objectives. The decision-maker evaluates these options and identifies omissions, misconceptions, and errors that are used during The Detailing Stage to develop tentative plans. Using the tentative plans, the decision-maker provides performance criteria that are used in the Evaluation Stage to project the costs and benefits of the alternatives. For the Installation Stage, the decision-maker chooses organizational design alternatives, such as reward systems, personnel selection, resource allocation, etc., to implement the preferred solution. The decision-maker judges field performance to determine success and terminate surveillance. At anytime, the decision-maker can choose to terminate the process.

As indicated in Figure 18-3, the formulation process, which is a subset of the overall organizational decision-making process, can overlap the Intelligence and Development Phases, i.e., some information gathering stages within the Intelligence Phase can occur before the formulation process begins and some information gathering stages within the Development Phase will occur before one or more options are finally targeted for development. These evaluations and choices by key decision-makers throughout the intelligence and development phases affect the direction of the decision making process. Direction guides subsequent activity. The earlier that any misdirection occurs; the more costly are its consequences. Therefore, support for direction setting and maintenance is critical for successful organizational decision-making.

Nutt (1993) provides an example of the formulation process with early misdirection:

A Toyota dealer has been getting disturbing signals after a long period of sales growth. Declines in the closing ratio (a measure of lost sales) were noted and profit had leveled off. The dealer judged these performance indicators to be important signals and linked them to staffing problems. Growth was thought to have forced the addition of sales people who were not acculturated into the dealer's approach to the car business. A sales manager position was created to train and supervise the sales force. After a year, the closing ration and profit continued to fall. The sales manager was fired and the dealership was back to square one. The Toyota dealer linked declines in the closing ration to sales force quality. The remedy was seen in terms of training. Given this direction no other option could be considered.

4.3   Decision Formulation Strategies

According to Nutt (1993), four formulation strategies that organizational decision-makers employ in descending order of success are:
- Reframing: Justify the need to act
- Objective-directed: Provide target
- Issue: "matter under dispute" - Infer solutions from problems and concerns
- Idea: Provide direction with a solution

While the overall decision length remains the same for these strategies, the degree of participation, iteration, and consensus building is also in descending order, i.e., reframing demands the most iteration and participation that requires more energy up front, but the total decision-making time to implementation remains similar for all strategies.

5.   STUDY PROCESS

Initially, a number of organizational decisions within a variety of organizations were identified. Organizational decisions are those that have a major impact on the organization, for example, the opening of new offices, acquisitions and mergers, or development of new business lines and opportunities. Using Nutt's model (1993), detailed information was collected on these decisions that recently occurred or were in-process. The data collection included interviews with people who were directly involved in the decision-making process. The people performing this investigation were Executive MBA students. These evaluators were mostly mid-level to senior level managers and many either actively participated or were actively participating in these decisions.

Armed with research-driven techniques, these evaluators reflected on these processes and gathered information to make sense within their given situation. By using insiders, the candidness achieved in these evaluations was unprecedented. Anonymity is critical due to the sensitivity of the information and will be strictly maintained in this report. The following section presents three diagnosing examples completed by insiders-as-researchers.

6.   ORGANIZATIONAL DECISION EXEMPLARS

In this section we review a sample of organizational decisions to demonstrate how the formulation process affects direction setting and the goodness of decision outcomes. The most important finding that is consistent with Nutt's (1993) work is the need to carefully and continually examine decision-making direction before committing. Figure 18-4 presents a schematic of an organizational decision to open a new office. Upon initial review, it appeared that the process followed the strategy of setting a goal to expand and then executing the objective to open a new office. However, upon further reflection, the commitment to the initial direction of opening up an office seriously affected the remainder of the decision-making process. Much of the work that occurred after this initial direction setting was wasted energy. The effort to place the new office within a new region while meeting cost considerations was unnecessary. The major unspoken assumption that affected this direction was related to company values. All major participants in the decision just assumed that to insure the propagation of the company culture in this new office, that they must open their own, "new" office, instead of purchasing an already existing office with an existing client base. The new office is not generating new business, and therefore this decision-making process was ineffective. Other factors that contributed to their decision to open a new office were their past experiences with opening offices, a failure to consider a changing regulatory environment, and "group think."

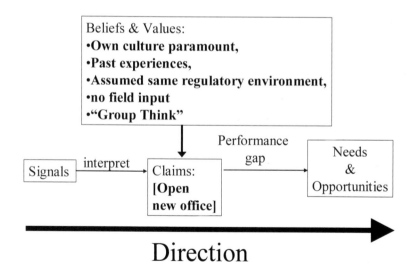

Figure 18-4. Opening a new office: Early misdirection

Figure 18-5 presents an organizational decision to merge two companies. The strategy employed was the least successful, but commonly applied strategy of providing direction with a solution. While previous investigations of merging these two institutions ended in decisions to not pursue mergers, the stature of an important stakeholder and his "belief" in his "business savvy" set the direction to pursue a merger, which ultimately failed at great cost.

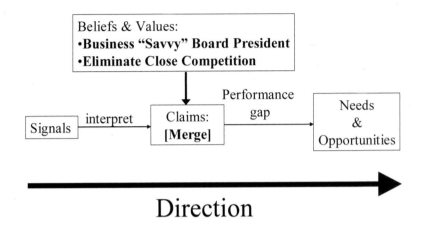

Figure 18-5. Merging organizations: Later misdirection

Figure 18-6 presents an organizational decision by one health care organization to respond to changing market pressures. In this exemplar, organizational decision-makers did an excellent job of engaging the organization to reframe their views about the health care environment and the need for the organization to respond in new ways to ensure their economic survival and growth. The misdirection in this decision-making process was the failure to engage responsible members in the organization in development of innovative solutions that were appropriate to their organization. Senior decision-makers, who perceived great urgency in the situation, relied on their solution perspective that was developed through interaction with health care professionals with similar responsibility in other organizations, and through their service on national organizations. "Best practices" from other organizations were accepted by senior decision-makers without any participation by organizational members below the executive level. As it turns out, this organization does not have the "deep pockets" of other organizations from which "best practices" were gleaned. While consensus was reached in the organization to ensure primary care physicians referred patients to this health organization, the unilateral decision to "control" physicians was both costly and ineffective. Physician practices that were purchased were expensive and were no longer profitable when physician-entrepreneurs no longer owned them. This exemplar demonstrates that direction setting must be monitored throughout the decision-making process.

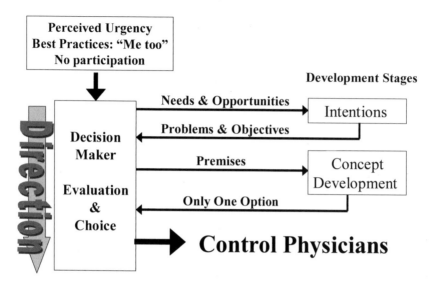

Figure 18-6. Controlling Physicians: Later Misdirection

7.   SUMMARY AND CONCLUSIONS

The responsibility for the research-role by researcher and practitioner within action research can vary along a continuum from where the researcher takes full responsibility for research-oriented tasks to where the researcher coaches the practitioner in fulfilling research-oriented tasks. This chapter explored the end of the continuum where the inside practitioner is provided with the theory and research structure to fulfill more of the research-oriented tasks. The ill-structured problem domain of business planning was used to illustrate.

While historically researchers show choice as the culmination of the decision process, decision-makers and stakeholders evaluate and make choices, sometimes tacitly, throughout the formulation process for organizational decisions. These evaluations and choices by key decision-makers throughout the intelligence and development phases affect the direction of the decision making process. Direction guides subsequent activity. The earlier that any misdirection occurs, the more costly it becomes. These kinds of decisions are usually sensitive, especially when not perceived as successful by all stakeholders. It may be difficult for outside researchers to gain sufficient trust or organizational knowledge in these situations to find out the true story available only to insiders.

Several organizational decisions within a variety of organizations were used to explore the value of insider-as-researcher. Executives, who are students within an Executive MBA Program and are also participants in organizational interventions, fulfilled the role of insider-as-researcher. Results indicate organizations can use Nutt's Choice in Direction Setting Model to analyze a situation and perhaps use it to modify direction setting behavior.

As noted at the beginning of the chapter, this chapter should not be considered a full report of an action research project. The purpose of the chapter was to explore the issue of providing insiders with some minimal set of knowledge and skill to fulfill more of the researcher role. We have not explored such issues as when the theory may be insufficient for the situation or intervention, what happens to the research the insiders generate, nor conflicts of interest that insiders may have. At the same time, the chapter does provide additional evidence that, even under these limited circumstances, insiders can take on more of the research role. They can provide access to sensitive data not available to external researchers and are capable of systematically evaluating organizational interventions.

ACKNOWLEDGMENTS

The insiders were critical to this study. Without their access and candidness much less would have been learned. I hope the chance to reflect on how their organizations make major decisions has helped them to be more effective. Peter Grillo was helpful in the background review of decision-making. In addition, the author thanks the helpful comments of the reviewers. This work was partially funded by the Lattanze Foundation.

REFERENCES

Baskerville, R., & Myers, M.D. (2004). Special issue on action research in information systems: Making IS research relevant to practice – foreword. *MIS Quarterly*. 28(3), 329-335.

Baskerville, R.L., & Wood-Harper, A.T. (1998). Diversity in information systems action research methods. *European Journal of Information Systems*. 7, 90-107.

Conklin, J. (1987). Hypertext: An introduction and survey. *IEEE Computer*. 20(9), 17-41.

Clark, P.A. (1972). *Action Research and Organizational Change*. London, England: Harper and Row.

Daft, R., & Lengel, R. (1986). Organization information requirements, media richness and structural design. *Management Science*. 32(5), 554-571.

Daft, R.L., & Weick, K.E. (1984). Toward a model of organizations as interpretative systems. *Academy of Management Review*. 9(2), 284-295.

Davison, R.M., Martinsons, M.G., & Kock, N.F. (2004). Principles of canonical action research. *Information Systems Journal*. 14(1), 65-86.

Dreyfus, H., & Dreyfus, S. (1986). *Mind Over Machine*. New York, NY: Free Press.

Heller, F. (1993). Another look at action research. *Human Relations*. 46(10), 1235-1242.

Iversen, J. H., & Mathiassen, L. (2003). Cultivation and engineering of a software metrics program. *Information Systems Journal*. 13(1), 3-20.

Iversen, J.H., Mathiassen, L., & Nielsen, P.A. (2004). Managing risk in software process improvement: An action research approach. *MIS Quarterly*. 28(3), 395-434.

Kock, N. (2003). Action research: Lessons learned from a multi-iteration study of computer-mediated communication in groups. *IEEE Transactions on Professional Communication*. 46(2), 105-129.

Kock, N., & Lau, F. (2001). Introduction to the special issue: Information systems action research serving two demanding masters. *Information Technology & People*. 14(1), 6-11.

Lee, D.L., & Brookes, C.H. (1993). *An innovative corporate intelligence system at the M.W. Kellogg Company*. Technical report. Houston, TX: M.W. Kellogg Company.

Levin, D.Z., Cross, R., Abrams, L.C., & Lesser, E.L. (2002). Trust and knowledge sharing: A critical combination. *IBM Institute for Knowledge-based Organizations*. http://www-1.ibm.com/services/strategy/e_strategy/trust.html.

Lindgren, R., Henfridsson, O., & Schultze U. (2004). Design principles for competence management systems: A synthesis of an action research study. *MIS Quarterly*. 28(3), 435-473.

Massey, A.P., & Clapper, D.L. (1995). Element finding: The impact of a group support system on a crucial phase of sensemaking. *Journal of Management Information Science*. 11(4), 149-176.

Mathiassen, L. (2002). Collaborative practice research. *Information Technology and People*. 15(4), 321-345.

Mintzberg, H., Raisinghani, D., & Theoret, A. (1976). The structure of 'unstructured' decision processes. *Administrative Science Quarterly*. 21, 246-275.

Myers, M.D. (1997). Qualitative research in information systems. *MIS Quarterly*. 21(2), 241-243.

Nutt, P.C. (1993). The formulation processes and tactics used in organizational decision making. *Organization Science*. 4(2), 226-251.

Parnes, S.J., Noller, R.B., & Biondi, A.M. (1977). *Guide to Creative Actions*. New York, NY: Scribner.

Simon, H.A. (1960). *The New Science of Management*. New York, NY: Harper and Row.

Weick, K.E, & Meader, D.K. (1993). Sensemaking and group support systems. J.M Jessup & J.S. Valacich, eds. *Group Support Systems: New Perspectives*. New York, NY: Macmillan.

Whitaker, R.D., Selvaraj, J.A., Brown, C.E., & McNeese, M.D. (1995). *Collaborative Design Technology: Tools and Techniques for Improving Collaborative Design*. AL/CF-TR-1995-0086. Wright-Patterson Air Force Base, Ohio: Air Force Materiel Command.

INDEX

Acroamatic   179–185, 187
Action planning   45, 46, 56
Action research (AR)   19–21, 23–40,
   62, 64, 69, 77–81, 83–85, 87, 88, 92,
   138–144, 147–155, 193–197, 200–
   213, 241–252, 280, 285, 287, 288,
   291, 299, 300, 328–343, 346–350,
   377–382, 384–392, 406, 407, 410,
   417, 418
Action research cycle   315, 316, 322
Action researcher   194–197, 203, 211–
   213, 247, 248, 250, 405, 406, 410,
   see also Researcher, Outsider
Action taking   45, 46, 58
Action-research framework   46,   *see
   also* DSAR framework
Adoption   256, 261, *see also* Implementation
Agency theory   245, 247, *see also* Principal-agent theory
Argyris   4, 6
Authority   20, 21, 23–29, 31, 33–39,
   see also Domination

Business planning   407, 408, 417
Business process   98, 107–110, 112,
   118, *see also* Organizational process
Business process redesign   277, 299,
   see also Process redesign

Business process re-engineering   277,
   279, 281, 291

Cancellations   196, 211, *see also* Pro-
   ject cancellation
Canonical action research (CAR)   201,
   202, 205, 208, 378–383, 390, 392
Challenges   218–220, 222, 236, 237
Change through action   380, 382, 383,
   386, 387
Claims   12, 13, 15, *see also* Outputs
Clans   317, 318
Client   237, *see also* Customer
Collaboration   168
Collaborative technologies   255
Commitment   221, 222, 224, 225, 228,
   235–237
Communication flow optimization model
   280, 283–286, 292, 297–300
Comprehensive framework   328,   *see
   also* Research framework, Frame-
   work
Consistency   370, 371
Constructivism   69, 71–74, 78, 79, 81,
   84
Consulting   378–380, 384–392, 396,
   397, 403, *see also* IS consulting
Contingency   100, 101, 104, 106, 115,
   121, 122

Control 361, 363, 366, 367, 369–373
Control issues 332, 345, 346
Cultural context 161, 162, 168, 170
Customer 217, 222, *see also* Client
Cycle 379, 381, *see also* Cyclical model, Cyclical process model
Cyclical model *see also* Cyclical process model, Cycle
Cyclical process 313, 314
Cyclical process model 380, 381, 386, 387, *see also* Cyclical model, Cycle

Data generation 256, 260
Decision making 408, 410, 412, *see also* Decision-making, Decision making process
Decision making process 413, 417, *see also* Decision making, Decision-making
Decision support systems (DSS) 246–249
Decision-making 410, 412–416, 418, *see also* Decision making, Decision making process
Definition 20, 36, 40, *see also,* Formalization
Design 331, 332, 343, 347, *see also* Study design
Designerly action research 62, 78, 80, 81, 89–91
Designerly ways of knowing 62, 68, 69, 74–76, 78–80, 85, 87
Design-science 46, 48, 49, 52, 54–58, *see also* DSAR framework
Diagnosing 45, 58, *see also* To diagnose
Dilemmas 318, 319, 324
Documentation 361, 362, 366, 367, 369–373
Domination 24, 28, 29, 33, 37, *see also* Authority
DSAR framework 49, 52, 54, 56, 58, 59, *see also* Design-science, Action-research framework
Dual imperatives 141, 142, 147, 148

Epistemology 8, 10, 12, 13, 15, 62, 64, 68, 75, 76
Evaluating 45, 46, 55, 58

Failed theory 321
Formal power 30–34, 37, *see also* Formalization
Formalization 23, 25–27, 30, 33, 35, 37, 39, *see also* Definition, Formal power
Framework 328–333, 336, 343, 346, 349, 350, 361, 364–367, 369–373, *see also* Research framework, Comprehensive framework

Gap between design and science 62, *see also* The Theory/Practice gap

Healthcare 241, 242, 244, 245, 248–250, *see also* Healthcare industry, Hospitals
Healthcare industry 245, 250, *see also* Healthcare, Hospitals
Healthcare professionals 241, 242, *see also* Practitioners, Physicians, Hospital administrators
Hospitals 244–246, 248–250, *see also* Healthcare, Healthcare industry
Hospital administrators 245–249, *see also* Practitioners, Healthcare professionals, Physicians
Hypotheses 5, 6, 8, 11, *see also* Hypothesis
Hypothesis 5, 7–9, 14, *see also* Hypotheses

Ill-structured problems 406, 407, 417
Implementation 260, 264, 265, 396, 397, 399, 400, 402, *see also* Adoption
Information systems (IS) 43–45, 59, 131–140, 142, 145, 146, 149, 155, 162, 168, 169, 171, 172, 174, 184, 185
Information systems research 336, *see also* IS research
Information technology (IT) 256, 272
Initiation 23, 26–28, 33, 35, 39
Innovations 396, 397
Insiders 406, 407, 410, 414, 417, 418, *see also* Practitioners
Interpretative 396, *see also* Interpretive

Interpretive 398, 403, *see also* Interpretative

Investigators 30, *see also* Researchers

IS consulting 385–388, 390, *see also* Consulting

IS research 327–329, *see also* Information systems research

Iversen 356, 361, 365, 367, 368, 372, 373, *see also* Jakob Iversen

Jakob Iversen 373, *see also* Iversen

Kaplan 396, 397

Keynes 5, 6, 14

Knowledge 168, 181, 185, *see also* Understanding

Knowledge production 62–64, 76, 80, 89, *see also* Production of knowledge

Kurt Lewin 4, 5, 98, *see also* Lewin

Leadership 222, 223, 228–230, 234, 237

Learner 259, 261, 263, 272, *see also* Trainee

Learning 313–315, 317, 324

Learning through reflection 380

Lewin 4, 97, 98, *see also* Kurt Lewin

Longitudinal case study 398

Media richness theory 108, *see also* Social influence model, Social presence theory

Members of the organization 20, *see also* Practitioners

Method of science 4, 5, *see also* Scientific method

Methodology 398, *see also* Research method

Mode 2 62–64, 79, 80, 84, 85, 88, 90, *see also* Mode 2 knowledge production

Mode 2 knowledge production 62–64, 80, *see also* Mode 2

Multiple iterations 103, 106, 107, 121

New product design 407, 408, *see also* New product development (NPD)

New product development (NPD) 194, 197–204, 208–213, 408, *see also* New product design

Object-oriented analysis 282, 299

Organisational context 131, 132, 134–140, 155

Organizational process 109, *see also* Business process

Ouchi 317

Outputs 12 *see also* Claims

Outsider 405, 406, *see also* Action researcher, Researcher

Participatory action research 316

Performance 397, 398

Personal telematics 202–205, 208, *see also* Telematics

Physicians 242, 245–249, *see also* Practitioners, Healthcare professionals, Hospital administrators

Physician's Profiling System (PPS) 242, 243, 245, 248

Positivism 69, 72, 79, 81, 82, 84

Positivist 6, 8, *see also* Positivist research

Positivist research 5, *see also* Positivist

Power 19–21, 24–34, 36, 37, 40, *see also* Structure of power

Power structure 22, 23, 26, 30–34, 37, 39, 40, *see also* Structure of power

Practical problem 313, 315–318, 321, 322, 324

Practitioners 19–21, 23–25, 35, 39, 242, 244, 248–250, 407, 417, *see also* Healthcare professionals, Hospital administrators, Insiders, Members of the organization, Physicians

Principal-agent theory 245, *see also* Agency theory

Process performance 194, 198, 200, 208

Process redesign 277–300, 306–308, *see also* Business process redesign

Product concept effectiveness 194, 198, 199, 208, 210

Production of knowledge 62, 63, *see also* Knowledge production

Project cancellation   196, 211, *see also* Cancellations
Projectified world order   186, 187
Prototypes   199, 202, 205–207, 209–212

Qualitative research   268
Quality of the experience   357, 365, 370

Raison d'être   44
Relatedness   367, 370
Relationship   221, 223
Relevance   44, 45, 56
Relevant data   256, 271, 272
Relevant theory   381, *see also* Theory, Theoretical framework
Research framework   328, 349, *see also* Framework, Comprehensive framework
Research method   397, *see also* Methodology
Research rigor   193, 331, *see also* Rigor
Research themes   9, *see also* Themes
Researcher   19–21, 23–26, 28–34, 37–39, 193–197, 201, 203, 205, 208, 209, 211–213, 241–251, 406, 407, 410, 414, 417, 418, *see also* Action researcher, Investigators, Outsider
Researcher-client agreement   380, 390, *see also* Researcher-client Infrastructure (CRI)
Researcher-client Infrastructure (CRI)   380, 381, 390, *see also* Researcher-client agreement
Rigor   44, 45, 56, 193, 195–197, 211, 330–332, 343, 349, *see also* Research rigor
Roles   361, 366, 367, 369, 370–373

Scientific knowledge   313, 319, 322
Scientific management   278, 279, 281, *see also* Scientific management method
Scientific management method   281, *see also* Scientific management
Scientific method   5, *see also* Method of science
Scientific research vs design   67, *see also* The Theory/Practice gap

Scientization   62, 65, 66, 74, *see also* Scientization
Scientization of design   62, 65, 66, 74, *see also* Scientization
Self-development   257, 261
Self-reflection   169, 171, 172
Social influence model   109, 112, 117, 119, 121, *see also* Media richness theory, Social presence theory
Social presence theory   108, *see also* Media richness theory, Social influence model
Social setting   397–399, 401–403
Sociotechnical   133, 134, 138, 139, 155, *see also* Sociotechnical discipline
Sociotechnical discipline   133, 134, *see also* Sociotechnical
Specifying learning   333, 348
Specifying the learning   45, 46, 57
Structure of power   19, 26, *see also* Power, Power structure
Study design   331, 332, 343, *see also* Design
Subjectivity   100, 102, 105, 117, 118, 121, 122
Sunk costs   237

Team membership   221, 222, 224
Team performance   227, 228
Telematics   201–205, 208, 209, *see also* Personal telematics
The Theory/Practice gap   64, *see also* Gap between design and science, Scientific research vs design
Themes   9, 11, 12, *see also* Research themes
Theoretical framework   382, *see also* Theory, Relevant theory
Theoretical sensitivity   269
Theory   379–383, 387, 406, 417, 418, *see also* Relevant theory, Theoretical framework, Theory-base
Theory-base   407, 410, *see also* Theory
To diagnose   55, *see also* Diagnosing
Total quality management   279, 291
Trainee   262–264, 269, 270, *see also* Learner
Transferability   361, 364–367, 369, 370, 372, 373

Trust   221, 234

Uncontrollability   100, 101, 106, 113,
    114, 121
Understanding   162, 168, 169, 171–174,
    180, 183–185, *see also* Knowledge
Unit of analysis   103–105, 121, 122
Usefulness   361, 363, 364, 366–373
Users   255, 272

Validation   397
Validity   3, 4, 6, 10, 11, 15
Value   228, 235, 236, 238
Vulnerability   169–172, 178, 183, 184

Walsham   168
Whole project   167